SAGE was founded in 1965 by Sara Miller McCune to support the dissemination of usable knowledge by publishing innovative and high-quality research and teaching content. Today, we publish more than 750 journals, including those of more than 300 learned societies, more than 800 new books per year, and a growing range of library products including archives, data, case studies, reports, conference highlights, and video. SAGE remains majority-owned by our founder, and after Sara's lifetime will become owned by a charitable trust that secures our continued independence.

Los Angeles | London | Washington DC | New Delhi | Singapore | Boston

India's
2014
Elections

India's 2014 Elections

Elections

A Modi-led BJP Sweep

Edited by
Paul Wallace

 www.sagepublications.com

Los Angeles • London • New Delhi • Singapore • Washington DC • Boston

First published in 2015 by

SAGE Publications India Pvt Ltd
B1/I-1 Mohan Cooperative Industrial Area
Mathura Road, New Delhi 110 044, India
www.sagepub.in

SAGE Publications Inc
2455 Teller Road
Thousand Oaks, California 91320, USA

SAGE Publications Ltd
1 Oliver's Yard, 55 City Road
London EC1Y 1SP, United Kingdom

SAGE Publications Asia-Pacific Pte Ltd
3 Church Street
#10-04 Samsung Hub
Singapore 049483

Published by Vivek Mehra for SAGE Publications India Pvt. Ltd, typeset in 10/13pt Berkeley by Diligent Typesetter, Delhi and printed at Chaman Enterprises, New Delhi.

Library of Congress Cataloging-in-Publication Data

Wallace, Paul.
    India's 2014 elections : a Modi-led bjp sweep / edited by Paul Wallace.
        pages cm
    Includes bibliographical references and index.
    1. Elections—India. I. Wallace, Paul, 1931– II. Title.
    JQ292.W35   324.954'0532—dc23   2015   2015008749

ISBN: 978-93-515-0187-9 (HB)

The SAGE Team: Rudra Narayan, Alekha Chandra Jena, Anju Saxena and Rajinder Kaur

Ramashray Roy expertly served as the co-editor
For the first four volumes of this series.
He continues as a valued colleague,
A continuing close friend, and
As an inspiration to continuing scholarship.
The book's dedication to him reflects his continuing presence.

Bulk Sales

SAGE India offers special discounts
for purchase of books in bulk.
We also make available special imprints
and excerpts from our books on demand.

For orders and enquiries, write to us at

Marketing Department
SAGE Publications India Pvt Ltd
B1/I-1, Mohan Cooperative Industrial Area
Mathura Road, Post Bag 7
New Delhi 110044, India

E-mail us at **marketing@sagepub.in**

Get to know more about SAGE

Be invited to SAGE events, get on our mailing list.
Write today to **marketing@sagepub.in**

This book is also available as an e-book.

Contents

PART I
Thematic Studies

Chapter 1
Paul Wallace

Chapter 2
Christophe Jaffrelot and Gilles Verniers

Chapter 3
Walter K. Andersen

Chapter 4
Rainuka Dagar

Chapter 5
Jyotirindra Dasgupta and Anshu N. Chatterjee

PART II
Analytical State Studies

A. Northern Cluster

B. Kashmir and Western Cluster

C. Eastern and Southern Cluster

D. North East

List of Tables

List of Figures

List of Abbreviations

AAMSU	All Assam Minorities Students' Union
AAP	Aam Aadmi Party
AASU	All Assam Students Union
ABMSU	All BTC Minority Students Union
ABSU	All Bodo Students Union
AD	Apna Dal
ADR	Association of Democratic Reform
AGP	Asom Gana Parishad
AIADMK	All India Anna Dravida Munnetra Kazhagam
AITC	All India Trinamool Congress
AIUDF	All India United Democratic Front
AKRASU	All Konch Rajbongshi Students' Union
AP	Andhra Pradesh
APHLC	All Party Hill Leaders Conference
BCs	Backward Classes
BIMARU	Bihar, Madhya Pradesh, Rajasthan, and Uttar Pradesh
BJD	Biju Janata Dal
BJP	Bharatiya Janata Party
BJS/JS	Bharatiya Jan Sangh
BKS	Bharatiya Kisan Sangh
BLD	Bharatiya Lok Dal
BLT	Bodo Liberation Tigers
BMS	Bharatiya Mazdoor Sangh
BPF	Bodoland People's Front
BPPF	Bodo Progressive Political Front
BSF	Border Security Force (BSF)
BSP	Bahujan Samaj Party
BTAD	Bodo Territorial Area District

BTC	Bodo Territorial Council
BVJA	Bhrashtachar Virodhi Jan Andolan
CPI	Communist Party of India
CPI-M	Communist Party of India (Marxist)
CM	Chief Minister
CSDS	Centre for the Study of Developing Societies
DHD-J	Dima Halam Daogah (Jewel)
DMK	Dravida Munnetra Kazhagam
EBCs	Extremely Backward Castes
ECI	Election Commission of India
FDI	Foreign Direct Investment
GII	Gender Inequality Index
GoG	Government of Gujarat
GSDP	Gross State Domestic Product
GTA	Gorkhaland Territorial Administration
IAC	India Against Corruption
IDC	Institute for Development and Communications
IRDP	Integrated Rural Development Programme
IT	Information Technology
ITI	Industrial Training Institute
JD(U)	Janata Dal–United
JKNPP	Jammu Kashmir National Panthers Party
KJP	Karnataka Janata Party
KMSS	Krishak Mukti Sangram Samiti
LBGT	Lesbian, Bisexual, Gay, and Transsexual
LeT	Lashkar-e-Taiba
LF	Left Front
LJP	Lok Janshakti Party
LSHPP	Lower Subansiri Hydroelectric Power Project
LUTF	Ladakh Union Territory Front
MBCs	Most Backward Castes
MKSS	Mazdoor Kisan Shakti Sangathan
MLA	Member of Legislative Assembly
MNS	Maharashtra Navnirman Sena
MP	Member of Parliament
MY	Muslim–Yadav
NBSS	Non-Bodo Suraksha Samiti

NC	National Conference
NCP	Nationalist Congress Party
NCPRI	National Campaign for People's Right to Information
NDA	National Democratic Alliance
NDFB	National Democratic Front of Bodoland
NES	National Election Study/Survey
NEW	National Election Watch
NGOs	Nongovernmental Organizations
NOTA	None Of The Above
NRC	National Register of Citizens
NREGA	National Rural Employment Guarantee Act
NSU	National Students Union
OBCs	Other Backward Castes
PC	Parliamentary Constituency
PCC	Pradesh Congress Committees
PDP	People's Democratic Party
PRP	Praja Rajyam Party
PSP	Praja Socialist Party
RJP	Rashtriya Janata Party
RPI	Republican Party of India
RSS	Rashtriya Swayamsevak Sangh
RTI	Right to Information
SAD	Shiromani Akali Dal
SAIS	Paul H. Nitze School of Advanced International Studies
SC	Scheduled Caste
SEZ	Special Economic Zone
SGPC	Shiromani Gurdwara Prabandhak Committee
SJA	Sanmilita Jatiya Abhibarttan
SJM	Swadeshi Jagran Manch
SP	Samajwadi Party
ST	Scheduled Tribe
SWRC	Social Work and Research Center
TDP	Telugu Desam Party
TMC	Trinamool Congress
TRS	Telangana Rashtra Samithi
ULFA	United Liberation Front of Assam
UMF	United Minority Front

UP	Uttar Pradesh
UPA	United Progressive Alliance
UPDS	United People's Democratic Solidarity
VAW	Violence Against Women
VHP	Vishwa Hindu Parishad
VKY	Vanbandhu Kalyan Yojana
YSR Congress	Yuvajana, Shramika, Rythu Congress
YSRCP	Yuvajana Shramika, Rythu Congress Party

Preface

In a world rent with crises, India continues to be a beacon for democratic politics. The peaceful transference of power as a result of its 16th national election highlights a notable degree of political maturity. The replacement of the Congress-led coalition after 10 years with the Bharatiya Janata Party (BJP) clear majority is one obvious result of this historic election.

The suggestion in Volume IV of this India national election series that the 2009 elections could enhance a 'state–nation' system evolving into a strong Center and strong states proved to be premature as the Center subsequently weakened. As a consequence of the 2014 elections, the emergence of a strong leader and a strong party coupled with continuing regionalism may provide a version of the state–nation system. The extent to which the new political structure coupled with India's diversity will shape society, politics, and governance within the next five years remains to be seen. The contributors of this volume provide in-depth national and state studies, which are critical to understanding the elections and their implications.

At the time this book would go to press, Prime Minister Narendra Modi would already have been confronted with his first challenge. The February 10, 2015 Delhi Assembly elections have raised fundamental questions about the Modi-led BJP sweep of the parliamentary elections and success in subsequent Assembly elections. Arvind Kejriwal's Aam Aadmi Party (AAP) upset the Modi juggernaut win of 67 of Delhi's 70 seats with 54 percent of the popular vote. BJP's turnaround is a huge 95 percent drop from the 60 assembly segments won in the 2014 Delhi parliamentary election. It is also a 78 percent loss from what the party won in the December 2013 Assembly election.

Election details are of less importance than the legitimacy and impact of the elections themselves. Just as the national elections validated the peaceful transfer of power from the dynastic Congress Party to Narendra Modi and his BJP as detailed in this book, the Delhi elections may have provided a brake to the strident new majority regime. Modi's clear Lok Sabha majority, increasing electoral power at the state level, and the passionate assertiveness of the *parivar* (family of Hindu organizations) led to concern for the secular, democratic Indian polity.

Delhi's election results may have been a minor blip on BJP's election successes. Or it may have conveyed an effective message to India's aspirational generation and other social groups that enthusiastically catapulted Modi and the BJP into power. They wanted him to emphasize his election messages of economic development and clean, effective government rather than societal discord. Prime Minister Modi, breaking a long silence, responded to these concerns within a week of the Delhi elections, stating that no religious group would be allowed to incite hatred against others, overtly or covertly, and that his mantra remains development. What concrete measures are taken to address this still remain to be seen.

Delhi's election as well as the earlier national election stands in a stark contrast to the inability of elections to cope with major concerns in adjoining countries. Pakistan had a technically successful election in 2013 with a civilian government having completed its tenure for the first time in its history. The Pakistan People's Party (PPP) peacefully transferred governmental power to its major opposition political party, the Pakistan Muslim League-Nawaz (PML-N). Nonetheless, the elections did little to resolve the role of the military, or that of *jihadi* groups like the Lashkar-e-Taiba (LeT) and Jaish-e-Mohammed. Even more threatening are the open assaults by Taliban groups. They killed 148 people including 132 children at a military-run school in Peshawar in December 2014, along with direct attacks on military installations and violence against minorities.

Bangladesh's 'battling Begums', Sheikh Hasina of the ruling Awami League and Khaleda Zia of the Bangladesh National Party, provide another example of elections that fail to cope with basic political and societal fissures. Sri Lanka also fit this category until the upset victory by Maithripala Sirisena over Mahinda Rajapaksa who called a snap general election in January 2015 in an attempt to further consolidate his already massive power. It now seems possible that the new political configuration can reconcile the island's Tamil minority with its Singhalese Buddhist majority.

Indian elections did resolve the authoritarian elements of Indira Gandhi's 21 months of emergency rule in 1975–77. However, India's situation in 2015 is not comparable to the serious situations in Pakistan and Bangladesh. Nonetheless, by Indian democratic standards, national and state elections continue to provide remarkable opportunities for nonviolently reconciling state and society.

Continued success for this election series is first and foremost due to the eminent contributors whose brief biographies are listed elsewhere in this volume. In their individual capacities, they represent notable scholarly institutions in India, the United Kingdom, France, Canada, and the United States. In addition, the Centre for the Study of Developing Societies (CSDS) in Delhi and the Institute for Development and Communications (IDC) in Chandigarh have been generous in providing quantitative data from surveys conducted throughout India. As always, the Election Commission of India provides electoral data for the 2014 elections and the means for comparative tables with all previous elections dating back to 1951. Our scholars are indebted to their institutions for assistance as well as to their colleagues at home and abroad. A newer generation of scholars is also emerging as evidenced by several of our authors and co-authors.

Special recognition must be accorded to SAGE for its enthusiastic support of this election volume. Shortly after the announcement of the election results in June 2014, I traveled to the SAGE head office in New Delhi. Since my past trips to SAGE, two changes have taken place. First, a relatively new modern Metro line buffered the ride to a far-off South Delhi. More importantly, instead of the usual one-on-one with an assigned staff person and a leisurely lunch in the vicinity, the elections stimulated an all-day royal durbar at SAGE headquarters. An intelligent discussion of the election, its possible ramifications, and excitement about the proposed volume resulted in a series of meetings with the various components of SAGE's burgeoning operations from the assigned three individuals and their departments to the marketing and other sections, and a laying on of hands from the CEO Vivek Mehra himself.

Rudra Narayan Sharma, the Commissioning Editor, provided continuous professional oversight including increasing decibel reminders of our mutually set deadlines. Compliments are also extended to Elina Mazumdar and R. Chandra Sekhar for being helpful, especially in the early discussions about the volumes and in their oversight of this project. Finally, Alekha Chandra Jena, the Production Editor, expertly piloted the last stage of the manuscript preparation.

India's 2014 election reminds us that elections are a necessary but not a sufficient element of democracy. Effective governance has now become an issue as 1.2+ billion people continue to test India's developing, pluralistic democracy.

PART I

Thematic Studies

1

Introduction: Single Party and Strong Leadership

Paul Wallace

Terms such as 'historic' and 'transformative' sprang forth from the May 16, 2014 election results of the 16th Lok Sabha. Narendra Modi is now a new iconic leader, as for the first time since 1984 a single party has won a majority in the Lok Sabha elections. With 282 seats out of 543, the Bharatiya Janata Party (BJP) has a clear majority of 51.93 percent, excluding 53 seats of its allies in National Democratic Alliance (NDA). The Indian National Congress (hereafter Congress or Congress Party) is reduced to 44 seats, an all-time low and less than 10 percent of the total number of seats.

According to the Attorney General's statement on July 25, 2014, at least 55 seats were needed to form the official opposition. A Lok Sabha petition signed by 60 members, including the Nationalist Congress Party (NCP), supported the Congress request to constitute the official opposition.[1] Two precedents can be cited here. Until 1969, and then again in the 1980s, there was no Leader of the Opposition.[2] It appears that once again there won't be an official opposition. See Table 1.1 for complete results and Table 1.2 for a comparison of the 16 leading parties in the 2014 Lok Sabha elections with those in 2009.

Table 1.1
Parties, Seats Contested, Seats Won, Number of Votes, and Percentages—Lok Sabha Elections 2014

Party Abbreviations	Party Name	Party Type	No. of Contestants	Seats Won	Votes by Party	Votes %
BSP	Bahujan Samaj Party	National	503	0	22,946,182	4.14
BJP	Bharatiya Janata Party	National	428	282	171,657,549	31
CPI	Communist Party of India	National	67	1	4,327,298	0.78
CPM	Communist Party of India (Marxist)	National	93	9	17,986,773	3.25
INC	Indian National Congress	National	464	44	106,938,242	19.31
NCP	Nationalist Congress Party	National	36	6	8,635,554	1.56
AAP	Aam Aadmi Party	State	432	4	11,325,635	2.05
AJSUP	AJSU Party	State	10	0	488,719	0.09
ADMK	All India Anna Dravida Munnetra Kazhagam	State	40	37	18,115,825	3.27
AIFB	All India Forward Bloc	State	39	0	1,211,418	0.22
AINRC	All India N.R. Congress	State	1	1	255,826	0.05
AITC	All India Trinamool Congress	State	131	34	21,259,681	3.84
AIUDF	All India United Democratic Front	State	18	3	2,333,040	0.42
AGP	Asom Gana Parishad	State	12	0	577,730	0.1
BJD	Biju Janata Dal	State	21	20	9,491,497	1.71
BPF	Bodoland People's Front	State	2	0	330,106	0.06

DMDK	Desiya Murpokku Dravida Kazhagam	State	14	0	2,079,392	0.38
DMK	Dravida Munnetra Kazhagam	State	35	0	9,636,430	1.74
HJCBL	Haryana Janhit Congress (BL)	State	2	0	703,698	0.13
INLD	Indian National Lok Dal	State	10	2	2,799,899	0.51
IUML	Indian Union Muslim League	State	25	2	1,100,096	0.2
JKN	Jammu and Kashmir National Conference	State	3	0	396,713	0.07
JKNPP	Jammu and Kashmir National Panthers Party	State	13	0	57,103	0.01
JKPDP	Jammu and Kashmir Peoples Democratic Party	State	5	3	732,644	0.13
JD(S)	Janata Dal (Secular)	State	34	2	3,731,481	0.67
JD(U)	Janata Dal (United)	State	93	2	5,992,196	1.08
JMM	Jharkhand Mukti Morcha	State	21	2	1,637,990	0.3
JVM	Jharkhand Vikas Morcha (Prajatantrik)	State	16	0	1,579,772	0.29
KEC(M)	Kerala Congress (M)	State	1	1	424,194	0.08
LJP	Lok Janshakti Party	State	7	6	2,295,929	0.41
MNS	Maharashtra Navnirman Sena	State	10	0	708,118	0.13
NPF	Naga Peoples Front	State	2	1	994,505	0.18
NPEP	National Peoples Party	State	7	1	576,444	0.1
PMK	Pattali Makkal Katchi	State	9	1	1,827,566	0.33
PPA	People's Party of Arunachal	State	2	0	47,018	0.01

(Table 1.1 Continued)

(Table 1.1 Continued)

Party Abbreviations	Party Name	Party Type	No. of Contestants	Seats Won	Votes by Party	Votes %
RJD	Rashtriya Janata Dal	State	30	4	7,442,313	1.34
RLD	Rashtriya Lok Dal	State	10	0	696,919	0.13
RSP	Revolutionary Socialist Party	State	6	1	1,666,380	0.3
SP	Samajwadi Party	State	197	5	18,672,916	3.37
SAD	Shiromani Akali Dal	State	10	4	3,636,148	0.66
SHS	Shiv Sena	State	58	18	10,262,982	1.85
SDF	Sikkim Democratic Front	State	1	1	163,698	0.03
TRS	Telangana Rashtra Samithi	State	17	11	6,736,490	1.22
TDP	Telugu Desam Party	State	30	16	14,094,545	2.55
UDP	United Democratic Party	State	1	0	106,817	0.02
IND	Independent	Independent	3,235	3	16,743,719	3.02
	Total contesting candidates*		6,201	527	515,425,190	98.85
				NOTA votes	6,000,197	1.08
	*Except NOTA			Total votes	521,425,387	100

Source: Election Commission of India, General Elections 2014. Data on May 17, 2014. Available online at http://eci.nic.in (Party-wise trends and result).

Notes: In addition to the national and state parties recognized by the Election Commission, the following won seats: All India Majlis-E-Ittehadul Muslimeen—1, Apna Dal—2, Yuvajana Sramika Rythu Congress Party—9. *NOTA: None of the Above. All 467 contesting parties are included in the following official ECI report.

Table 1.2
Party-wise Number of Seats: Top 16 in 2014 Compared with 2009

	2014	2009
Bharatiya Janata Party	282	116
Indian National Congress	44	206
All India Anna Dravida Munnetra Kazhagam	37	9
All India Trinamool Congress	34	19
Biju Janata Dal	20	14
Shiv Sena	18	11
Telugu Desam	16	6
Telangana Rashtra Samithi	11	2
Communist Party of India (Marxist)	9	16
Yuvajana Sramika Rythu Congress Party	9	—*
Nationalist Congress Party	6	9
Lok Janshakti Party	6	—*
Samajwadi Party	5	23
Aam Aadmi Party	4	—*
Rashtriya Janata Dal	4	4
Shiromani Akali Dal	4	4

Sources: Election Commission of India, General Elections 2014. Data on May 17, 2014. http://eci.nic.in (Party-wise trends and result).
Election Commission of India-General Elections 2009. Party-wise No. of Seats: Data on: June 23, 2009. http://eci.nic.in/results/FrmPartyWise-TrendsAndResults.aspx.
Note: *Not listed in 2009.

Voting percentages are less impressive with the BJP securing 31.4 percent or a total of 38.3 percent of the votes with its allies in NDA.[3] Nonetheless, data in Table 1.3 provide evidence of BJP's large victory margin over the Congress' 19.3 percent with the next highest being 4.1 percent. This table also provides the number of absolute votes ranging from over 171.6 million for the BJP and approximately 106.9 million for the Congress to 22.9 million for the Bahujan Samaj Party (BSP). BSP

Table 1.3
2014 Elections—Highest to Lowest: Party Vote Percentage and Vote Count

Party	Votes	Vote Count
BJP	31.0%	171,657,549
INC	19.3%	106,938,242
BSP	4.1%	22,946,182
AITC	3.8%	21,259,681
SP	3.4%	18,672,916
ADMK	3.3%	18,115,825
CPM	3.2%	17,986,773
IND	3.0%	16,743,719
TDP	2.5%	14,094,545
YSRCP	2.5%	13,991,280
AAP	2.0%	11,325,635
SHS	1.9%	10,262,982
DMK	1.7%	9,636,430
BJD	1.7%	9,491,497
NCP	1.6%	8,635,554
RJD	1.3%	7,442,313
TRS	1.2%	6,736,490
JD(U)	1.1%	5,992,196
SAD	0.7%	3,636,148
INLD	0.5%	2,799,899
AIUDF	0.4%	2,333,040
LJP	0.4%	2,295,929
DMDK	0.4%	2,079,392
PMK	0.3%	1,827,566
RSP	0.3%	1,666,380
JMM	0.3%	1,637,990
VM	0.3%	1,579,772
MDMK	0.3%	1,417,535

Source: Election Commission of India, General Elections 2014. Data on May 17, 2014. Available online at http://eci.nic.in (Party-wise trends and result).

was in the third place with 4.1 percent of the votes; despite that it failed to secure any seat! By contrast, Mamata Banerjee's regional All India Trinamool Congress (AITC) with 3.8 percent and 21.2 million votes in fourth place won 34 seats in West Bengal. None of the above (hereafter NOTA) polled slightly more than 6 million. In 2013, the NOTA option was made mandatory by the Supreme Court so that voters could reject all candidates without giving up their right to a secret vote. Staggering election statistics include a franchise of 814 million with a historic turnout of 66.4 percent.

A comparison of voter turnout for all national elections from 1951 till 2014 supports the historic high percentage total of the 2014 Lok Sabha elections. It is also impressive that no vote percentage falls below 55. The vote percentage from the 1998 to 2014 elections ranges between 58.08 and 66.4; see Table 1.4.

The major change in the system is that coalition politics has been replaced by the majority party rule or as one commentary neatly summarizes: The country is transiting from problems of coalition government to those stemming from one-party majority rule under a strong leader.[4] By contrast, the former ruling coalition and dominant party are shadows of their previous pre-eminence. Perhaps the strongest change from the past decade is that a leader who has dominated his party as well as the country has now replaced weak leadership. In what directions this will take India to will be charted during its five-year mandate.

Table 1.4
Voter Turnout Trend in Percentages, 1951–2014

1950s	1951: 61.17	1957: 62.23		
1960s	1962: 55.42	1967: 63.04		
1970s	1971: 55.27	1977: 60.49		
1980s	1984: 64.01	1989: 61.95		
1990s	1991: 55.88	1996: 57.9	1998: 61.97	1999: 59.99
2004–14	2004: 58.08	2009: 58.21	2014: 66.4	

Source: Compiled from Election Commission of India, various years. Available online at http://eci.nic.in.

Three Factors in the BJP Landslide Victory

Three major factors that led to BJP's massive win over the ruling UPA are the following:

- *Economy.* *Piaaz* (onion) is the most iconic item responsible for high inflation, slowing growth, and especially raising food prices. Their price increased by over 400 percent during the Congress Party/United Progressive Alliance (UPA) period of inflationary rule. As James Carville wrote on Bill Clinton's bathroom mirror during his first successful election campaign for the US Presidency, "It's the economy, stupid."

- *Corruption.* In 2011, Anna Hazare raised the issue of corruption, converting it into a national movement as he mobilized huge crowds in New Delhi and elsewhere in India. Arvind Kejriwal, one of his leading followers, took up the cause founding the Aam Aadmi Party (AAP) or common man party resulting in his becoming the chief minister of the Delhi state for 49 days in 2014. He resigned citing the failure of the Congress-led national government to pass his version of an anti-corruption law, but continued his movement by fielding over 400 AAP candidates for the Lok Sabha throughout India. Corruption continued as an albatross against Congress providing voters with an alternative for the BJP and its allies, particularly in Punjab where the AAP won four seats, its only victories.

- *Presidential campaign.* Thirdly, and arguably the most important, Gujarat Chief Minister Narendra Modi ran a largely positive presidential, plebiscitary style campaign in a parliamentary system. BJP's unexpected majority in the Lok Sabha is ascribed to Modi personally as a Tsunami or in local parlance combining his first and last names, as a 'TsuNaMo'.[5] Criss-crossing India with relentless energy and a brilliant campaign, he softened his association with right-wing Hindu slogans such as Hindutva emphasizing his record of economic development and governance as a chief minister of Gujarat. He tapped elements of the population that had responded three decades earlier to Indira Gandhi's message promising "a government that works" that resulted in her landslide victory in 1980, also seen as a plebiscitary election.[6]

By contrast, dynasty heir apparent Rahul Gandhi leading the Congress Party lacked the charisma and political skills of Narendra Modi. Britain's *The Economist* sharply criticized Rahul "as a dud: earnest but lacking in energy, ideas, strategy and, crucially, the ability to connect with party workers and voters." Modi, on the other hand, "is red-blooded and presidential."[7] Congress' Youth Congress so assiduously developed by Rahul since 2008 proved to be a major failure. It boasted of having more than 13 million members in May 2012. Two years later the *Hindustan Times* concluded: "It's war but Rahul Gandhi's young army ... has gone missing." For various reasons, 'a huge migration' took place to other parties including the AAP. Weak commitments consequent upon buying votes for internal elections are also alleged.[8]

Astute analyst Ramachandra Guha, the author of *Gandhi Before India*, arguably provides the most trenchant criticism of Rahul Gandhi:

> Lacking in energy and ambition, he (Rahul) may be the first member of his family not to command the respect even of his own party colleagues. In the decade he has been in politics, Mr Gandhi has conspicuously failed to motivate cadres (and voters) while campaigning in state (and national) elections.[9]

Congress Prime Minister Manmohan Singh did not fill the political gap, as he appeared to be a non-participant in the campaign. An iconic description of Manmohan Singh's role is captured by Mizoram's chief minister, Lal Thanhawla, in a meeting of Congress workers following the election results: "The former PM is an educated man, but he was always silent."[10]

Several major questions will receive close attention as the Modi-dominated BJP engages in its five-year term as a single party dominant government rather than compromised by a weak alliance. Will Prime Minister Modi successfully reinvigorate India's economy as he continuously promised emphasizing much needed changes to India's infrastructure? Clean water, sanitation, roads, harbors, electricity, and cleaning the Ganges River as he promised during his successful campaign in Varanasi are on the priority list. Varanasi, Hindus' most holy city, and the adjoining areas comprise an industrial complex dumping untreated wastes into the revered Ganges River.

In each of the over 400 constituencies that Modi addressed, his very able campaign staff provided him with specific local information spelling out development and good governance promises that he delivered personally and additionally in holographic appearances that many in his audiences accepted as real. Facebook and Twitter also became important elements of the BJP's adroit use of social media. NaMo, as he is often referred to in the media, tirelessly engaged in the longest campaign in India's electoral history comparable to a presidential race.

Development, good governance, and a perception of successfully engaging in the fight against corruption will mark a successful regime. If the promises, however, are too herculean, then the aura of Prime Minister Modi can fade, and then the question of maintaining his new base will arise. Will Modi whose socialization occurred as a dedicated RSS (Rashtriya Swayamsevak Sangh) monastic figure begin to dominate? Will he appeal to communal passions like some of his followers during the campaign?

The term 'dream catcher' widely used to capture Modi's dilemma speaks to these two dimensions. Positively, he borrowed a key phrase of Barack Obama's rhetoric in his successful campaign for the United States presidency in 2008: "Yes I can." Modi promised in a roaring manner adding, "Yes, I will" to enthusiastic crowds. Negatively, 'dream catcher' invokes the hard realities of problems and politics within India, and the global economy that are incapable of satisfying the high expectations that are raised.

Are the Congress and the Dynasty Finished?

Another major question revolves around India's political system itself. Whether the dynastic politics of the Nehru–Gandhi family and the 'Congress System' ended with the Congress Party's crushing defeat? Forty-four seats are a little more than half of what BJP won in Uttar Pradesh (UP) alone. Motial Nehru, a nationally prominent lawyer, founded the political family in the early 1900s during British rule. His son, Jawaharlal Nehru, became second only to Mahatma Gandhi in India's nationalist movement. Following independence in 1947, Nehru became India's first prime minister and a major architect and tutor of India's essentially secular constitutional parliamentary system. Nehru's daughter Indira, following Lal Bahadur Shastri, in 1966 became India's third prime minister. Earlier, she had married Feroze Gandhi, a Parsi who was not related to Mahatma Gandhi, though the surname has been politically helpful for the dynasty. Thus, it became the Nehru–Gandhi dynasty.

After Indira Gandhi's assassination in 1984, her son Rajiv Gandhi continued the political dynasty as a prime minister. His assassination in 1991 led Rajiv's Italian wife Sonia Gandhi to bringing back the party to power as the head of the UPA-ruling coalition in the past two terms with a non-political economist serving as the prime minister. Sonia's son Rahul reluctantly and ineffectively led the Congress Party to its worst ever defeat in 2014. Her daughter Priyanka's notable efforts in the last part of the campaign came too late, although she is credited with helping Rahul to win his parliamentary seat.

Dynastic dynamics, nonetheless, may lead to the disparate elements of the Congress Party and its allies turning to Priyanka the latest of the clan, especially one who looks like Indira Gandhi and also has a good deal of her grandmother's charismatic appeal. Or, will new leadership outside of the dynasty emerge in a reconstituted Congress Party? As could be anticipated, defections from and threats to the Congress Party have been taking place from Congress leaders in several states, for example, Maharashtra, Assam, West Bengal, and Jammu and Kashmir.[11]

Three reasons revolving around memory, in addition to the leadership deficiencies, are proposed by Ramachandra Guha as particularly relevant to the near collapse of the Congress Party in the 2014 elections. First, the charisma of Jawaharlal Nehru and Indira Gandhi is not remembered by India's largely young electorate. Secondly, neither do they remember their 'brutal assassinations'. Thirdly, in an "increasingly aspirational society, one cannot invoke ... (its) ancestors to justify one's own pre-eminence."[12]

The option of a dominant one-party system in which the BJP exercises the post-independence Congress role is possible. Certainly, that is the thrust of Modi's drive as he personally led the BJP to Assembly victories in Haryana and Maharashtra in October 2014, while publicly planning conquests in future state elections. Even more likely is the resumption of two national parties, whether under the Congress leadership or new alignments that do or do not involve a major role for the Congress Party, but do include powerful regional parties largely relegated to individual states.

Civil Society and the Elections

Civil society is well developed in India. Election data reveal that the better educated, higher income, rapidly urbanizing and more modern parts of the economy, including large and small business, as well as throngs of professionals from India and abroad supported Modi's landslide victory. Increasingly, they as well as other segments of the population are being described as the 'aspirational class'. Over 100 million new voters were part of the world's largest franchise of 814 million people. The highest ever participation rate of 66.4 percent of the 550 million voters who cast their ballots validated the election run by an independent, unbiased Election Commission.

Criticism has taken place of the model code of conduct by major political parties, of the system of representation resulting from the first past the post electoral system, and of the Election Commission itself.[13] Nonetheless, no one disputes the election results. India's Election Commission provides an excellent model for transparent, fair elections elsewhere and is a vital component of India's democracy.[14] Civil society should help shape the Modi-led BJP regime toward a more secular, development-oriented direction. But, will it? On the one hand, Prime Minister Narendra Modi's place in history will primarily result from India developing 'soft power' stemming from a strong economy and a forward-looking population. On the other hand, inevitable economic problems perhaps stemming from global factors as in 2008 as well as domestic politics can make it tempting to play the communal card.

South and Southeast Regionalism Increases

South and southeast states largely resisted the Modi wave even as the BJP continues to build its bases. Regional satraps such as J. Jayalalithaa in Tamil Nadu and Mamata Banerjee in West Bengal highlight the political distinctiveness of the south and southeast from north, central, and west India. Odisha's Naveen Patnaik and his regional party, the Biju Janata Dal (BJD), now has entered this elite category winning an impressive fourth term in Odisha State Assembly elections and sweeping those for the Lok Sabha. A new regional leader is K. Chandrasekhar Rao of the Telangana Rashtra Samithi (TRS) who triumphed in Telangana, which in June became India's 29th and the newest state. Kerala also resisted the Modi–BJP wave as Congress maintained control. A case can also be made for Karnataka, another southern state.

Language relates to India's diversity as a significant factor for continuing regionalism in south and southeast India. Hindi is the first language spoken by 420+ million of India's 1.2+ billion population, less than a majority. Bengali numbers over 80 million, Telegu over 74 million, and Tamil 60+ million according to the 2001 census.[15] Kannada and Malayalam are the other major regional languages in the south.

North and West

By contrast, just six states in the north and west account for 194 of BJP's total of 282 seats, that is, 69 percent. They consist of UP (71 of 80), Bihar (22 of 40), Rajasthan (25 of 25), Gujarat (26 of 26), Madhya Pradesh (27 of 29) and Maharashtra (23 of 48). Strike rate and competitive party are two concepts employed by one analyst to explain the voting efficiency of BJP's dominance in these areas:

> The *strike rate* of a party refers to the proportion of constituencies the party wins for a given set of constituencies, and a party is deemed to be *competitive* in a constituency if it is one of the top two vote getters in that constituency.

In these states, the strike rate of the BJP is a massive 91 percent in the constituencies it contested. Similarly, in 189 constituencies where the BJP and Congress were the top two competitors, the BJP won 166 of them for a strike rate of 88 percent. As a consequence, there were very few BJP 'wasted votes'.[16] BJP's sweep of seven out of seven seats in Delhi, all five seats in Uttarakhand and three seats from Jammu and Kashmir enhanced these results.

Punjab provided a more complex result in a three-party election featuring two anti-incumbency reactions. One reaction was against the alliance of the rural Sikh-based Shiromani Akali Dal (SAD) and the urban Hindu-based BJP, and the second was against the Congress Party, its major competitor. The ruling alliance dominated by the SAD won only six seats, while the Congress opposition in the normally two-party state won only three out of a total of 13 seats. That provided an opening for the new AAP to win four seats—its only Lok Sabha seats. Captain Amarinder Singh, head of the state Congress Party, defeated the national BJP leader Arun Jaitley in Amritsar in a highly publicized contest. Jaitley, nevertheless, became Finance as well as Defence Minister in the new national government.

Social Categories, Major Losers and Policy Concerns

Social Categories: Documenting BJP's Positive Nation-wide Trend

All categories reflect BJP increases compared to 2009. Most notable for a party earlier associated with upper castes is its increase among Other Backward Castes (OBCs). Narendra Modi identified himself as an OBC. *India Today's* survey registers an 11 percent increase over 2009, while the Centre for the Study of Developing Societies (CSDS) National Election Study (NES) has a comparable gain of 12 percent. A further disaggregation of the OBC data by CSDS lists the BJP gain in the lower OBC category as 20 percent. Increases among women (14 percent), rural (14 percent), urban (13 percent), upper castes (18 percent) and especially schedule castes (26 percent) provide evidence of broad support. See Table 1.5.

A partial explanation of BJP's increase among the poor may be provided by a detailed study including rich quantitative and qualitative data that focus on how elite parties attract poor voters. Hindu nationalists, the author concludes, recruited the poor through their movement affiliates, while allowing them to maintain their linkages with rich and core elite supporters including those based on religion and ideology. Two major Hindu nationalist wings are cited for the provision of social services. The *Seva Bharati* (Service to India) and *Vanvasi Kalyan Ashram* (Association for the Welfare of Tribals) provide services ranging from schools

Table 1.5
BJP Percentage Increases in Social Categories

	2009	2014
Women	19	33
Rural	20	34
Urban	16	29
Upper Castes	28 [29]*	46 [47]*
OBC	19 [22]*	30 [34]*
Muslims	10 [4]*	17 [8]*
Scheduled Castes	18	34

Sources: Ashok K. Lahiri, "The End of Identity Politics," *India Today*, May 26, 2014, pp. 24–26. Data from the Centre for the Study of Developing Societies. Shreyas Sardesai, "Muslims Marginalised as OBCs Shift Allegiance" and Sanjeer Alam, "OBC Support for BJP Signals the End of 'Caste Politics'" *Hindu*, June 1, 2014, p. 12.

Note: *National Election Study is provided in brackets.

to blood banks, medical dispensaries, and vocational training centers. The larger number or concentration of these welfare networks providing local public goods correlates with BJP's support.[17]

Major Losers

The Communist Party of India (Marxist) (CPI-M) with nine total seats is reduced to heading the tiny state of Tripura and two seats in its former bastion, West Bengal. Along with the Communist Party of India (CPI) with one seat, they have been highlighted as the biggest losers among national parties. The Left Front's (LF) 10 seats are a shadow of its 60 seats following the 2004 Lok Sabha elections. Then, they were a significant element supporting the UPA coalition from the outside so as to keep the BJP out of power. Revival or even survival is its post-2014 election mission.

BSP's Mayawati who had aspirations of leading a Third Front did not win any seats in her UP base, even though her party won 19 percent of the state's votes. The ruling Samajwadi Party (SP) in UP did slightly better—or less worse—by winning five seats, all by family members, with 22.2 percent of the state's votes.[18] Sharad Pawar's Nationalist Congress Party (NCP) winning only four seats in Maharashtra is also a big loser.

Policy Concerns

Policy concerns of a civil society include the following:

- Laws and protection concerning minorities, that is, inclusive governance.
- Women's issues include rape, police treatment, harassment in public places and political representation.
- Educational textbooks involve rewriting with a Hindu nationalist bias.
- Censorship against academic books about Hinduism, which took place during the 'secular' Congress-led UPA administration.
- Continuance of Article 370 of the Constitution providing special rights for Kashmiris in Kashmir.

Policy concerns of the Hindu (Hindutva) Right (RSS, VHP) include the following:

- Construction of the Ram temple at Ayodhya.
- Uniform Civil Code.
- Cow protection
- Repeal of Article 370 regarding Jammu and Kashmir.

Policy concerns of business include the following:

- Fast-track approval of business plans, that is, reducing bureaucratic delays.
- Reducing corruption especially in licensing approval.
- Selling or reducing government enterprises, that is, reforms.
- Encouraging foreign direct investment (FDI) without alienating BJP's base, for example, box stores.
- Most important is effectively tackling infrastructure problems in transportation, electricity and ports.

Policy concerns of all of India's population, including 100 million new voters and half of the population under the age of 25:

- Control inflation
- Jobs
- Economic growth
- Good education
- Clean water
- Pollution
- Housing

Volume IV of this India national election series suggested that the 2009 elections could enhance a 'state–nation' system that appeared to be evolving into a strong Center and strong states.[19] That forecast proved to be premature as the Center subsequently weakened. As a consequence of the 2014 elections, a strong leader and a strong party coupled with continuing regionalism may provide a new version of the state–nation system. India's diversity will shape the nature of the present regime change within the next five years. Various perspectives emerge from the notable scholars in the following chapters, all of whom provide their own analyses and conclusions. Part I of this volume plays a thematic role consisting of all-India studies, while Part II is focused on states' analysis.

Part I: Thematic All-India Studies

Continued regionalism is Christophe Jaffrelot's and Gilles Verniers' theme in Chapter 2. They emphasize that "the apparent nationalisation of Indian politics should be treated with caution" as regional parties remain 'resilient' especially in the non-Hindi areas. Nonetheless, they open the possibility of a change in Center–state power relations at the expense of regional parties if BJP wins more Vidhan Sabha elections, thus becoming dominant in the Upper as well as Lower House of Parliament. BJP's centralization, they conclude, will continue to have to contend with regional parties and how the Congress adapts to the 'changing landscape'.

Chapter 3 focuses on the BJP based partly on Walter Anderson's pre-election interviews with Narendra Modi and senior members of the BJP and the RSS. He emphasizes Modi's central role in the campaign that appealed to the "young and poor … and their demand for jobs." In taking command of the various organizations that constitute the 'Parivar', Modi "studiously avoided Hindutva themes during the campaign and publicly rebuked those who did." A 'significant deviation' from this pattern is the appointment of Amit Shah to head the UP campaign, which occasioned a rebuke by the Election Commission for Shah's extremist Hindutva statements. In his final sections, Anderson examines six major governance challenges for Modi. They include India, the BJP, the economy, Muslim confidence, foreign policy and calibrating "a productive balance of power between central and regional pressure groups."

Gender and especially women provide the central issues for Chapter 4. Rainuka Dagar states that the elections were contested on the "three fault-lines of governance, development and secularism … across competing parties." In this context, "Women … were lobbied across all three fronts.…" Gender and women are examined in detail from various sociatal and electoral perspectives. Longitudinal electoral tables show an increased turnout of women voters. In 2014, there was also a lessening of the gender gap between men and women voters from previous years with women outnumbering men voters in 16 of the 35 states/union territories. Nevertheless, election discourse and manifestos acknowledged the deep problems women face including sexual violence, health and sanitation, education and representation. Dagar concludes that: "Political efficacy for legitimate concerns remains a goal … faultlines across identities of gender, caste and religion in a fragmented polity need to be redefined."

Civic scrutiny related to democratic consolidation is the topic addressed by Jyotirindra Dasgupta and Anshu Chatterjee in Chapter 5. The promise of decisive governance resulting from the elections, they maintain, will have to address the concerns of a 'scam weary' public and the need for 'transparency and accountability'. Scrutinizing promises, policies and implementation are essential. India's rich arrays of civic organizations are presented, illustrated by case studies, as the major instruments of accountability, especially for the 'disadvantaged population'. The key to their success in democratic politics is that they offer "a modest way of complementing the existing democratic institutions and not supplanting or overturning them" as compared to the impatience of Kejriwal and the AAP.

Part II: Analytical State Studies

Sudha Pai and Avinash Kumar in Chapter 6 explain BJP's near sweep in UP, arguably the most important state in the elections, with detailed tables and figures that complement the qualitative text. BJP's 'spectacular victory' was due to the 'revival of its organization and social base'. Modi led the new leadership, replacing the old guard including Vajpayee and Advani with the support of the Sangh Parivar. In addition to upper caste support, the BJP made deep inroads into the backward and Dalit base of the formerly dominant 'strong identity-based parties', the SP and BSP for a broad 'Hindu vote bank'. A key to the victory, they argue, is that it "was not so much a BJP as a Modi victory in UP due to a two-pronged ... campaign by him and his confidante Amit Shah, using both Hindutva and development" so as to appeal to all sections of the population including non-Hindus. The election also "witnessed the return of communal mobilization and violence," particularly in western UP.

BSP proved to be the major competitor with 20 percent of the votes as it maintained its core Dalit base. It could not, however, win any seats due to multi-cornered contests as well as a loss of some of its previous support. Anti-incumbency based on poor governance resulted in the ruling SP being relegated to its five family seats. "Internal decay" led to a divided party with "criminal links ... numerous factions" and disappointment with Akhilesh Yadav as a chief minister after its 2012 Assembly victory. Congress' "crushing defeat" resulted from the "absence of a strong organization, social base and effective leadership." The dynasty, concludes the authors, "can no longer substitute for performance." Given the volatility of UP politics, the real test of the "new BJP vis-à-vis the state parties" will be in the 2017 Assembly elections.

Chapter 7 on Bihar in its major outlines parallels UP. Maneesha Roy and Ravi Ranjan emphasize BJP's success in consolidating the Hindu identity in its favor, with the partial exception of Yadavs, and a "shift in community Identity" in a triangular election. Narendra Modi, Nitish Kumar, and Lalu Prasad Yadav provided powerful leaders, each with niche alliance partners. The Modi wave emphasized the same successful themes of leadership and development in the context of attacks against the incumbent UPA as in the rest of India, along with a tailored criticism of the Nitish Kumar regime. BJP, in addition to its upper caste base, made significant gains among Dalits and OBCs. New alliance configurations between former state-level antagonists appear to be forming as a reaction to BJP's dominant election victory.

Delhi's election is part of the BJP sweep of India's north and west. Ravi Ranjan analysis in Chapter 8 is within the context of its historical and demographic background as well as detailed tables. BJP led in 60 of the Assembly segments. Delhi has a volatile history of sweeps relating to national patterns. Year 2014, however, provided a three-party context that included the AAP. It failed to repeat its 2013 success that established it in power for 49 days, but the AAP retains its aspirations. Congress, which ruled Delhi for 15 years, was decimated with a "poor third in all seven seats." Muslims split between the AAP and Congress as BJP consolidated upper caste and OBC votes.

Chapter 9 by Pramod Kumar on Punjab examines the one state in the north and west that did not succumb to the Modi wave. Punjab featured an unusual double anti-incumbency movement that reacted against the Congress/NDA nationally as well as the Shiromani Akali Dal (SAD)/BJP alliance at the state level. That political dynamic became possible with the entrance of the AAP into what is normally a two-party contest. Voters, therefore, had an option that they exercised in electing four AAP candidates, helping to explain the only wins in the AAP's nation-wide efforts. As a consequence, "Modi's leadership as a factor became secondary to anti-incumbency."

Modi's strategy in Punjab, as well as nationally, has been "to regionalize the national elections and nationalize the regional agenda." Assembly elections in Haryana and Maharashtra three months after the Lok Sabha elections followed this pattern. Punjab is described and analyzed in detail providing a series of longitudinal tables computed from the Election Commission as well as attitudinal variables from studies conducted by Kumar's Institute for Development and Communications research organization.

Jammu and Kashmir, Chapter 10, falls into the north and west pattern of a major BJP victotry by winning three of its six seats, two in Jammu and one in Ladakh. Reeta Tremblay and Mohita Bhatia detail BJP's following national trends. These include high voter turnout, the Modi factor, frustration with the incumbent regime's inability to push development and its tolerance of corruption as well as its poor governance. Suprisingly, the

National Conference (NC) and the Congress were "wiped out." Congress previously had won the Jammu seats eight times.

Nevertheless, each of the state's three regions manifest distinctive demographic patterns. Jammu with 65+ percent Hindus, the Valley with 97+ percent Muslims, and Ladakh split between Muslims and Buddhists each have different identities with "unique perceptions and experiences relating to a number of dimensions." Detailed background information and ananlysis are provided for Article 370 as well as its contemporary relevance.

Gujarat, not unexpectingly, features Narendra Modi in Chapter 11 who used the 2012 Assembly elections to prepare for 2014. In addition to Modi's personal contributions, Ghanshyam Shah emphasizes BJP's professional marketing and management skills versus fragmented Congress' defeatism and decline. The Sangh Parivar groups, religious organizations and impressive voter mobilization effectively reached a broad spectrum of social groups, with the exception of lower classes and minorities. Modi achieved the target he set of winning all the 26 Lok Sabha seats.

Chapter 12 by Suhas Palshikar and Nitin Birmal emphasizes the importance of the BJP-led NDA coalition winning 42 seats in Maharashtra to its clear national majority as well as the continued decline of Congress and its ally, the Nationalist Congress Party. In addition to presenting the major issues resulting in the NDA sweep, they examine the implications for interparty competition between the BJP and Shiv Sena as well as the Congress and NCP. The situation offers the possibility of "the rise of a clear single-party dominance in the state in the near future." Major concerns include the distribution "over vast networks of resources built by the Congress factions" and the "fragmentation of the Maratha community," about 30 percent of Maharashtra's population. New social alignments are possible. A postscript examines the October 24, 2014 Assembly election.

Chapter 13 on West Bengal highlights the decline of the LF after being the dominant party for 34 years. Trinamool Congress (TMC) has established itself in place of the LF as the dominant party with Chief Minister Mamata Banerjee joining the other major regional leaders of east and south India. Amiya Chaudhuri provides the background for the CPI(M)-led LF gradual and then rapid decline particularly as a consequence of the Nandigram and Singur movements led by Mamata Banerjee.

According to Andrew Wyatt in Chapter 14, Tamil Nadu characterized arguably India's most regional pattern of politics in 2014 as "this was the first Lok Sabha election since 1967 in which national parties were excluded from the alliances led by the Dravidian parties" that dominate the state's politics. Thus, it is an "an ironic outcome" that contrasts starkly with the Modi and BJP narrative dominating the national election discourse. He does anticipate that national parties will be able to re-engage in alliance politics in the future. Wyatt explains how and why the state deviated from the national trend as he concentrates on the regional parties, local issues and the relevance of Sri Lanka to alliance dynamics. Jayalalithaa could not translate All India Anna Dravida Munnetra Kazhagam's (AIADMK) winning of 37 of the state's 39 seats into her leading a national coalition due to BJP's majority. Wyatt does, however, closely examine the bases of her state power, its competition with the Dravida Munnetra Kazhagam (DMK) and the DMK leadership problems. In an epilogue, he also reacts to the post-election bombshell announcing a court decision finding Jayalalithaa guilty of corruption resulting in making her ineligible to hold a government office and the probability of a jail term. Implications in regard to the DMK also are examined.

Chapter 15 could easily be two chapters as Karli Srinavasulu explains the election politics behind the bifurcation of Andhra into two with Telangana becoming a separate state. One focus on how a "weak Telangana Rashtra Samithi (TRS) could win the 2014 elections with a convincing majority on its own." Regional identity and regional interests dominated the elections. Major attention is paid to Hyderabad in terms of its 'concentrated growth' and thus as a major precipitant of the Telangana demand for separation. Chandrababu Naidu re-emerges as a major political actor as he once again became a chief minister, this time of residuary Andhra and returned to an alliance with the BJP, but without Hindutva overtones. TRS, however, contested alone and successfully in Telangana. Strong regional parties, Srinavasulu concludes, nonetheless, "cannot be seen as a reflection of narrow regionalism."

Karnataka as presented by S.S. Patagundi and Prakash Desai in Chapter 16 reports that national issues including the Modi wave were not very influential as local 'complex politics' dominated the electoral outcome. Five years of unpopular BJP rule highlighted by "corruption, infighting and a leadership crisis" led to its rejection in the 2013 Assembly elections. Congress, on the other hand, successfully shifted from the dominant Lingayats and Vokkaligas to the OBCs, Dalits and minorities. BJP rebounded in 2014 to win 17 of the 28 seats, by far its best southern result. Congress did win nine seats and 40.8 percent of the votes, good compared to Congress results elsewhere, but far below the party's expectations as well as major polls. Caste alignments including solid Lingayat support, the Sangh Parivar and Modi's role in urban areas contributed significantly to BJP's turnaround, especially in Malnud and the coastal areas where it did poorly in 2013.

Assam in Chapter 17, by Akhil Datta, is another state where BJP rebounded from poor results in Assembly elections. It won only five out of 126 Assembly seats in 2011, but won seven of the 14 seats in the 2014 Lok Sabha elections, while Congress won only three seats. BJP benefitted from a spectacular voter turnout of 80.3 percent fueled by a "reaction against the incumbent (Congress) government," Modi's campaign, and political changes involving the Bodos and their ethnic opponents. Election results are "almost a deathblow to the hegemonic domination by the fractured minority Bodo community" in the Bodo Territorial Area Districts combined with a united non-Bodo majority.

Four thematic chapters follow this introduction exploring national themes and the elections in regard to regionalism, the BJP, gender and civic scrutiny. Then, 12 state studies provide the bulk of this volume in an altered political landscape. Regime change has replaced an unsuccessful Congress-led alliance with a majority BJP as well as weak to strong leadership. It has also changed the political geography of India so that our state chapters are divided according to the results of the 2014 Lok Sabha elections into:

- A northern and western cluster reflecting BJP's sweep.
- An eastern and southern cluster reflecting continued regionalism.
- The Northeast, which represents India in its range from Assam, included in this volume, to Tripura as well as in its diversity and pluralism.

Notes and References

1. Ghulam Nabi Azad, a Congress leader in the Rajya Sabha said it was 'most unfortunate' that Congress had not been given the opposition leadership status in the Lok Sabha. Bhadra Sinha, *Hindustan Times*, July 25, 2014, p. 1, http://www.hindustantimes.com/india-news/no-case-for-congress-to-claim-leader-of-opposition-in-ls-ag/article1-1244630.aspx (accessed on July 25, 2014).
2. Karan Thapar, "Congress may not deserve it, but give it the LoP post." *Hindustan Times*, July 13, 2014, http://www.hindustantimes.com/comm5ent/karanthapar/it-may-not-deserve-it-but-give-congress-the-post/article1-1239690.aspx (accessed on July 15, 2014).
3. India's first-past-the-post electoral system, as in the United Kingdom and the United States, strongly rewards the first place finisher and geometrically punishes the losers. Congress benefitted in 2009 when it won 38 percent of the seats on its vote share of 29 percent. Similarly, in the 2012 UP state elections the SP won 224 seats with 29.15 percent of the vote, while the BSP won only 80 seats with 25.91 percent of the vote. Neelanjan Sircar, "The Numbers Game: An Analysis of the 2014 General Election," Center for the Advanced Study of India, June 16, 2014, https://casi.sas.upenn.edu/iit/nsircar (accessed on July 16, 2014).
4. Neerja Choudhury, "Big Boss Takes Charge," *Times of India* (Chandigarh edition), February 28, 2014, p. 14.
5. Aroon Purie, Editor-In-Chief, *India Today*, May 26, 2014, p. 3.
6. Paul Wallace, "Plebiscitary Politics: India's 1980 Parliamentary Elections in Punjab and Haryana," *Asian Survey*, Vol. 20, No. 6 (June 1980), pp. 612–33.
7. "Congress after the cataclysm," *Economist*, June 21, 2014, p. 42.
8. *Hindustan Times*, April 18, 2014, p. 1.
9. Ramachandra Guha, "The past and future of the Congress Party," *Hindustan Times*, August 2, 2014, http://www.hindustantimes.com/StoryPage/Print/1247609.aspx 1/2 (accessed on August 2, 2014).
10. Adam Halliday, *Indian Express* (Chandigarh edition), May 31, 2014, p. 10. *Economist* headlines an article about him: "Man out of time." It cites a biography by Sanjaya Baru, a former spokesman, that "chronicles a leader who is unassertive in a cabinet, nearly powerless in hiring or firing ministers in a broad coalition and passive to a fault ... (while) giving just three full press conferences in ten years." May 3, 2014, pp. 33–34.
11. "Challenge for Rahul Gandhi as Congress battles revolts, desertions in many states," *Times of India*, July 21, 2014, http://timesofindia.indiatimes.com/india/Challenge-for-Rahul-as-Congress-battles-revolts (accessed on August 2, 2014).
12. Ramachandra Guha, "The past and future of the Congress party," *Hindustan Times*, August 2, 2014, http://www.hindustantimes.com/StoryPage/Print/1247609.aspx 1/2 (accessed on August 2, 2014).
13. Major criticisms of the election campaign and of the Election Commission itself is provided in *Frontline*'s extensive cover story by V. Venkatesan, an interview by T.K. Rajalakshmi with H.S. Brahma, Election Commissioner; an interview by V. Venkatesan with S.Y. Quraishi, former Chief Election Commissioner; state-wise coverage by various reporters as well as other items. pp. 3–33.
14. See Quraishi, Shahbuddin Yaqoob (2014). *An Undocumented Wonder: The Making of a Great Indian Election* (Delhi: Rainlight/Rupa). The author was a member of the Election

Commission from 2006 to 2010 and Chief Election Commissioner from 2010 to 2012. I personally can testify to his intelligence and non-partisan democratic commitment as a consequence of long discussions with him in New Delhi and Chandigarh.

15. Subodh Varma, Like it or not, you just can't do without English," TNN, *Times of India*, August 6, 2014. The 2011 census data have not yet been released. http:// timesofindia.indiatimes.com/india/Like-it-or-not-you-just-cant-do-without-English/ articleshow/39724110.cms?utm_source=newsletter&utm_medium=referral&utm_ campaign=digest_section (accessed on August 6, 2014).

16. Neelanjan Sircar, "The Numbers Game: An Analysis of the 2014 General Election," *Center for the Advanced Study of India*, June 16, 2014 (https://casi.sas.upenn.edu) (accessed on June 17, 2014).

17. Tariq Thachii, "Elite Parties and Poor Voters: Theory and Evidence from India," *American Political Science Review*, Vol. 108, No. 2, May 2014, pp. 454–77.

18. Election Commission of India, General Elections 2014. Data on May 17, 2014.

19. Paul Wallace, "Introduction: Political Stability and Governance Coherence," in Paul Wallace and Ramashray Roy, *India's 2009 Elections: Coalition Politics, Party Competition and Congress Continuity* (New Delhi: SAGE Publications, 2011), pp. 10–11.

2

The Resistance of Regionalism: BJP's Limitations and the Resilience of State Parties

Christophe Jaffrelot and Gilles Verniers

The 16th Indian general elections have been extolled as a resounding success: more than 815 million voters were called to the ballot and 66 percent of them exercised their franchise, an all-time high in India. The 2009 general elections' turnout was 58 percent, and the previous record, 64 percent in 1984, also occurred in exceptional circumstances, in the wake of Mrs Gandhi's assassination. The outcome of the 2014 elections has also been hailed as historic, or a landmark in Indian politics, as for the first time in the last 30 years, a non-Congress party succeeded in obtaining a single majority of seats in the Lok Sabha on its own. The performance is all the more remarkable in that national politics in India has been marked by an intense fragmentation of both the party system and the electorate.

Does this result mean that India and its voters have turned fragmentation into the nationalization of the party system? Are we witnessing a turning point in Indian politics as far as some of the major trends of Indian politics—including its regionalization—are concerned? Or do we have yet another outcome of a fragmented political scene—an unlikely one or one that few thought would be possible—which would leave the future far more open than the current BJP victory would lead to think? There is no doubt that the Modi campaign has brought novelty to campaigning practices in India: the media blanket, the winner's unprecedented level of campaign expenditures, the projection of Narendra Modi as a providential and solitary leading figure and so forth. But do the outcome and the processes that led to it display the same novelty?

One way to assert this is to scrutinize the performance of both the BJP and other parties, mainly the regional ones. The strong embeddedness of the BJP in the Hindi Belt and the resilience of regional parties as a whole, as will be argued here, will show that the tales of the apparent nationalization of Indian politics should be treated with caution.

The BJP: A Dominant but Non-hegemonic Party

To call BJP's victory a complete triumph would be an exaggeration. The party benefited fully from the inherent disproportionality effect of the electoral system: it won 52 percent of the seats with only 31 percent of the votes, the lowest figure ever to achieve such a result (Table 2.1). This is for the first time in India, where no party—barring the Congress in 1952—ever succeeded in winning a majority of seats with less than 40 percent of votes. In 2014, the BJP won 1.67 seats for each percentage of votes, while the Congress won only 0.47 seats by the same yardstick. In other words, 60,000 votes sufficed on an average for the BJP to win a seat, while the Congress' average touched the 240,000 mark.

This amplification of BJP's victory can be explained by the noticeable geographical concentration of the BJP vote. While it is true that the BJP progressed remarkably in areas where it did not use to perform, such as West Bengal, where it nearly tripled its 2009 vote share (from 6.1 percent to 16.8 percent), Assam (from 17.2 percent to 36.4 percent), Jammu and Kashmir (from 18.6 percent to 32.4 percent), and, to a lesser extent, Kerala (from 6.3 percent to 10.3 percent, its 1999 level), its expansion did not translate into many seats (one in Kerala, two in West Bengal, and three in Jammu and Kashmir).

Table 2.1

Single-majority Parties' Performance

	1967 INC	1971 INC	1977 BLD	1984 INC	2014 BJP
Vote share	40.78%	43.68%	41.32%	49.10%	31.01%
Seat share	53.85%	67.95%	54.51%	74.59%	52.12%

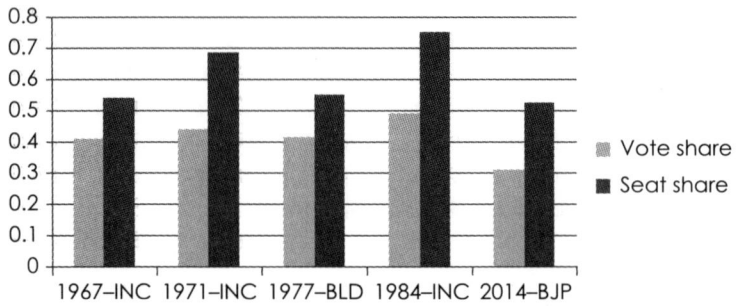

Source: Adapted from Election Commission of India (ECI) and G. Verniers' election data.

The BJP scored largely in areas where it is traditionally strong. It won 190 of the 225 seats of the Hindi Belt: UP, Bihar, Madhya Pradesh, Chhattisgarh, Rajasthan, Haryana, Himachal Pradesh, Delhi, and Jharkhand, that is, 84 percent of the seats. That figure increases to 86 percent if one adds Gujarat and decreases to 80 percent if one adds Maharashtra. If one includes the performance of allies—Lok Janshakti Party (LJP) in Bihar and the Shiv Sena in Maharashtra—the NDA is seen to bag 86 percent of the seats in their regions. Two other partners—the Shiromani Akali Dal in Punjab and the Telugu Desam Party in Andhra Pradesh—won 4 and 16 seats, respectively. Three small parties add seven further seats gave the National Democratic Alliance a comfortable majority of 332 seats (272 being the majority threshold). However, the BJP remained largely absent in the South—barring Karnataka, where it did not shine—the Eastern Coast and the Northeast, barring Assam and Arunachal Pradesh.

BJP's vote share levels in the Hindi Belt are noteworthy. Nationally, the party bagged 31 percent of vote share, whereas in the Hindi Belt states (and Gujarat), it won 45 percent of the average vote share (Table 2.2). In UP, where the party won an unprecedented 71 seats, it surpassed the combined vote share of its three opponents (Congress, BSP, and SP)

Table 2.2
*Vote Share and Seat Share of National Parties in the Hindi
Heartland and Gujarat (1967–2014)*

	Seat Share		
	INC	*BJP*	*BLD*
1967	57.38%	13.52%	
1971	72.43%	9.05%	
1977	4.76%		93.25%
1980	71.03%		
1984	95.63%	0.40%	
1989	14.68%	29.76%	
1991	25.40%	42.46%	
1996	17.86%	53.17%	
1998	17.86%	55.95%	
1999	15.87%	52.38%	
2004	23.02%	36.51%	
2009	35.71%	30.95%	
2014	3.19%	86.06%	

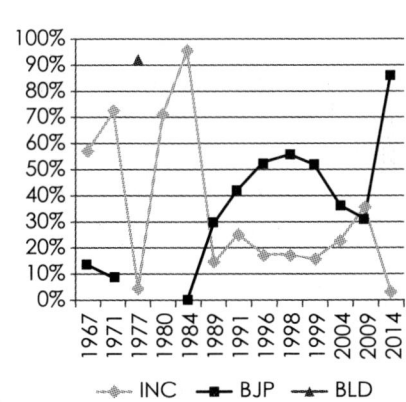

	Vote Share		
	INC	*BJP*	*BLD*
1967	35.86%	16.70%	
1971	45.30%	14.09%	
1977	27.36%		62.10%
1980	39.74%		
1984	52.05%	13.32%	
1989	33.03%	18.76%	
1991	28.10%	30.49%	
1996	20.13%	32.59%	
1998	20.56%	35.98%	
1999	25.41%	34.24%	
2004	24.31%	31.30%	
2009	29.25%	27.91%	
2014	19.54%	45.31%	

Source: Adapted from ECI and G. Verniers' election data.

in 22 constituencies. The analysis of the geography of the results suggests that the BJP appears more as a meta-regional party than a truly national party.

It can also be noted that BJP's performances were significantly stronger in urban areas. The BJP emerged as an urban party, a characteristic it had somewhat lost in the previous election and regained in the 2014 elections. Overall, the BJP obtained 42 percent of the urban vote share,[1] far above its average vote share of 31 percent. In cities the BJP took giant strides—28 percent increase in the vote share of urban seats as compared to 5 percent increase in that of rural seats.[2] The success rate of BJP candidates in cities was 84 percent, against 63 percent in rural areas.

In contrast, the Congress suffered the worst defeat in its history. The party was reduced to 44 seats, with 19 percent of the votes, which is 60 seats less than in its first defeat against the BJP in 1998, or 6 percent less than that in the 1999 elections. The defeat was so comprehensive that the party failed to reach even the 10 percent seats bar required to obtain the status of Leader of the Opposition. Even the 1977 defeat, after the 'Emergency', was not as thorough. The opposition then gathered under the Janata Party banner won in the Hindi Belt—setting the precedence—where the Congress had been reduced to 12 seats, compared to 7 in 2014.

Thus, 45 percent of the votes in the Hindi Belt brought the BJP and its allies 86 percent of the seats. The Congress, in contrast, obtained only 3 percent of the seats with 19.5 percent of the votes. If we compare the two national parties' performance in 2014 with that in 2009, we can see that in 2014 the BJP is three points above the Congress, whereas in 2009 the Congress was one point above the BJP (Figure 2.1). This huge swing amplified the disproportionality effect of the electoral system and enabled the BJP to achieve a clear majority.

The Resilience of Regional Parties

The resilient actors of these elections have been the regional parties, though in a contrasted manner. Two striking numbers reveal that they have on the whole, including the northern states, withstood the Modi wave—in terms of votes rather than seats, however. All regional parties combined have

Figure 2.1
Vote Share and Position of BJP and Congress Candidates in the 2014 General Elections

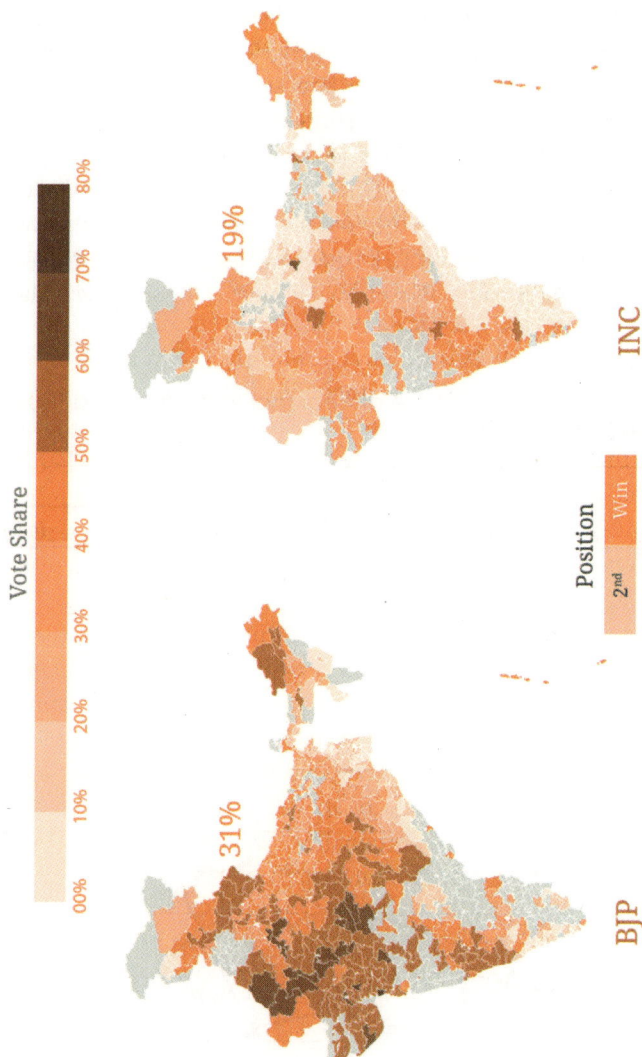

Source: Adapted from ECI data and G. Verniers' election data. With QGIS.
Disclaimer: This image has been redrawn by the authors and is not to scale. It does not represent any authentic national or international boundaries and is used for illustrative purposes only.

obtained the same number of seats as in the previous elections (212), with the same combined vote share (46.6 percent) (Table 2.3).

This stability, however, hides important contrasts of performance. Regional parties in the South and the East—AIADMK in Tamil Nadu, BJD in Odisha, and TMC in West Bengal—have swept the polls, even though the BJP was contesting in these states.

In comparison, the regional parties in the northern states—the SP and BSP in UP, Nitish Kumar's Janata Dal–United (JD[U]), and Laloo Prasad's Rashtriya Janata Dal (RJD) in Bihar—have been decimated in terms of seats, even though they did not perform poorly in terms of vote share, garnering 3.4 percent, 4.1 percent, 1.1 percent, and 1.3 percent, respectively, at the national level, but far more at the state level. Mayawati's

Table 2.3
Vote Share and Seat Share of Regional vs. National Parties (1991–2014)

| | Seat Share | | | |
	INC	*BJP*	*Regional*	*Independent*
1991	232	120	168	1
1996	140	161	233	9
1998	141	182	214	6
1999	114	182	241	6
2004	145	138	255	5
2009	206	116	212	9
2014	44	282	212	3

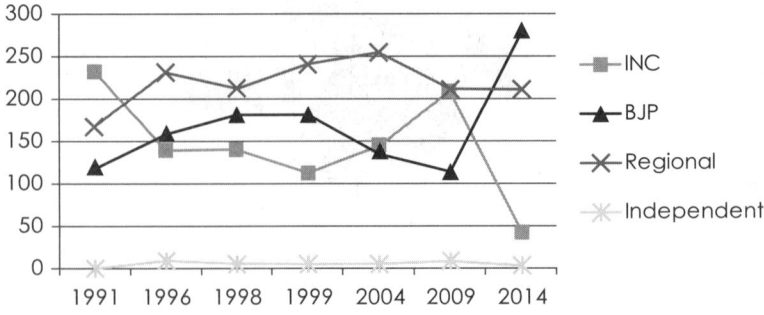

(Table 2.3 Continued)

(Table 2.3 Continued)

	Vote Share			
	INC	*BJP*	*Regional*	*Independent*
1991	36.26	20.11	39.44	4.03
1996	28.8	20.29	44.22	5.98
1998	25.82	25.59	45.79	2.32
1999	28.3	23.75	44.76	2.69
2004	26.53	22.16	46.76	4.24
2009	28.52	18.84	46.77	5.19
2014	19.3	31.1	46.6	3

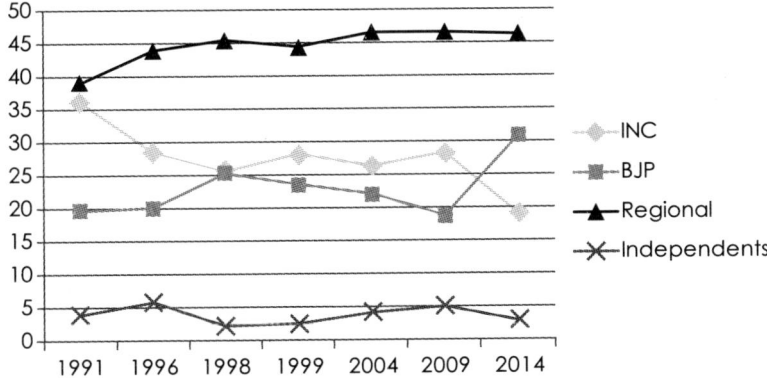

Source: Adapted from ECI data.

BSP did not get a single seat for its 19 percent of votes and Mulayam Singh Yadav's SP could secure only two seats despite having received 24 percent of the votes.

In Bihar, RJD and JD(U) outpolled the BJP with 20.14 percent and 15.78 percent, respectively, but wrested a scant four and two seats, respectively. The only regional player who scored a success was Ram Vilas Paswan's LJP (six seats with 6.40 percent of the votes), though this was on account of its alliance with the BJP, with which it had a seat-sharing agreement in seven constituencies, winning all but one seat.

Regional parties swept states where the BJP is not traditionally a strong contender. In Tamil Nadu, Jayalalithaa's AIADMK doubled its 2009 vote share (44.3 percent) and won 37 seats. The two other seats were won by the BJP and its local ally Ambumani Ramadoss's Pattali Makkal Katchi. The DMK did not win any seat in spite of its share of valid votes: 1.7 percent nationally and 23.58 percent at the state level.

In Andhra Pradesh, the carving of Telangana and the fragmentation of the party system that preceded it led to a scattered distribution of votes, from which the Congress emerged as the greatest loser. The Telangana Rashtra Samithi more than doubled its vote share (from 6.14 percent to 13.93 percent) to win 11 seats, against 2 in 2009. The Telugu Desam Party (TDP) increased its vote share by 4 percent (29.15 percent) and gained 10 additional seats (16), owing to its concentration in coastal Andhra. The Yuvajana, Shramika, Rythu Congress (YSR Congress), a breakaway faction of the Congress led by Jagan Mohan Reddy, son of late Congress Chief Minister Y.S.R. Reddy, finished a close second, tailing the TDP in vote share with 28.9 percent of the total vote share. They score, however, only nine seats, owing to the dispersion of its votes. The residual Congress won 11.5 percent of the votes—85 percent of which are attributed to Telangana—scoring two seats.

In Odisha, Naveen Patnaik's strategy to keep distance from the BJP—which enabled him to win the 2009 elections—paid off, as the BJD gained six additional seats (20 out of 21) with a 7 percent vote share increase—bringing it to 44 percent as compared to its 2009 performance. The BJD repeated this performance in the Vidhan Sabha elections as well, which was contested simultaneously. There, the party won 80 percent of the seats (117) with 43 percent of vote share. The Congress came second with 26 percent of vote share and reached the runner-up position in most of the coastal constituencies. The BJP, third with 21.5 percent, was ahead of the Congress in most of the interior constituencies.

In West Bengal, Mamata Banerjee's TMC consolidated its grip with 39.3 percent of the votes, an 8 percent gain from 2009. The Communist Party India (Marxist) or CPM registered its worst performance, winning only two seats but with 22.71 percent of the valid votes. In Kolkata, the BJP came second, before the CPM. The saffron party came third overall, making unprecedented inroads into this eastern state. Both BJP and CPM won the same number of seats (2).

Kerala provided some relief to the Congress, which came first with eight seats out of 20, with 31 percent of the votes. In Karnataka too, the Congress resisted very well, with 41 percent of vote share, 2 percent behind the BJP. The BJP still suffered from past divisions, dating from the preceding Assembly elections, in which the former Chief Minister B.S. Yeddyurappa broke away from the party and contested under his own banner. He subsequently rejoined the BJP, but the traces of this rift were too fresh to heal in time for the campaign.

In all these other states, the decline of the Congress and the fragmentation of the political scene carved spaces that the dominant regional parties could occupy. In many cases, BJP's rise contributed to the further fragmentation of already divided landscapes, reinforcing the dominant regional parties.

In 2009, seat-sharing agreements between the Congress and some regional allies had helped the UPA to secure a number of seats.[3] In 2014, the uncertainty of the outcome at the precampaign phase led most parties—the Congress first among them—to go to the polls on their own. Thus, former allies and splintered factions of the Congress (as in the case of Andhra Pradesh) neutralized each other in a number of constituencies. Taken together, the UPA parties represent 23 percent of the total vote share, with 59 seats. The NDA parties represent 38 percent of the total vote share, with 332 seats. It would be difficult to argue that seat-sharing agreements among UPA and former UPA members would have affected the outcome in any significant way, but one might assume that the amplitude of the rout might have been in some cases somewhat attenuated.

As a result, and despite the overall resilience of regional parties, there are slightly fewer parties represented in the Lok Sabha (36 parties—26 having two MPs or more—against 39 in 2009). In addition, the decimation of the Congress and the regional parties in the North led to a considerable shift of the balance of power between national and regional parties, not only due to the fact of BJP's majority in the Lok Sabha but also because of the reduction of the number of significant players.

Vote Consolidation?

Beyond main parties' performances, the 2014 elections also showed smaller but significant shifts in voting behaviors. Political observers who spend time on the field asking voters who they are going to vote for are often struck by a response that has become more and more generic: respondents say that they are going to vote "for the winner." In other contexts, it would be considered presumptuous, if not hazardous, to claim the status of the victor before the polling takes place. Why vote for a candidate X if he or she is bound to win anyway? But in India, it is important to project an image of a victor in order to catch indecisive voters, sometimes called the *hawa* (wind), in order to consolidate a winning wave.

These elections have also confirmed a trend that was visible in the previous State Assembly elections in Rajasthan, Madhya Pradesh, and Chhattisgarh. The share of votes, which is usually distributed among small parties, local, and independent candidates or branches of other states' regional parties, has substantially diminished in favor of national and regional parties (Table 2.4). A similar phenomenon was observed in

Table 2.4

Performance of Regional Parties (Vote Share and Seats) in the 2009 and 2014 General Elections

	2009		2014	
	Vote Share	*Seats*	*Vote Share*	*Seats*
Trinamool	31.18%	19	39.35%	34
CPM	32.11%	9	22.71%	2
BJD	37.23%	14	44.08%	20
AIADMK	22.88%	9	44.28%	37
DMK	25.09%	18	23.58%	0
TDP	24.93%	6	29.15%	16
TRS	6.14%	2	13.93%	11
YSR Congress	0.00%	0	28.94%	9
SP	23.26%	20	22.19%	5
BSP	27.42%	23	19.63%	0
SHS	17.00%	11	20.64%	18
NCP	19.28%	8	15.04%	4
JD(U)	24.04%	20	15.78%	2
RJD	20.13%	4	20.14%	4
LJP	6.96%	0	6.40%	6
SAD	33.85%	4	26.27%	4

Source: Adapted from ECI data.

the 1999 general elections, polls that followed rapidly the 1998 elections. This is an indication that voters tend to want their votes to count and are less ready than before to 'lose' their votes on hopeless candidates or parties (Table 4.5).

Particularly striking is the poor performance of the BSP outside UP (Table 4.6). The Dalit party had made inroads into neighboring states in preceding elections, particularly in Delhi, Haryana, and northern Madhya Pradesh, banking on a consolidated Dalit support. The decline was particularly pronounced in Haryana and Delhi, where the AAP drew a substantial part of its electorate among the poorer segments of the electorate.

Finally, new players have not been able to impact the competition, contrary to expectations. The AAP obtained 2 percent of the total vote share and four seats, all in Punjab. Its vote share was concentrated in this

Table 2.5
Vote Share of Independent Candidates and Small Parties in 2014 General Elections

	1998	1999	2004	2009	2014
Independents	2.37%	2.74%	4.25%	5.19%	2.99%
Small parties	14.93%	4.12%	5.33%	7.92%	4.99%
Total	17.30%	6.86%	9.58%	13.10%	7.97%

Source: Adapted from ECI data.

Table 2.6
Performance of the Bahujan Samaj Party in Five States (Vote Share and Number of Seats) in the 2014 General Elections

	2009	2014
Uttar Pradesh	27.42% (23)	19% (0)
Delhi	5.7% (0)	1.2% (0)
Haryana	15.7% (0)	4.6% (0)
Madhya Pradesh	5.8% (1)	3.8% (0)
Rajasthan	3.4% (0)	2.4% (0)

Source: Adapted from ECI data.

state and in Delhi,[4] where it increased its tally, compared to the Fall 2013 Assembly elections. It failed to make inroads in India's larger cities and in the periphery of Delhi, where it represented less than 5 percent of vote share on average. In Karnataka, the AAP scored lower than the NOTA option, which was introduced for the first time in a general election.

Therefore, far from showing a sure sign of nationalization of the party system, the 2014 results just show how fragmented the vote was. The vote was fragmented precisely because the BJP was able to win 282 seats with just 31 percent of the votes. In other words, the BJP victory does not mean that there has been a structural transformation of the polity but that we have yet another product of fragmentation, which has characterized Indian politics for the last 30 years. This is not to say, however, that these elections were a simple continuation of past trends. Two new phenomena at least—among others and too early to call them trends yet—have emerged.

Class versus Caste

First, parties that are explicitly caste-based have suffered more than the regional parties who incarnate a regional identity and are not associated—or not exclusively associated with specific vote banks. The BSP in UP is a case in point, but a similar erosion affected the SP and the JD(U). These parties' past successes were built on electoral strategies based on the formation of caste-based local alliances between their core electorate—Dalit, Yadav, or Kurmis—and specific segments of the local voting population, also defined along caste lines. The 'transferability of vote bank' strategy brought the BSP to power several times and was emulated by other parties. This time, the BJP wave neutralized its competitors' alliance strategy by drawing voters from most of the groups that do not constitute a traditional vote bank for these regional parties—upper caste and lower OBCs for the most part. Thus, the relative success of the BSP and SP in terms of vote share can be explained by their ability to maintain the support of their core electorate, but their defeat can be explained by their inability to build successful local alliances, due to BJP's successful campaign.

Of course, these explicitly caste-based parties are also located in northern states, where the BJP has been traditionally stronger than in other regional party-dominated states. But these caste-based parties might have suffered more from the Modi wave than other regional parties, such as AIADMK, BJD, and TMC, for other reasons as well. For instance, these parties tend to differ also in terms of leadership style. Jayalalithaa and Mamata Banerjee are embodiments of the same kind of strong leadership as Narendra Modi, and the voters were certainly asking for more political authority after 10 years of a rather self-effacing prime minister and of a government perceived as essentially corrupt. This may not be a perfect explanation as Mayawati is also a decisive leader, an embodiment of power and authority, and Naveen Patnaik, the chief minister of Odisha, is not particularly known for having authoritarian tendencies. This did not prevent the former from losing and the latter from winning decisively. These chief ministers also effectively centralize executive powers and govern through the bureaucracy—kept on a tight leash—rather than through their party organizations. Lack of access to the bureaucracy makes it difficult for other parties to perform their expected role of service provider often assigned by voters to politicians. But again, the same could be said of Mayawati or Nitish Kumar in Bihar.

The decline of the explicitly caste-based regional parties may also reflect a more structural, societal evolution of India's polity, which the BJP has cannily exploited. After a decade of economic growth and rapid urbanization, low-caste-based parties have lost some of their appeal. Dominant groups—such as the dominant OBCs in UP and Bihar—have reaped most of the benefits from their states' economic transformation. Not only has the recent growth taken place in some specific economic sectors—construction, mining, local industry—and not so much in the agricultural sector, but also the growth's benefits has usually been reaped mostly by the local economic elites, often equated with the local political elites aligned with the dominant parties. The perception of the SP in UP being a self-serving organization at the service of Yadavs and minorities might have aroused the resentment and perhaps even the wrath of other segments of the electorate.

Furthermore, these parties find it difficult to keep mobilizing voters on their previously successful campaign themes. Reservations have reached a saturation point in public debate and these regional parties are themselves not particularly keen on expanding the current regime. In any case, reservations or further reservations did not figure very high in the priority list of OBCs and Dalit voters, who tend to migrate toward cities or intend to do so in the near future. These voters want jobs in the industrial and services sectors, which are largely privately owned. They aspire to join the ranks of the middle class and in Narendra Modi they found an embodiment of their aspirations. Narendra Modi claimed in his campaign that he represented a 'neo middle class' made up of these newly urbanized aspiring categories. This might have attracted voters who used to consider themselves as Dalits or OBC first. Recent figures of the Centre for the Study of Developing Societies (CSDS) indeed show that the richer and the more urbanized UP Dalit voters were, the less they voted for the BSP and the more for the BJP. This trend was also observed among the OBCs of UP and Bihar at the expense of the SP and the JD(U), although the latter two parties retained the support of their core electorate.

Thus, emerges a class factor in the support of the BJP, a factor reinforced by the attractiveness of the Hindutva discourse to this new category; the 'neo middle class' OBCs and Dalits. In UP, the 2013 Muzaffarnagar riots polarized voters along communal lines and fostered the Hindu identity of Jats and other lower caste voters, again at the expense of the BSP (which had performed much better in western UP in 2009 and 2012) and the Rashtriya Lok Dal, which was wiped off the electoral map. An examination of vote share density of the BJP in UP reveals that the BJP got its highest vote share—between 50 percent and 60 percent—in most of the urban seats and in all the western UP seats surrounding Muzaffarnagar.

Does this mean that caste is waning as a mobilization vehicle or as a determinant of electoral behavior? BJP's support in UP was strongest among the upper castes and the lower OBCs. The saffron party also suc-ceeded in attracting votes from other groups, particularly from the youth. But the SP and BSP's core electorates, which have been slightly diluting in previous recent elections, have remained intact overall, indicating that caste polarization remains a salient feature of politics in these regions.

Redundant State Parties?

The second new feature is that for the first time since 1989 state parties are not necessary for the survival of the Union government. Over the past 25 years, the fulfillment of India's federal potential had become largely dependent on the support or the opposition of regional parties to the Central government. Now the BJP has a clear majority on its own. Given the political style of Narendra Modi, the new balance of power has already resulted in a more centralized form of governance. However, it would be too hasty to dismiss the importance of state-based parties and, more broadly, of state politics. Three reasons can attenuate this new form of centralization. First, Narendra Modi, as a Chief Minister of Gujarat, has for 13 years fought the 'Delhi Sultanate' in the name of demanding greater autonomy for the states. Second, the states have acquired a clear sense of their capabilities and a culture of independence that may not be easily thwarted. Third, the BJP lacks a majority in the Rajya Sabha. In the Upper House, the Congress is still number 1 with 68 seats. The BJP comes second with only 46 seats, the rest being divided among 26 parties, of which only three hold more than 10 seats: the BSP (14), the TMC (12), and AIADMK (10). The SP, the JD(U), and the CPI(M) have nine seats each. The Modi government will need to engage with some of these parties to ensure the passage of its Bills in the Rajya Sabha.

The most important regional parties are all located in non-Hindi-speaking states, and the recent pro-Hindi and pro-Sanskrit decisions taken by the Modi government and the relative absence of ministers from the South and the East of the country will surely be irritants to their relation with the Center.

For all these reasons, the era of coalitions is far from over. Indeed, in spite of the fact that the BJP has an absolute majority in the Lok Sabha, the Modi government includes members of state parties that have been allies in their respective regions. Shiv Sena, Akali Dal, the TDP, the LJP, and various other inconsequential minor formations have been accommodated, their ministers being in charge of minor portfolios, but still kept on board.

Conclusion

The rise of the BJP needs to be qualified not only because it pivoted largely upon the popularity of Narendra Modi, but also because it was not the landslide victory that the number of seats won by the party initially suggested. No party has won so many seats with so few votes in the past. BJP's success was, in fact, due to the concentration of its supporters in the north and the west of the country, at the expense of the Congress and a few state parties of the Hindi Belt. BJP's success, similar to its prior successes, was essentially located in the Hindi Belt.

While the Congress was routed in northern and western India (even though it retained more votes than the BJP did in 2009), regional parties (like the TMC) withstood the 'Modi wave' rather effectively, even when they were declared opponents of BJP's champion. Their resilience shows a clear continuity in the fragmentation of the electorate and the party system, a defining feature of Indian politics.

Nonetheless, the 2014 Lok Sabha elections have seen the defeat of explicitly caste-based parties and the resilience of regional parties appealing to broader segments of the electorate. In that sense, they may mark a turning point, which would be verified if caste-based parties in the Hindi Belt continue to lose ground in upcoming state elections, due to the attractiveness of BJP's class and Hindutva-oriented discourse over caste compulsions. In that case, the BJP may become a dominant party in the north of India, where the state parties do not have a strong regionalist identity on which they could capitalize and oppose national parties. In contrast, the ethno-linguistic roots of southern regional parties may contribute to their resilience.

The 2014 Lok Sabha elections may also prove to be a milestone if the balance of power between the Center and the states is transformed at the expense of the regional parties because of India's return to a dominant party system. Today, the BJP needs the support of state parties in the Rajya Sabha, but if it wins Vidhan Sabha elections in the coming years, that dependence will automatically reduce, thus reinforcing BJP's domination.

A dominant BJP, however, would not take India back to the heydays of the 'Congress system' in terms of the Center–state relations. As Rajni Kothari showed in the 1960s, this 'system' gave great autonomy to the Pradesh Congress Committees (PCC) and the state governments whose leaders were represented at the Congress Working Committee. On top of it, the Congress was its own opposition in many states—where the faction leader at the helm of the PCC was the main rival of the chief minister. Modi's BJP is a far more centralized party then the Congress ever was, evident from the appointment of Amit Shah, Narendra Modi's right-hand man, as the new party president. In the absence of a second national party, deprived of an effective organization and more importantly, of a salient political narrative, the opposition to the centralist tendencies of the BJP will come from the states and from the regional parties. How these parties will coordinate their efforts and how the Congress will adapt itself to this profoundly changed landscape will determine the course of India's democracy in the coming decade.

Notes and References

1. That is in constituencies with 75 percent plus urban population.
2. Rural seats being defined as constituencies with less than 25 percent urban population.
3. See Christophe Jaffrelot and Gilles Verniers, "Re-nationalization of India's Political Party System or Continued Prevalence of Regionalism and Ethnicity?," *Asian Survey*, 51 (6) 2011, pp. 1090–1112.
4. Fifty-four percent of their total vote share comes from these two states.

3

The Bharatiya Janata Party: A Victory for Narendra Modi

Walter K. Andersen

The recent national elections can be characterized as pivotal. They launched Narendra Modi, former chief minister of the state of Gujarat, to the national stage, and his goal is to remain in power until he achieves his goals of a rapidly developing and secure country. The Bharatiya Janata Party (BJP) is the first political party in three decades to have a parliamentary majority on its own and, thus, has considerable room for maneuver. Its victory provides a springboard for the party to make an aggressive push to expand both its electoral and social base. The long-dominant Congress Party was decimated and its European-style social welfare agenda rejected. In its place, the BJP pledged to place greater emphasis on private enterprise and less on government.

The new prime minister, moreover, is different socially from his predecessors as he is not from the elite upper class that has dominated Indian politics at the national level till now. The BJP's success in appealing to the lower levels of the Hindu caste hierarchy in this election may alter its presently high-caste orientation. These elections made Modi the most influential figure in a group of affiliated Hindu nationalist organizations referred to as the Sangh Parivar. His task is to get these groups to adopt more inclusive policies that would attract the support of religious minorities, especially Muslims. He studiously avoided Hindutva themes during the campaign and publicly rebuked those who did. His personal campaign appeal was to the young and poor generally and their demand for jobs. With over 50 percent of the 850 million voters between 18 and 35 years old, this was Prime Minister Modi's target group, and polls show that the support of the youth gave him an electoral victory. His major challenge will be to satisfy their demands.

I would like to thank the many senior members of the BJP and the Rashtriya Swayamsevak Sangh (RSS) who agreed to meet with me over the past several months to give me their insights regarding the recent political campaign and Mr Modi's rise in the party, and this includes time that Mr Modi himself gave to me to question him about these issues. I take full responsibility for any mistakes in fact or interpretation that might appear in this analysis. In addition, I would like to thank the following colleagues at Paul H. Nitze School of Advanced International Studies (SAIS), some are my students in the South Asia Studies program, for their generous help in compiling the data and reviewing my text: Rebecca Aman, Allison Berland Kaul, Thomas Schuyler Sturm, Shrey Verma, and Constantino Xavier.

Introduction

The BJP and its National Democratic Alliance (NDA) partners have won what is for them an unprecedented victory in the 2014 Lok Sabha election, with a major shift of popular votes (from 18.8 percent in 2009 parliamentary elections to 31 percent in 2014 for the BJP, and from 29.28 percent to 39 percent for the NDA) and seats (from 116 in 2009 to 282 for the BJP and from 181 to 336 for the NDA).[1] Winning a convincing majority of the parliamentary seats on its own, the BJP has replaced the Congress Party as the preeminent national party and has returned to power after 10 years. It is the first time that a political party, other than the Congress, has received a parliamentary majority on its own.[2] Moreover, this is also the first time that the BJP has demonstrated significant support in all parts of the country.[3]

Four factors seem to have worked in the BJP's favor and they will form the core of this discussion. First was the ability of the BJP candidate, Narendra Modi, to take firm control of the BJP and generate among its core support base a commitment to support him, and by extension, his party, the BJP. Second was the construction of a campaign organization involving thousands of volunteers working together in a closely supervised effort to reach the voters. Third was the anti-incumbency factor fueled by the widespread perception of corruption, lack of development, and poor governance by the ruling Congress Party. Fourth was the BJP's very effective campaign strategy that combined a focus on economic development and jobs that were particularly relevant to India's rapidly growing aspirant population[4] and on Modi himself as the person who could revive India economically. Modi and the BJP campaign were virtually silent on divisive Hindu nationalist issues (e.g., building a Ram temple at Ayodhya and creating a unified civil code) that could have stalled the surge in support for Modi and the BJP and reminded voters of his inability or unwillingness as chief minister of the state of Gujarat to stop the communal rioting in 2002 that left over a thousand people, mainly Muslims, dead.

BJP: Campaign Themes

The BJP Manifesto, in a delayed release on April 7, the first day of polling, reflected the issues Modi had raised during his hundreds of speeches all over the country.[5] It was ideologically centrist, and many commentators, including some in the Congress Party, even compared it to the Congress Manifesto.[6] The document calls for improved policy implementation and focuses on economic growth, job creation, reducing corruption, and keeping prices under control. On economic growth, it emphasizes a developing labor-intensive industry and removing bureaucratic impediments that have slowed decisions on critical economic projects, especially large-scale infrastructure plans. It makes special mention of infrastructure development, reflecting Modi's own focus as chief minister of Gujarat. There are a number of specific actionable proposals, such as raising education appropriations to 6 percent of GDP, connecting Jammu and Kashmir with a rail freight corridor, initiating a National Health Assurance Scheme, creating a National Agricultural Market, transforming Employment Exchanges into Career Centers, establishing institutes of technology and administration in all states, and building

100 smart cities. However, the Manifesto does not support foreign direct investment in retail trade as part of the larger effort to increase such investment throughout the economy, a clear effort to please the party's constituency of small shopkeepers.

Reflecting the campaign itself, there is comparatively little on foreign policy. While no specific countries are mentioned in the document, Modi himself has referred to Japan on the campaign trail as a country with whom India should seek greater involvement.[7] Among the more significant specific foreign policy/security questions raised in the Manifesto is the suggestion of a possible revision of India's no-first-use policy of nuclear weapons. However, just one month after Modi's swearing in, his government affirmed the commitment of the previous government to back the Additional Protocol that would enable the International Atomic Energy Agency to have greater access to India's civilian nuclear program, and, thus, signaled the new government's seriousness in implementing the 2008 Indo-US nuclear deal.[8] The Manifesto also calls for a more muscular policy when required in dealing with provocations from neighboring countries, a likely reference to border incidents over the past year involving Pakistan and China.

Only at the end does the Manifesto refer, and then in a cursory fashion, to such Hindutva issues as the construction of a Ram Temple at Ayodhya and a uniform civil code. At the same time, this Manifesto goes far beyond any previous BJP statement in proposing programs designed to help Muslims, pledging to improve the economic, cultural, and educational well-being of Muslims, including a "permanent interfaith consultative mechanism" and the "preservation and promotion of Urdu." Yet, Muslim suspicion of Modi remained deep throughout the campaign and Modi will have to seek to calm Muslim anxieties to avoid a polarization that would stand in the way of his development objectives.[9]

Intemperate remarks by some of his senior campaign workers, such as Amit Shah, head of the campaign in Uttar Pradesh, worked against his message of inclusiveness, though these comments may also have been calculated to attract additional Hindu support. The BJP won 71 of Uttar Pradesh's 80 parliamentary seats, an unprecedented number of seats for the party in India's most populous state. After the elections, Shah was made president of the BJP, a move calculated both to strengthen Modi's hold on the party and to broaden its message. The choice is potentially risky as the Prime Minister will need to ensure that future election tactics fit a model of national stability; an inclusiveness if his economic goals are to be achieved. The complexity of Indian society, however, nudges any party seeking power at the federal level to ideological moderation, a process that characterized the previous BJP-led government under Atal Bihari Vajpayee (1999–2004).[10]

Modi: Consolidating Control over the BJP

Setting the groundwork for the BJP's electoral victory was the successful move of Modi to assert control over his party, the BJP, perhaps more completely than the previous popular BJP prime minister, Atal Bihari Vajpayee.[11] Modi seems, moreover, to be in the process of transforming the BJP to make it much more inclusive both geographically and socially—and much less collegial. Infighting among senior party leaders in the wake of the party's loss of the 2004 and 2009 national elections gave this regional leader, elected chief minister of Gujarat four times, a major opportunity to grasp the party's levers of power from the established national leadership and subsequently to reshape his party—and ultimately the 2013–14 political campaign—around himself.[12] The BJP campaign was the closest any Indian major party has come to waging an American-style political campaign, and Modi's advisers recognized early on the benefits of a more personalized campaign around his charismatic persona and of pitting him against the much younger, and less popular, Rahul Gandhi from the Congress Party.

Modi achieved a similar transformation earlier at the state level in Gujarat after the deadly communal rioting in early 2002 that elicited criticism of his governance both within the BJP and within the larger Indian political system. He moved to reshape the state unit of the party, employing what one astute analyst of Modi has said was a deliberate policy of replacing the "old style, 20th century Gujarat-based Rashtriya Swayamsevak Sangh (RSS) chapter that brought him into public life,"[13] with a new strategy that was development oriented. Modi promoted loyalists who had an activist commitment to development rather than to those advocating older, more divisive Hindutva issues that took a jaundiced view toward Muslims and other minorities.[14] His was a hands-on government in which he took direct control of several of the most important ministries over his long tenure as chief minister. He seems to be applying this same hands-on technique to the new cabinet at the Center. The BJP's Parliamentary Board announcement on September 13, 2013 that Modi would be their party's prime ministerial candidate conclusively underscored his eclipse of the party's national oligarchs. But in retrospect, this rise had started much earlier and he developed the reputation of a tough political infighter against those who opposed him or his policies.

In May 2012, for example, Modi maneuvered to remove his longtime rival from Gujarat, Sanjay Joshi, from the powerful General Secretary position of the national BJP, thus, effectively destroying Joshi's career in the party. Modi's growing clout in the party was again demonstrated when, on March 31, 2013, he was appointed to the BJP's Parliamentary Board by Rajnath Singh,[15] who had earlier dropped Modi from that body during Singh's first term as its President (2006–09).[16] Modi's consolidation of power was virtually complete a few months later in September when the Parliamentary Board named him the party's candidate for prime minister. The old guard within the party, many with their own local bases of support, grumbled about being sidelined, though Modi was careful to show them public deference and to appear with them on public platforms— and later to appoint most of them to his cabinet. Modi's choices suggest he finds it important to keep potential critics close to him, as witnessed by his choice of Sushma Swaraj, one of his more outspoken critics as external affairs minister.

Modi's dominance was conclusively demonstrated in the closely supervised candidate selection process in the early spring of 2014 when several of the party's most senior leaders were obliged, often against their wishes, to accept a shift from their traditional parliamentary constituencies or dropped. Among the more prominent was Dr Murli Manohar Joshi, who was shifted from Varanasi to make way for Modi. Other examples include the former cricketer Navjot Singh Sidhu (the sitting MP from Amritsar), who was denied a ticket from his constituency, which he had successfully won in both 2004 and 2009, to make way for Arun Jaitley, a long-time Modi supporter and sometime legal advisor.[17] Former External Affairs Minister Jaswant Singh was denied a ticket in his home state of Rajasthan and was expelled from the party for six years for his open protest.

The most dramatic example of discontent over a seat selection was that of L.K. Advani, who was denied the Bhopal seat in Madhya Pradesh that he reportedly wanted,[18] and told to keep the Gandhinagar seat in Modi's own state of Gujarat. Even party president and Modi loyalist Rajnath Singh was moved to Lucknow within the state of Uttar Pradesh from his Ghaziabad constituency, though, perhaps as a reward for his loyalty to Modi, he made a public statement suggesting that Modi wanted him to stay on as party president after the elections.[19] Except for Jaswant Singh, the former oligarchs accepted the verdicts and stayed within the party's big tent, perhaps a result of their earlier socialization within the Hindu nationalist RSS with its emphasis on loyalty to comrades and the organization.[20]

Modi also seems to be transforming the party's long-time association with the Hindu nationalist RSS, which in the past has served as a kind of arbitrator of intra-party disputes, ideological mentor, and source of full-time party organizers (of whom Modi had been one) and volunteers during electoral campaigns. While himself emerging from the ranks of full-time RSS workers,[21] Modi himself sometimes has had an uneasy relationship with the RSS establishment both as the chief minister in Gujarat and as a national party leader, in part because he does not conform to its model of collegial decision making and because he progressively removed those with a hard Hindutva style from positions of importance in the Gujarat BJP to make way for persons who were development-oriented, who were personally loyal to him, and who were less divisive on sectarian issues. An earlier Hindutva-oriented era in the BJP party in Gujarat conclusively came to a close with the decision, almost certainly vetted by Modi, to deny parliamentary tickets to Harin Pathak and Rajendrasinh Rana, two former colleagues in the Gujarat unit of the RSS who used a hard Hindutva style to help bring Modi to power in 2001 and who had repeatedly won in their own respective constituencies.[22] Despite this demotion, they did not leave the party.

The one significant deviation from this pattern of keeping some distance from political figures with a public Hindutva orientation is Amit Shah, a close confidant, who had served as home minister in the Gujarat government under Modi and has a reputation as a tough, hard-knuckles strategist with a very public Hindu nationalist record. Modi, relying on Shah's organizing skills, placed him in charge of the party's campaign in the all-important state of Uttar Pradesh, which elects 80 members to parliament. His alleged outspoken Hindutva comments led India's Election Commission on April 11 to ban his participation in political rallies,[23] a ban that was lifted a few days later when Shah offered an apology and assured the Commission that it would not happen again. Modi also sought to place some distance between himself and the inflammatory anti-Muslim remarks of some prominent supporters by criticizing their statements in tweets released on April 21, 2014, of which one stated, "I disapprove any such irresponsible statement and appeal to those making them to kindly refrain from doing so."[24] This was almost certainly a reaction to the public furor that developed over anti-Muslim comments attributed to Bihar BJP leader, Giriraj Singh, and by Pravin Togadia, a leader in the Vishwa Hindu Parishad and a member of the RSS, in the last month of the campaign.

Despite Modi's distancing himself from advocates of hard Hindutva in Gujarat and his studious avoidance of Hindutva issues in the national campaign, he was able to arouse something bordering on adulation from the RSS's ordinary members, those who faithfully attend the daily training sessions and participate in other RSS activities. The enthusiastic support for Modi from the RSS cadre forced an initially reluctant national RSS leadership to accept Modi as leader of the BJP, to commit RSS personnel to his campaign, and eventually to perform its traditional mediatory role for the sake of party unity in an effort to calm down those party leaders who saw Modi's rise as a threat to their ambitions.[25] Especially instrumental in supporting Modi within the senior ranks of the RSS was Suresh Soni, the Joint General Secretary of the RSS, who was to become the major contact between the RSS and the Modi campaign. So enthusiastic was the RSS cadre backing for Modi that Mohan Bhagwat, its national leader, considered it necessary to publicly advise them to remember their primary loyalties were to the RSS and not to an individual.[26]

Modi: His Tactics

Modi proved himself to be an adept strategist who waged a highly effective parliamentary political campaign that managed to focus the discussion on development and on Modi's personal leadership rather than on more problematic considerations like identity and social welfare. This was a shrewd reading of the public mood on both issues. On the issue of development, one pre-election survey conducted by the Lok Foundation and the University of Pennsylvania's Center for the Advanced Study of India, administered between October and December 2013,[27] found that about 25 percent of the respondents identified economic growth as the number one issue, closely followed by corruption (21 percent) and inflation (18 percent).[28]

Modi was also helped by the widespread concern, especially among the large cohort of young voters, about their job prospects. According to the Indian Election Commission, around 50 percent of the population is between the ages of 18 and 25 and about 10 percent of some 814 million electorate voted for the first time in the recent election.[29] In a February Pew poll, some 69 percent of the youth (18–29 years) said the BJP would do more to create jobs compared to just 17 percent who said so for the Congress.[30] In a campaign almost presidential in style, Modi focused on the comparison between his significant economic achievements as three-term chief minister of Gujarat and Rahul Gandhi, the vice president of the Congress Party, who had never held any public administrative position.

In a direct appeal to the aspirations of the tens of millions of poor young Indians, he drew a sharp distinction between his humble origins and experience as a tea seller, and those of Rahul Gandhi, heir to the most prominent political dynasty in India. According to a Pew poll[31] from February, 78 percent had a favorable view of Modi while only about 50 percent had a favorable impression of Gandhi. In both cases, the popularity of the candidate outstripped support for their respective parties: 63 percent for the BJP and only 19 percent for the Congress.[32] To supporters of Narendra Modi, the rapid economic development of Gujarat during his long tenure as chief minister provides some of the best evidence that his leadership will help India regain its economic momentum. Two prominent Indian–American Columbia economists, Jagdish Bhagwati and Arvind Panagariya,[33] have been strong defenders of Modi's 'Gujarat' model, often responding publicly to criticism of Modi's record. They argue that the rapid economic growth in Gujarat has led to substantial reductions in poverty, malnutrition, and illiteracy. They are especially critical of data ranking Gujarat among the Indian states with the highest rates of malnutrition and poverty.

Critics, however, have called the state's record into question, claiming that Gujarat's growth trajectory was set long before Modi took office, that Modi himself has not had a significant role,[34] or that the state's economic growth has not included the poor, the disadvantaged, and minorities. Foremost among these critics have been left-leaning economists Amartya Sen and Jean Druze who have claimed that Gujarat's growth statistics mask a severe shortage of social infrastructure.[35] Others maintain that the 'Gujarat model' depends on business subsidies and concessions of public goods to companies investing in the state. Although both the inclusiveness of Gujarat's economic success and then Chief Minister Modi's role in that success are subject to debate, Gujarat's growth has been higher than most other states and that period of accelerated growth has coincided with Modi's tenure in office.[36] What is relevant here is that a large part of the voting public accepted Modi's claims and saw them as proof of the positive benefits his leadership could bring to India.

The significant BJP victories in the November–December 2013 State Assembly elections in Rajasthan, Madhya Pradesh, and Chhattisgarh (with the prominent exception of Delhi) made the cadre even more convinced that an all-out effort for the 2014 national election would bring victory.[37] At the same time, Modi guided the efforts to work out pre-polling alliances to enable the BJP to form a coalition government if it did not get the required majority of 272 votes. He could rely on remnants of the old NDA, like the Shiv Sena in Maharashtra and the Akali Dal in Punjab, two of the 15 allied parties that enabled Atal Bihari Vajpayee to form his coalition government in 1999.

As the party's prospective victory loomed, the BJP worked out alliances with former allies, such as that with Dalit leader Ram Vilas Paswan and his Lok Janshakti Party in Bihar, and the Telegu Desam in what had been the state of Andhra Pradesh. As the election drew closer and all polls showed a significant BJP victory, several more parties joined, though not the large regional parties in Uttar Pradesh, Odisha, West Bengal, and Tamil Nadu. While the BJP received an unexpected parliamentary majority on its own, Modi dealt with these allies as if they were coalition partners and several members of these allied parties were given cabinet posts.

The Meaning of the Electoral Results

The BJP's landslide victory in the 2014 Indian parliamentary elections marks a tectonic shift in Indian politics. Led by Narendra Modi, the BJP is the first non-Congress political party in India's history that has won a simple majority on its own and the first time since 1984 that a single party has had a majority in the Lok Sabha, the lower and more powerful house of parliament. The decisive mandate in favor of Narendra Modi and the BJP has challenged traditional political assumptions of caste and religion. Modi's success at articulating an economic agenda and turning it into an electoral rallying point that transcends barriers of caste and religion is a precedent in Indian politics.

The BJP's impressive victories in the states of Uttar Pradesh and Bihar (the BJP and its allies won 104 seats out of 120 in the two states) point toward a social churning that is taking place in India's populous Hindi-speaking heartland. Election results indicate a sizeable shift toward the BJP from voters from two key categories: the Other Backward Classes (OBC) and the Dalits. This shift could be altering the support base of the BJP from a largely high-caste party to one drawing significant lower-caste support. Estimates suggest, at the national level, 45 percent of lower OBCs and 33 percent of upper OBCs voted for the BJP, while more than 26 percent of Dalit votes were polled in favor of the party—more than the Bahujan Samaj Party, which got less than 20 percent votes among the Dalits at the national level.[38] Narendra Modi and the BJP have success-fully tapped into the aspirations of a young population that is seeking jobs and new opportunities for upward mobility.

A promise of development, combined with a broad social coalition of upper castes, sections of OBCs, and Dalits, has played an important role in ushering a BJP victory in the 2014 general elections. Belonging to the OBC community himself, Narendra Modi has leveraged his economic achievements in Gujarat to successfully outmaneuver traditional caste politics of the Mandal era. Building on this electoral success, the BJP and the RSS will almost certainly look to make inroads into constitu-encies that have constituted the main electoral base of regional caste-based parties. The 2014 mandate, thus, provides the BJP a springboard to make an aggressive push for an expansion of its electoral base, both in terms of geography and social base.

The Challenge of Governance

Six major challenges Modi faces as Prime Minister:

1. Can he continue to use his personalized style of leadership to govern a country far more complex than his home state of Gujarat?
2. Can he reshape the BJP into a loyal instrument of power with the tacit approval and continued support of the RSS?
3. Can he significantly move the Indian economy forward to satisfy the longing for development, jobs, and alleviation of poverty, and, thus, satisfy the high expectations from him?
4. Can he build Muslim confidence in his leadership and work to prevent communal violence? A number of prominent Muslim public figures, such as the journalist/author M.J. Akbar, have joined the BJP and bring to the new administration an expertise in allaying Muslim suspicions and encouraging the party to nominate more Muslims to positions of authority. This conciliatory approach may be one of the new prime minister's most difficult challenges. He will need to rein in the anti-Muslim Right among the group of associations loosely affiliated to each other and the RSS, often referred to as the Sangh *Parivar* (the Sangh family). Perhaps the most outspoken figures are from the Vishwa Hindu Parishad, a member of the RSS family of organizations that works with the Hindu ecclesiastical world. One of its leaders, Pravin Togadia, issued a number of inflammatory statements during the campaign that embarrassed Modi and prompted a public rebuke from him regarding such statements. The Prime Minister will need to use his influence with the Sangh Parivar to broaden the message of Hindu nationalism to make it more inclusive and, thus, more acceptable to non-Hindus, perhaps emulating the Christian parties of Europe after World War II, which did this by emphasizing an inclusive social message based on Christian principles.[39] He could do this by emphasizing the RSS message of *Karmayoga* (social work on behalf of the nation) which he employed during the campaign.
5. Can Modi's government shape Indian foreign policy so that it buttresses his goal of faster economic growth at home? His 'Look East' orientation has already elicited both favorable comment

and pledges of economic cooperation from Japan and China, two countries that he visited on several occasions during his tenure as chief minister of Gujarat. His successful invitation to the seven regional SAARC prime ministers/presidents, including Prime Minister Nawaz Sharif of Pakistan, to his May 26, 2014, swearing-in ceremony underscored his goal, often stated on the campaign trail, of bringing the South Asian states together jointly to work on projects to develop the region economically. This commitment was underscored by his choice of Bhutan as his first overseas visit. His engagement on foreign policy was further underscored by the contacts world leaders made to him after his election. In quick succession, the leaders of China, Japan, and the United States invited him to visit, and he accepted all three. Chinese Foreign Minister Wang Yi visited India on June 8 and 9, just weeks after Modi's swearing-in ceremony, to discuss bilateral relations and to invite him to visit China in the fall.[40]

6. The BJP's massive victory has tempered fears about increasing party fragmentation and regional parties' veto power, blocking the central government's economic reforms and foreign policy agenda, but Prime Minister Modi will have to bring India's regional states on board to execute his ambitious program. Under the previous government, key policy initiatives, such as opening the retail sector to foreign investment, a water-sharing agreement with Bangladesh, and normalizing relations with postwar Sri Lanka, all faltered due to regional leaders' opposition and internal coalition pressure. Only four previous prime ministers had served as chief ministers, and Narendra Modi is the only one to have completed more than one term at the helm of a regional government (Gujarat: 2001–14), thus, giving him ample experience and insight on how to calibrate a productive balance of power between central and regional pressure groups.

Conclusion

Overall, Narendra Modi's solid parliamentary majority gives him far greater room for maneuver than that possessed by his predecessors. His early style of leadership as prime minister suggests that it will be as hands-on as was his leadership in Gujarat. In a move in this direction, one of Modi's first acts as prime minister was to eliminate most of the inter-ministerial groups of ministers committees, which were typically used to defer decisions and avoid addressing divisive issues. These committees had the effect of blurring policy choices.

If Prime Minister Modi can achieve this agenda reasonably well, his chances of a lengthy tenure are good and he will have the time to transform the BJP into a loyal instrument of power and an agent of change. He has repeatedly said he needs two terms (10 years) to do this.

Notes and References

1. Election Commission of India, General Elections 2014. Data on May 17, 2014, http://eci.nic.in/eci_main1/ElectionStatistics.aspx (accessed on June 3, 2014)
2. Comparing seats won by the BJP since the party emerged with its present name in the 1984 elections, the successive parliamentary seat counts were 2, 85, 120, 161, 182, 138, 116, and 282 in the most recent election.
3. The BJP has long had a strong base of support in the Hindi-speaking center and north of India, but with marginal to no support in the south and east.
4. The term 'aspirant' is taken from a McKinsey study analyzing the future growth trends in India in the context of the more rapid growth of the Indian economy after the adoption of market reforms in the 1990s. It concludes that this lower-middle-class group is the fastest growing segment of the population. S. Sankhe, April 2012, McKinsey & Company. http://www.mckinsey.com/insights/urbanization/urban_awakening_in_india (accessed on June 3, 2014).
5. The campaign manifesto, whose English title is "Time for Change, Time for Modi," was released from the party headquarters in Delhi. While technically chaired by senior party leader Dr Murli Manohar Joshi, Narendra Modi according to party interlocutors was personally involved as he wanted a document that could serve as a blueprint for action if he emerged as Prime Minister. The consultative mechanism put together to offer ideas resembled that of the party's ideological parent, the Rashtriya Swayamsevak Sangh, with requests for suggestions from all segments of society and institutions and passing that information up through the ranks to the senior leadership. Bharatiya Janata Party, "Manifesto 2014", n.d. www. bjp.org/manifesto2014 (accessed on June 13, 2014).
6. M. Sharma, "The Very Real Differences Between the BJP and Congress Agendas," *Business Standard*, April 7, 2014, http://www.business-standard.com/article/elections-2014/the-very-real-differences-between-the-bjp-and-congress-agendas-114040700680_1. html (accessed on April 14, 2014). "10 Differences Between Congress, BJP Manifestos," NDTV, April 8, 2014, http://www.ndtv.com/elections/article/election-2014/10-differences-between-congress-bjp-manifestos-505486 (accessed on June 13, 2014); *First Post*, "Here's a Word Cloud Comparison of BJP's and Congress's Manifesto," April 7, 2014, http://www.firstpost.com/politics/heres-a-word-cloud-comparison-of-bjps-and-congresss-manifesto-1468801.html (accessed on June 13, 2014).

7. Shri Narendra Modi memorial lecture in Chennai on "India and the World," YouTube. com, October 18, 2013, https://www.youtube.com/watch?v=zRgeAR2jXpE (accessed on June 13, 2014); B. Einhorn and B. Shrivastava, "India Under Narendra Modi Could Be Japan's Best Friend," *Bloomberg Businessweek*, April 10, 2014, http://www.businessweek.com/articles/2014-04-10/india-under-narendra-modi-could-be-japans-bestfriend (accessed on June 13, 2014); S. Verma, "Big in Japan: Why Abe Is Rooting for a Modi Win," *Foreign Policy Magazine* (South Asia Channel), February 20, 2014, http://southasia.foreignpolicy.com/posts/2014/02/20/big_in_japan_why_abe_is_rooting_for_a_modi_win (accessed on June 13, 2014).

8. R. Sood, "Agenda for Nuclear Diplomacy," *Hindu*, June 27, 2014, http://www.thehindu.com/opinion/lead/agenda-for-nuclear-diplomacy/article6152407.ece?homepage=true (accessed on July 7, 2014).

9. A. Varshney, "Hearing the Silence," *Indian Express*, April 14, 2014, http://indianexpress.com/article/opinion/columns/hearing-the-silence/2034581/ (accessed on June 13, 2014).

10. L. Rudolph and S. Rudolph, *In Pursuit of Lakshmi: The Political Economy of the Indian State* (Chicago: University of Chicago Press, 1987), pp. 38–44.

11. Modi has exercised more influence in the party than any BJP leader since Deendayal Upadhyaya, who died under mysterious circumstances on February 10, 1968, while traveling on a train from Lucknow to Patna. Upadhyaya was a revered figure in the party, then called the Bharatiya Jana Sangh, from its formation in the early 1950s until his death. For a discussion of the Bharatiya Jana Sangh and Upadhyaya's commanding role in it, see Walter K. Andersen and Shridhar D. Damle, *The Brotherhood in Saffron: The Rashtriya Swayamsevak Sangh and Hindu Revivalism* (New Delhi: Vistaar Publications, 1987).

12. Modi's success in becoming the center of the political campaign nationally is underscored by the decision of Arvind Kejriwal of the Aam Aadmi Party to contest from the city of Varanasi, Uttar Pradesh, soon after the BJP announced that Modi would contest from this city. His appeal to the rank and file worker is witnessed by the widespread use of 'NaMo' (abbreviation of Narendra Modi) to underscore that the party and Modi are linked. The party, capitalizing on his personal popularity, made him the focus of the campaign with the launching of its Bharat Vijay Rallies from March 26, scheduling Modi to address 185 rallies targeting 295 parliamentary constituencies. For an analysis of the strategy, see *Firstpost Politics*, "From Today, Modi to Address 185 'Bharat Vijay Rallies'," March 24, 2014, http://www.firstpost.com/politics/from-today-modi-to-address-185-bharat-vijay-rallies-1448363.html (accessed on April 14, 2014).

13. S. Bhatt, "Why Modi Had to Get Rid of Harin Pathak," *India Abroad*, April 4, 2014, pp. A22–A23.

14. A prominent exception to this general policy of sidelining people associated closely with Hindutva issues is Modi's retention of Amit Shah, his campaign manager in the key state of Uttar Pradesh.

15. M. Reddy, "Modi Marches into Rajnath's Team 2014," *Hindu*, March 31, 2013, http://www.thehindu.com/news/national/modi-marches-into-rajnaths-team-2014/article4566873.ece (accessed on June 16, 2014).

16. Rajnath Singh and Modi were later to develop a close relationship and the former worked within the party to facilitate Modi's rise receiving the critical Home Ministry in the new cabinet.

17. Jaitley lost his contest, but still was named to two of the most important cabinet ministries, Finance and, at least temporarily, Defense.
18. P. Joshi, "Modi to Contest from Vadodara Too; Advani Denied Bhopal," *Hindu BusinessLine*, March 19, 2014, http://www.thehindubusinessline.com/news/politics/modi-to-contest-from-vadodara-too-advani-denied-bhopal/article5806334.ece (accessed on June 16, 2014).
19. Press Trust of India, "Will Continue as BJP Chief if Party Comes to Power: Rajnath Singh," *Indian Express*, March 28, 2014, http://indianexpress.com/article/india/politics/will-continue-as-bjp-chief-if-party-comes-to-power-rajnath-singh/ (accessed on June 16, 2014).
20. Telling is the fact that of the senior leaders who were denied tickets or told to shift constituencies, the only one who openly rebelled and left the party was the person with no RSS background, Jaswant Singh. There is speculation within senior BJP circles that Jaswant Singh may return to the BJP.
21. Modi started attending the daily training sessions of the RSS when he was eight years old, and this experience, he later wrote, gave him the self-discipline and national commitment to make him what he now is. He rose through the ranks, including the rigorous three-year training course, and became a full-time worker (*pracharak*) of the RSS from 1970. He was pracharak for Ahmedabad by the time he was 24 and simultaneously worked for a Master's degree in Political Science at Gujarat University. In 1985, the RSS assigned him to the BJP, and two years later, he formally joined the party. For a review of his earlier career, see "Narendra Modi: From Tea Vendor to PM Candidate," *Times of India*, September 13, 2013, http://timesofindia.indiatimes.com/india/Narendra-Modi-From-tea-vendor-to-PM-candidate/articleshow/22554466.cms (accessed on April 12, 2014). Several of his biographies of varying quality have been published over the past year.
22. Bhatt, "Why Modi Had to Get Rid of Harin Pathak."
23. F. Daniel, "Election Commission Bans Rallies by Amit Shah over Religious Hatred," Reuters, New Delhi, April 12, 2014, http://in.reuters.com/article/2014/04/11/election-commission-amit-shah-azam-khan-idINDEEA3A0DU20140411 (accessed on April 14, 2014); Anant Zanane, "Amit Shah's 'Revenge' Remark in Riot-Hit Area Sparks Controversy," NDTV, April 5, 2014, http://www.ndtv.com/elections/article/election-2014/amit-shah-s-revenge-remark-in-riot-hit-area-sparks-controversy-504771 (accessed on April 14, 2014); Surabhi Malik, "Amit Shah to Seek Review of Election Commission's Ban on His Rallies in UP," NDTV, April 12, 2014, http://www.ndtv.com/elections/article/election-2014/amit-shah-to-seek-review-of-election-commission-s-ban-on-his-rallies-in-up-507596 (accessed on April 14, 2014); "Ishrat Jahan Case: Court Grants Time to CBI on Plea to Make Shah Accused," *Economic Times*, March 26, 2014, http://articles.economictimes.indiatimes.com/2014-03-26/news/48594857_1_amit-shah-cbi-judge-geeta-gopi-ishrat-jahan (accessed on April 14, 2014); Walter Andersen and Allison Berland Kaul, "Election 2014: It's Mission 50+ for Modi," *Hardnews*, April 9, 2014, http://www.hardnewsmedia.com/2014/04/6275?page=show (accessed on April 14, 2014).
24. *FirstPost*, April 23, 2014, http://www.firstpost.com/politics/modi-raps-petty-togadia-on-twitter-for-his-irresponsible-statements (accessed on April 24, 2014).
25. Party interlocutors tell me that this is the first time that a movement from below has forced the national leadership of the RSS to throw its support to someone as the BJP's prime ministerial choice and to commit the organization so thoroughly to a political campaign.

26. Bhagwat made these comments in an address to the Pratinidhi Sabha (the chief deliberative body of the RSS), meeting in Bangalore on March 9, 2013, in response to a participant's suggestion that the RSS should be to the BJP what the statesman Chanakya was to the emperor who built the Mauryan Empire in the 4th century BC. Some senior BJP officials went even further in their public praise of Modi, such as Party President Rajnath Singh, who reportedly compared Modi to Lord Ram, perhaps the most popular incarnation of the Divine in Hindu theology. "RSS Can't Chant 'NaMo, NaMo': Mohan Bhagwat to Cadre," *Zee News*, March 11, 2014, http://zeenews.india.com/news/nation/rss-can-t-chant-namo-namo-mohan-bhagwat-to-cadre_917174.html (accessed on April 6, 2014); "Rajnath Singh Compares Narendra Modi with Lord Rama," NDTV, December 30, 2013, http://www.ndtv.com/article/india/rajnath-singh-compares-narendra-modi-with-lord-rama-464750 (accessed on April 6, 2014).

27. Lok Foundation and Center for the Advanced Study of India, n.d., Center for the Advanced Study of India. Retrieved from Lok Pre-Election Survey: http://casi.sas.upenn.edu/system/files/Lok_2014_Short_Report_wMoEs.pdf; http://casi.sas.upenn.edu/system/files/Lok_Survey_Methodological_Note.pdf (accessed on April 13, 2014).

28. M. Vaishnav, D. Kapur, and N. Sircar, "Growth Is No 1 Poll Issue for Voters, Shows Survey," *Times of India*, March 16, 2014, http://timesofindia.indiatimes.com/home/lok-sabha-elections-2014/news/Growth-is-No-1-poll-issue-for-voters-survey-shows/articleshow/32112319.cms (accessed on April 6, 2014).

29. S. Shah, "Vital Facts and Numbers About 2014 Indian Polls," *International News*, March 28, 2014, http://www.thenews.com.pk/Todays-News-2-240768-Vital-facts-and-numbers-about-2014-Indian-polls (accessed on April 6, 2014).

30. Banyan, "India's Election: Gauging Opinion," *Economist*, April 2, 2014, http://www.economist.com/blogs/banyan/2014/04/indias-election (accessed on April 6, 2014).

31. Y. Raj, "Modi More Popular, Rahul Far Behind: US Survey," *Hindustan Times*, February 2, 2014, http://www.hindustantimes.com/specials/coverage/myindia-myvote/chunk-ht-ui-myindiamyvote-countdownto2014/unhappy-indians-clamour-for-change-at-lok-sabha-election-poll/sp-article10-1188604.aspx (accessed on April 6, 2014).

32. A subsequent poll (conducted by Zee Media through the Taleem Research Foundation) showed that 46.1 percent supported Modi for prime minister and only about 21.2 percent reported support for Gandhi. See: Zee News, "Narendra Modi Most Popular for PM's Post: Zee–Taleem Poll Survey," March 14, 2014, http://zeenews.india.com/news/nation/narendra-modi-most-popular-for-pm-s-post-zee-taleem-poll-survey_918028.html (accessed on April 6, 2014).

33. A. Panagariya, "Here's Proof that Gujarat has Flourished Under Modi," *Tehelka*, March 29, 2014, http://www.tehelka.com/heres-proof-that-gujarat-has-flourished-under-modi/ (accessed on May 5, 2015).

34. M. Ghatak and S. Roy, "Modinomics: Do Narendra Modi's Economic Claims Add Up?," *Guardian*, March 13, 2014, http://www.theguardian.com/commentisfree/2014/mar/13/modinomics-narendra-modi-india-bjp (accessed on May 5, 2014).

35. A. Srinivas, "Gujarat Has not Been a Leading State." *Hindu Business Line*, July 24, 2013, http://www.thehindubusinessline.com/opinion/gujarat-has-not-been-a-leading-state/article4949463.ee (accessed on May 5, 2014).

36. For a good assessment of the state's economic performance and Modi's role, see Milan Vaishnav, "The Modi Debate Worth Having in India." http://carnegieendowment.org/2013/10/09/modi-debate-worth-having-in-india/gpfj.

37. The BJP gained a significantly enhanced representation in Rajasthan: 162 versus 78 (of 200) in 2008, in Madhya Pradesh: 165 versus 143 (of 230) in 2008, and lost 1 seat in Chhattisgarh, retaining a majority. See http://eciresults.nic.in/PartyWiseResult.htm (accessed on April 15, 2014).

38. S. Kumar, "How the BJP Stole Congress' thunder," *Hindustan Times*, May 17, 2014, http://www.hindustantimes.com/elections2014/election-beat/tectonic-shift-how-the-bjp-stole-congress-thunder/article1-1220206.aspx (accessed on June 17, 2014).

39. See discussion of the Christian Democratic effort to broaden its appeal in Katherine Adeney and Lawrence Saez, *Coalition Politics and Hindu Nationalism* (London: Routledge, 2005), pp. 254–64.

40. C.R. Mohan, "The Great Game Folio: A Modi Twist," *Indian Express*, June 7, 2014, http://indianexpress.com/article/opinion/columns/the-great-game-folio-31/ (accessed on July 7, 2014).

4

Gender Narratives and Elections: Mandate for Safety, Development, or Rights?

Rainuka Dagar

Gender in Indian elections continues to remain under-represented in numbers and ideological persuasions. Women interests, however, formed an engaged part of mainstream electoral politics rather than being presented as standalone issues as in the earlier elections, even though gender interests were not represented as "acting in the interests of the represented, in a manner responsive to them," as first proposed by Hanna Pitkin.[1] The 2014 Parliament elections in India were contested across three fault lines of governance, development, and secularism within a performance versus brand measure across competing parties. Political violation of rule of law, corruption, skewed distribution of income, rising inflation, and divisive identity-based politics were targeted and branded promises were marketed.

Women rather than gender issues were lobbied across all three fronts to emerge as a point of reference. Women's safety was promoted as an indicator for good governance, women were projected as part of an inclusive growth model, and gender as a site of intra-group contestations claimed the need for women's security on physical, economic, and social parameters. Gender in this election has been decoded at three levels. The first filter explores how the broadening of democracy through a homogenizing discourse of 'development for all' addresses the distinct historical positioning and interests which place population groups in relational hierarchy. Conventional categories of religion, caste, gender, and urban–rural divides were replaced with an all-encompassing citizen category, with services to be delivered according to shortfall, not vulnerability. In specific, what tensions emerge for gender positioning and its intersectionality in a fragmented polity? With the electoral pitch shifting to a citizen-based barometer for access to developmental benefits, these became the criteria of delivery in a governance frame.

This leads to the second layer of analysis—shorn of identity, what issues does the politics of presence denote for gender rights? This is particularly relevant as the public protests against sexual violence were a momentum against a gender manifestation that was enfolded into the electoral campaign. What does this contrast, of recognition to a gendered nature of victimization on the one hand and an identity-blind citizen agenda on the other, imply for gender interests? The form of violence, discrimination, or inequality provides the evidence of injustice and legitimacy for intervention. The vulnerability that generates the form is subsumed under a development criterion that imposes neutrality by overarching distribution of goods for all and recategorizes the electorate as service users pledging their rights to basic utilities. Gender roles and differential positioning as considerations for women's discrimination remained unaccounted for.

This weaves the third issue that explores electoral politics in emerging democracies as a change process for gender equalities. Have these elections been able to shape the 'engagement of women issues' within democratic processes particularly for inclusive policy outcomes?

The first section of this chapter maps the gender markers in this election and the second analyzes the tensions that the gender narrative unfolds for a rights-based governance.

Gender Markers: An Overview of 2014 Elections

Political Presence: Gaining Ground

The politics of presence in voter numbers and electoral candidates has registered an upswing for women. There has been an increased turnout of women voters and also a lessening of the gender gap between men and women voters from previous years (67 percent for men and 66 percent for women, see Table 4.1). Women outnumbered men voters in 16 of the 35 states/union territories. This was happening for the first time in Bihar, Rajasthan, Odisha, Tamil Nadu, and Uttarakhand, while in the northeastern states of Manipur, Meghalaya, and Sikkim, a higher share of women voters has been recorded in earlier elections. The share of women contestants rose, though nominally, from 7 percent to 8 percent, which is the highest in all elections (see Table 4.1).

In terms of numbers, 658 women candidates entered the electoral fray. An analysis of availability of women candidates per constituency shows that the 2014 elections had the highest (1.2) candidates. In other words, the voters had increased options to elect women candidates in these elections (see Table 4.2).

The trend of increased women participation is also reflected in most national party candidatures. The women-headed All India Trinamool Congress (AITC) from the Left bastion of West Bengal with a 19 percent share of the total candidates provided the most access to women, followed by the new Aam Aadmi Party (AAP) which had a gender diversity of 13 percent in its candidature (see Table 4.3). The highest proportion of elected candidates also belonged to AITC (32 percent), though in numbers and total share from elected women it was the Bharatiya Janata Party (BJP) (47 percent) banner that provided most women to Parliament. Elected women candidates numbering 62 recorded a marginal increase to 11 percent of the total (see Table 4.1), significantly lower than the global average of 22 percent. Neighboring states of Nepal (29.9 percent) and Pakistan (20.7 percent) post higher women presence in their parliaments, though supported by a legislated candidate quota.[2]

A shift from a descriptive representation of women drawn from family-based political strongholds to personal leadership took place in 2014.

Table 4.1

Gender-wise Participation in Lok Sabha Elections, 1951–2014

Election Year	Contestants			Elected		Registered Electors over Total Registered Electors (%)		Votes Polled over Total Votes Polled (%)		Votes Polled over Registered Electors (%)	
	Men	*Women*	*Other*	*Men Elected over Total Seats (%)*	*Women Elected over Total Seats (%)*	*Men*	*Women*	*Men*	*Women*	*Men*	*Women*
1951						55.0	45.0	–	–	–	–
1957	1,473 (97.04)	45 (2.96)		467 (94.53)	27 (5.47)	52.8	47.2	61.7	38.3	–	38.8
1962	1,919 (96.68)	66 (3.32)		463 (93.72)	31 (6.28)	52.7	47.3	60.2	39.8	63.31	46.6
1967	2,302 (97.17)	67 (2.83)		491 (94.42)	29 (5.58)	52.0	48.0	56.6	43.4	66.63	55.5
1971	2,686 (97)	83 (3.0)		494 (95.37)	24 (4.63)	52.3	47.7	57.7	42.3	60.90	49.1
1977	2,369 (97.13)	70 (2.87)		523 (96.49)	19 (3.51)	52.0	48.0	56.4	43.6	65.62	54.9

(Table 4.1 Continued)

(Table 4.1 Continued)

Election Year	Contestants			Elected		Registered Electors over Total Registered Electors (%)		Votes Polled over Total Votes Polled (%)		Votes Polled over Registered Electors (%)	
	Men	Women	Other	Men Elected over Total Seats (%)	Women Elected over Total Seats (%)	Men	Women	Men	Women	Men	Women
1980	4,487 (96.93)	142 (3.07)		501 (94.71)	28 (5.29)	52.1	47.9	56.9	43.1	62.16	51.2
1984	5,320 (96.85)	173 (3.15)		498 (92.1)	43 (7.95)	51.8	48.2	55.6	44.4	68.17	58.6
1985						54.3	45.7	54.6	45.4		71.7
1989	5,962 (96.79)	198 (3.21)		501 (94.53)	29 (5.47)	52.5	47.5	56.1	43.9	66.13	57.3
1991	8,420 (96.24)	329 (3.76)		495 (92.70)	39 (7.30)	54.1	45.9	57.0	43.0	61.58	51.3
1992								59.8	40.2		21.0
1996	13,353 (95.71)	599 (4.29)		495 (92.52)	40 (7.48)	52.3	47.7	56.0	44.0	62.06	53.4
1998	4,476 (94.23)	274 (5.77)		505 (92.15)	43 (7.85)	52.3	47.7	55.6	44.4	65.86	57.7

Year											
1999	4,364 (93.89)	284 (6.11)		497 (91.03)	49 (8.97)	52.3	47.7	55.7	44.3	63.96	55.6
2004	5,080 (93.47)	355 (6.53)		500 (92.08)	43 (7.92)	52.0	48.0	55.6	44.4	61.66	53.6
2009	7,514 (93.11)	556 (6.89)		484 (89.13)	59 (10.87)	52.3	47.7	54.2	45.8	60.20	55.8
*2014	7,593 (92.03)	654 (7.93)	4 (0.05)	481 (88.58)	62 (11.42)	52.4	47.6	53.0	47.0	67.09	65.6

Sources: Computed from Election Commission of India's statistical reports of Lok Sabha Elections for the years 2009, 2004, 1999, 1998, 1996, 1992, 1991, 1989, 1985, 1984, 1980, 1977, 1971, 1967, 1962, 1957, and 1951. eci.nic.in/eci_main1/ElectionStatistics.aspx (accessed on 5th August 2014).

Notes: Data on participation of women is not available for 1951 elections.

*For 2014: Registered electors, votes polled over total votes polled, and votes polled over registered electors are computed from statistics given in eci.nic.in/eci_main1/GE 2014/STATE_WISE_TURNOUT.htm, accessed on August 3, 2014. Elected candidate are calculated from 164.100.47132/LssNew/Members/partywiselist.aspx, accessed on August 5, 2014. Contestants are calculated and researched from Election Commission of India. affidiavitarchive.nic.in/DynamicAffidavitDisplay/FrmElectionAffidavit.aspx, accessed on August 10, 2014.

Table 4.2
Availability of Women Candidates per Constituency, 1962–2014 Lok Sabha Elections

Year	No. of Male Candidates	No. of Female Candidates	No. of Parliament Constituencies	No. of Male Candidates per Constituency	No. of Female Candidates per Constituency	No. of Voters per Constituencies
1962	1,919	66	494	3.88	0.13	227,211
1967	2,302	67	520	4.43	0.13	293,701
1971	2,686	83	518	5.19	0.16	292,542
1977	2,369	70	542	4.37	0.13	358,421
1980	4,487	142	529	8.48	0.27	383,276
1984–85	5,320	173	541	9.83	0.32	473,743
1989	5,962	198	530	11.25	0.37	583,114
1991–92	8,420	329	534	15.77	0.62	535,312
1996	13,353	599	535	24.96	1.12	641,697
1998	4,476	274	548	8.17	0.50	685,113
1999	4,364	284	546	7.99	0.52	680,713

2004	5,080	355	543	9.36	0.65	717,021
2009	7,514	556	543	13.84	1.02	767,576
*2014	7,593	654	543	13.98	1.20	1,019,893
Total	77,318	3,899	7,960	9.71	0.49	516,970

Sources: Computed from Election Commission of India's statistical reports of Lok Sabha Elections for the year 2009, 2004, 1999, 1998, 1996, 1992, 1991, 1989, 1985, 1984, 1980, 1977, 1971, 1967, and 1962, eci.nic.in/eci_main1/ElectionStatistics.aspx, accessed on August 5, 2014.

Note: *For 2014, contestants are calculated and researched from Election Commission of India, affidiavitarchive.nic.in/DynamicAffidavit-Display/FrnElectionAffidavit.aspx, accessed on August 10, 2014.

Table 4.3

Contestants and Elected Women Candidates by Major Parties, 1996–2014

	1996		1998		1999		2004		2009		2014*	
	Contested	Elected	Contested	Elected	Contested	Elected	Contested	Elected	Contested	Elected	Contested	Elected
Bharatiya Janata Party (BJP)	27	14	32	15	25	15	30	10	44	13	36	30
%	(5.72)	(8.81)	(8.25)	(8.24)	(7.37)	(8.24)	(8.24)	(7.25)	(10.16)	(11.21)	(8.41)	(10.64)
% Total Female	(4.51)	(35.0)	(11.68)	(34.88)	(8.8)	(30.61)	(8.45)	(23.26)	(7.91)	(22.03)	(5.47)	(48.39)
Communist Party of India (CPI)	3	1	6	2	4	1	2		4		6	
%	(6.98)	(8.33)	(10.34)	(22.22)	(7.41)	(25)	(5.88)		(7.14)		(8.96)	
% Total Female	(0.5)	(2.5)	(2.19)	(4.65)	(1.41)	(2.04)	(0.56)		(0.72)		(0.91)	
Communist Party of India (Marxist) (CPI(M))	5	1	8	3	5	3	8	5	6	1	10	1
%	(6.67)	(3.13)	(11.27)	(9.38)	(6.94)	(9.09)	(11.59)	(11.63)	(7.32)	(6.25)	(10.75)	(11.11)
% Total Female	(0.83)	(2.5)	(2.92)	(6.98)	(1.76)	(6.12)	(2.25)	(11.63)	(1.08)	(1.69)	(1.52)	(1.61)
Indian National Congress (INC)	49	16	38	10	51	14	45	12	43	23	60	4
%	(9.25)	(11.68)	(7.97)	(7.09)	(11.26)	(12.28)	(10.79)	(8.28)	(9.77)	(11.17)	(12.93)	(9.09)

	1	2	3	4	5	6	7	8	9	10	11	12
% Total Female	(8.18)	(40.0)	(13.87)	(23.26)	(17.96)	(28.57)	(12.68)	(27.91)	(7.73)	(38.98)	(9.12)	(6.45)
Nationalist Congress Party (NCP)					9	1	5	2	7	2	4	1
%					(6.82)	(12.5)	(15.63)	(22.22)	(10.29)	(22.22)	(11.11)	(16.67)
% Total Female					(3.17)	(2.04)	(1.41)	(4.65)	(1.26)	(3.39)	(0.61)	(1.61)
Female-headed Parties												
Bahujan Samaj Party (BSP)			5	10	1	11	1	20	1	28	4	29
%			(2.37)	(3.98)	(20.0)	(4.89)	(7.14)	(4.6)	(5.26)	(5.6)	(19.05)	(5.77)
% Total Female			(0.83)	(3.65)	(2.33)	(3.87)	(2.04)	(5.63)	(2.33)	(5.04)	(6.78)	(4.41)
All India Trinamool Congress (AITC)					4	2	6	1	6	4	25	11
%					(13.79)	(25)	(18.18)	(50)	(17.14)	(21.05)	(19.08)	(32.35)
% Total Female					(1.41)	(4.08)	(1.69)	(2.33)	(1.08)	(6.78)	(3.8)	(17.74)
All India Anna Dravida Munnetra Kazhagam (ADMK)	1	1	1	2	–	2	–	2	–	4	–	4
%	(5.56)	(4.35)	(5.56)	(6.9)	(10.0)	(6.06)	(8.7)	–	–	(10.0)	–	(10.81)
% Total Female	(2.5)	(0.36)	(2.33)	(0.7)	(2.04)	(0.56)	(0.36)	–	–	(0.61)	–	(6.45)

(Table 4.3 Continued)

(Table 4.3 Continued)

	1996		1998		1999		2004		2009		2014*	
	Contested	Elected	Contested	Elected	Contested	Elected	Contested	Elected	Contested	Elected	Contested	Elected
					New							
Aam Aadmi Party (AAP)	–	–	–	–	–	–	–	–	–	–	57	–
%	–		–		–		–		–		(13.19)	–
% Total Female	–		–		–		–		–		(8.66)	–

Sources: Computed from Election Commission of India's statistical reports of Lok Sabha Elections for the years 2009, 2004, 1999, 1998, and 1996. eci.nic.in/eci_main1/ElectionStatistics.aspx, accessed on August 5, 2014.

Notes: *For 2014, elected candidates are calculated from the Election Commission of India, 164.100.47132/LssNew/Members/partywiselist.aspx, accessed on August 5, 2014.
For 2014, contestants are calculated and researched from the Election Commission of India, affidiavitarchive.nic.in/DynamicAffidavitDisplay/FrmElectionAffidavit.aspx, accessed on August 10, 2014.

In 2009, 62 percent of elected women had either family connections in politics (48 percent) or belonged to an elite (14 percent) stature. In 2014, this share dropped by 12 percent to 50 percent for elected women in contrast to 27 percent of male legislators. Half the women legislators had neither an elite reservoir nor family-led political preserves of winnability, but forged these from their party commitments and individual capacity (see Table 4.4).

Conditions of representative democracy provided access, and in the case of BJP, the party provided institutional support with a higher proportion drawn from individual leadership. The candidature and campaign of Smriti Irani, a television actor turned BJP party spokesperson who led the party charge against Rahul Gandhi, the Congress prime ministerial candidate, illustrates this shift. The campaign was an effective challenge for a 'popular vote' to gain 'popular control' in the bastion of the most successful political party. Rather than the politics of gender or family links, it was independent ability that selected a number of female candidates.

Other examples include Meera Sanyal, CEO and chairperson of the Royal Bank of Scotland, tribal leader Dayamani Barla involved in the anti-mining movement from the AAP, and Vasundhra Raje Scindia performing as a genderless chief minister delivering all of Rajasthan's seats to the BJP. It provided space to a gender-blind rather than a gender-neutral or engendered political opportunity and structure. It is a move away from traditional political behavior, which has been critiqued as being gender-blind with male as the only experience, implicitly promoting the male norm as citizen interests.[3–5] But, women's presence across a multisectionality of myriad identities and experiences located in institutional structures is no guarantee for promoting gender interests,[6–9] Anne Philips argues that it is the politics of ideas promoted through political accountability that counters the risk of narrow interest-based politics.[10] It is neither neutrality nor presence, but the inclusion of identities and difference as a dynamics of presence that remains to be strengthened for an egalitarian Indian democracy.

Widening Democracy: Acknowledging Diversity

Following an Election Commission order of November 2009, Indian elections for the first time provided for political inclusion of the third gender. It prescribed for a third gender choice 'Other' on voter registration forms

Table 4.4

National and Female-headed Party-wise Background of Elected Candidates for 2009 and 2014 Lok Sabha Elections

Background	Type	Party	2009			2014		
			M	F	T	M	F	T
Elite	National Parties	BJP	3 (2.91)	1 (7.69)	5 (4.31)	42 (16.67)	4 (13.33)	47 (16.67)
		BSP	–	–	–	–	–	–
		CPI	–	–	–	–	–	–
		CPM				1 (12.5)	1 (100)	2 (22.22)
		INC	15 (8.2)	5 (21.74)	20 (9.71)	6 (15)		6 (13.64)
		NCP	–	–	–	2 (40)		2 (33.33)
	Female Headed	ADMK	–	–	–	–	–	–
		AITC	3 (20)		3 (15.79)	6 (26.09)	4 (36.36)	10 (29.41)
	Others		7 (5.15)	2 (18.18)	9 (6.12)	19 (15.83)	2 (18.18)	21 (16.03)
	Total		**28 (5.77)**	**8 (13.79)**	**37 (6.81)**	**76 (15.8)**	**11 (17.74)**	**88 (16.21)**

Political Background							
National Parties	BJP	12 (11.65)	3 (23.08)	15 (12.93)	19 (7.54)	5 (16.67)	24 (8.51)
	BSP	4 (23.53)	4 (100)	8 (38.1)	–	–	–
	CPI	–	–	–	–	–	–
	CPM	3 (20)	1 (100)	4 (25)	1 (12.5)	4 (100)	1 (11.11)
	INC	45 (24.59)	12 (52.17)	57 (27.67)	8 (20)		12 (27.27)
	NCP	4 (57.14)	2 (100)	6 (66.67)	–	1 (100)	1 (16.67)
Female Headed	ADMK	–	–	–	2 (6.06)	–	2 (5.41)
	AITC	2 (13.33)	1 (25)	3 (15.79)	2 (8.7)	4 (36.36)	6 (17.65)
Others		25 (18.38)	5 (45.45)	30 (20.41)	21 (17.5)	6 (54.55)	27 (20.61)
Total		**95 (19.59)**	**28 (48.28)**	**123 (22.65)**	**53 (11.02)**	**20 (32.26)**	**73 (13.44)**

(Table 4.4 Continued)

(Table 4.4 Continued)

Background	Type	Party	2009			2014		
			M	F	T	M	F	T
Others	National Parties	BJP	88 (85.44)	9 (69.23)	96 (82.76)	191 (75.79)	21 (70)	211 (74.82)
		BSP	13 (76.47)	–	13 (61.9)	–	–	–
		CPI	–	–	–	–	–	–
		CPM	12 (80)	–	12 (75)	6 (75)	–	6 (66.67)
		INC	123 (67.21)	6 (26.09)	129 (62.62)	26 (65)		26 (59.09)
		NCP	3 (42.86)	–	3 (33.33)	3 (60)		3 (50)
	Female Headed	ADMK	9 (100)		9 (100)	31 (93.94)	4 (100)	35 (94.59)

AITC	10	3	13	15	3	18
	(66.67)	(75)	(68.42)	(65.22)	(27.27)	(52.94)
Others	104	4	108	80	3	83
	(76.47)	(36.36)	(73.47)	(66.67)	(27.27)	(63.36)
Total	**362**	**22**	**383**	**352**	**31**	**382**
	(74.64)	**(37.93)**	**(70.53)**	**(73.18)**	**(50)**	**(70.35)**
Grand Total	**485**	**58**	**543**	**481**	**62**	**543**
	(100.0)	**(100.0)**	**(100.0)**	**(100.0)**	**(100.0)**	**(100.0)**

Sources: Background of candidates compiled from the Election Commission of India's statistical report of Lok Sabha Election 2009. eci.nic.in/eci_main1/statistical report.aspx, accessed on August 5, 2014.
For 2014, data compiled from eci.nic.in/eci_main1/eci.nic.in/eci_main1/statistical_report.aspx, accessed on August 10, 2014.

to recognize transgender individuals to vote and run for office under their distinct identity. There were 28,341[11] transsexual voters and four candidates (see Table 4.1) registered in the election fray. This recognition pre-empts a landmark ruling by the Supreme Court to create a third gender category identifying transgendered people in official documents. It gives identity to 2 million transsexuals, acknowledging their specific interests and different living conditions. However, this does not include the entire lesbian, bisexual, gay, and transsexual (LBGT) category that has acquired a global identity. By a divided acceptance of the larger category, the electoral message is that diversity is a political category and not a human category evolved over shared interests and history.

Sexual Violence Protests Provide a Unifying Agenda

Protests against sexual violence are critical processes for policy change. Laura Weldon in a global study demonstrates that the women's movement is an important promoter for policy outcomes on violence against women (VAW) issues, even more than the traditional electoral avenues of higher women representation in government.[12] In India, the agitation against the Mathura rape in 1977 and more recently the popular protests against the Nirbhaya incident have spurred legal reform, improvement in the justice delivery mechanisms, and increased reporting of incidents.[13-15] The sexual violence protests not only reflected shared concerns across citizens, but provided a unifying electoral agenda on three dimensions.

One, difference of interests across divides of urban–rural, gender, caste, and class were homogenized by the brutal violence to present a people's agenda for VAW. This needs to be placed in the context of people's frustration and non-performance of the United Progressive Alliance with rising inflation and the burden of price rise crippling the common person, while in contrast, rampant and unabated corruption defined the lifestyle of the ruling political class. Government apathy to peoples' plight was vented against the brutal Nirbhaya incident, providing a common ground for protest across various interest groups—students, the middle class, women, civil society activists, and the urban workforce. These became part of the citizen categorization that the electoral campaigns targeted rather than the conventional electoral categories of caste, religion, or rural–urban slum vote banks.

Second, this 'normative legitimacy' mobilizing public opinion was marshaled into a political force with parties making it an electoral issue either questioning the competence of the state to maintain rule of law or the promise of improved state security. The repeated question by Modi, "Are your sisters and daughters safe—do you not worry till they get home?"[16] or the Congress assertion of legislating criminal justice changes, the promise for one-stop crisis centers[17] to ensure the citizens that their concern for safety of their women were resonated in the electoral arena. They unified the peoples' agenda, the women's movement, and electoral agenda.

Third, women safety became a rallying point to seek good governance, not only integrating gender into the governance debate, but making it an indicator of performance. It combined 'normative legitimacy' with 'political efficacy', with parties promising government accountability and pledging that future state actions would express this will of the citizens.[18] Electoral mobilizations of the sexual violence protests welded women interests to public interests by framing them as an issue within the spectrum of good governance.

Gender Rights Unfolded across Fault Lines of Caste Rather than Religion

Religious sectarianism was raked as a campaign issue, but in the context of gender rights, caste rather than religion took precedence in the electoral discourse. There were two overriding agendas: one symbolically targeting the marginalized SC/ST (scheduled caste/scheduled tribe) castes, and the other being women activists and the media demanding a political commitment and legal action against intra-caste cultural practices conferring VAW. The BJP strategically targeted SC/ST votes to storm the Hindi heartland in particular. The more backward among the Dalits were brought into its fold through a 'social harmony campaign' as documented by Badri Narayan through ticket distribution to Gonkars, Pasis, and Rawats, by symbolically addressing their identity with references to Dalit heroes, and subcaste meetings through RSS-affiliated social organizations. BJP promised benefits such as reservations in education and employment through the implementation of the social justice committees report prepared by BJP-led Uttar Pradesh government.[19] The party pledged provisions of basic facilities, particularly sanitation and education, linking these to conditions undermining the dignity and rights of women. In India, less than 53 percent households have toilet facilities, which decrease to about 31 percent in rural India. The Hindu heartland states from where BJP made huge gains have less than 22 percent households in rural areas with toilet facilities—Uttar Pradesh (21.8 percent), Rajasthan (19 percent), Madhya Pradesh (13.1 percent), and Bihar (17.6 percent).[20] These states have high proportions of SC populations and it is these populations on the margins of poverty and social hierarchy that do not have access to toilets who were the targeted electoral constituency.

The second issue raised by activists focused on intra-caste atrocities of rape and 'honor killing' by the so-called self-styled traditional councils.[21] Rape sanctioned by a panchayat in the interiors of West Bengal and the violence unleashed against couples marrying within the subcaste under Khaap jurisdiction in Haryana provided the precipitating factors.[22,23] They drew attention to women's conduct being policed by caste councils. The exercise of choice against acceptable sexual and reproductive behavior unsheathed grave sanctions of rape and death. Both issues reinforced the physical protections for women; while one extended the discourse to universal rights for all citizens, the other addressed specific needs in exclusion to collective living.

Electoral Claims and Emerging Issues for Gender Access and Rights

The election pitch seeking change on gender issues was specific in its articulated claims. Access to education for the girl child, employment opportunities for women, leadership representation in the Parliament, health and sanitation for women on the margins, and a legal armory with efficient law enforcement machinery to protect women from sexual abuse formed the gender flashes in the electoral discourse. The manifestos of political parties were more detailed, with the Congress theme evolving around a victimology frame—promising one-stop crisis centers, functioning helplines, in-camera proceedings, and land rights for women, specially single women and women-headed households. Congress promises also included "land for women whose husbands have migrated away," "clear pending compensation of women with missing husbands in areas of unrest and conflict," or special schemes for young women and tribals facing sexual exploitation. The BJP proclaimed women as national nurturers, broadening the typed family care industry to a national domain. The campaign weaved symbolic ties to typed gender constructs, glorifying the female gender with national pride and Hindu cultural idioms—purifying of mother Ganga/Yamuna, the Banarasi sari that protects women's dignity, alluding to women candidates as mothers and sisters.

Other parties, such as the AIADMK, had a listed scheme for providing the Indian symbol of married women, a *thirumangalyama* (gold ornament), for their marriage.[24] Within this larger cultural ethos, the promises and demands for women were for a specific distress or gap and isolated from the interdependencies of a social order, relations, or pattern of survival. This is fraught with tensions between legal rights, social order, executive authority, and the neoliberal market. It is within this interplay that gender rights within the wider development policies, governance system, and sociocultural contexts have to emerge.

The electoral mandate seeking change to deliver on gender claims made during the elections has to negotiate three basic challenges, these being the contentions between good governance and rights-based governance, collectivity claims and women autonomy, and inclusive development and identity-based equality.

Sexual Violence: A Rights-Based Governance Issue

Public protests and distress over rapes and sexual abuse was reflected in 7 percent of the electorate stating women's safety was an electoral issue. This was significant with corruption, unemployment, and inflation forming 40 percent, 31 percent, and 23 percent of people's agenda, respectively (see Table 4.5). Physical abuse of women ranked above developmental needs of electricity, sanitation, and quality education. Popular concern of woman's sexual abuse was captured by electoral politics. It sounded alarm bells over the inability of incumbent governments

Table 4.5
Respondent Opinions on Issues They Want Addressed by Their Elected Representatives

Issues	Rural	Urban	Total
Corruption	123	138	261
	(36.5)	(44.23)	(40.22)
Lack of livelihood	99	103	202
	(29.36)	(33.17)	(31.19)
Inflation	81	70	151
	(24.04)	(22.44)	(23.27)
Women safety	19	25	44
	(5.64)	(8.01)	(6.78)
Drinking water	12	20	32
	(3.67)	(6.44)	(5.0)
Electricity	20	8	28
	(5.96)	(2.48)	(4.29)
Education	11	12	23
	(3.26)	(3.85)	(3.54)
Health services	12	8	20
	(3.67)	(2.48)	(3.1)
Sanitation	8	6	14
	(2.29)	(1.98)	(2.14)
Drug abuse	8	2	10
	(2.37)	(0.64)	(1.54)
Total	337	312	649
	(100)	(100)	(100)

Source: Institute for Development and Communication (IDC), Chandigarh. Field Survey, Assam, Gujarat, Haryana, and Punjab, October–April 2014. The total number of respondents was 649. Due to multiple responses, the sum of all is not equal to the total number.

to provide a safe and secure environment for its citizens with women being the acclaimed vulnerable section. Along with corruption, dynastic rule, and criminalization of politics, women's insecurity in public spheres strengthened the assertions against the inept rule of law. The discourse challenged the institutional legitimacy of the state in providing an enabling democracy with an effective safety and security apparatus. By linking the safety of sisters, daughters, and mothers to hooliganism and criminalization of politics, it was the honor of the patriarchal stronghold that was sought to be protected through improved law and order under an able Modi government.[25]

While decreasing the fear and risk of abuse are measures of accountable and effective governance, it is the conditions of gender inequality that require the prior transformation, as is evidenced in Mulayam Singh, leader of a prominent regional party, commenting, "Boys commit mistakes. Will they be hanged for rape?",[26] or his party's senior member Abu Azmi who opined, "Any woman who, whether married or unmarried, goes along with a man, with or without her consent should be hanged,"[27] or the public molesting of Congress candidate actor Nagma by an elected state legislator of the party.[28] In a society where the female form has acquired the status of a trading stock, it is not only in Bollywood, the advertisement or the fashion industry, but even in the popular conception of males and females mirrored in politics that the female body is singled out for attention. While Rakhi Sawant, an outspoken actress, was reported to attract more attention for her clothes than her political issues,[29] the Chandigarh election was labeled a glamour contest between the Bollywood celebrity candidates of AAP (Gul Panag) and BJP (Kirron Kher). Parties were replete with Bollywood candidates and women celebrities acting as crowd magnets.[30] The female form is used as a resource by the parties themselves, and then when the 'product' is abused as sexual merchandise, promises to bolster legal mechanisms for a safe environment for women are made. The 'body beautiful' cannot be delinked from the male gaze as a 'targeted tactic of power' that declares the female as a physical object of male desire. She becomes limited to a commodity for both warranted and unwarranted attention. It was only the brutality of rape, not the sexual appreciation, labeling, or its use that came under the campaign cacophony.

Sexual abuse is not the only violence women face. Reported crimes against women that reflect a proportion of violence women face point out that besides rape, molestation, sexual harassment, dowry harassment, there are rampant dowry deaths, female infanticide–feticide, trafficking, and domestic violence. In fact, dowry-related crimes have a higher preponderance than sexual abuse.[31] The missing girl child phenomenon is growing and has now impacted all Indian states.[32] The female gender is not only unsafe on the streets, but also in their homes. However, this larger issue did not form part of the electoral landscape. While specific forms were raised in previous elections and party manifestos, it was the imagery of brutal rape that captured the electoral pitches in 2014. Female feticide that saw attention in the previous election was limited to slogans of 'Educate the girl child, save the girl child'. By building this capacity or resource, a female can contribute to an economy—of a nation or of her in-laws, but continues to be a resource drain, both social and material in her natal family. The birth family chooses to negate the burden of the 'other', as a member who will contribute to another household. Women are not chance victims of wife-beating or rape by antisocial elements or hooligans, but it is their social position and commodification of the female body that projects them for abuse. The legal achievements will remain in contention with the social order unless the conditions of that order are addressed. Consider the creation of the Nirbhaya fund and its non-utilization. It was cited as another example of a nonperforming government. But, neither the non-utilization nor the creation of state schemes under the Nirbhaya banner, such as pink and white taxies in Kerala, Bhopal's Police mobile unit, helpline in Delhi or women only buses in Assam, are in a position to change the conditions of gender violence. Relief and redressal in terms of an efficient legal criminal system have to be linked to security and safety provisions in institutions and delivery systems, such as harassment policies, codes of conduct, and sensitization mechanisms.

Additionally, these have to be linked to prevention programs and schemes that promote just gender positioning and rearrange social order.

Consider also the governance constraints with tension between executive authority, state policy, and gender entitlements in an identity-fragmented polity. A centrally aided government scheme provides for the prevention of atrocities against SC/ST populations, which includes, among others, compensation to rape victims. Punjab at 32 percent has the highest proportion of SC population, Himachal Pradesh has 25 percent and Uttar Pradesh has 20.7 percent.[33] In strongly polarized states, such as Uttar Pradesh where caste identity is a political entity, all compensation gets distributed to the rape victims during the 10th and 11th plans.[34] States like Himachal Pradesh or Punjab do not distribute this compensation to SC rape victims. In fact, in Punjab, the head gets transferred to non-Plan expenditure in the 12th plan.[35]

Mayawati, when she headed Uttar Pradesh's Bahujan Samaj's government, paid special attention to this constituency, increasing the relief amount to ₹2.0 lakh while the Central Government provides for ₹25,000. This is relevant since rapes against SCs constitute 30 percent of the reported cases in Uttar Pradesh in contrast to all over India where these account for 6 percent of the cases.[36] Post election, Mayawati strives to be the beneficiary of this voter base.[37] While rapes are still not decreasing, the compensation gets distributed according to perceived relevance of group in state politics and fragmented identities get strengthened. The point is that legal reform, increasing efficiency, effectiveness of the criminal justice system, policy provisions, and protective mechanisms in themselves cannot change social relations and hierarchies. Rather than good governance, rights-based governance remains the challenge.

Collectivity Claims and Gender Entitlements

In the gender domain, these elections were about women safety. The principal voice was protecting women from sexual violence. What was contested was the accommodation or targeting of collectivities, such as the rural Haryana Khaaps or the West Bengal caste panchayats that harbor or issue dictates for 'honor killing' or gang rape as sanctions against erring members. No polity can accede to a death or rape as being anything other than a grave violation, and in a rights-based constitution, it is the individual life that has irrevocable sanctity. The contention arises if violations to life and dignity are to change from practice. The women's movement and rights activists including the media denounced the collectivities, labeling these as Kangaroo courts, backward and barbaric. Political parties shied away from acknowledging the link of gender conduct codes to collectivity assertions—these were dealt with as incidents that were denounced.

After all, Indian elections are about vote bank politics. Both views avoid the real issue. The collectivities are a lifeline for a population's access to basic services, safety nets, and women's security, in other words, a lack of governance outreach, which is provided by these collectivities. In a crisis—death of the only earner, dowry harassment of a daughter, or even money to buy a buffalo, treat an illness or a malfunctioning tractor—who tides the family? It is not the insurance company, the police, the bank or health services that provide the cover to bear the loss. It is the family and social support system that regroups to provide protection. An emergency routine is in place; only it is not state mechanisms, but an informal standby.

The British administration in colonial India recognized the collectivity as the lifeline in rural Haryana.[38] This social capital continues to be relevant. Haryana, which claims a high per capita income (62,078, ranked third)[39] and low poverty (11.6 percent, in comparison to all India rates of 21.92 percent),[40] has liabilities that are met through social networks and their reciprocal exchange. Rural life is plagued by debt (53.1 percent of farmer households have outstanding loans),[41] health access is below the Indian average, and it has a rising misery index,[42] a difficult survival, and low safety of women. For the majority of the rural families, this network provides the only safety valve in times of crisis and struggle. This support was acknowledged by Modi when he referred to the turmoil of unemployed youth being forced to migrate from his village, farms, friends, and family: "He is worried where should he go, who will hold his hands, who will save him...!"[43] That this support mechanism continues to be operational and banked upon can be evidenced from 42 percent of the electorate for whom trust in caste/religious leadership remains a point of call for women rights. This dependence rises for rural populations (see Table 4.6). In spite of government machinery in place with counselors, legislatures, police, and governance systems, the traditional authority systems continue to be relied upon.

Defined rules of conduct, interaction, and reciprocity are drawn by these collectivities. If these are transgressed to challenge the social order and survival of the collectivity, human rights and individual life chances are violated.[44] Such norms of social living are practiced because they work, and no alternative has been created. It is these issues of governance that need to be tackled to ensure survival across the life cycle and a dignified life, with growth and sustenance not only of individuals, but also identities that have historically nurtured and shaped group living. It is with alternatives that combine the social reservoirs of the informal identity-based networks with the rule of law that gender entitlements can be delivered.

Table 4.6
Citizens' Trust in Different Stakeholders in Regard to Women's Rights

Stakeholders	Rural	Urban	Total
Local government council	216	139	355
	(59.67)	(48.43)	(54.70)
Local police	180	147	327
	(49.72)	(51.22)	(50.38)
Representative leaders of your caste/tribe	171	104	275
	(47.24)	(36.24)	(42.37)
Leaders of your religion	172	101	273
	(47.51)	(35.19)	(42.06)
Political leadership	114	98	212
	(31.49)	(34.15)	(32.67)
NGO/civil society	67	145	212
	(18.5)	(50.52)	(32.66)
Community-policing initiative	3	13	16
	(0.83)	(4.53)	(2.46)

Source: Institute for Development and Communication (IDC), Chandigarh. Field Survey, Assam, Gujarat, Haryana, and Punjab, October–April 2014. The total number of respondents was 649. Due to multiple responses, the sum of all is not equal to the total number.

Inclusion and Gender Rights in the Development Agenda

Women's empowerment was a catchphrase in this election used as part of a development agenda. Rahul Gandhi was spoofed for his constant reference to the term. Party leaders sprinkled the word in context to freebies of basic needs of health and education for women on the margins, employment, and representation in governance forums. In the BJP posters, the concept of empowerment was linked to making public spaces safe, promises of education and skill development, and gender participation in decision-making. Linking safety with respect for women, the Congress promised 25 percent female representation in the police force and small soft loans as a development focus in their poster campaign. There was a liberal use of the word empowerment assuring women's development with an undertaking for narrow interventions. The women-related development narrative in this election occupied two fronts—(a) claiming women as part of an inclusive growth agenda and (b) as a promise of specific benefits for women, such as education and toilet facilities in homes linked to safety and survival.

An inclusive development was proclaimed as an adherence to the principle that inequalities, gender in this instance, disadvantage not only the interests, but the society as a whole. Modi proclaimed, "Unless women are empowered the country cannot develop," or "Women are equal partners in development." Rahul Gandhi cautioned, "We can only be half a superpower if our women are not empowered."[45] This discourse was in tune with the post-2015 United Nations development agenda. Highly unequal societies tend to grow more slowly than those with low income inequalities, are less successful in sustaining growth over long periods and recover more slowly from economic downturns.[46] Women's rights to skills and increased access to employment projected them as part of the well-documented incremental argument, that increasing women's share in resources and opportunities advances other development goals. 'Educate the girl child, save the girl child' may well have been the call for national asset creation. Investment in girls' education is being extolled by some development agencies as the highest return investment available in the developing world as a business case for smart economics.

Naila Kabeer and Luisa Natali argue that there is evidence that gender equality, particularly in education and employment, contributes to economic growth, but growth-led change in gender hierarchies remains doubtful.[47] The forces of free market operate with competitive pressures, which marginalize women for increased productivity, costs of maternity benefits, crèches, and harassment fallouts. Political parties claim to promote pay parity and social insurance,[48] promotions or sexual protection to which all parties are in agreement. These do not impact the conditions of work, as Jayanti Ghosh argues, since the market conditions are not conducive.[49] How can gender-sensitive provisions to tackle structural imbalances be addressed when economic development focuses on issues of poverty and growth rather than inequalities and redistribution? Such a focus, Philips has been arguing, registers a retreat from the discourse of equality.[50]

The politics of sanitation lead by BJP was the other face of development agenda for women. Framed across three parameters of women safety, basic needs, and girl child education, it reinforced the pledge to make women safe—in particular within the SC segment for whom open toilets and use under dark have been sites of abuse. Toilets were used as a symbol of denied basic rights (even after 60 years of independent governance) linked to non-performance and women's dignity. "In the 21st century, 90 out of 100 houses do not have toilets in this area.... Is it a matter of shame? How much our mothers and sisters suffer! Do we want our mothers–sisters to face this?"[51] This basic facility was parried with the incumbent government's continued inattention to these facilities with a boogie on secularism: "We say what about toilets, they say it is the time of secularism."[52] Lack of toilets for girls in schools was cited as a reason for dropouts and this declaration provided a tangible target.

Open toilets are a site of abuse, but denial of a site does not change the dynamics of hierarchies or historical use of women's bodies as an expression of that power. Nor does the provision of toilets in girls' schools change the practice to regulate the sexuality of girls entering puberty or role-based responsibilities that may be encouraging the dropouts. Both narratives sought political legitimacy, one within the global development politics promising inclusive development necessary for economic growth and the other in marginalized population groups where lack of basic women's rights questioned the development obligations to label the incumbent as non-performing.

Increased access to equality parameters is, however, no guarantee against women's safety. Sweden is ranked second on the gender inequality index (GII) in contrast to India at 132.[53] Sweden, the most equal of societies, had high rape rates of 66.5 in comparison to India's 4.26 in 2012 and these continue to increase as top GII ranking is maintained.[54,55] While there are arguments that macroeconomics reforms negatively impact on women by burdening their reproductive and care roles,[56–58] other scholars have noted that women's increased employment, access to credit, land and cash transfers has positive impact on poverty, children's welfare, and productivity.[59–61] In either situation, there is no evidence of change in gender positioning and hierarchies, the evidence being that development parameters do not ensure gender rights.

Conclusion

The 2014 elections linked select outcomes of gender inequalities to poor development and governance. The discourse sought public accountability for states' inability to protect and provide for women. Political efficacy for legitimate concerns remains a goal. Non-accessibility, discrimination, and violence faced by women is an expression of their social placement. It is based on gender roles and its intersectionality with caste, religious and ethnic positioning interlaced with market forces. It is not access or development, but gender that is the basis of inequalities. Men and women perform different functions within the family and collectivity, particularly reproductive roles, and have associated responsibilities. The male kinship with intergenerational interdependence generates social capital, and survival mechanisms for members, both men and women. These social relations need to be revamped in changed conditions of survival for equality outcomes. Improved incomes, legal safeguards, reservations in decision-making, and life-enhancing provisions are the right of every citizen. For women to enjoy access to these, the social relations and the fault lines across identities of gender, caste, and religion in a fragmented polity need to be redefined. For this, the domain of engagement has to extend from state policy and mechanisms to stakeholders of democracy; in other words, creation of 'gender capital'.[62] This includes gender-sensitive capacities of state institutions, political support, rights-based groups, and community networks, including identity interest groups. The policy challenge remains to renegotiate and manage social relationships to promote gender rights.

Notes and References

1. Hanna F. Pitkin, *The Concept of Representation* (Berkeley, CA: University of California Press, 1967), p. 209.
2. Inter-Parliament Union (IPU), *Women in Parliament in 2013: The Year in Review* (Geneva: Switzerland, 2013).
3. Susan C. Bourque and Jean Grossholtz, "Politics on Unnatural Practice: Political Science Looks at Female Participation," *Politics and Society* 4(1974): 225–66.
4. S. Carroll and L. Zerilli, "Feminist Challenges to Political Science," in A. Finifter (ed.), *Political Science: The State of the Discipline II* (Washington: APSA, 1993), pp. 55–78.
5. V. Randall, *Women and Politics*, 2nd edition (Basingstoke, UK: MacMillan, 1987).

6. R. Charles Beitz, *Political Equality: An Essay in Democratic Theory* (Princeton, NJ: Princeton University Press, 1989).
7. H. Britton, "The Incomplete Revolution: South Africa's Women's Struggle for Parliamentary Transformation," *International Feminist Journal of Politics* 4, 1(2002), 43–71.
8. H. Britton, *Women in the South African Parliament: From Resistance to Governance* (Urbana, IL: University of Illinois Press, 2006).
9. I.M. Young, *Justice and Politics of Difference* (Princeton, NJ: Princeton University Press, 1990).
10. Anne Philips, *The Politics of Presence* (New York: Oxford University Press, 1995).
11. Shashank Chouhan, "Facts and Figures for India's 2014 General Elections," Reuters, April 3, 2014.
12. Laura S. Weldon, *When Protest Makes Policy: How Social Movement Represent Disadvantaged Groups* (Ann Arbor: The University of Michigan Press, 2012).
13. Nikita Doval, "Trial and the Trial," *Week*, April 7, 2013, pp. 40–46.
14. Dwaipayan Ghosh, "Jump in Reporting of Rape Cases," *Times of India*, Delhi, March 24, 2013, p. 1.
15. Satya Prakash and Harish V. Nair, "16/12: A Crime that Changed Rape Laws in India," *Hindustan Times*, New Delhi, September 11, 2013, p. 5.
16. Narendra Modi, "Vijay Shankhnad Rally," Meerut, India, February 2, 2014, https://indiatoday.intoday.in/story/narendra_modis_speech_in_meerut_full_text/1/341308.html (accessed on 24 July, 2014).
17. Indian National Congress. 2014. "Your Voice: Our Pledge—Lok Sabha Election Manifesto," p. 25, indiatoday.intoday.in/story/narendra-modi-speech-in-meerut-full-text/1/341308.html (accessed on July 25, 2014).
18. Nancy Frazer, *Scales of Justice: Reimagining Political Space in a Global World* (New York: Columbia University Press, 2010).
19. Badri Narayan, "Remaking the BSP," *Indian Express*, May 26, 2014.
20. Institute for Development and Communication (IDC). 2014. "Benchmarks for Inclusive Growth: For Informed Policy Formulation." Punjab Development Report. Chandigarh: IDC, p. 55.
21. Sujoy Dhar, "Bengal Gang Rape Case: Victim and Her Family Placed Under Police Protection," *India Today*, January 26, 2014.
22. Jason Bueke, "Village Justice in West Bengal: This Is Our Way. We Don't Go to the Police," TheGuardian.com, January 24, 2014 (accessed on April 26, 2014).
23. Sandeep Rai, "I Back Khap Stand Against Same Gotra Marriage: Ex Top Cop Satyapal Singh," *Times of India*, Meerut, March 20, 2014.
24. All India Anna Dravida Munnetra Kazhagam (AIADMK). 2014. "Lok Sabha General Election Manifesto."
25. See note 21.
26. *Hindustan Times*, "Mulayam Singh on Rape: Boys Make Mistakes, Why Hang Them?," April 11, 2014, p. 1.
27. Sandhya Soman and Mohammad Wajihuddin, "Punish Women Too in Rape Case: SP Leader Abu Azmi," *Times of India*, Mumbai, April 12, 2014, p. 1.
28. *Daily Post*, "MLA Molests Congress Candidate Nagma in Public at Hapur," *Daily Post*, March 25, 2014, p. 1.
29. *Hindustan Times*, "Rakhi Sawant to Contest Lok Sabha Polls as an Independent from Mumbai," March 26, 2014.
30. Priyadarshini Sen, "Super Trouper," *Outlook*, April 14, 2014, pp. 38–39.

31. Dowry-related abuse had a rate of 21.42, sexual abuse a rate of 28.51. The rate of violence is the number of incidents per 100,000 of population. Rape was 10.29 percent of the reported crime against women (52.24) in 2013 (computed from data provided by NCRB). See, National Crime Record Bureau (NCRB). 2013. *Crime in India*. New Delhi: Ministry of Home Affairs.

32. Rainuka Dagar, *Gender Identity and Violence: Female Deselection in India* (New Delhi: Routledge, 2014), p. 18.

33. GoI. 2011. *Census of India*. New Delhi: Office of the Registrar General and Census Commissioner.

34. Socio-Economic and Educational Development Society (SEEDS), *Study Report: Crimes and Atrocities Against SC and STs with Special Reference to Implementation of the Protection of Civil (PCR) Act, 1955 and the Prevention of Atrocities (POA) Act, 1989 in the States of Andhra Pradesh, Gujarat, Maharashtra, West Bengal and Orissa* (New Delhi: Planning Commission, 2013).

35. GoI. 2013–14. *Annual Plan, Volume 71—Statements*. Chandigarh: Department of Planning, p. 217.

36. NCRB. 2013. *Crime in India*. New Delhi: Ministry of Home Affairs.

37. *Indian Express*, "Badaun Gang Rape: Mayawati Meets Victims Family, Alleges 'Jungle Raj' in Akhilesh in U.P.," June 1, 2014, Lucknow.

38. The British colonial governance in the Rohtak gazetteer of 1884 noted, "The ancient village communities ... are admirably adapted to resist the evil effect of bad seasons, epidemics and other evils incidental to the country. Bound together by ties of blood connection and above all common interest ...," these continue to be relevant more than a century later (Government of Punjab. 1884. *Gazetteer of Rohtak District, 1883–84*. Calcutta: Calcutta Printing Press).

39. See note 11, p. 8.

40. Ibid., p. 58.

41. NSSO. 2005. "Selection Assessment Survey of Farmers: Indebtedness of Farmers Household," NSSO 59 Round (January–December 2003), National Sample Survey Organisation, A-102.

42. Ibid., p. 64.

43. Narendra Modi, "Vijay Shankhnaad in Kashi—Hum Vade Nahi Iraade Lekar Aaye Hai," Kashi, India, December 2013, https://www.narendramodi.in/complete_speech_shri_narendra_modi_addressing_vyay_shankhnaad_rally_in_varanasi_up/ (accessed on July 25, 2014).

44. To provide protection and services, a system of social organization and authority is in place. The bloodline demarcates each individual and family responsibility to the members. Resources are exchanged and shared within the father lineage and, as is common in India, in a one-way transfer from the bride's family to the groom's. Within the bloodline, all are extended family members with responsibilities to each other in the life cycle of birth, marriage, death, and the struggle for survival. If couples marry within the bloodline, the tenacious lifeline collapses. Also, within this closed patriarchy, if girls are provided land rights, both the bloodline demarcations and the father–son interdependence is threatened, as her husband and children are from another lineage and do not contribute to the patriliny. It provides women both safety and security, but within the shackles of patriarchy. Rape is unacceptable and justice through criminal proceedings collectively pursued and culprits socially ostracized. However, intercaste marriages break the social order (see note 32, p. 183).

45. *Times Now*, "Frankly Speaking with Rahul Gandhi," January 27, 2014, http://www.timesnow.tv/Frankly-Speaking-with-Rahul-Gandhi—1/videoshow/4446831.cms (accessed on February 2, 2014).
46. United Nations. 2012. "UN System Task Team on the Post-2015 UN Development Agenda: Addressing Inequalities, the Heart of the Post-2015 Agenda and the Future We Want for All."
47. Naila Kabeer and Luisa Natali, "Gender Equality and Economic Growth: Is There a Win–Win?," IDS Working Paper, vol. 2013, no. 2017 (2013), pp. 1–58, Institute for Development Studies, Brighton, UK.
48. Communist Party of India (Marxist). 2014. "Manifesto for the 16th Lok Sabha Elections."
49. Jayanti Ghosh, "Macro Economic Growth and the Development Paradigm," in Christa Witcherech (ed.), *In Search of Economic Alternatives for Gender and Social Justice: Voices from India* (Brussels: Women in Development Europe, 2010), pp. 9–14.
50. Anne Philips, "Multiculturalism, Universalism and the Claims of Democracy," in M. Molyneux and S. Razavi (eds), *Gender Justice, Development and Rights* (Oxford: Oxford University Press, 2002), pp. 115–38.
51. Narendra Modi, "Bharat Vijay Rally," Basti, India, May 2, 2014, modilive.in/watch_shri_narendra_modi_addressing_bharat_vijay_rally_in_basti_uttar_pradesh/ (accessed on July 25, 2014).
52. Narendra Modi, "Bharat Vijay Rally," Khalilabad, India, May 2, 2014, www.bjp.org/sh_modi_s_vision_speeches/3133_shri_narendra_modi_addressing_bharat_vijay_rally_in_khalela_uttar_pradesh_2nd_may_2014 (accessed on July 25, 2014).
53. United Nations Development Programme (UNDP), *The Rise of South: Human Progress in a Diverse World*, Human Development Report, New York, 2013, pp. 156–58.
54. National Crime Record Bureau (NCRB), *Crime in India* (New Delhi: Ministry of Home Affairs, 2012).
55. United Nations Office on Drugs and Crime (UNODC). 2013. *Statistics on Crime*, http://www.unodc.org/unodc/data-and-analysis/statistics/crime.html (accessed on August 3, 2014).
56. D. Elson, *Male Bias in the Development Process* (Manchester: Manchester University Press, 1991).
57. Valentine M. Moghadam, *Modernising Women: Gender and Social Change in the Middle East* (London: Lynne, 2003).
58. P. Sparr, *Mortgaging Women's Lives: Feminist Critiques of Structural Adjustment* (London: Zed Press, 1994).
59. A. Barrientos and J. De Jong, "Reducing Child Poverty with Cash Transfers: A Sure Thing?," *Development Policy Review* 24,5(2006), 537–52.
60. R.L. Blumberg, "Women's Economic Empowerment as the 'Magic Potion' of Development," paper presented at the 100th Annual Meeting of the American Sociological Association, August, Philadelphia, 2005.
61. N. Kabeer, *Mainstreaming Gender and Poverty Eradication in the Millennium Development Goals* (London: Commonwealth Secretariat/Ottawa: International Development Research Centre, 2003).
62. See note 32, pp. 240–65.

5

Civic Scrutiny, Organized Action, and Democratic Consolidation

Jyotirindra Dasgupta and Anshu N. Chatterjee

A clear electoral verdict of 2014 in favor of decisive governance led by a strong prime minister set a new direction for Indian politics. The formative phase of this new development offers a new opportunity to raise some basic questions. How will the new authority deal with the public sense of despair and distrust regarding the discretionary conduct of and abuse of power by the political and administrative elites? When the citizens delegate authority to elected representatives, who will ensure transparency and accountability during the long interval between elections? A scam-weary country can reasonably ask these questions with great concern since the dark trail of effects left by the previous regime cannot be easily erased.

There are no simple answers. But the developing public space in India should encourage concerned citizens to scrutinize all the major new promises, policy processes, implementation effects, and issues of suffering and redress of especially poor people.[1] Our work is concerned with the role of civic organizations in scrutinizing the ways of authorities in order to find proper measures of accountability to satisfy citizens.

We attend to civic groups because, unlike parties and politicians, they do not seek political power. They are not tied to big business or political establishments. Their goal is to organize people, and make authorities listen, respond, and engage, if necessary, in struggles to ensure redress, especially for the disadvantaged population.

We present some selected cases and try to indicate how these civic processes may offer a reserve line of institutional resources to serve people, and in the process, ensure democratic consolidation for the country. Our focus on civic associations includes popular movements, nongovernmental organizations (NGOs), and other groups formed by qualified persons who primarily seek to work with people and not for profit or power.[2] We attend to selected areas of action and issues, such as elections and party conduct, livelihood policy for the poor, and information and transparency issues. Our discussion will also imply that such popular activation may be a source of resistance to any future attempts to violate civic rights, basic freedoms, and public interest.

Watching Elections and Representatives

A small group of faculty members, mainly from the Indian Institute of Management, Ahmedabad, founded the Association of Democratic Reform (ADR) in 1999. Their objective was to present reliable information on the election processes in order to enable voters and citizens to make well-grounded choices.[3] Though small in size, the ADR was fortunate to gain a supportive hearing from the highest levels of India's judicial system. Judicial activism in India, after the emergency phase, made it possible for concerned citizens to represent a victimized group if it was unable to afford access to legal services.[4] These public interest litigation cases not merely unfolded new avenues of redress for highly disadvantaged groups in society but also encouraged collaboration among "legal aid organizations, NGOs, and public interest advocates."[5]

The ADR filed public interest litigation in 1999 asking for disclosure of criminal, financial, and educational background of candidates for elections. The Supreme Court responded in 2002 and later in 2003 making background disclosure mandatory for candidates in affidavits revealing criminal, financial, and educational background to be submitted with the

Election Commission of India.[6] This link with the independent statutory authority of the Election Commission, which enjoyed a high reputation in the country, aided the ADR's continued effectiveness in its pursuit of transparency in electoral and party processes.[7] From 2002, the ADR has regularly conducted and, with support from about 1,200 NGOs from all over the country, sponsored an elaborate dissemination of candidates' background information for almost all state and parliamentary elections.

Praja organization in Mumbai is an example of city-level organizations that support ADR's activities. These programs are part of a civil society organizational network called National Election Watch (NEW) along with coordinated Election Watch systems in every state. Besides conducting information campaigns to alert voters and expose unsavory elements involved in electoral processes, these civic associations also engage in advocacy activities with the Election Commission in order to build public opinion and pressure on political parties.[8]

What happens after the elections is equally important for these civic associations. The representatives and their support bases remain under their scrutiny. Watching the conduct of political parties, their sources of finance, and exploring the prospects of their regulation are some of the key functions of the ADR and other NEW partners.[9] They have demonstrated that the Lok Sabha is increasingly becoming a privileged playfield where millionaires enjoy numerical majority.[10] These reports also suggest that in the same recent Lok Sabhas, nearly a third of the members were tainted with serious pending criminal cases.[11] Meanwhile, the disturbing conduct of the 15th Lok Sabha (2009–14) raised painful issues for Indian democracy. While many civic organizations' scrutiny of candidates exposed some of the seamier side of the electoral processes, the actual record of the conduct of the elected members in parliament was distressing. A nine-time member of parliament felt that the 15th Lok Sabha was the worst that he had ever seen.[12] The Lok Sabha of the 1950s conducted sessions for about 127 days a year; the corresponding figure after the year 2000 was about 72 days.[13] From 1962 to 1991, every Lok Sabha registered more than 100 percent of "actual duration of sessions against total allotted time" but the corresponding figure for 2009–14 was only 63 percent.[14]

As for the time spent for legislation, the first Lok Sabha (1952–56) devoted 49 percent of the total available time while its 15th counterpart brought the figure down to 13 percent.[15] Fewer debates on major policies and more emphasis on creating disruptions or other dramatized episodes that were ready to be picked up by the national media appeared to engage their major attention. Each disruption in the 15th Lok Sabha cost the country about ₹250,000 a minute; this was the most expensive parliament in India's history. The 15th Lok Sabha, however, was not always marked by inaction. In 2010, for instance, its members energetically "gave themselves a 200 percent raise in salary."[16]

Civic Engagement and Constructive Participation

The depressing record of the later years of the UPA (United Progressive Alliance) regime made many observers feel that the 'democratic space' was 'shrinking', and that "the state is being manipulated by forces not visible to" citizens.[17] A major source of worry for many civic groups was that business interests were "behind most government decisions and debates."[18] Fortunately, these civic associations offered a responsible oppositional initiative, concerns for accountability, and above all, a constructive drive for influencing policy processes to make an urgent impact on basic livelihoods. In India, most laws recently designed for improving the livelihood of the poor generally appear to take four to six years or longer, especially if they happen to be highly controversial. Extensive public discussions are needed at different stages of the relevant policymaking processes. These processes, however, have increasingly benefited from productive participation of relevant stakeholders, including those who represent local, regional, or deprived ethnic groups. As one study points out, "This is partly due to strong civil society voice that has emerged in the last two decades...."[19] It is not surprising that in the last 15 years one may find "... the central role of the civil society ... in lawmaking" that has affected the livelihoods of deprived people.[20]

The selected examples, cited in the study and elsewhere, include laws connected with "the Right to Education, Forest Rights, Right to Information (RTI), Food Security, Right to Employment, (and) those addressing disabilities or domestic violence."[21] In addition to aiding the process of law making, civic associations at the grassroots level closely scrutinized the extremely important processes of implementation and delivery. Studies of the working of intervention regarding livelihoods and social protection, involved in the National Rural Employment Guarantee Act (NREGA), have noted that rather than the architecture of the law, it is the monitoring and collective pressure of civil society that determines the quality of delivery.[22] The NREGA of 2005 and the programs associated with it represent India's largest and most ambitions social protection and public works enterprise for the rural poor.

Unlike the previous employment programs, NREGA in 2005 made access to work a matter of legal right. This is also a demand-driven program that is based on a system that guarantees employment for 100 days per household, within 15 days of applying for work.[23] It is expected that the work will be provided within 5 km of the worker's place of resident. If work is not provided within 15 days, the worker will be entitled to unemployment allowance. The average wage, allowing for some variation in states, was about ₹120 a day around 2013–14. The budget allocation for these employment programs for 2013–14 was about ₹33,000 crore.[24] This refers to the Union Government's allocation, which represents the major share of the expenditure for the program.[25]

The employment generation aspect also needs to be seen in the context of durable asset creation in the rural areas. While ensuring employment and income for semi-skilled or unskilled workers in the villages, these programs are directed to accomplish labor-intensive productive tasks relating to water conservation, drought relief, irrigation, land development, and other forms of asset creation. The responsibility of preparing, monitoring, and auditing of the actual shelf of work for the job seekers is vested in the decentralized participative institutions like the *Gram Sabhas* and panchayats. Given the enormous scale of organization involved in accomplishing such tasks, it is not surprising that there are many serious concerns regarding the feasibility or at least about the quality of the impact of the projects. It is reasonable to assume that the problems of relatively low awareness about the provisions of the programs and low transparency in the administrative system dealing with poor people will reduce the levels of efficacy of implementation for some years to come.

However, many reports have already recorded several positive features of these programs in practice that merit our attention. The Comptroller and Auditor General's report of 2013 indicates that by 2012, the average number of days of employment per rural household per year was 43.[26] The corresponding figure was 54 by 2010. Perhaps a better delivery or implementation system can restore or even improve this figure in future.[27] Much depends on the quality of the administration, political will, and the development of civil organizations in states with respect to what the beneficiaries can expect from these programs. Already, the beneficiary profile of this program is encouraging. Surveys of beneficiaries conducted before 2009 report that nearly 73 percent of families that benefited belong to scheduled castes and scheduled tribes. The same report indicates that about 50 percent of these beneficiaries are women, who indicate that their ability to personally retain wages aids their economic independence.[28]

Both the beneficiary profile and the productive outcomes of the NREGA programs seem to significantly improve when civil associations actively scrutinize the implementation processes at local levels through organized social audit. This process of public hearing, participated by local citizens who get a chance to review official records of finances and procedures, and to collectively question officials, with the able assistance of civil leaders, significantly helps to fight corruption and improve the performance of the projects. Besides social audit, active civic assistance to use the weapon of information to serve public interest and accountability has helped reduce the incidence of abuse of political authority in states like Rajasthan, Kerala, and Gujarat. The careful and critical method of such action, mostly lacking media appeal, made it increasingly clear that these social protection programs with proper organized support can amount to much more than a mere survival scheme for the rural poor.[29]

There were also more dramatic modes of civic engagement, to promote the rights and resources of poorer people. The Jan Satyagraha movement of the *Ekta Parishad* (Unity Association) was designed to attain people's control over livelihood resources and local governance using nonviolent methods of popular struggle.[30] The Ekta Parishad, beginning in 1991 in Madhya Pradesh, gradually extended its activities in Bihar, Orissa, and other states. It has a special concentration on tribal land rights and other issues concerned with women, and cultural and economic problems of deprivation.

Ekta Parishad has, over the years, staged many impressive satyagraha campaigns to persuade mainly state-level authorities to respond to its demands. In 2012, it organized an impressive "long march of 60,000 plus landless laborers and marginal farmers to Delhi" that yielded a significant agreement on legal entitlement of land for landless families and a new land reform policy.[31]

In fact, time and again during recent decades, popular movements and civic campaigns have filled in the valuable areas of public space that the vote-seeking parties and interest-chasing pressure groups have failed to cultivate. When crucial struggles of the poor against unfair land acquisition, or popular campaigns for rehabilitation and resettlement of poor people, were crying for organized leadership, the leaders of parties did not respond. It was the *Narmada Bachao Andolan*, or the popular movements connected with Singur and Nandigram issues in West Bengal that conducted popular struggles in different parts of the country to fight for land and livelihood rights of the poor.[32] These had a positive, though slow-paced, impact on national land legislation. To be sure, the passage of Land Acquisition Bills from 2007 through the 2013 Act was not expected to deliver ideal results. At least, it was reassuring that the public space offered relevant room for the voices of the rural poor.

Information and Citizen Activation: Transparency Issues

It took at least a decade of struggle led by the National Campaign for People's Right to Information (NCPRI), beginning in 1996, to create the ground for legislative processes leading to the enactment of the historic RTI Act of 2005. The national campaign consisted of social activists, lawyers, journalists, retired administrators, and academics. NCPRI collaborated with the Press Council of India to formulate the first draft of an RTI law and sent it to the Government of India in 1996. The civic leaders were disappointed with the long delays and frustrating amendments to their carefully drafted inputs that marked the legislative process for a number of years. They considered the Freedom of Information Act of 2002 as "a very watered down version" of the Bill drafted by them in

1996.[33] They were interested in stronger transparency provisions and a wider jurisdiction.

When a new government in 2004 promised a more comprehensive legislation, once again they offered their suggestions for amending the 2002 Act. There was extensive discussion and negotiation with the new leaders in power. But the new RTI Bill as introduced in Parliament in 2004 turned out to be much weaker than the promised version. Among the weaknesses of the 2004 version, the most distressing one for NCPRI was the limited jurisdiction envisaged; it applied only to the Union Government.

Once again, it took another round of civic campaigns, negotiations, and giving evidence before a Standing Committee of Parliament by several members of the NCPRI, that the new RTI Act of 2005 came into effect on October 13, with a jurisdiction covering the whole of India. It was not easy to deal with the Congress-led coalition government or its predecessor. It is also historically interesting that most of the time, official interest in legislation for RTI has come from non-Congress ruling coalitions as in 1977–79, 1989–90, and 1996–98.[34] Yet, the Congress Party leaders of the UPA proudly used the RTI enactment as one of its greatest accomplishments during the election campaigns of 2014. They forgot the story of the contributions of the civil associations.

In fact, the relentless struggles conducted by one of the most respected civic organizations working in North India at the grassroots level, seeking to connect the people's RTI with the basic livelihood issues of the poor, provided the most important support base for the NCPRI for the RTI legislation. The *Mazdoor Kisan Shakti Sangathan* (MKSS), the Workers and Peasants Power Organization, located in Rajasthan and led by some of the most creative civic leaders in India including Aruna Roy, has performed an exemplary role.[35]

It is this movement's watchful eyes that made sure that the scope of the RTI Act extended to both the national and the regional levels, along with additional state-level RTI legislations, foiling the attempts of the UPA government to limit its application to the Union Government's jurisdiction alone.[36] The extensive scope of the RTI in India, covering the federal, state, and local levels, is especially important, because at relatively lower levels, it also enables poor people to gain information held by the state that is frequently connected with their crucial livelihood concerns.[37]

With caring attention of organizations like the MKSS, the RTI provides a formidable weapon for the weaker social segments against the veil of secrecy that protects the local alliance of privilege.

The MKSS began its anti-corruption campaigns in the 1990s, not with accusatory statements but rather with a focus on specific local issues such as fraud in the government draught-relief program that deprived day laborers of their fair share of wages.[38] Uncovering such accounts of deprivation required access to documents containing official information, revealing discretionary billing practices, wage bills for ghost workers, inflated payments for inferior substitutes of contracted materials, and gross discrepancies between official records and workers' experiences, and other instances. Campaigns for systematic formal channels of information yielded in 2000 a state-level RTI that significantly aided struggles against bureaucratic resistance to popular demand for information, just as the later wider RTI Act of 2005 opened greater facilities for access to official records.

More than access, it was actually the new system of sharing and collectively verifying the information in organized rural public hearing (*jan sunwai*) with open access that marked a milestone of civic scrutiny in the country.[39] The assembled villagers while participating in such social audit sessions came across hard evidence about who deprived them so as to benefit powerful persons. If these institutional processes of accountability did not always bring about commensurate compensation or ideal redress, at least they generated a sense of efficacy of collective action.

Fortunately, MKSS had extensive support from a prestigious NGO in Rajasthan known as Social Work and Research Center (SWRC) predating the MKSS. Their different ways of working and support bases, however, turned out to be mutually useful. The elite background, political contact resources, and distinguished local and national performances of leaders like Sanjit (Bunker) Roy of SWRC, Aruna Roy, and Nikhil Dey of MKSS and others, were not easy to match.[40] But there are also other types of effective leadership and organizational resources that can endow strength to comparable civic movements. The Ekta Parishad leadership, discussed above, reflected a less Westernized and more Gandhian background.

The *Bhrashtachar Virodhi Jan Andolan* (BVJA), or the People's Movement Against Corruption, beginning in 1991 in Maharashtra, was led by

Anna Hazare whose rural origin and underprivileged social background stood in sharp contrast to those associated with SWRC, MKSS, or other civic association leaders.[41] He began his civic engagement with a successful struggle against a collusive move of a band of forest officials and timber merchants to deplete public resources in his state. Like the MKSS, his BVJA was deeply involved in rural development work and struggles. The movement against corruption was a part of the larger program of working for the livelihood requirements of the poor people. Anna's growing goodwill in the field of social work earned him good political contacts and sources of information. The BVJA used these and other resources along with organized scrutiny of the work of public agencies at various levels of state administration to make sure that the poor people in rural areas get a fair deal.

As in the case of the MKSS, the BVJA was significantly supported by the resources of a prominent peer association, the Hind Swaraj Trust. Anna's involvement in that well-funded NGO ensured a mutually supportive role that was important for both these organizations.[42] However, unlike the MKSS, the strategies of interaction with the statewide authorities or with other organizations in Maharashtra followed by the BVJA leadership seemed to lack the prudence and consistency that the MKSS was able to maintain over time in Rajasthan.[43] Perhaps Anna's Gandhian modes of mass politics needed a larger stage. A suitable ground soon emerged due to a number of factors that set a new course for his leadership in public space.

Discontent, Resentment, and Redress

By the second year of the second UPA rule, popular discontent with the economic situation and disclosures of massive corruption in the corridors of power created a deep sense of national distress. All the scams and scandals, including those related to 2G telecom, Commonwealth Games, coal block allocation, and many others, seemed to be a normal part of the art of decimating public resources using a democratic cover. When the politicians and officials were busy playing their big money games, there were many other private players sadly earning the country the title of the 'Bribe Republic'.[44]

But this was also the country where the people by this time were learning to express anger and channel resentment against the public sources of corruption. The RTI Act of 2005 discussed above was one channel that particularly proved useful as more people learned to use it, and at times more effectively with the aid of civil society organizations. In fact, a review committee estimated that in the initial two-and-a-half years of the Act's implementation, citizens filed nearly 2 million requests for information.[45]

To be sure, many of these attempts were to probe possibilities of redressing grievances of the poor, but they also frequently yielded relevant information about corruption in public authorities and, occasionally, also ways of securing compensation. If this does not sound dramatic, it surely indicates a practical way of connecting poor citizens' livelihood agenda and transparency issues with the proximate authority that matters for their daily life. Thanks to pressures from civic associations, one of the largest rural development programs, the NREGA discussed above, officially includes transparency rules designed to minimize corruption and promote civic scrutiny of projects.[46]

By 2011, an angry India appeared to be ready for a more stirring version of an anti-corruption movement. It was not surprising that the India Against Corruption (IAC) movement of this time was led by Anna Hazare whose Gandhian techniques of struggle and earlier (BVJA) reputation helped assemble a wide range of support in Delhi and elsewhere. The concerted efforts of major civic associations, leaders of popular struggles, and others strengthened the anti-corruption movement to a degree of popularity that probably surprised the ruling authorities.[47]

However, the IAC and Anna Hazare's unflinching focus on a Jan Lokpal Bill, seeking to establish a powerful and comprehensive guardian safeguarding the country against corruption, reflecting a version of Sweden's Ombudsman as an independent government office dealing with corruption, raised many questions that did not yield easy answers even for many avid partners of the movement.[48] Lokpal Bills had been introduced several times in the Lok Sabha since 1968 without any major excitement or success.[49] This time, however, anger all over the nation offered a more favorable setting for using it as a politically organizing mission.

The evocative sentiments connected with the fasting of a dedicated but frail leader helped. But a stronger aid to the movement was delivered by a grossly inept government, and its rarely audible prime minister, who kept changing their response to Anna Hazare from compromise first, then later arrogantly arresting, improperly imprisoning, hastily releasing, and discussing with him once again in mellow terms. Finally, when the Lokpal and Lokayukta Act of 2013 came into force in January 16, 2014, the UPA regime was already mired in a deep state of distress.[50] However, what the new act was actually going to accomplish was unclear. Even the original version pressed by Anna and his team, with its demand for covering the prime minister and all government servants, and additional provisions to ensure a selection process for the Lokpal requiring a significant independence from the government, may not prove to be very productive in practice.

Fighting corruption in government may either ideally entail radically redesigning the administrative job or, as under the present system, to prosecute an official after detecting corruption.[51] The Lokpal or Ombudsman type of authority probably would be more attentive to investigation and filing of charges, but due to the complex and dragging criminal justice system, securing successful conviction would be more difficult. In fact, an empirical study of cases handled by a state Lokayukta between 1995 and 2011 indicates, that given the present administrative system and an overburdened legal structure guided by archaic laws, new agencies can only make modest improvement.[52]

Parting Ways: A Party to Change System

The moderate draft Lokpal Bills, including the one prepared by the NCPRI, were not unaware of these limitations. But the Anna Team, and more so, its organizational architect Arvind Kejriwal, was less interested in reason. Kejriwal and his close associates were increasingly losing faith in the politics of negotiation with an adversary whose reliability, in their perception, was doubtful. By the beginning of October 2012, they were ready to make public their intention to part ways with Anna Hazare and the limited agenda of civil society movements. They realized that the focus now needed to be on "fundamental systemic changes" that would necessarily call for a "political instrument of their own."[53] Thus, the Aam Aadmi Party (AAP) was launched on November 26, 2012, apparently to offer an alternative to "the entire political establishment,"[54] as stated by Yogendra Yadav, a prominent political science scholar, and a core philosopher–leader of the party. The sensational debut of this small party in Delhi and the story of its encounter with the national political processes deserve special attention.

Kejriwal's passion for waging a relentless war against corruption from within the conventional electoral system was timed for right resonance in 2013 for India in general and Delhi in particular. From his IIT student days, he had a fascination for the anti-corruption zeal of leaders like V.P. Singh, and distaste for religious politics of the kind associated with the Ram Mandir movement.[55] When he joined the elite Indian Revenue Service, his attention was devoted to building a civil organization, Parivartan, to ensure transparency in tax process.[56] His leaving the elite job, joining the Anna team, and forming the AAP told a story that served as an appealing credential for leading a new mode of politics.

But perhaps the most renovating feature of the new political formation was the fact that it did not call for any visible support from any caste, class, ethnic, or religious group. In a country where the electoral incentive for cultivating particularist support tends to be high, the political compulsion for compromising with the seamy conduct of representatives may be unavoidable. To the extent, the AAP can disconnect itself from such unsavory leverage, it will promise a new assurance to a new generation of citizens. This kind of assurance may be particularly interesting for the expected growing importance of the Indian middle class, which by 2015–16 is likely to consist of 267 million people.[57] The new politics may gain from such people "who are beyond the poverty line but not in the category of the rich" because they will possibly be more attached to "rights based claims for economic justice" than "charitable notion of economic redistribution."[58]

The AAP's spectacular electoral performance in December 2013 in the Delhi Assembly elections, its seven weeks of power with outside support, and unexpected resignation of Chief Minister Kejriwal on February 14 earned it excited admirers as well as concerned critics.[59] The level of excitement sharply diminished when its adventure in the national Lok Sabha elections in 2014 earned it only 4 seats—all in Punjab—out of its 434 candidates.[60] Even the Delhi seats eluded the AAP this time. The party had attracted a large number of volunteers before the elections,

350,000 nationwide by one estimate, but it declined to about 50,000 after its defeat.[61] Public contributions to its funds considerably declined. Some party leaders left. There were charges of leadership cult and coterie domination of major decision-making processes. In fact, many of the claims of new directions in party-building also appeared to be less credible now.

However, some of the innovative institutional contributions, especially in Delhi, like the *mohalla sabhas* or local councils, consisting of about 4,000 voters in each area, serving as participatory bodies with channels of communication with administrative officials, are still being nurtured.[62] Not everything is lost. The main leadership is still around. If it did not follow through all the principles of swaraj or self-rule in its own party-building process, it can correct its course.[63] As Yogendra Yadav assures his critics, there is a serious attempt to build the party from below, and that the AAP is the only party which has "the energy and will to take on Modi and BJP over the next five years."[64]

However, the AAP may find that other parties are already preparing the ground for a credible opposition to the BJP. Only three months after the big victory in the Lok Sabha elections, the BJP suffered a big reversal of fortune when it lost 6 out of 10 seats in Bihar in the August 21 by-elections in 2014. It also faced unexpected setback in 2 seats each in Karnataka and Punjab. In these elections, the regional parties and the Congress Party demonstrated that they should be taken seriously, even if the number of seats involved in these elections was not large.

Besides elections, the internal notes of dissent within the party may reveal signs of strain that may disturb the party leadership. It is interesting that some of these voices of dissent on policy issues have emerged from its leaders who work with labor or peasant unions. The Bharatiya Mazdoor Sangh (BMS) is "upset with the series of amendments approved by the Modi Cabinet to relax labor norms."[65] The Bharatiya Kisan Sangh (BKS) is worried that there may be attempts to "tinker with the land acquisition law passed by the UPA government which makes it tougher for industries to get land."[66] If these policy issues based on important material concerns of workers and peasants gain prominence in the party, how will it impinge on the role of religious ideology as the basic bond of organizational unity? These internal voices of dissent may one day turn into prospective resources for a broad band of opposition that the AAP or other parties would like to imagine.

Concluding Observations

The civic style, and its modest pace and practicable scale, may not satisfy those who, like Kejriwal, seek to replace the establishment or the system. As we have noted, the key to the success of the civic mode lies precisely in the fact that it offers a modest way of complementing the existing democratic institutions and not supplanting or overturning them. When the elections are over, and the winners are busy maximizing their returns on political investment for five years, increasingly, it is the civic associations that can come to the aid of the poorer people in different parts of India.

As we have tried to show, civic workers or leaders with education, motivation, and compassion try to hear, represent, organize, and strategize the manifest, or even the unarticulated, voices or aspirations of the disadvantaged people. These voices are incorporated into actionable issues deliberated in the limelight of the public space. This is how deprived groups, whether in distant forests, remote villages, or neglected areas of towns or cities, get organized to make a public presence and to prepare for negotiation, struggle, and hopefully, redress. This is the way the civic associations strive to connect people to power.[67] The associations in civil society do this job better than politicians because they do not seek power or profit. Their prize is the successful realization of neglected collective aspirations, earnestly following, if not enriching, democratic rules of politics.

Notes and References

1. See Iris Marion Young, *Inclusion and Democracy* (Oxford: Oxford University Press, 2000), p. 173. Young's discussion of Jurgen Habermas and other theorists is useful. For us, public space refers to a communicative network where information and views of collective interest are openly exchanged and discussed. See ibid., pp. 170–74. For Habermas, see Jurgen Habermas, *Between Facts and Norms* (Cambridge: MIT Press, 1996), pp. 360–63.
2. See for NGOs, William F. Fisher, "Civil Society and Its Fragments" in David N. Gellner, ed., *Varieties of Activist Experience, Civil Society in South Asia* (New Delhi: SAGE Publications, 2010), p. 254. Also, see the discussion in Mary Katzenstein, Smitu Kothari, and Uday Mehta, "Social Movement Politics in India," in Atul Kohli, ed., *The Success of Indian Democracy* (Cambridge: Cambridge University Press, 2001), pp. 249–50. Estimated numbers of NGOs before the end of the 20th century ranged up to

100,000 (see ibid., p. 248). Some are nationally coordinated. For example, one may refer to the National Alliance of People's Movements or NAPM, formed in 1995 (ibid., p. 250). Foreign funds of NGOs have been officially watched since 1981 (ibid., pp. 249–50).

3. See Association for Democratic Reforms (ADR), *Annual Report, 2012–2013* (New Delhi: ADR, 2013), pp. 2–6.

4. For the beginning of this tradition, see Granville Austin, *Working a Democratic Constitution* (New Delhi: Oxford University Press, 1999), pp. 439 ff.

5. Modhurima Dasgupta, *Courting Development* (Saarbruken: VDM Verlag Dr Muller, 2009), p. 114.

6. ADR, *Annual Report, 2012–2013*, pp. 2–4.

7. The authority is derived from Article 324 of the Indian Constitution.

8. ADR, op.cit., 2013, pp. 4–5.

9. See, for example, ADR, Proceedings of the 9th National Conference on Electoral and Political Reforms, Jaipur, March 22–23, 2013, esp. pp. 12–15.

10. 58 percent of the 2009 elected members of the Lok Sabha were millionaires (or *crorepati* as normally reported), while the corresponding figure was 82 percent for the 2014 Lok Sabha (http://adrindia.org/research-and-reports/lok-sabha/2009/pdf-of-national-level-analysis; http://adrindia.org/research-and-report/election-watch/lok-sabha/2014/lok-sabha-2014-winners-analysis-criminal-and-finan (accessed on July 15, 2014)).

11. NEW reports of July 2014 indicate 185 members of the 2014 Lok Sabha and 158 members of the 2009 Lok Sabha had declared serious criminal cases. It should be noted that, generally, only a small proportion of these pending cases lead to actual conviction. See Bhaskar Dutta and Poonam Gupta, "How Indian Voters Respond to Candidates with Criminal Charges, Evidence from the 2009 Lok Sabha Elections," *Economic and Political Weekly*, vol. XLIX, no.4, January 15, 2014, p. 45.

12. Jayant Sriram and Kaushik Deka, "Bringing Down the House," *India Today*, March 3, 2014, p. 28.

13. See ibid., p. 30. Source: PRS Legislative Research, Delhi, pp. 26–32.

14. Ibid., pp. 26–27 and 30.

15. Ibid., p. 28.

16. Ibid., p. 28.

17. Ibid., inset, p. 3. The reference is to Aruna Roy's speech in the March 2013 conference. She is one of the most respected leaders in the national civil society.

18. Ibid., inset, p. 3.

19. Ashok Kumar Sircar, "Policy Initiatives and Policy Paralysis," in *State of India's Livelihoods Report 2013* (New Delhi: SAGE Publications, 2014), p. 63.

20. Ibid., p. 43.

21. Ibid., p. 43.

22. See ibid., p. 46.

23. See Savitha Suresh Babu and Kirti Vardhan, "Social Protection and Livelihoods," in *State of India's Livelihoods Report 2013* (New Delhi: SAGE Publications, 2014), p. 93 ff. for an excellent analysis.

24. See ibid., p. 93. The budget for 2012–13 was also the same. There was no increase in allocation for 2013–14, not even allowing for adjustment for inflation. From 2005 to 2012, the NREGA "has generated 1,348 crore person days of employment and had involved an expenditure of around ₹2 lakh crore" (lakh equals 100,000). This study

estimates that, as of 2013, nearly 5 crore (crore equals 10 million) "households across India have accessed employment through the Act" (ibid., p. 93).

25. The Union Government's share is 75 percent; the State Government's share is normally 25 percent. It may vary to favor smaller states.

26. CAG Report 2013's performance audit of MGNREGA, http://saiindia.gov.in/english/home/our_products/audit_report/Government_Wise/union_audit/recent_reports/union_performance/2013/Civil/Report_6/chap_13.pdf (accessed on August 29, 2014).

27. Smaller states like Manipur, Mizoram, and Tripura were able to raise the figure (of days of employment) to 80, ibid. It is interesting that some state ruling parties, with strong ideological concern for the disadvantaged groups in rural areas, have remained weak performers with respect to NREGA implementation. See Atul Kohli, *Poverty Amid Plenty in New India* (Cambridge; Cambridge University Press, 2012), p. 175 (for Uttar Pradesh under Mayawati leadership before 2010) and p. 208 (for West Bengal under Communist Party of India (Marxist) leadership; around 2008–09).

28. See Babu and Vardhan, "Social Protection and Livelihoods," pp. 94–95. This part of their report is based on the work of Jean Dreze and Reetika Khera as cited on p. 94.

29. See Aruna Roy and Nikhil Dey, "Much More than a Survival Scheme," *Hindu*, August 31, 2012, http://www.thehindu.com/opinion/lead/much-more-than-a-survival-scheme/article3840977.ece (accessed on August 16, 2014). Here, the authors claim among other benefits of the NREGA projects, as of 2012, the fact that they helped "decrease gender differential in wages," and increase real wages, productivity, and growth.

30. The Ekta Parishad leader P.V. Rajagopal has a strong Gandhian commitment (www.ektaparishad.com, accessed on July 24, 2014).

31. A.K. Sircar, "Policy Initiatives and Policy Paralysis," p. 36.

32. For the Land Acquisition legislation process, see ibid., pp. 46–48. The *Narmada Bachao Andolan* (Save the Narmada River Struggle) and its leaders, including Medha Patkar, have attracted wide scholarly attention. For West Bengal cases, see Amiya K. Chaudhari, "Making a Political Challenge," in Paul Wallace and Ramashray Roy, eds., *India's 2009 Elections* (New Delhi: SAGE Publications), esp. pp. 196–97.

33. National Campaign for People's right to Information (NCPRI), "Brief History of RTI," http://righttoinformation.info/about-us/brief-history-demand-for-the-right-to-information (accessed on May 19, 2014).

34. For details, see Rob Jenkins and Anne Marie Goetz, "Accounts and Accountability: Theoretical Implications of the Right-to-Information Movement in India," *Third World Quarterly* 20, 3(1999): 611 ff.

35. Ibid., pp. 603–21; Rob Jenkins, "Civil Society Versus Corruption," *Journal of Democracy* 18 (April 2007): 55–69, esp. p. 63.

36. NCPRI, "Brief History of RTI," p. 2.

37. The scope of the RTI Act in India is much wider than that of, for example, the Freedom of Information Act of the United States as adopted in 1966, which applies only to the national government. See Alasdair Roberts, "A Great and Revolutionary Law? The First Four Years of India's Right to Information Act," *Public Administration Review*, November/December 2010, p. 925.

38. See for details Rob Jenkins, "Civil Society Versus Corruption," pp. 59–60.

39. Ibid., pp. 60–61. Many of the MKSS materials are extensively covered in the works of Rob Jenkins and his collaborators.

40. Aruna Roy left the Indian Administrative Service to work with civic associations. She began to work with SWRC founded by Sanjit (Bunker) Roy (later her husband) who became famous as a leader of the Barefoot College Movement. All three of them went through the elite school system in India, and in Nikhil Dey's case, also law school (http://upakriti.org, accessed on July 31, 2014).

41. Anna Hazare was born in a village that didn't have a primary school. His poor relatives' efforts to finance his education elsewhere were not good enough to let him complete high school. Later, his training and experience in the army and social work proved to be useful.

42. See Rob Jenkins, ed., "In Varying States of Decay," in *Regional Reflections* (New Delhi: Oxford University Press, 2004), esp. pp. 221–26.

43. For details, see ibid., esp. pp. 243–49. Note the comment on "… the tendency for Anna to befuddle his followers with erratic decision-making…," on p. 249.

44. See Damayanti Datta, "The Bribe Republic," *India Today*, July 22, 2013, pp. 18–25, for the staggering details of everyday corruption. See also Maya Chadda, "India in 2012," *Asian Survey* 53, 1(January/February 2013), 52–53.

45. See Roberts, "A Great and Revolutionary Law," pp. 926–27.

46. Ibid., p. 932. However, not all the locations or states can claim to have developed the necessary infrastructure.

47. Besides the civic movements discussed before, the notable joiners included Medha Patkar, the leader of the Narmada Bachao Andolan, Agrarian Laborers Movement led by Swami Agnivesh, Arvind Kejriwal and his Parivartan movement, working class leaders, and others. See Shafi Rahman, "Start of a Surge," *India Today*, April 18, 2011, pp. 50–51.

48. For example, the National Campaign for Peoples' Right to Information (NCPRI) had a more moderate approach to the Lokpal issue. See Dhiraj Nayyar, Priya Sahgal, and Mihir Srivastava, "Parliament," *India Today*, September 12, 2011, pp. 22–36, esp. pp. 31 and 34 (Nikhil Dey's statements).

49. Most of the time the initiatives came from non-Congress coalition governments of short duration (see ibid., pp. 30–31).

50. *Lokayukta* refers to the state-level anti-corruption institution while *Lokpal* stands for the national-level; both terms convey a sense of a guardian role.

51. See P.G. Babu, Vikas Kumar, and Poonam Mehra, "Prosecuting Corruption in India, Evidence From Karnataka," in S. Mahendra Dev, ed., *India Development Report 2012–13* (New Delhi: Oxford University Press, 2013), pp. 266–85, esp. pp. 267, 268.

52. See ibid., pp. 282–83.

53. See Yogendra Yadav, "Ethical Cleansing, Not Ritual Purity," *Outlook*, October 15, 2012 (www.outlookindia.com, accessed on June 18, 2013).

54. Yogendra Yadav's interview with Revati Laul, "Our Real Strength…," *Tehelka Magazine*, http://www.tehelka.com/our-real-trial-of-strength-will-be-the-2013-delhi-election/ (accessed on June 18, 2013).

55. See Kunal Pradhan and Bhavna Vij-Aurora, "An Uncommon Life," *India Today*, January 6, 2014, p. 30.

56. Ibid., p. 31.

57. See Ashok K. Lahiri, "The Middle Class and Economic Reforms" *Economic and Political Weekly* XLIX, 11(March 15, 2014), 37–38.

58. Ibid., p. 43.

59. See Sandeep Unnithan, "AAP Eclipse," *India Today,* June 23, 2014, pp. 24–31, esp. pp. 30–31. In Delhi Assembly, it won 28 out of 70 seats and Kejriwal defeated a formidable incumbent chief minister by more than 21,000 votes. The Congress Party provided the outside support for forming the government.

60. These four seats in Punjab and 25 percent of popular vote in 2014 were won by the recently organized AAP, which lacked money, muscle, or dynastic support. See Harjeshwar Pal Singh, "How the AAP Won Punjab," http://kafila.org/2014/05/17/how-the-aap-won-punjab-harjeshwar-pal-singh (accessed on May 19, 2014).

61. Ibid., p. 24.

62. For details of local council systems in Delhi including mohalla sabhas, see Aditya Mohanty, "From Bhagidari to Mohalla Sabhas in Delhi," *Economic and Political Weekly* XLIX, 4(April 5, 2014), 16–18.

63. Self-rule or swaraj is also a guiding principle of the AAP's 'model for the nation'. See Arvind Kejriwal, *Swaraj* (New Delhi: Harper Collins, 2012), esp. pp. 109–45.

64. Asit Jolly, "Interview, Yogendra Yadav," *India Today*, June 23, 2014, p. 27.

65. See Ravish Tiwari and Kaushik Deka, "The Swadeshi Warriors," *India Today*, August 18, 2014, p. 30, pp. 26–32. In English, BMS refers to Indian Labor Union.

66. Ibid., p. 30. In English, BKS refers to Indian Peasant Union.

67. See Marion Young, *Inclusion and Democracy* (Oxford: Oxford University Press, 2000), pp. 173–74 and 177–180 for an analysis of how these connections tend to make democracy "strong and deep."

PART II

Analytical State Studies

A. Northern Cluster

6

Understanding the BJP's Victory in Uttar Pradesh

Sudha Pai and Avinash Kumar

The 2014 Lok Sabha election introduced significant shifts in Uttar Pradesh (UP), a key state that reflects the sweeping political change in the country. UP was the electoral battleground from where two principal contenders—Narendra Modi and Rahul Gandhi—fought the election. The Bharatiya Janata Party (BJP) won a spectacular victory in all regions of the state, reducing the Congress and the Samajwadi Party (SP) to their family strongholds. It also penetrated deep into the backward and Dalit base of the two well established and strong identity-based parties, the SP and the Bahujan Samaj Party (BSP).

This chapter seeks to understand the reasons underlying the spectacular victory of the BJP in UP. We propose that its victory was due to revival of its organization and social base. A new leadership led by Narendra Modi and his selected aides with the support of the Sangh Parivar has been replacing the older leaders/founders of the party Atal Bihari Vajpayee and L.K. Advani. Among the new generation leaders in the BJP, Modi was able to take control of the party due to his three successive victories in the Gujarat Assembly elections and his close association with the RSS. In fact, we argue that in 2014, it was 'not so much a BJP as a Modi victory in UP' due to a two-pronged, well-organized, and strategized campaign by him and his confidante Amit Shah, using both Hindutva and development. Modi stressed the lack of development under UPA-II and the ruling SP in UP and promised its rapid development based on the 'Gujarat Model'.

The party cadres, following a different path, employed communal strategies—used at times by Modi himself—to create a broad Hindu vote bank encompassing the upper castes, the backwards, and also the Dalits.

The ideology of Hindutva under Modi has undergone change despite the changing socio-political context in the country in the wake of globalization and the rise of a new and more demanding aspirational middle class. While under Vajpayee, development and economic reforms was prioritized over religious mobilization, as evident during the 1999 and 2004 national elections. Modi, in addition to addressing the aspirations of the frustrated young generation of voters due to the lack of development in UP, also revived religious mobilization on issues such as the Ram Mandir in 2014. Further, toward the end, it also realized that it was important to address in a more inclusive manner development of all sections of the population, not only the Hindus.

However, an equally important factor affecting the election was the changed political context in UP skilfully harnessed by Modi. The weakening of the two well-established state-level parties are particularly important. The ruling SP suffered from slow development, poor governance, and failure to control communal riots, while the BSP's popularity fell due to its *Sarvajan* (everybody) experiment leading to its defeat in the 2012 Assembly elections. Decline of the two major state parties provided Modi room to mount his campaign. Hence, we argue that two factors were responsible for the victory of the BJP: first, longer-term factors such as the continuing decline of the Congress, and, second, weakness of state-level parties visible in their lackluster campaigns. However, the victory of the BJP also lies more importantly in the ideological and organizational changes introduced by its new leadership and their long, well-organized, and planned campaign. Thus, it is through the lens of the new 'avatar'of the BJP that we attempt to understand its phenomenal success vis-à-vis the poor performance of other parties in UP.

Analyzing the Results

Victory of the BJP in UP

The magnitude of the victory of the BJP was surprising as the party has been on decline in UP from the mid-1990s after the Babri Masjid issue lost importance following its destruction. As Table 6.1 shows, its seats

Table 6.1

Position of Parties in the Lok Sabha Elections in UP since 1989

Name of the Party	2009 Won (Contested) Vote %			2004 Won (Contested) Vote %			1999 Won (Contested) Vote %			1998 Won (Contested) Vote %			1996 Won (Contested) Vote %			1991 Won (Contested) Vote %			1989 Won (Contested) Vote %		
BSP	20	(80)	–	19	(80)	24.67	14	(85)	22.08	4	(85)	20.9	6	(85)	20.61	1	(67)	8.7	2	(75)	9.93
BJP	10	(71)	–	10	(77)	22.17	29	(77)	27.64	57	(82)	36.49	52	(83)	33.44	51	(84)	32.82	8	(31)	7.58
INC	21	(69)	–	9	(73)	12.04	10	(76)	14.72	0	–	6.02	5	(85)	8.14	5	(80)	18.02	15	(84)	31.77
SP	23	(75)	23.25	35	(68)	26.74	26	(84)	24.06	20	(81)	28.7	16	(64)	20.84	JD 22 (73) 21.27 Janata Party 4 (81) 10.84			Janata Dal 54 (69) 35.9		

Source: Election Commission of India.

in Parliament dropped from 57 in the 1996 to 29 in the 1999 and 10 in the 2009 Lok Sabha elections. In the 2012 UP Assembly elections, the party had won only 47 seats (with barely 15 percent of the total votes polled) and was forced to forfeit deposits in 229 seats. In contrast, in the 2014 election, the BJP obtained 71 seats with 42.3 percent votes and its ally Apna Dal (AD) won two seats in eastern UP. It also stood second in all the seven constituencies that it lost (Figure 6.1). In terms of assembly segments, together with the AD, it gained the highest number of votes in 337 out of 403 assembly constituencies and finished as the trailing party in another 63 seats (Figure 6.2). Together, they swept nearly 84 percent of the assembly segments of UP.

Moreover, as Figure 6.3 shows, the BJP had the lowest average margin of loss (169,828 votes). This declines sharply if we leave the disproportionate margin of loss for BJP candidate (more than 3.5 lakh votes) contesting against Sonia Gandhi, from Raebareli.

The BJP gained, as the Lokniti–Centre for the Study of Developing Societies (CSDS) National Election Study (NES) in Table 6.2 reveals, substantial votes from all caste groups over the 2009 elections—over 70 percent of the Brahmins and other upper castes, 60 percent of the Other Backward Classes (OBCs), 53 percent of the Kurmis, and 45 percent of the other Dalits—cutting into the vote share of all parties.[1] The study points to no clear class factor. Voters of all ages, educational backgrounds, economic statuses, and genders supported the BJP and

Figure 6.1

Second Position Gained by Parties Out of Total Seats Lost by Them in the Lok Sabha Elections 2014 in UP

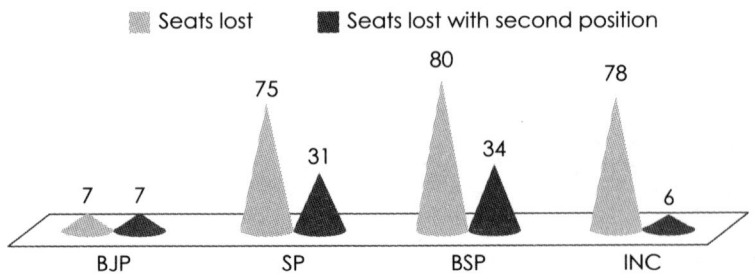

Source: Compiled from the data of the State Election Commission, UP.

Figure 6.2
*Position of BJP and Its Ally (Apna Dal) in the Assembly Segments
during the Lok Sabha Elections 2014 in UP*

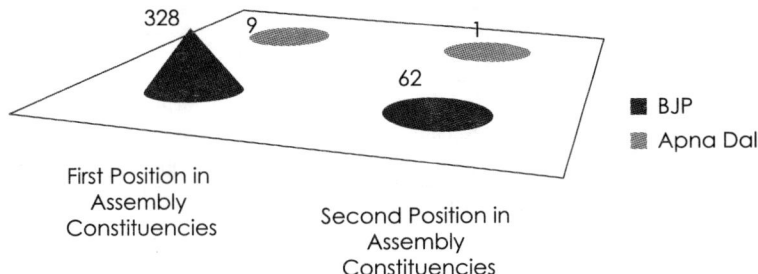

Source: Compiled from the data of the State Election Commission, UP.

Figure 6.3
Average Loss Margin

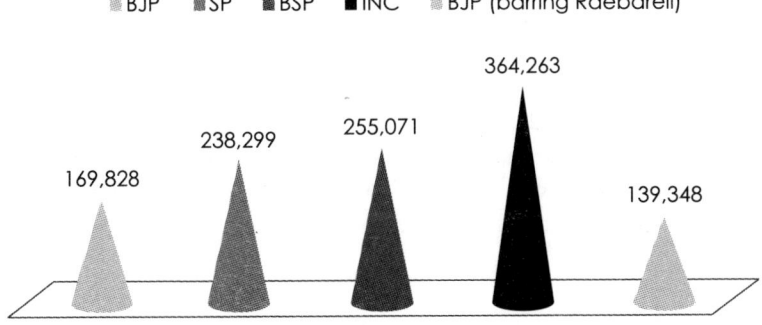

Source: Compiled from the data of the State Election Commission, UP.

its prime ministerial candidate Modi. The highest support (47 percent)
came from the first-time voters (18–22 years).[2]

Defeat of Other Parties in UP

The Congress Party, which had obtained 20 seats and 12.04 percent in
the 2009 Lok Sabha elections, reached a historic low in 2014, winning
only two family seats, Raebareli and Amethi, held by Sonia Gandhi and
Rahul Gandhi, respectively. It finished at second position in less than

Table 6.2

Support to Various Political Parties across Castes/Communities in 2014

Castes/Communities	Congress +RLD		BJP+AD		BSP		SP	
	2014	Swing from 2009	2014	Swing from 2009	2014	Swing from 2009	2014	Swing from 2009
Brahmins	11	−20	72	28	5	−4	5	0
Rajputs	7	−9	77	33	5	−2	8	−4
Other Upper Castes	9	−16	76	20	3	−8	7	−1
Yadavs	8	−2	27	21	3	−2	53	−20
Kurmis/Koeris	16	−12	53	35	4	−14	17	−1
Other OBCs	8	−9	60	32	11	−8	13	−12
Jatavs	2	−2	18	14	68	−16	4	−1
Other Dalits	4	−12	45	37	29	−35	10	0
Muslims	11	−14	10	7	18	0	58	28
Others	10	−8	51	31	20	−3	17	−2

Source: NES 2014, conducted by Lokniti-CSDS (A.K. Verma, Mirza Asmer Beg, and Sudhir Kumar, "A Saffron Sweep in Uttar Pradesh," *Hindu*, May 23, 2014).

Notes: Sample size was 2,324. Votes are in percentage and swing in percentage points. Figures have been rounded off.

10 percent of the seats (Figure 6.1) and gained only 7.5 percent of the total votes polled. Its average margin of loss (364,263 votes) was the highest (Figure 6.3), and it was confined to only 45 assembly segments (Figure 6.4). Congress candidate in Varanasi, pitted against Modi, finished a distant third, forfeiting his deposit. The party lost the confidence of all sections that had supported it during the 2009 Lok Sabha elections (Table 6.2, column 3).

The reasons for the collapse of the Congress lie in the deep decline of the organization and social base of the party in UP since the late 1980s. Efforts made first in 1998 by Sonia Gandhi and in the 2000s by Rahul Gandhi to revive the party in UP have yielded little success.[3] They faced an

Figure 6.4

Position of Non-NDA Parties in the Assembly Segments in UP in Lok Sabha Elections 2014

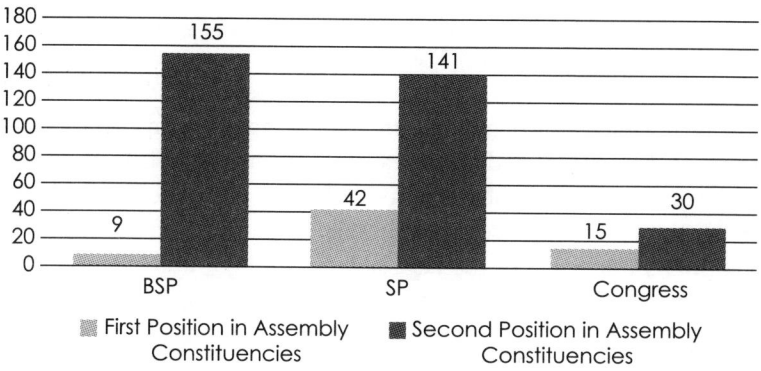

First Position in Assembly Constituencies   Second Position in Assembly Constituencies

Source: Compiled from the data of the State Election Commission, UP.

uphill task as the party had no social base or structural linkages between grassroots workers and the state leadership. Massive organizational changes were attempted to infuse young blood, reduce endemic factionalism, build disciplined cadres, and identify key constituencies where it could concentrate its strength in elections. However, rebuilding its Brahmin–Muslim–Dalit base proved difficult as these groups had shifted their allegiance to newer political parties in the state.

In the 2014 elections, apart from the anti-incumbency against UPA-II, Rahul Gandhi and his team in UP failed to provide leadership and direction. The selection of candidates was poor, the campaign remained lackluster, and the party's unwillingness to declare Rahul Gandhi as the prime ministerial candidate also proved unpopular. The attempt to form a national alliance with the BSP in January 2014 did not materialize with Mayawati preferring to contest the elections alone. Nor did the decision to provide reservation to Jats in UP and neighboring states help the party in western UP. In fact, in Amethi, a stronghold of the Gandhi family, Modi's belligerent campaign was able to swing votes toward the BJP candidate Smriti Irani, a new entrant into politics, reducing Rahul Gandhi's victory margin from 370,198 in 2009 to 107,903 votes.

With both the Congress and BJP in decline in the 1990s, it was the SP and BSP—two strong identity-based parties—that dominated UP politics in the 2000s (Table 6.1). Until the 2012 Assembly elections, people had showed faith in the larger backward class leadership, and had rejected the manifestations of both the national parties.[4] SP and BSP together won over 300 seats (i.e., 75 percent) in first position and nearly two-third (BSP at 210 seats and SP at 77) even at the second position, leaving only marginal space for all others. However, both performed badly in 2014. The SP obtained only 5 family seats, all by narrow margins.[5] Out of total seats lost (74), it finished as the trailing party in 31 parliamentary seats and its average margin of loss was significant (see Figures 6.1 and 6.3). In assembly segments, despite being the ruling party in the state with 226 MLAs (Members of the Legislative Assembly), it gained the highest number of votes in only 42 seats and remained the trailing party in 141 (see Figure 6.4). It could gain only 53 percent of its core Yadav vote which was 20 percent less than 2009 and lost considerable support among all other sections of the backwards (Table 6.2).

Mulayam Singh Yadav formed the SP in 1992 by uniting socialist groups, agrarian interests, and the Backward Classes (BCs), combined with support by the Muslim community unhappy with the Ram Mandir movement. By the early 2000s, the SP faced decline due to its inability to homogenize all sections of the backwards, and internal decay into a family fiefdom with criminal links and numerous factions. More recently, there has been disappointment with Akhilesh Yadav, appointed as chief minister after the victory in 2012, as soft and inexperienced, unable to maintain law and order, provide clean governance or development, or maintain control over an internally divided party.[6] Consequently, the SP lost the confidence of both the Muslims and the Hindus who, disliking the support given by the SP to the former, moved toward the BJP. Its increased support among the Muslims could not get translated into seats.

The BSP, despite gaining almost 20 percent of the votes in UP, could not win even a single seat. Its average margin of loss was over 250,000 votes (see Figure 6.3). It gained 7.22 lakh more votes in 2014 compared to the 2009 polls, spread over 46 seats across the state (Figure 6.5). Its vote share fell primarily in the western UP and some parts of Bundelkhand.

By securing second position in 34 constituencies, as shown in Figure 6.4, the BSP was the biggest challenge to the 'Modi wave' in UP. It also performed well in all the reserved constituencies, increasing its vote

Figure 6.5
*Change in Vote Share Percentage (%) of BSP in UP Lok Sabha
Constituencies in 2014 over 2009*

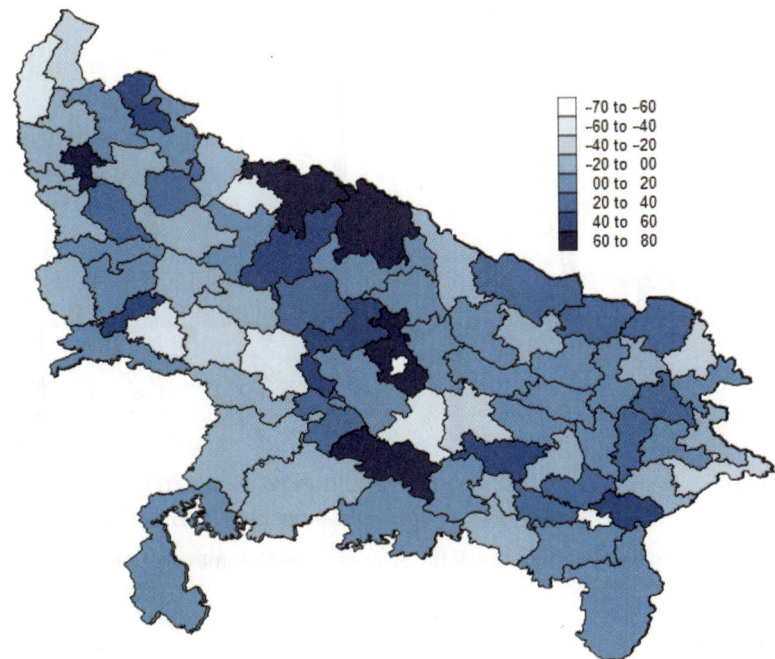

Source: Adapted from ECI. Credit: Aafaque R.K., Ashoka University Political Data
Center.
Disclaimer: This image has been redrawn by the authors and is not to scale. It
does not represent any authentic national or international boundaries and is used
for illustrative purposes only.

share in 14 out of 17, and was the trailing party in 11 seats (Figure
6.6). In five districts, which have over 30 percent Scheduled Caste (SC)
population (Kaushambi, Sitapur, Hardoi, Unnao, and Raebareli), BSP
increased its absolute votes in all by significant margins except Raebareli,
won by Sonia Gandhi (Figure 6.7). Yet, as Table 6.2 shows, there was
a significant shift of the BSP's Dalit vote base over the 2009 national
elections toward the BJP: 16 percent of the Jatavs and 35 percent of
the other Dalits. It also lost the support of all other social groups, particularly the Most Backward Castes (MBCs), and its Muslim vote base

Figure 6.6
Change in BSP's and SP's Absolute Vote Share in Lok Sabha
Elections 2014 over Lok Sabha Elections 2009 in the Reserved
Constituencies

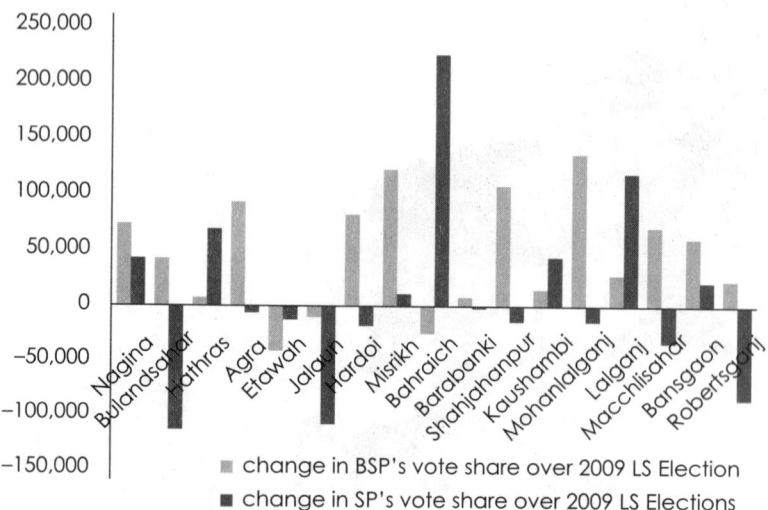

Source: Compiled from the data of the State Election Commission, UP.

Figure 6.7
Change in Absolute Vote Share of BSP and SP in Constituencies
with More Than 30 Percent of the SC Population in Lok Sabha
Elections 2014 over Lok Sabha Elections 2009

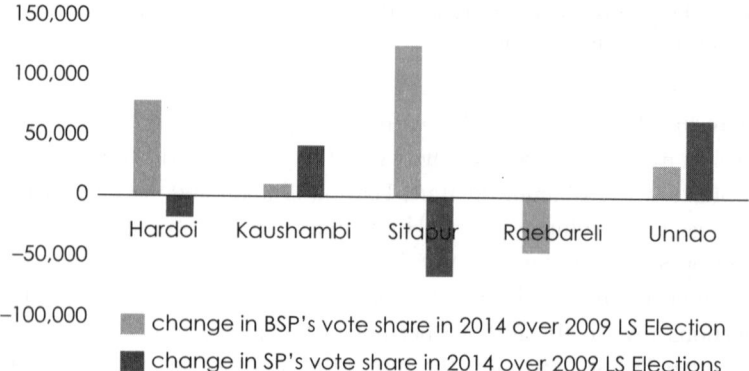

Source: Compiled from the data of the State Election Commission, UP.

remained almost the same as in 2009. But detailed analysis would show that the party's Dalit base remains secure despite some drop in votes. The party could not translate votes into seats due to multi-cornered contests in a first-past-the-post system.[7]

The defeat of the BSP in the 2014 elections is mainly due to the manner in which the party's mobilizational/electoral strategies have evolved in recent years. In the 1990s, the BSP attempted to widen its social base by giving tickets to the backwards and upper castes.[8] After the mid-2000s, based on its Sarvajan strategy, it began to directly mobilize the Brahmins and upper castes, Muslims, and MBCs to vote for the party, promising them a share in positions of power and the benefits of economic development, which provided it a majority in the 2007 elections.

Once in power, Mayawati attempted to implement an inclusive agenda covering the needs of all social groups, instead of solely Dalit-oriented policies, as in the past. Since the party had captured power alone after many years of struggle, Dalits expected that their needs would be given priority. But the government's inability to fulfil the developmental needs and aspirations of all sections of Dalits led to unhappiness among them. In fact, balancing the aspirations and providing equal distribution of resources between upper and lower castes and between Dalit subcastes became difficult for Mayawati. Subsequently, there developed anger against the BSP among some sections of the Dalits and they started moving toward the BJP.

Analyzing the BJP's Victory

The BJP, aware of the importance of UP if it was to capture power at the Center in 2014, began preparations in the state over a year in advance. The electoral campaign began with the shifting of Amit Shah from Gujarat to in charge of UP in early May 2013.[9] This was followed by the announcement of Narendra Modi as the BJP's prime ministerial candidate in September 2013, and closer to the elections, his decision to contest from Varanasi. The spectacular performance of the BJP in UP, according to Shah, was the "cumulative effect of a host of factors."[10] However, it can be traced to reorientation of the Hindutva ideology and revamping of its organization which enabled a well-planned campaign on the ground.

Ideological Underpinnings: Hindutva Redefined

In the early 1990s, during the Babri Masjid/Ram Janma Bhoomi dispute, Hindutva was conceived as a largely religious ideology used for political mobilization and identified with mainly upper-caste Hindus. But during the 2014 electoral campaign, Modi seemed to have redefined this ideology by including rapid economic development to create a strong and stable nation and greater inclusiveness through improving the lives of all castes and communities. This does not mean that the BJP abandoned or did not use its strategy of communal mobilization to secure the Hindu vote, but it was combined with a discourse of development, which appealed to a larger section of the electorate.

During the campaign, Modi on several occasions criticized the role of caste in politics and countered it with his pan-India plans. This idea emerged from his belief that in UP caste calculations would not suffice and addressing the developmental aspirations of the electorate, particularly the younger generation, was required. Most of his speeches at rallies dealt with issues of corruption, slow growth, and poor governance, both nationally by the Congress-led UPA-II and the SP in UP. While speaking about the latter, he pointed out that availability of jobs in Gujarat attracted large number of migration workers from UP. At a rally in Bahraich on November 8, 2013, he held, "There is no district, tehsil of UP, whose youth don't stay in Gujarat. When they can do wonders for Gujarat, UP can also utilise their skills."[11] With development projected as the prime agenda, Modi assured them of being their *sevak* (servant) and the nation's *chowkidaar* (guard). Reports about development in Gujarat were also brought home by the migrant workers.[12] In this way, he focused on arousing the frustrations and aspirations of voters, especially the unemployed youth in UP.

However, this does not mean that Hindutva in 2014 became free of communal and caste mobilization. At the RSS–BJP meeting held on September 9, 2013, it became clear that the core agenda of Hindutva—the Ram Temple, Common Civil Code, and Article 370—would be used. Unable to create statewide communal polarization as in 1991, the BJP–RSS cadres, which had started working on the ground much earlier, attempted to orchestrate Hindu–Muslim tension prior to the elections by taking advantage of the numerous low-key communal symbols:

- The slogan 'Jai Shri Ram' was used in most of Modi's rallies.
- The choice for Modi to contest in the holy city of Varanasi was significant.
- Modi's campaign in western UP was organized by the RSS-managed Vidya Bharati educational institutions.[13]
- RSS cadres circulated magazines that held the SP responsible for the riots creating unhappiness among the Yadavs.[14]

Equally important was the stage-managed confrontation over the Chaurasi Parikrama Yatra organized by the Vishwa Hindu Parishad (VHP), between the SP and the BJP in August 2013, with the former banning it and the latter supporting the efforts of the VHP. The Muzaffarnagar riots provided the BJP an opportunity to mobilize all Hindus, particularly the backward castes and Dalits, who had moved following the decline of the BJP and the Congress toward the SP and BSP. Amit Shah held small, quiet meetings in remote villages largely directed at Hindus to take 'revenge'. Addressing the Jats during his campaign on April 4, 2014, in Shamli village, the epicenter of the Muzaffarnagar riots, Shah reportedly said that the election, especially in western UP, was "one of honour ... an opportunity to take revenge and to teach a lesson to people who have committed injustice."[15] An FIR was filed by the district election officers of Shamli and Bijnor against Shah for spreading enmity based on caste and religion, and a notice issued by the Election Commission for violating of the model code of conduct.[16]

The impact of the communal campaign on the election can be understood from the fact that all BJP leaders who were implicated in the Muzaffarnagar riots and were given tickets won their seats with large margins. The riot-affected areas that went to poll in the first phase registered the highest polling and provided the highest victory margin for BJP in the state (Figure 6.8).

For the first time in UP, no Muslim candidate was elected from the state. The BJP won all the seats where the Muslim population is more than 20 percent, and the victory margin of the party, although significant in all these seats, was the highest in constituencies with Muslim population between 20 and 30 percent (Figure 6.9).

At the same time, Shah did not ignore the caste factor and devised strategies to reach out to the Dalit and backward caste voters. The party

Figure 6.8
Phase-wise Total Vote Percentage and Victory Margin of BJP in UP

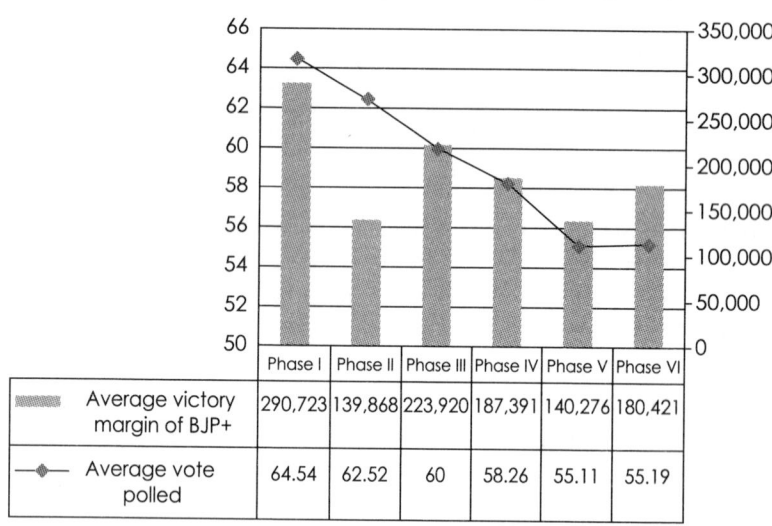

	Phase I	Phase II	Phase III	Phase IV	Phase V	Phase VI
Average victory margin of BJP+	290,723	139,868	223,920	187,391	140,276	180,421
Average vote polled	64.54	62.52	60	58.26	55.11	55.19

Source: Compiled from the data of the State Election Commission, UP.

Figure 6.9
Average Victory Margin of BJP vis-à-vis Other Parties in Constituencies with More Than 20 Percent Muslim Population in UP

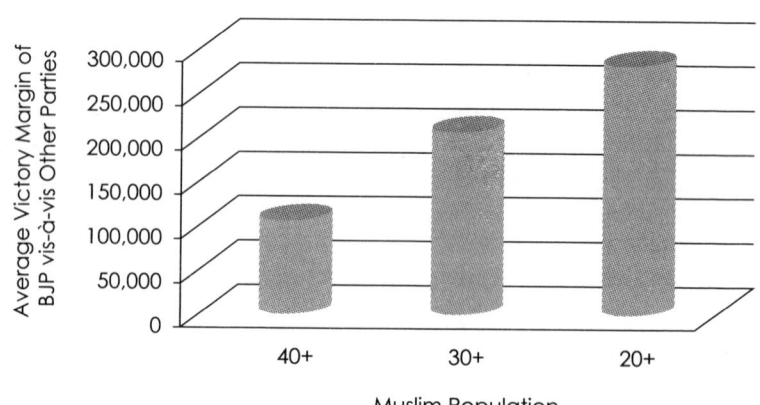

Source: Compiled from the data of the State Election Commission, UP.

gave 28 tickets to OBCs and importance to OBC leaders such as Kalyan Singh, Uma Bharti, Satyendra Kushwaha, Rameshwar Chaurasia, and Rajveer Singh. The party's decision to field Modi from Varanasi, projecting him as a backward caste *chaiwala* (tea seller) and the first OBC prime minister helped BJP obtain OBC votes. To obtain Dalit votes, especially that of non-Jatavs (Balmiki, Pasi, Dhobi, Koris, etc., who constitute 9 percent of the total population of UP), the BJP decided to appropriate the legacies of B.R. Ambedkar and other Dalit icons. Shah organized meetings in several Dalit villages and promised Bharat Ratna for the BSP founder Kanshiram. Modi addressed his second 3D rally, telecasted live at several locations across India on April 14, 2014, with garlanding the statue of B.R. Ambedkar. However, the prime focus was on obtaining the support of the MBCs, which led to the alliance with the AD, and provided a base for Modi in Varanasi and in some other Poorvanchal seats with high BC voters.

Revamping the Organization and the Campaign

The revival and redefinition of Hindutva enabled Modi to take firm control of the BJP with the help of the RSS, revamp the organization, and mount a well-planned, highly competitive, and aggressive campaign organized by Amit Shah. Shah took a number of steps that considerably strengthened the organization and improved the BJP's readiness for the election. An outsider, based on consultation with local leaders, he established a core team that analyzed the reasons for earlier electoral defeats. Meetings with party candidates who had lost elections enabled him to make decisions that set aside vested interests of state leaders and reach out to loyalists. Shah decided to replace veteran leaders from secure seats with new leaders loyal to Modi, and shifted the former to new constituencies; this reshuffling increased the party's chances of winning additional seats.[17] It also helped ensure that ticket distribution was based purely on a candidate's winnability factor. No candidate, except in a few places (Chandouli and Ghosi), was awarded a party ticket who had lost elections more than twice. Defunct district units were revived and committees were formed for over 80 percent of the booths in the state.

Certain features of the campaign in UP contributed to the BJP's excellent performance. It covered the state extensively, was tightly controlled by Modi and Shah with excellent funding, and was technology-driven with good media coverage. The campaign covered the state at two levels. The first, as Figure 6.10 shows, organized 40 massive rallies led by Modi with high media coverage across the state over a period of six months. Beginning with the *Vijay Shankhnaad* (Victory Declaration) rally at Kanpur on October 19, 2013, he addressed 12 rallies before the first phase of the election began on April 10, 2014, followed by another 28 rallies spread over the next one month. His campaign concluded with the *Bharat Vijay* (Conquering India) rallies at four constituencies in eastern UP,

Figure 6.10
Forty Constituencies Where Modi Held His Rallies during the Election Campaign in 2014

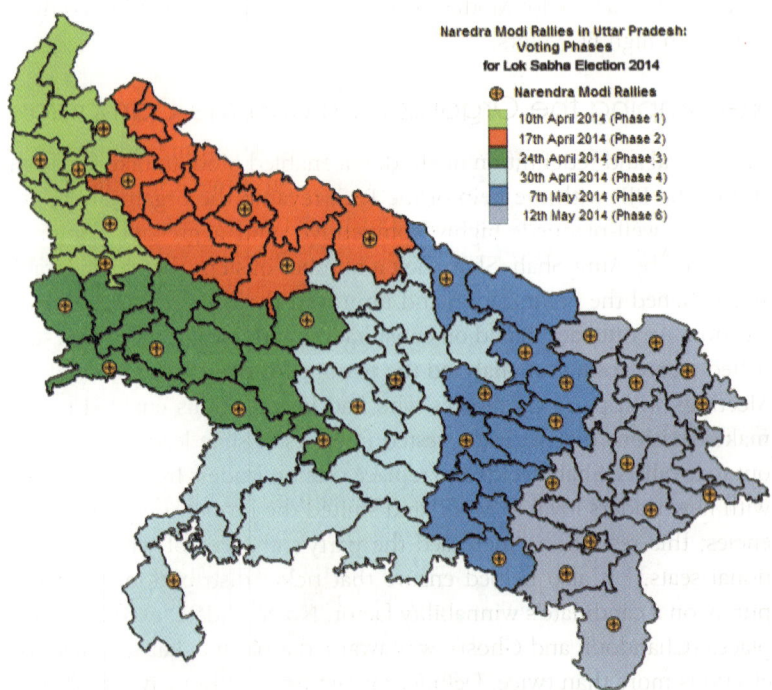

Credit: Aafaque R.K., Ashoka University Political Data Center.
Disclaimer: This image has been redrawn by the authors and is not to scale. It does not represent any authentic national or international boundaries and is used for illustrative purposes only.

Kushinagar, Ballia, Deoria, and Robertsganj, on May 10, 2014. At the end of all Modi's rallies, groups of RSS-recruited volunteers were found approaching people to gain their feedback which was then sent directly to the district RSS office.[18]

Second, Amit Shah extensively toured the state, planning Modi's campaign. He divided UP into eight zones, comprising of 21 clusters, of three to five seats, devising distinctive strategies for each. Young volunteers from 13,000 college campuses were recruited. For each rally, people were brought from a radius of 175 km with a target set of 10 people per booth. Good crowd management helped Shah consolidate the perception in the media of a 'Modi wave'. For areas beyond media's reach, classifying them as 'dark zones', Shah's team arranged more than 400 GPS-installed 'Modi vans' with campaign material and a 16-minute video on his personality, speeches, and BJP's manifesto that traversed more than 100,000 villages across the state.[19] Social media such as SMS, WhatsApp, e-mail, Facebook, and Twitter were used to create a 'Modi Brand'[20] through a 'Social Media War Room' at the BJP's Lucknow headquarters manned by young volunteers from Information Technology institutes under Sunil Bansal, a full-time RSS functionary and ABVP's national co-organization secretary. In sum, Modi ran a hi-tech, US presidential style, plebiscitary campaign, with extensive media coverage, in which the focus was mainly on him leaving out the party and other senior leaders.

Conclusion

The 2014 Lok Sabha elections in UP have introduced highly significant changes in the state's politics. The election has witnessed the return of communal mobilization and violence, largely absent since the early 1990s. Following the destruction of the Babri Masjid and the decline of the BJP, although the Ram Mandir issue was raised during elections, the two lower-caste parties the SP and the BSP were able to contain the BJP and communalization of state politics throughout the 2000s. However, numerous low-intensity, communal incidents since 2012 and the Muzaffarnagar communal violence in particular show that political parties, particularly the SP and BJP, have attempted to revive/strengthen and use their Muslim and Hindu vote banks, respectively, to create tension and win seats. An important reason for the victory of the BJP has been the communal campaign by the BJP–RSS cadres, Amit Shah, and at times by Modi himself. That the chasm polarizing the religious communities in UP is widening everyday has been exemplified by the continual riots in sites such as Moradabad and Saharanpur (in July 2014) even after the elections. The absence of Muslim MPs (Members of Parliament) from UP, a state with 18 percent Muslim population, is itself a matter of grave concern for the democratic functioning of the state.

In keeping with the changed ideological outlook, the promise of rapid development and good governance was a central feature of Modi's campaign, contributing to the victory of the BJP. It also has its roots in the gradual weakening of identity politics in the Hindi heartland and importance being accorded to developmental aspirations of the people. There is a growing frustration and unhappiness among the youth and middle classes as they see themselves left behind compared to other states. Consequently, the two issues of identity and development now seem to coexist along a political spectrum, with both being used at different points of time by the BJP depending on need during the election campaign. The humiliating defeat of the SP and the BSP, which have strong identity bases, point in the same direction. For such parties, dependence on caste alone, ignoring development, may no longer remain an option.

The revival of the Congress Party given its crushing defeat in UP seems difficult in the absence of a strong organization, social base, and effective leadership. The low margin of victory in the Gandhi strongholds demonstrates that the dynasty can no longer substitute for performance. Following the decline of the Congress and the BJP in the 2000s, there was a bipolar contest and turnover of power between the two state-level parties, the SP and the BSP. Failure of the BSP's experiment of Sarvajan, the SP's poor record of governance, and Congress's inability to revive provided room for the BJP to sweep the state using a combination of both communal mobilization and development.

However, UP has been a volatile state experiencing endemic political instability during the 1990s due to two competing strategies of caste and communal mobilization under the BJP, the BSP, and the SP. In contrast, during the 2000s, the electorate has chosen to give its mandate to a different party over successive elections, each with its own ideology and agenda. In the 2007 Assembly elections, the state witnessed a break from the past as the BSP was voted to power with a full majority and the party completed its full term. In the 2012 Assembly elections, the SP defeated the BSP and formed the government. The 2014 national election has witnessed the defeat of both these parties and the emergence of a rejuvenated BJP under Modi. Consequently, this has introduced a change in the state party system. While earlier the state-level parties with their specific social bases dominated state politics, in 2014 a national party, the BJP, has been able to sweep the election. The 2014 election witnessed very high levels of contestation between political parties to gain control over state politics and thereby control the Center. However, given the record of volatility that the state has witnessed over the past few decades, it remains to be seen if the BJP translates the 2014 victory into domination over state politics or it remains short-lived. The real test of the new BJP vis-à-vis the state parties in UP will only be in the 2017 Assembly elections.

Notes and References

1. A.K. Verma, Mirza Asmer Beg, and Sudhir Kumar, "A Saffron Sweep in Uttar Pradesh," *Hindu*, May 23, 2014.
2. Ibid.
3. Sudha Pai, ed., "The Congress Party in Uttar Pradesh: Dominance, Decline, and Revival?" in *Handbook of Politics in Indian States: Region, Parties, and Economic Reforms* (New Delhi: Oxford University Press, 2013).
4. Avinash Kumar, "Understanding the UP Mandate," *Hindu Business Line*, March 8, 2012.
5. Two won by Mulayam Singh Yadav, one by his daughter-in-law, and two by his nephews.
6. Sudha Pai, "Uttar Pradesh: Competitive Communalism Once Again," *Economic and Political Weekly* XLIX, 15(April 12, 2014), 16–19.
7. Sudha Pai, "Understanding the Defeat of the BSP in Uttar Pradesh National Election 2014," *Studies in Indian Politics* 2, 2(2014), 153–67.
8. Sudha Pai, *Dalit Assertion and the Unfinished Democratic Revolution: The BSP in Uttar Pradesh* (New Delhi: SAGE Publications, 2002).
9. Modi and Shah worked together in the early 1990s under the then chief minister of Gujarat, Keshubhai Patel. It is widely believed that Shah was instrumental in Modi's effort to dethrone Patel from Gujarat in 2001. When Modi became the chief minister in 2002, he appointed Shah as MoS (Home) and gave him 10 portfolios, the most for any minister.
10. At the Idea Exchange programme organized by the Indian Express group on May 13, 2014. See http://indianexpress.com/article/india/politics/50-55-for-bjp-bsp-second-in-up-amit-shah/ (accessed on June 25, 2014).

11. http://www.india272.com/2013/11/08/modi-charms-baharaich-vijayshankhnadrally/ (accessed on June 27, 2014).

12. Gujarat is the third preferred destination of the migrant workers from UP after Delhi and Maharashtra. See R.B. Bhagat, and S. Mohanty, "Emerging Pattern of Urbanization and the Contribution of Migration in Urban Growth in India," *Asian Population Studies* 5, 1(2009), 5–20.

13. See http://indianexpress.com/article/cities/mumbai/rss-takes-charge-of-modis-meerut-rally/ (accessed on June 27, 2014).

14. These were *Muzaffarnagar Danga* and *Faisla Aapka? Bharat: Darool Harabya Darool Islam*. See Lalmani Verma, "RSS Magazine Defends Jat Youths, Blames Akhilesh Government," *Indian Express*, New Delhi, January 6, 2014.

15. He is also reported to have claimed, "When Modi becomes PM, Mullah (Muslim cleric) Mulayam's government in UP would fall on its own the very next day" (TNN, "EC Issues Notice to Amit Shah for Poll Code Violation," April 8, 2014).

16. Ibid.

17. Rajnath Singh shifted to Lucknow vacating the Ghaziabad seat for former Indian Army Chief General V.K. Singh; Murli Manohar Joshi vacated Varanasi for Modi and shifted to Kanpur; Kalraj Mishra was sent to Deoria, while Kesarinath Tripathi, former assembly speaker, was asked to work for the party.

18. Badri Narayan, "Modi's Modus Operandi in the 2014 Elections," *Economic and Political Weekly* XLIX, 20(May 17, 2014), 12–14.

19. Rohini Singh, "Election Results 2014: How Amit Shah Swept Uttar Pradesh for BJP," *Economic Times*, May 17, 2014.

20. From Modi T-shirts to cups, from masks to sweets, *chai pe charcha* campaigns and the most impressive of all, the 3D hologram rallies were a few of these tools.

7

Saffron Deluge Inundates Masters of Mandal Politics in Bihar*

Maneesha Roy and Ravi Ranjan

The massive mandate for the BJP in the 2014 Lok Sabha elections has reversed trends evident in Indian politics since the demise of Congress dominance and the era of coalitions. These trends were:

- The emergence of state-based political parties as key players in national politics.
- The lack of an important overarching ideological/programmatic perspective.
- The absence of a powerful national leader enjoying pan-India popularity and influence.[1]

Much of the credit for BJP's spectacular success must go to the key states of Bihar and Uttar Pradesh (UP). Given its limited presence in the southern states, the chances of the Narendra Modi-led NDA (National Democratic Alliance) forming a national government largely depended on the two largest states in the Hindi heartland. UP and Bihar account for a fourth

* We are grateful to Dr Ramashray Roy, a leading specialist on Bihar, for his key insights that helped us improve our chapter.

of India's population, around 300 million people, and 120 (22 percent) of the 545 members in the Lok Sabha. BJP won 93 of the 120 seats. Its ally Apna Dal in UP got 2, while in Bihar, Ram Vilas Paswan's Lok Janshakti Party (LJP) and Upendra Kushwaha's Rashtriya Lok Samata Party (RLSP) won 6 and 3 seats, respectively.

Is the breakup between the BJP and the Janata Dal (United) (JD[U]) the root of JD(U)'s defeat? Was it an aspirational vote for the BJP standing above considerations of caste and creed? Was the Modi wave the critical factor? Does a rejection of Bihar's ruling party raise questions about Nitish Kumar's development work? Or does it mean that the Bihar voter is making a clear distinction between the Lok Sabha and the Assembly polls? These are a few questions this chapter seeks to analyze. It can be contested that the BJP–JD(U) breakup made only a dent in the power position in the state with JD(U) continuing to be the ruling party in the Bihar Assembly. A combination of factors, some of them engrained in Bihar's socioeconomic situation, Nitish's strategy to build reliable and durable support based on caste and religion along with factors which came into play at the time of elections need to be taken into account.

A New Cleavage in Bihar's Politics: Triangular Fight of 2014

The 2014 election was Bihar's first in a quarter century to be fought by three powerful parties and regional politicians: Chief Minister Nitish Kumar, the leader of the JD(U); BJP's prime ministerial aspirant Narendra Modi; and the veteran Lalu Prasad Yadav, the head of Rashtriya Janata Dal (RJD). Lalu singlehandedly altered Bihar's political landscape in the 1990s by politically empowering the Backward Castes. NDA's landslide victory in Bihar won 31 out of 40 seats in 2014; BJP alone won 22 while LJP and RLSP won 6 and 3 seats, respectively. The ruling party, JD(U), and the Congress were reduced to only 2 seats each, whereas Lalu's RJD managed to win 4 seats but failed to retain the Saran seat as Rabri Devi lost to BJP candidate Rajiv Pratap Rudy.

Campaigning in Bihar was launched in 2013. Modi himself framed the Bihar election strategy forming alliances with caste-based groups, and with clever use of his own OBC caste card and the party's aspirational message of development. Moreover, Modi's candidature in Varanasi in eastern UP improved the party's prospects in Bihar. The verdict in UP and Bihar was a setback for the masters of Mandal politics: Mulayam Singh Yadav's Samajwadi Party (SP) and Mayawati's Bahujan Samaj Party (BSP) in UP, and Sharad Yadav's JD(U) and Lalu Yadav's RJD in Bihar.

The significance of the 2014 Lok Sabha elections lies in the fact that the NDA which represented, as Paul Wallace characterized it, "a broad catch-all spectrum of parties"[2] emerged as a well-integrated and determined fighting political machine. An aggressive and well-designed campaign focusing on development, good governance, and decisive leadership as key issues catapulted the NDA to power. Through his clever multimedia messaging and indefatigable campaign, Modi not only relentlessly drove home the UPA government's flaws, but he was also able to convey three messages.

One, pedigree does not matter. He highlighted his humble origin as a tea seller who worked his way up through sheer hard work and determination that caught the attention of the poor and laborer-class Bihari voters. Two, Modi boasted that in Gujarat he could deliver and transform a state. In a backward state like Bihar, Modi with his mantra of development emerged as a shining beacon that could pull the state out of the darkness of poverty and underdevelopment. Three, he was successful in showcasing himself as a decisive leader capable of tackling intractable issues like poverty, unemployment, price rise, and inflation, thereby becoming the symbol of change that India in general and Bihar in particular was yearning for.[3]

In Bihar, Modi became the first candidate whose personal brand trumped party affiliation at the national level. The Modi wave symbolized and personified the anti-incumbency rage against the misrule of the UPA at the Center and betrayal of JD(U) in Bihar. Shattering the provincial and party traditions of Indian politics, Modi thoroughly eclipsed his Congress rival Rahul Gandhi. Bihar was among the key battleground states that scripted Modi's amazing win. He also benefitted from the failure of Nitish's strategy of support building and consolidation. After JD(U) split from the NDA on June 16, 2013, the 2014 elections represented a make-or-break election for Nitish as he ended up with the weakest caste coalition among the three front-ranking parties. Accordingly, Shaibal Gupta characterized it as a 'paradigm shift election' as for the first time, a constituency of Mahadalits, *pasmanda* Muslims, and women has been carved out in Bihar. It remains to be seen how they will vote in the future because they have remained loyal to Nitish Kumar.[4]

The JD(U)'s electoral rout, a distant third position, is unexplained. When the JD(U) parted ways with the BJP, the gesture was intended to win the confidence of Muslims, who constitute a significant 16 percent of the population. As Lalu was jailed and disqualified to fight the Lok Sabha election and the Congress had become unpopular nationally, the UPA appeared a spent force. The real battle in Bihar, it seemed, was between the BJP and the JD(U). But RJD chief Lalu's release on bail made the electoral battle very competitive by consolidating the UPA and making the election a triangular fight.

From Upper Caste Dominance to Congress Decline: The Changing Character of Caste Politics

Apart from being a constituent of what is popularly known as BIMARU (Bihar, Madhya Pradesh, Rajasthan, and Uttar Pradesh) state, Bihar also represents a complex mosaic of castes differentiated in terms of income, worldly possessions, social status, and political power. The rigidity of the traditional feudal social structure did not provide any internal mechanism or avenues for status mobility within the caste framework inhibiting initiative and innovations. Social status ranking remained fixed despite commendable achievements by low-caste individuals. Economically, the distribution of wealth was highly skewed in favor of the upper strata of society. As a result, power too was very unevenly distributed, concentrating heavily at the upper echelons of the caste-based society.

In the wake of representational politics, caste started determining the number-based power configuration in Bihar which is largely dominated by the OBC vote. Many political commentators feel that caste prevents the modernization and democratization of politics, preventing the resolution of social conflicts and making governance in Bihar very difficult. The Indian political class and elite theorists of democracy now accept these propositions. Though the backward castes constitute nearly 60 percent of Bihar's electorate, they were politically insignificant until the 1970s. Their turning point was in 1977 when the Janata government introduced reservation for backward castes in government service. In Bihar, three basic caste groups emerged—forward castes, backward castes, and Scheduled Castes (SCs) and Scheduled Tribes.[5]

The Congress Party ruled over Bihar continuously until 1990, except for brief periods in the late 1960s and late 1970s. The upper sections of society ruled,[6] both caste-wise and class-wise, notwithstanding the fact that some of its chief ministers belonged to the OBC, SC, and Muslim communities. Though socialist parties exercised considerable influence in Bihar in the initial phase after independence, backward-caste politics gained and lost ground in the political spectrum of the state intermittently until the 1980s. The defeat of the Congress in 1990 marked the end of an era in Bihar's politics that can be best described as 'feudal democracy'.[7] It failed to deliver the promises of independence—land reforms, poverty alleviation, welfare, individual rights, fair treatment, plus freedom from indignity, humiliation, and discrimination. Leadership in Bihar supported the status quo in the society, politics, and economy.

For the first time, backward castes in the late 1960s were able to forge internal solidarity and convert it into numerical superiority in Bihar. A disjunction between economic power and political power seemed possible for the first time when economic dominance no longer guaranteed dominance in politics. The number of Members of Legislative Assembly (MLAs) and Members of Parliament (MPs) belonging to the OBCs, particularly the upper OBCs like Yadavs, Kurmis, and Koeris, went up dramatically, surpassing the number of upper-caste elected representatives by a large margin.[8] The Assembly election of 1990 marks a watershed in terms of electoral transformation. For the first time, the numbers of OBC MLAs were more than upper-caste MLAs in Bihar, 34.9 against 34.6 percent. Upper castes dominance declined to only 25.6 percent of Janata Dal MLAs, whereas the backward castes constituted 43.8 percent of the party MLAs. From 1985 to 1995, the number of OBC MLAs doubled to 50 percent while the number of upper-caste candidates more than halved to 17 percent, marking a profound alteration in the process

Table 7.1
Bihar: Party Results in Lok Sabha Elections 1989–2014

Gen Election	INC	BJP	JD	RJD	SAM	JD(U)	Others	Total	Remark
1989	4	8	32				10	54	(left front 5 JMM 3)
1991	1	5	31				17	54	(Left front 9 others 8
1996	2	18	22		06		06	54	Others 3, Left Front 3
1998	5	20	1	17	10		01	54	
1999	4	23		7	18		02	54	Others 3 Left Front 1
2004	3	05		22		06	04	40	LJP 4
2009	2	12		04		20	02	40	2 Independents
2014	2	22		04		2	10	40	LJP 6, RLSP 3, NCP 1

Source: Aggregated from Election Commission of India official election results.

of political claim-making. In 1995 Assembly elections, only 61 forward caste candidates returned to Bihar Vidhan Sabha as against 165 backward caste members (Table 7.1).[9]

The local institutions of power that remained in the firm grip of the upper-caste landlords started eroding with a new caste consciousness. Left organizational efforts tried to transform the 'caste social' into 'class political', which changed during the 1990s. 'Caste political' magnifies caste within the class and actively pursues caste-conflict to challenge the dominance of upper castes in electoral politics. Caste appeared in a new avatar, 'caste political', which has increasingly been used as an instrument of political assertion bringing returns in other spheres too. Class was a difficult route; caste was handy. This was impressively articulated by the idiom of *ijjat* (dignity). Caste political is not so much about ascription, but more about aspiration, dominance, aggression and reaping the resources of governance. Scriptural caste has less relevance as it now tends to reside more in the hurt pride of the upper castes. Caste political does not allow the same practice of derogation, contempt, humiliation and subjugation; rather it uplifted the social caste (of lower castes) by celebrating it rather than being ashamed of it. This is what Michelluti calls "vernacularization of democracy" in India in relation to caste.[10]

Political Journey of Social Justice to Social Engineering of Developmental Governance

In post-independent India democratic politics began to play a major role in distributing power resources. Due to this reason the rigidity of the caste structure began to be eroded. Two factors account for this:

a. The need of the contending political parties to widen and consolidate their power base; and

b. Politics as the avenue of status improvement and mobility.

If the former pushed the boundary of political mobilization to the farthest limit of caste structure, the latter created a vested interest in politics making it necessary for depressed caste groups to join politics in order to modify and, if possible, improve their worldly possessions. The interaction of these two factors had the effect of shifting, within a period of half a century beginning from 1990s onwards the power resources from the upper castes to middle and lower castes. It is the overall consequence of the interaction of these two factors that Lalu and his wife Rabri could displace the upper castes from power positions and rule over Bihar uninterrupted and unchallenged for 15 years from 1990 to 2005.

With the formation of Janata Dal government in 1990, under the leadership of Lalu Prasad, a new era of the rise and consolidation of backward castes began. A powerful social equation of OBCs–Muslims emerged in the electoral algebra with partial support from a section of Rajputs and Dalits. The new foundational change in Bihar politics has changed the ways in which institutions and various apparatuses of the government, procedures, rules, tactics, symbols, slogans, and language were rewritten in relation to caste that highlights some dimensions of social engineering of Lalu's regime of 15 years. Bihar's electoral history since 1990 demonstrates that Lalu Prasad emerged as a giant on Bihar's political firmament and won the 1990, 1995, and 2000 Assembly elections due to his social justice plank.

What is interesting about the long tenure of the Lalu–Rabri regime is that even when the question of development was sidetracked by the argument that development would bolster the revolution of rising expectations, their political stranglehold did not slacken. Even after he was arrested in 1997 for alleged embezzlement, Lalu made his wife the chief minister and ruled de facto. Yadav's 15-year misrule spawned massive crime, lawlessness, and corruption. Yet, his opponents—the Congress, whose state government he had routed in 1990, the BJP, and his former socialist comrades—failed in repeated efforts to dislodge him until 2005.[11] The reason for this lies in two factors of social engineering:

1. The Muslim–Yadav (MY) political alliance crafted by Lalu was firmly behind RJD. 16 percent Muslims and 14 percent Yadavs together account for about 30 percent of Bihar's electorate. Raising the slogan of MY, Lalu exhorted his supporters to literally wipe out the upper castes with the slogan 'Bhura baal saaf karo', bhura baal being an acronym for Bhumihars, Brahmins, Rajputs, and Lalas (Kayasthas). The formidable MY alliance ousted the upper castes from leadership of the state's politics. After the 1990 Assembly election, 19.1 percent of the MLAs were Yadavs, which increased to 25.8 percent Yadav MLAs after the 1995 Assembly election.
2. The issue of the honor (ijjat) of the OBCs, especially the Yadavs and the Dalits. Besides the Muslims and the Yadavs, Lalu had a huge following among 23 percent most backward classes and 10 percent non-Paswan SCs due to his social justice plank.

However, by creating subcategories among the backwards and the Dalits, Nitish stole Lalu's place as the natural leader of all non-upper castes. Nitish excluded the Yadavs (and sundry others) as a sort of creamy layer, playing Santa Claus for the rest, that is, the extremely backward castes (EBCs). In addition, of Bihar's 22 Dalit subcastes, Nitish Kumar categorized 21 as 'Mahadalits', leaving out the dominant Dalit subcaste of Paswan. The JD(U)–BJP ruling coalition, under the leadership of Nitish, proceeded to not only heal the deep wounds inflicted upon Bihar by the misrule of the Lalu–Rabri combine, but also put Bihar on the highway of accelerated and unprecedented development. In Nitish's words: "This is the beginning of our campaign ... to throw him (Lalu) out and deliver Bihar back to those who live up to the high standards of JP (Jayaprakash Narayan) and Karpoori (Thakur) and to the wishes of the people."[12]

Overthrowing Lalu with his messiah-like popularity necessitated splitting the Backward Caste vote and aligning with the BJP at the cost of his socialist and secular persuasions. Nitish also pursued a strategy of development and coupled it with social engineering. Being a pragmatic politician, he realized that development alone would not guarantee a durable and loyal support base. He realized that if he could not break the support base of other parties, he must create a new support base for himself. He, therefore, pursued a three-pronged strategy: (a) Special privileges to EBCs (about 100 scattered castes) and to Mahadalits constituting about 28 percent of the vote; (b) formation of a Mahadalit Commission to identify and extend special benefits to the most underprivileged among Dalits incorporating 18 Dalit sub-castes, excluding Chamars and Dusadhs, under the Mahadalit rubric and transferring resources and opportunities to them; (c) dividing the Muslim community by promoting *Pasmanda* (Muslims against high-caste Muslims).[13] The success of Nitish's strategy resulted in a massive electoral victory inasmuch as the JD(U) won 20 Lok Sabha seats out of the 25 it contested in 2004.

Moreover, the 15-year-long Lalu–Rabri rule witnessed a deterioration of public life in Bihar, the failure of institutions including politico-administrative machinery, the breakdown of law and order, and a surge in corruption. Lalu himself became implicated in corruption cases and was later found guilty and jailed for his role in the embezzlement of ₹950 crore in the fodder scam. Besides the fact that no one in Bihar thought that Lalu could actually provide good governance, the most backwards were also angry with Lalu because his party had primarily empowered the Yadavs providing government resources. Finally, the lack of development and lawlessness led to the defeat of RJD resulting in the alliance of JD(U) and BJP winning the 2005 Assembly elections.

After becoming chief minister in 2005, Nitish cultivated four constituencies: EBCs who form 35 percent of the states' electorate, Mahadalits, the poorest among the Muslims (known as the *pasmanda musalman*), and women, reserving 50 percent seats in all panchayats for them. His inducements for the backwards and the Dalits included scholarships and hostels, especially for their girls who were also given uniforms and bicycles to ride to school, building boundary walls for Muslim graveyards to protect them, and giving freebies such as radio transistors. But more than the handouts, Nitish's government was able to develop a widespread feeling of political empowerment by creating the special categories of the EBCs and the Mahadalits. As Binoy Shankar Prasad notes, Nitish Kumar skillfully steered the NDA of the JD(U) and the BJP to a resounding electoral success.[14]

Bihar until recently has been acclaimed as a fast-developing state under Chief Minister Nitish Kumar. Bihar not only successfully overcame the ravages of 15 years of the Lalu–Rabri rule, but also made giant strides toward economic and political health. He won two Assembly elections back-to-back in 2005 and 2010, the second more spectacularly than the first, and led his JD(U) to superb results in the 2009 Lok Sabha elections. RJD won 22 out of the 26 Lok Sabha seats it contested in 2004 against the 6 of the 24 Lok Sabha seats JD(U) contested. However, the reverse occurred in the 2009 Lok Sabha elections as JD(U) won 20 out of the 25 Lok Sabha seats it contested, while the RJD could only win 4 out of the 24 seats it fought. Lalu himself lost 1 of the 2 seats he contested.

It is true that Bihar in recent years has maintained a high degree of development. The achievement of a higher and consistent rate of Gross State Domestic Product (GSDP) does not, however, conceal the fact that Bihar still remains very low on important indicators of development. For example, 34 percent of Bihar's population is below the poverty line as compared to the national average of 22 percent. School dropout rate is 62 as against the county's 49, infant mortality rate is 34 as against India's 28, and maternal mortality rate amounts to 219 as against India's 178. Rural Bihar's monthly per capita expenditure is ₹970 as against rural India's ₹1,397, and in urban Bihar it is ₹1,287 compared to urban India's ₹2,477.[15]

This suggests that the existing inequalities in the distribution of wealth and status have not declined much despite some significant socioeconomic gains by deprived socioeconomic interests. Moreover, with a poor industrial base, Bihar relies heavily on agriculture.[16] However, agriculture has not received sufficient capital inputs to compensate for the loss of its industrial base after the separation of Jharkhand. Furthermore, the higher growth in GSDP does not seem to be benefitting the poor as is reflected in the high rate of poverty. This demonstrates that there is a dissonance between what the politicians thought people should have and what the people actually wanted to have.[17]

Nonetheless, it goes to Nitish's credit that Bihar overcame the trauma of the Lalu–Rabri regime and made substantial progress toward economic development and social change. Under Nitish, Bihar was the best performing state in terms of GSDP at 15 percent in 2012–13, and the average GSDP growth between 2005 and 2012–13 was 9.9 percent.[18] In addition, infant mortality rate was brought down from 61 per thousand in 2005 to 43 per thousand in 2013.[19] Nitish also built roads and promoted the education of the girl child. On the social front, he promoted the EBCs, created a new caste category of Mahadalits along with the poorer sections of the Muslims, and raised the percentage of reservations for women in Panchayati Raj institutions from 30 to 50 percent. He, thus, consolidated his political position by pursuing the twin strategy of development with social engineering.[20] These are no mean achievements. However, they did not gain the necessary voter support. There are primarily two reasons for this: shortcomings in his overall strategy of development with social engineering, and the breaking up of the BJP–JD(U) alliance.

How Nitish Scripted His Own Defeat

Nitish, it appeared, had been successful in creating a new Bihari identity that overarched caste and creed and endorsed development. His nine years of governance, nonetheless, could not win for him the 2014 Lok Sabha elections. JD(U) contested 8 seats, but won only 2. Nitish's dream of creating a Naya Bihar (new Bihar) seems to have unraveled. Why did Nitish's JD(U) do so badly despite his record of good governance?[21] It is true that Modi's charisma had a lot to do with JD(U)'s rout. However, it would not have been so effective if certain other factors endemic to Bihar politics in general and Nitish's strategy in particular were not operative.

A major problem was Nitish's unilateral decision to break JD(U)'s 17-year-old alliance with the BJP in June 2013. The parting was bitter and acrimonious, ending months of feuding between the two erstwhile partners. The JD(U) maintained that they were forced to end the alliance as they did not want to compromise the party's 'basic principles', a political euphemism to mean they would never accept a BJP led by Modi on the grounds of the latter's anti-Muslim sectarian image. The BJP called the breakup the worst kind of political opportunism and a virtual 'betrayal' of the people's mandate. Even while in alliance with the BJP, Nitish kept himself distant from the Hindutva agenda of the BJP to safeguard his secular image. He always kept the BJP on a tight leash in their seven-plus years of running a coalition government. This earned him the trust of Muslims in Bihar. Nitish was also pinning his hopes to be victorious in 2014 on a widespread feeling of empowerment his government had triggered off by officially creating the special categories of EBCs and Mahadalits.

Nitish thought the political arithmetic favored him. On paper, the 29 percent EBC communities, a majority of the 17 percent Muslims, and 12 percent Mahadalits, all part of the new social base that he had created with targeted social welfare schemes, made him appear formidable. In effect, he only ended up further fragmenting Bihar's already caste-ridden society. His own caste, the Kurmis, are a tiny 2.5 percent of the state's electorate and, hence, politically insignificant. Also, he could not bank upon the support of the other prominent backward caste group, the Koeris, who are around 4 percent of the population, as one of their leaders, Rajya Sabha MP Upendra Kushwaha, had quit earlier because he was sidelined by Nitish.

Moreover, Nitish did not have the support of any of the 'aggressive castes'. These include the Bhumihars and the Rajputs among the upper castes, the Yadavs among the backwards, and the Paswans among the Dalits. The support of one of these castes is important because they bring the EBCs, the Mahadalits, and others at the lower social spectrum to the polling booths. The BJP–JD(U) alliance had succeeded in caste-ridden Bihar because it bagged the support of both upper castes and most backward caste communities forging a 'coalition of extremes' who otherwise competed against each other. The upper castes had developed a deep dislike for Nitish soon after he reserved 20 percent panchayat seats for the EBCs in 2006. This move evicted the upper-caste communities who traditionally controlled the panchayats. But the upper castes still voted for the Nitish-led NDA in the 2009 Lok Sabha and 2010 State Assembly election as he was in alliance with the BJP.

With Nitish severing ties with the BJP, the upper castes deserted him. The numerically strong MY sided with Lalu, further marginalizing Nitish. The JD(U)'s Kishanganj candidate, Akhtarul Iman—a turncoat from RJD—delivered a body blow to Nitish by withdrawing from the contest to 'strengthen secular votes', a move that impacted the Muslim vote across the state. He lost Dalit votes when Ram Vilas Paswan's LJP aligned with the BJP. With Modi usurping the title of development icon from Nitish who was known as *Sushasan Babu*, and BJP projecting him as a backward caste prime ministerial candidate, a large number of EBCs switched sides. Thus, three monumental miscalculations involving communal politics, caste politics, and misreading of the political scene led him to defeat.[22]

Moreover, Nitish's campaign strategy, focused primarily on development and special status for Bihar, failed to enthuse voters and also paled in comparison to the Gujarat model of development.[23] He compounded his mistakes by ignoring the fact that while he was the face of the NDA alliance in Bihar, it was the committed BJP cadre that had helped him at the ground level by bringing voters to the booth.

Nitish's JD(U) was not well-integrated, relying on the glue of power to unite disparate elements in the party. With the prospect of severe defeat looming, internal dissentions came out in the open, resulting in desertions. Former bureaucrat N.K. Singh quit the JD(U) and joined the BJP, crediting the NDA as a whole and not just the Bihar CM alone for the recent recovery of the state.[24] Singh criticized the JD(U) saying its governance matrix had got "distorted" to exclusively focus on a "survival-centric strategy than a development-centric strategy" that forced him to quit.[25] Many in the party accused Nitish of authoritarianism; so one day before the announcement of the Lok Sabha poll results, five ministers did not attend the cabinet meeting.[26] The situation threatened to split the JD(U) which could be prevented only after Nitish stepped down as chief minister and a Mahadalit, Jitan Ram, was chosen as the new chief minister.[27]

Nitish Kumar, offering a non-Congress and non-BJP alternative to the country, was counting on the support of former socialist party members, including Paswan. But with the LJP supremo aligning with the BJP, Nitish lost one anti-Modi voice in the state and about 4.5 percent of Dalit votes. Meanwhile, the BJP had also reached an important understanding with OBCs in Bihar. It had reached an alliance with Upendra Kushwaha's RLSP who parted with Nitish. Kushwaha was considered to have a grip over 6 percent of the Kushwaha community electorates in the state. With Kushwaha gone too, Nitish lost another addition to his federal front. According to political analysts, the BJP commands a majority (around 17 percent) of the 'upper caste' votes and a sizable portion of 'Baniya' votes (7 percent) in the state. Separating from the JD(U), the BJP also wasn't weighed down by an expected anti-incumbency wave. Yet Nitish cannot be entirely written off from Bihar's political landscape.

Why the RJD and Congress Combine Could Not Stage a Comeback?

If Nitish had to face his self-created demons in the 2014 electoral battle, Lalu was still paying for his past sins of misrule. The political dexterity of the indefatigable Lalu has often forced many political pundits to err on the side of caution. Lalu's chances of reviving his sagging political career looked up when the BJP and JD(U) ended their alliance. That coalition had won 32 seats in 2009. Since the 2014 elections were a triangular contest, Lalu believed that the RJD was well placed to beat the BJP and the JD(U). In their most recent electoral faceoff—the 2010 Assembly election—the RJD got 19 percent votes, only 3 percent behind the JD(U)'s 22 percent and ahead of BJP's 17 percent. In 2009, the RJD placed second in as many as 19 Lok Sabha seats, losing 6 of them by less than 30,000 votes. The RJD had hoped to make big political gains from the growing disenchantment with the Nitish-led JD(U) government. There were signs that the popular mood was swinging back in favor of the RJD.

An enthused Lalu made grand electoral plans for his party. However, he was politically hurt when he was convicted by a special CBI court in the fodder scam corruption case that disqualified him from Parliament and rendered him ineligible for contesting elections for at least six years. It was evident that Lalu was facing the toughest fight of his political career spanning over four decades. His conviction meant he lost his House membership and could not contest elections. This forced his wife and daughter to enter the electoral arena. With him in jail, his party was fighting a battle for survival. His problems were compounded by the fact that he had not allowed a second line of leadership to grow within the party. It was unclear who would lead the party in his absence as his wife had been discredited earlier.

Ominous signs of factionalism came to the fore with attempts by the JD(U) to engineer defections from RJD's 22 MLAs. These efforts succeeded when the RJD split and 13 of its MLAs announced their decision to quit the party. Six of them later claimed they were not part of the breakaway faction and three more subsequently returned to the RJD. The MLAs who quit pledged support to Nitish's government.[28] MLA Chaudhary Samrat spearheaded the rebellion as he had been denied a ticket from Khagaria.[29] What weakened Lalu further was the decision of LJP's Ram Vilas Paswan to ditch Lalu and Congress in favor of the BJP. From being the champion of social justice and messiah of minorities, Lalu had become battered and lonely.

Lalu got a reprieve from the court granting him bail in December 2013. This meant that he could go plead his case directly to the people. He toured the state on a chopper from morning to evening in a high-voltage campaign projecting him as the only alternative to Modi's 'divisive politics'. Since both the RJD and the Congress could not hope to win the Lok Sabha polls alone, they needed to forge an alliance to enlarge their support base. The Congress had fought the 2004 elections in alliance with the RJD and LJP, winning 29 of the 40 parliamentary seats. In 2009, the Congress had fought alone without the RJD and LJP. The results were disastrous for all three parties with RJD winning only 4 seats, Congress 2, and LJP zero.

Therefore, an alliance between the RJD and the Congress became a political necessity for both in 2014. What made this alliance attractive was the fact that despite heavy electoral reverses, Lalu's support base had not undergone any significant erosion. His steadfast commitment to secularism and OBC assertion were expected to prove beneficial in the election. The coming together of the RJD and the Congress was expected to consolidate the MY vote behind their alliance. Lalu worked hard to woo the Congress in order to put up a joint 'secular front' to take on both BJP's Narendra Modi and his old bête noire JD(U) leader Nitish.

RJD, Congress, and the Nationalist Congress Party (NCP) announced an alliance for the Lok Sabha polls in Bihar in which Lalu would contest

27 seats, the Congress 12, and NCP 1. Most polls gave Lalu between 10 and 15 seats. However, this alliance was doomed for various reasons. There was a tussle regarding seat-sharing as Congress wanted to contest 15 seats and the RJD was only willing to offer 11. The Madhubani seat had become a bone of contention between Congress and RJD and was a major irritant because in the finalization of the tie-up it had finally gone to RJD. Congress leaders feared that the RJD would swallow the Congress. The alliance didn't work in a coordinated fashion as Lalu was conspicuous by his absence from both Rahul's and Sonia's election rallies in Aurangabad and Sasaram. The three leaders didn't campaign jointly even once.[30] Local Congress leaders resented the unholy alliance and felt that after his conviction in the fodder scam Lalu was a political liability.

Despite all the hard work that Lalu put in, he could not resurrect his charisma or play his victim card beyond a point. The continued defection of his close associates with varied caste profiles to both the JD(U) and BJP including those from his famed MY left him shattered. At just 4 seats, his performance was worse than the last polls when he got 4 despite breaking the alliance with Congress and LJP. To add insult to injury, both his wife Rabri Devi, contesting from Saran, and his daughter Misa Bharti, contesting from Patliputra, lost. The verdict was as much a statement on the limitations of the MY combine (30 percent of the votes in Bihar) as it was a result of the Modi wave. Of the 17 seats in the state where Muslims have more than 15 percent of votes, BJP won 12. The rest were shared by the RJD–Congress and NCP alliance, and JD(U) which got 1 seat. RJD has been in a state of decline since 2000. It remains to be seen if BJP has, perhaps, hit the final nail in the coffin.

The Saffron Upsurge

An NDA powered by the Modi-driven saffron wave struck gold in Bihar, inundating the Nitish-led JD(U) and Lalu-led RJD. The NDA won 31 seats, an increase of 19 seats. With an overwhelming 44 percent vote share for BJP, up 30 percent from 2009, the party alone won 22 of the 30 seats it fought. Ram Vilas Paswan's LJP won an astounding 6 of 7 seats it contested, while RLSP bagged all 3 it fought. The overall tally of NDA missed the 2009 mark, when the BJP had partnered Nitish Kumar's

JD(U), by just 1 seat. The main opponents, the RJD–Congress–NCP combine, won just 7, while JD(U) posted only 2, down 18 from the 2009 polls. This remarkable electoral feat was the result of several factors. Congress and its allies were subject to backlash from the anti-incumbency of the 10-year regime. UPA-II was weighed down by charges of poor governance, administrative ineptitude, and corruption scandals, as well as spiraling inflation and stagnant growth. Despite internal differences on policy matters and personality tussles, BJP managed to skillfully project Modi as the prime ministerial candidate and succeeded in generating a nationwide campaign and debate on his political personality and the development model he had espoused in Gujarat.[31] Modi galvanized his party after being appointed BJP's campaign committee chief in June 2013. Two consecutive Lok Sabha defeats had sparked factionalism and leadership crisis in BJP.

Modi lost no time in lifting the spirits of the cadres by using spectacular rallies. He kicked off his Bihar campaign with a massive *Hunkar* rally. His vast media outreach targeted his bête noire Nitish, picked on Congress's chinks, and showcased his strengths as a leader capable of fulfilling the aspirations of 10.5 crore Biharis. His 'growth and development' plank won back the urban middle class and youth. As the first OBC contender for the prime minister's mantle, he drew in sections of backwards, even Dalits, to the party. Modi made his humble roots a campaign plank. His intelligent use of his underprivileged OBC background, complemented by the nomination of a large number of backwards as Lok Sabha candidates, planted him at the heart of the politics of 'social justice'. His win has forced the post-Mandal champions of backward castes like Lalu to rethink their OBC strategy. In contrast to the quota-driven, freebie-promising OBC leaders, Modi led a vitriolic anti-Congress campaign from an ideologically opposite tent, capturing the imagination of the multitudes, especially the backwards in Bihar and UP.

His success with backwards is surprising because he is the antithesis of the OBC school of politics. He is anti-reservation, the defining idiom of the social justice era, opposes doles, and is an unapologetic market reformer whose mantra is 'minimum government, maximum governance'. His 'rags to riches' story has found resonance in backward Bihar, particularly among the youth. As social scientist Shiv Vishvanathan observed, "He first spoke of being a tea vendor, then spoke about Ambedkar and then brought up his OBC roots at the very end of the election campaign. It is more about class, and recognition of his aspirational journey."[32] His late, opportunistic drift to 'backwardism' came once he realized that it was the weapon of choice in the post-Mandal battlefields of Bihar and UP. Modi never found the need to play up his OBC roots in Gujarat, but in Bihar and UP where caste trumps all other achievements and considerations, he grabbed the opportunity that Priyanka Gandhi presented him and waved his Ghanchi caste card with aplomb while remaining wedded to his Hindutva brand of politics. Modi was successful in taking the Mandal–Kamandal cohabitation to a new level by adding to it his basic Hindutva appeal, and his positioning as an administrator and a market reformer. It is this composite positioning that swelled the Hindutva kitty by bringing in the aspirational youth who yearn for jobs, infrastructure, and education, in short, a better life.

Another factor that propelled Modi's win was 'reverse polarization', which made Muslim votes redundant. In Bihar, despite concerted efforts by the 'secular' parties to get Muslims to vote en bloc against the BJP, the saffron challenger prevailed because of counter-polarization due to the bid for consolidation of MY vote in favor of the RJD. Consequently, Lalu who was expected to offer stiff resistance to the BJP did poorly. In 17 seats where Muslims have more than 15 percent of votes, the BJP won 12. The remaining 5 have been shared by the RJD–Congress–NCP–JD(U) alliance.[33] BJP leader Giriraj Singh's controversial statements targeting Muslims also emerged as an important factor. It led to Muslim consolidation behind Lalu, hurting Nitish's hope of attracting a sizable chunk of the Muslim vote.

The RJD chief appeared a better bet for those opposed to Modi with his solid hold over the Yadavs who account for 14 percent of the population and vote en bloc. The consolidation of Muslims helped BJP in a big way because there was a corresponding rallying among Hindus. At the same time, there were limits to what Lalu could do to attract support beyond the MY combination. The lawlessness and misgovernance associated with his regime were still fresh in the collective memory of the people, especially the EBCs and the Mahadalits. The upper castes as always did not show any inclination to align with Lalu or Nitish as they were largely driven by the Modi factor.

The fact that BJP stitched a new 'coalition of extremes' with allies like Ram Vilas Paswan and Upendra Kushwaha helped in augmenting the party's traditional base among the upper castes and Vaishyas. The LJP and the RLSP added a significant number of votes of the subcastes they represented to the NDA. The post-poll survey by the Centre for the Study of Developing Societies (CSDS) suggests that the BJP's social engineering paid off handsomely: 68 percent of Dusadhs—the Dalit subcaste Paswan belongs to—voted for the NDA. The NDA also wooed the EBCs, which constitute around 30 percent of Bihar's population and have traditionally voted for the JD(U); 53 percent of them reportedly voted for the NDA. This massive shift in the EBCs' support to the BJP was partly due to Modi's backward caste origins that the BJP kept trumpeting during its campaign in Bihar.

The upper castes, as expected, voted for the BJP en masse. Moreover, the Dalits not only voted for Modi in Bihar, they are also shifting toward the BJP as the new aspirational social group among Dalits wishes to be as much a part of the growth story as the traditional upper castes. Here, it is much less of the Hindu identity as it is about a perceived universalism of the benefits of growth and governance.[34] However, we did not see a similar kind of polarization among other Dalit castes. Upper castes supported the BJP with more than 80 percent of Brahmin, Rajput, Bhumihar, or Kayastha voters favoring the BJP–LJP alliance. A unique combination of caste realignment, the word-of-mouth spreading of Modi's achievements in Gujarat, and communal polarization in rural areas ensured the NDA's historic victory in Bihar. The CSDS survey shows that a significant percentage of votes across castes went to the NDA: upper castes 78, Yadav 19, Kurmi and Koeri 26, lower OBC 53, Dusadh 68, and Mahadalits 33. However, only 2 percent of Muslims in Bihar voted for the NDA.

Another less-talked-about factor that helped the NDA mobilize the backward castes and Dalits is the massive reduction in violent caste-based conflicts after Nitish assumed power in 2005. This scale of mobilization would have been unthinkable in the 1990s when the caste-based militia would indulge in frequent killing of people from each other's caste. Nitish made a concerted effort to kindle a subnational Bihari identity by downplaying caste and focusing on development. It could be argued, therefore, that Modi successfully rode on Nitish's achievements.

Figure 7.1
Bihar: Caste-wise Political Party Candidates for 2014 Lok Sabha Elections

BIHAR	BJP			Cong+NCP			RJD			JD(U)			LJP			Others	Total
	C	E	W	C	E	W	C	E	W	C	E	W	C	E	W		
Brahmin	3	3	100	1	0	0	1	0	0	2	0	0	0	0	0	2	9
Rajput	7	5	71	1	0	0	3	0	0	2	0	0	1	1	100	2	16
Bhumihar	3	3	100	1	0	0	-	-	-	3	0	0	1	1	100	6	14
Kayastha	1	1	100	0	0	0	1	0	0	1	0	0	0	0	0	4	7
Yadav	4	4	100	1	1	100	9	2	22	6	0	0	0	0	0	6	26
OBC	7	4	57	1	0	0	3	0	0	11	2	18	1	0	0	8	27
MBC/EBC	4	2	50	0	0	0	2	1	50	2	0	0	1	0	0	4	13
Dalit	3	3	100	5	0	0	2	0	0	6	0	0	3	3	100	8	27
Muslim	1	0	0	2	2	100	6	1	17	5	0	0	1	1	100	4	19
Sikh	0	0	0	1	0	0	0	0	0	0	0	0	0	0	0	0	1
ST	0	0	0	0	0	0	0	0	0	0	0	0	0	0	0	1	1
Total	30	25	83	13	3		27	4	23	38	2	5	7	6	85	42	160

Source: Times of India, May 19, 2014. http://epaperbeta.timesofindia.com/Article.aspx?eid=31808&articlexml=THE-HINDI-HEARTLANDS-CASTE-IN-STONE-19052014012063 (accessed on May 20, 2014).
Note: C = Contested; E = Elected; W = Percentage of contested candidates who won.

Despite a spectacular win, the BJP suffered severe losses in sitting seats of Bhagalpur, Purnia, Katihar, and Banka. Bhagalpur was a shock loss for party leader Shahnawaj Hussain. Besides, it suffered a total wipeout in Muslim-dominated Seemanchal in Bihar's northeast, which took away the shine from the complete sweep in most other areas (Figure 7.1).

Post 2014: Secular Realignment or Reconfiguring the Caste Coalition

Today, Biharis consider themselves as global citizens who are part of an emerging economic superpower. But the reality is that politics in Bihar is still mired in caste and religion. Candidates are often chosen on the basis of whether they are Dalit, OBC, Thakur, Bhumihar, Brahmin, or Muslim. In a state that continues to remain a metaphor for backwardness, development may be the latest slogan. However, caste remains the lowest common denominator for doing electoral arithmetic.

Keeping this in mind, Nitish made a tactical move by resigning from the chief ministership, making a Mahadalit Bihar CM, and negotiating support from Lalu in the Assembly. In doing this, he did save his thin majority government from collapsing but, more importantly, he symbolically played out his revenge on the upper castes that ignored him in favor of the BJP. Together, the JD(U) and the RJD can consolidate nearly three-fourths of the state's votes, which does not include the upper castes for the Assembly elections. Also, as the CSDS survey shows, this time, over one-fourth of the total voters in Bihar voted for the 'national interest'. It is expected that a majority of them would go back to the JD(U) for the state-level elections. So, while Nitish's attempt to carve out a niche at the Center failed, in Bihar he is down but by no means out.

Assembly by-elections held in September 2014 show that a reunification of Lalu Prasad and Nitish Kumar could do well in Assembly elections. Together, the two powerful OBC leaders polled more votes in the Lok Sabha elections, 47 percent, than the resurgent BJP backed by Ram Vilas Paswan and Upendra Kushwaha. The BJP alliance won nearly 39 percent of the votes. In the 2014 election the RJD and JD(U) alliances together polled some 28 lakh votes more than the NDA. It was merely a difference of around 8.6 percent votes between the NDA and the Lalu-led front that tilted the balance to the NDA.

In the 2009 Lok Sabha election, NDA secured 38 percent and the UPA 36 percent. A similar vote share had brought the NDA a similar number of seats in 2009, though the constituents were different. JD(U) and BJP together won 32 seats with 38 percent of the votes in 2009. BJP replicated that together with LJP and RLSP in 2014. On both occasions, Lalu was the principal opponent. His party in fact improved on its vote share from 19 percent to nearly 21 in 2014. If Lalu and Nitish come together, there will be a consolidation of OBC, Dalit, and EBC votes, creating a very formidable, secular front. At the same time, recalling its Samata Party days, JD(U) is planning to appease the upper castes, particularly Rajputs and Bhumihars, to split the BJP voter base. The RJD camp has also reconciled itself to the fact that a strong MY consolidation has not by itself been enough to stop the BJP juggernaut. Therefore, an alliance between the RJD, JD(U), and Congress would be a robust social combination if it could occur.

Conclusion: Consolidation of Communal Identity and Shift in Community Identity in a Multi-Polarized Election

As the 2014 election was for 'Delhi', not 'Patna', nearly 28 percent of voters in the state voted for a change of the central government. A large section of them voted on the issue of lack of development in Bihar and some in anticipation of better facilities like roads or better supply of electricity or drinking water. Due to shift in castes' political loyalty and religious polarization, Bihar also witnessed very sharp reverse polarization as a little over two-thirds of MY voters voted for the RJD–Congress alliance.[35] However, in the 2014 triangular fight, the BJP had a chance to consolidate the Hindu vote. The ruling JD(U) asserted that the BJP has succeeded in communalizing the state. They also played the caste card to consolidate this communal polarization in their favor.

Along with the upper caste vote, the BJP has attempted to add the Dalits and OBCs to its total by alliances with Paswan and Upender Kushwaha. The 'upper caste' communities, Brahmins, Kshatriyas, Bhumihars, and Kayasthas, who make up about 15 percent of the population, are considered the dominant opinion makers in Bihar. Nitish Kumar, who was being touted as the messiah of Bihar before he walked out of the NDA, is now being painted as a loser, thanks largely to the efforts of the articulate sections among the upper-caste communities. The BJP believes it holds complete sway over this 15 percent vote in Bihar.

BJP attempted to simultaneously break a sizable chunk from the other backward castes and from Nitish's formerly winning combination of EBCs and Mahadalits. The switching over of JD(U) leaders such as Jai Narain Nishad and Purnamasi Ram was aimed at seizing the EBC and Mahadalit votes from the JD(U). The BJP also made a valiant effort to wean away the Yadavs from the RJD. The candidature of Lalu's one-time confidante Ramkripal Yadav from Pataliputra is an example of this move. BJP Bihar Chief Nand Kishor Yadav also ensured that the party got a share of Yadav votes. The BJP has been successful in its efforts to claim credit for whatever development the state has seen in the past nine years.

Formation of a 'grand alliance' by old socialist friends, Lalu and Nitish, in Assembly by-polls after opposing each other and losing the general elections indicates further consolidation of caste and polarization on religious lines. BJP's gain in the Lok Sabha should not be counted as a complete loss for secular forces in caste-ridden Bihar. Rather, it may be a temporary shift toward the fluid 'political identity' of development and governance epitomized by the BJP in its 2014 election campaign that may change in the future. It may also succumb to the 'permanent identity' of caste and religion.

Notes and References

1. Ramashray Roy, "Regional Base and National Dream: Alliance Formation, 2009 National Elections," in Paul Wallace and Ramashray Roy (eds), *India's 2009 Elections: Coalition Politics, Party Competition, and Congress Continuity* (New Delhi: SAGE Publications, 2011), p. 28.
2. Paul Wallace, "Introduction: The New National Party System and State Politics," in Paul Wallace and Ramashray Roy (eds), *India's 1999 Elections and 20th Century Politics*, (New Delhi: SAGE Publications, 2003), p. 5.
3. Ruchir Sharma, "The Monophonic Voice of India," *Times of India*, May 14, 2014.
4. *Frontline*, 2 May 2014.
5. Ravindra Kumar Verma, "Caste and Bihar Politics," *Economic and Political Weekly* 26, 18(May 4, 1999), 1142–44.
6. According to the 1931 Census, upper castes constituted only 13.7 percent of the total state population (5 percent Brahmins, 3 percent Bhumihars, 4.4 percent Rajputs, and 1.2 percent Kayasthas). The other backward castes can broadly be distinguished as upper OBC and extremely backward castes (EBCs). The upper OBC constituted 20.3 percent of Bihar's population (11.7 percent Yadavs, 4.4 percent Koeris, 3.5 percent Kurmis, and 0.6 percent Baniyas). The EBCs constituted 18.2 percent of the state population. There were 15 caste groups under this category.
7. Jeffrey Witsoe, "Corruption as Power: Caste and the Political Imagination of the Postcolonial State," *American Ethnologist* 38, 1(2011), 73–85.
8. Manish K. Jha and Pushpendra, "Governing Caste and Managing Conflicts in Bihar, 1990–2011," Policy and Practice Paper Series, Calcutta Research Group, Kolkata, 2012.
9. Robin Cyril, "Bihar: The New Stronghold of OBC Politics," in Christopher Jaffrelot and Sanjay Kumar (eds), *Rise of the Plebeians? The Changing Face of Indian Legislative Assemblies* (New Delhi: Routledge, 2009).
10. Lucia Michelutti, "The Vernacularization of Democracy: Political Participation and Popular Politics in North India," *Journal of the Royal Anthropological Institute* 13 (2007): 641.
11. "Lalu, Nitish, Modi—Three Men and a Vote," www.tehelka.com (accessed on August 22, 2014).
12. Sankarshan Thakur, *Single Man: The Life and Times of Nitish Kumar of Bihar* (New Delhi: Harper Collins, 2014).

13. Binoy Shankar Prasad, "Identity Politics Recycled: 2009 Lok Sabha Election in Bihar," in Paul Wallace and Ramashray Roy (eds), *India's 2009 Elections: Coalition Politics, Party Competition, and Congress Continuity* (New Delhi: SAGE Publications, 2011), pp. 325–329.

14. Ibid.

15. *Times of India*, April 6, 2014.

16. *Hindustan Times*, March 29, 2014. Also see "Despite Super Show Nitish Headed for Defeat," *Hindustan Times*, May 5, 2014.

17. "Politicians-Voter Discontent in Bihar's Poll Priority," *Hindustan Times*, April 24, 2014.

18. "Bihar Best Performing State in Terms of Growth Rate: Survey," *Times of India*, July 9, 2014.

19. *Times of India*, May 4, 2014.

20. Ibid.; Prasad, "Identity Politics Recycled," pp. 325–27.

21. "Modi Factor Changes Poll Fate of Bihar's Transformer Nitish Kumar," *Times of India*, May 4, 2014.

22. *Times of India*, May 12, 2014.

23. "How Brand Nitish and His Campaign for Special Category Status for Bihar Failed to Take Centre Stage," *Times of India*, April 6, 2014.

24. Sanjay Kumar, "National Election Study 2014—Bihar: Interpreting the Massive Mandate," *Hindu*, March 21, 2014.

25. "Former JD(U) MP N.K. Singh Joins BJP," *Hindu*, March 22, 2014.

26. *Hindustan Times*, May 16, 2014.

27. "Nitish Stares at Prospect of Rebellion as His Ruling JD(U) Got Only 2 Out of 40 Lok Sabha Seats in Bihar," *Times of India*, May 19, 2014.

28. "Lalu Prasad Yadav Accuses Nitish Kumar of Hatching Conspiracy to Break RJD," PTI, http://articles.economictimes.indiatimes.com/2014-02-25/news/47670704_1_rjd-leader-rjd-legislature-party-lalu-prasad-yadav (accessed on June 10, 2014).

29. *Hindustan Times*, February 25, 2014.

30. "Gaya Craves for Stars, Skips Rallies," *Telegraph*, April 1, 2014.

31. *Frontline*, Election Special, May 16, 2014, pp. 4–5.

32. Shiv Viswanathan, "NaMo Thrust BJP Forward among Backwards in UP, Bihar," *Times of India*, May 17, 2014.

33. "Election Results 2014: Meira Kumar, Misa Bharti Bite Dust, Chirag Paswan Wins," *Times of India*, May 17, 2014.

34. Ajay Gudavarthy, "A Rightward Shift in Dalit Politics," *Hindu*, September 13, 2014.

35. http://www.livemint.com/Opinion/ngZRP3dgVn0PJHh256eDsI/Role-of-polarization-in-BJPs-big-victory.html (accessed on June 12, 2014).

8

Reclaiming the Capital: BJP's Clean Sweep in Delhi

Ravi Ranjan

Following the national trend, Bharatiya Janata Party (BJP) candidates in Delhi swept all the seven Lok Sabha seats with a 65.07 percent turnout. This replicates its sweep in 1999 when the BJP also came to power at the Center.[1] This chapter provides a historical and demographic background, and addresses four important aspects of the election:

1. A constituency-wise analysis of the electorate's mood swing.
2. Delhi's move from a two-party to a three-party system.
3. Ways in which the emergence of the Aam Aadmi Party (AAP) has changed Delhi's electoral politics.
4. Congress Party's situation following the BJP's massive victory.

India's is an historic election in five ways.[2] First, it was the most expensive election, as India spent ₹3,426 crore,[3] a 131 percent increase over the 2009 Lok Sabha elections. Second, it took 36 days. Third, 27 percent of the candidates have a worth over ₹1 crore, 11 percent more than in 2009. Fourth, 17 percent of the candidates were charged with criminal cases as against 15 percent in 2009.[4] Fifth, for the first time, alternative media played a crucial role with 45 percent of the citizens going online to talk politics. Similarly, this election also reflected Delhi's swing in a short span of less than six months from the Assembly elections in December 2013 to parliamentary elections in 2014.[5]

Distinctiveness of Delhi: Win the Capital and Govern the Country

In most of India's parliamentary elections, the political mantra to govern India is "win the capital and govern the country." Past election results substantiate this. The National Capital Territory of Delhi was reorganized by the 69th Amendment in 1990 and Delhi was reconstituted as a state under the provisions of Government of National Capital Territory of Delhi Act 1991.[6] Delhi subsequently faced six national elections. The National Democratic Alliance (NDA) or United Progressive Alliance (UPA) national coalition that won nationally also won Delhi. In 1998, the first victorious BJP-led NDA coalition under Atal Bihari Vajpayee won six out of seven seats. The next year, the BJP won all seven seats. The Congress won six seats out of seven seats in 2004 when it led the UPA victorious coalition and then in 2009 it won all seven seats. In 2014, as in 2009, the BJP won all seven seats in a triangular contest including the AAP.

Delhi always has been a swing state as in parliamentary elections. Delhi voted for non-Congress parties like Bharatiya Lok Dal (BLD), BJP, and erstwhile Bharatiya Jan Sangh (BJS/JS). In the first general election in 1952, Delhi's four parliamentary seats were won by BJS and the Kisan Mazdoor Praja Party with one each, and two by the Congress. The Congress swept all four seats in 1957 and five in 1962. The Congress came down to one seat in the new total of seven in 1967 as BJS won the other six. In 1971, the Congress returned with all seven seats. In the 1977 elections following the declaration of emergency by Indira Gandhi, all seven seats were won by BLD. The Congress returned to national power in 1980 and won six of Delhi's seven seats. Vajpayee won the New Delhi constituency.

Indira Gandhi's assassination and the consequent sympathy wave in 1984 led to a national Congress landslide and its Delhi sweep of all seven seats in spite of or aided by the anti-Sikh riots. In 1989, the Bofors and other alleged scandals led to another national coalition supported by the BJP. Delhi reflected the swing with five seats won by the BJP–Janata Dal

Table 8.1
Party-wise Parliamentary Election Results since 1967

Party	1967	1971	1977	1980	1984	1989	1991	1996	1998	1999	2004	2009	2014
Congress	1	7	0	6	7	2	2	2	1	0	6	7	0
BJP	–	–	–	0	4	5	5	6	7	1	0	7
Janata Party/Dal	–	–	–	1	–	1	–	–	–	–
BLD	–	–	7	–
JS/BJS	6	0	–

Source: Centre for the Study of Developing Societies (CSDS) Data Unit. Election Commission of India, http://eci.nic.in. *Frontline*, Vol. 16, November 5, 1999.

Notes: Total Lok Sabha seats: 7.
Turnout (2014): 65.07 percent; Turnout (2009): 51.85 percent; Turnout (2004): 47.09 percent; Turnout (1999): 43.7 percent.
Change in turnout as compared to 2009: +13.28 percentage points.

combine and only two by the Congress. Similar results in 1991 and 1996 resulted in the BJP winning five seats and the Congress two. In 1998, the BJP won six seats and in 1999 it won all seven for the first time. The BJP went to polls in 2004 with its 'India Shining' slogan and high expectations. The Congress, however, upset the BJP nationally and won six seats in Delhi. In 2009, the Congress repeated nationally and won all of Delhi's seven seats. After 10 years, the BJP has returned to power in 2014, winning all of Delhi's seats. In all of the 16 Lok Sabha elections, Delhi registered a clean sweep in seven elections. The Congress won in 1957, 1962, 1971, 1984, and 2009, while the BLD swept Delhi in 1999 and the BJP swept in 2014 (see Table 8.1).

Decoding Delhi's Political History

Delhi as India's capital continuously provides a magnet for migrants. As a result, its population has registered an increase from 17.4 lakh (1.7 million) in 1951 to 16.7 lakh (16.7 million) (see Table 8.2 for India-wide and Delhi decennial data). The electorate numbered 11,936,360 in

December 2013 when the Assembly elections were held. By April 2014, another 124,133 voters were added for the parliamentary elections. Changing demography has influenced the city's politics. In the first four decades since 1951, the decadal growth rate of population was more than 50 percent and then 47 percent in 2001. However, it came down to 21 percent in 2011.

This decreasing trend may be attributable to implementation of various employment promotion programs like MNREGA and welfare schemes like pension to senior citizens and widows by the central and state governments that reduce the incentive to migrate. Another major limitation to migrate to Delhi includes the development of NCR priority towns including Gurgaon, Faridabad, Sonipat, Noida, Ghaziabad, and Meerut.[7] The rate of population growth in Delhi during the last decade, nevertheless, was higher than the national level. Delhi's average annual growth rate was 3.93 percent in 1991–2001 and 1.92 percent in 2001–11; during the same period, average annual exponential growth for India was 1.97 percent and 1.64 percent, respectively.[8] The percentage of Delhi's population at the national level increased from 0.48 percent in 1951 to 1.38 percent in 2011 (Table 8.2).

Table 8.2

Population of India and Delhi and Their Growth, 1951–2011

						in lakhs (100,000)
		Delhi		India		Share of Delhi's
S. No.	Years	Population	Growth (%)	Population	Growth (%)	Population in All India
1.	1951	17.44	–	3,610.88	–	0.48
2.	1961	26.59	52.44	4,392.35	21.64	0.61
3.	1971	40.66	52.93	5,481.60	24.80	0.74
4.	1981	62.20	53.00	6,833.29	24.66	0.91
5.	1991	94.21	51.45	8,464.21	23.87	1.11
6.	2001	138.51	47.02	10,287.37	21.54	1.35
7.	2011	167.53	20.96	12,101.93	17.64	1.38

Source: Census of India, *Various Issues and Provisional Population Totals*, NCT of Delhi Series 8, Paper 1 of 2011.

Delhi had an unbalanced sex ratio of 868 females to 1,000 males in the 2011 census, which compares with the national average of 940 females per 1,000 males. With a total population of 16,314,838, Delhi is among the most highly populated cities in India. The literacy rate is 86.43 percent, slightly higher than the national average. The per capita annual income in the national capital is ₹2.01 lakh, which is three times the national average and is the highest in the country.[9]

Prior to 1991, Delhi was governed by the Delhi Administration Act, 1966, and for a very short time was a state with 48 Assembly members. Chaudhary Brahm Prakash served as the first Chief Minister.[10] Delhi had its first Assembly election in 1993 for 70 seats after its reconstitution as a state in 1991. In 2006, seven Lok Sabha seats assigned to Delhi included one for scheduled castes (SCs). Twelve of the 70 Assembly seats were designated for SCs. A large discrepancy between constituencies has been rectified. In 1967, for example, the smallest, Chandni Chowk, had an electorate of 20,000 while South Delhi with 300,000 had the biggest. Each parliamentary constituency (PC) now covers 10 Assembly constituencies and the imbalance of size has been eliminated.[11] The radically changed political map of the city had split some vote banks and diluted others. The Muslim vote, prominent in the pre-delimitation constituencies, now stands diluted significantly after delimitation.

Constituency-wise Analysis of 2014 Election Results

For the 2014 parliamentary election, Delhi had 12,060,493 voters (66.98 percent of total population); 226,833 were first-time voters. The most important new political development was the formation of the AAP, which formed the Delhi government in its very first election. It lasted 49 days. Parliamentary elections attracted 302 candidates. Northeast Delhi constituency with 60 candidates had the highest number, while Northwest Delhi with 30 had the lowest. Delhi followed national trends with the BJP winning all seven seats followed by the AAP and the Congress in number of votes.[12] The BJP's campaign sought votes on a one-point Modi-for-PM agenda, and its mix of newcomers and sitting MLAs benefitted from a massive pro-change wave that saw the party emerge

Table 8.3

Constituency-wise Voter Turnout in 2014 General Election in NCT Delhi

PC Name	Total Electorate (in Lakh)	Male Turnout	Female Turnout	Total Turnout	Muslim Voters
1 - Chandni Chowk	14.5	69.61%	65.72%	67.84%	20%
2 - North East Delhi	19.6	68.65%	65.62%	67.29%	21%
3 - East Delhi	18.3	66.12%	64.46%	65.39%	18%
4 - New Delhi	14.9	65.79%	64.19%	65.08%	8%
5 - North West Delhi	21.9	62.43%	61.02%	61.79%	8%
6 - West Delhi	20.4	67.04%	64.97%	66.10%	4%
7 - South Delhi	17.5	63.50%	62.08%	62.90%	7%
State Total		66%	63.93%	65.07%	

Source: Election Commission of India, http://eci.nic.in. Centre for the Study of Developing Societies.

victorious in a three-cornered contest. The BJP bucked predictions of the exit polls that gave the AAP two to three seats in Delhi. The AAP did replace the Congress as the alternative to the BJP. Four of the seven sitting Congress MPs including a Union Minister lost their security deposit.[13] The high voter turnout of 65.09 percent, a nearly 14 percent jump over 51.81 percent in 2009, was a decisive vote for change (Table 8.3).

Chandni Chowk Parliamentary Constituency

Being one of the oldest constituencies in the country, it has been represented from the beginning by many prominent political leaders. Not only is it very densely populated, but it also covers historically significant regions going back to the Mughal period in the culturally important Shahjahanabad area. It extends from Lahori Darwaza to Chowk Kotwali, covering Chandni Chowk and ending in Fatehpuri Masjid. Traders and the business community dominate it. Chandni Chowk electorate always demand better business facilities, development of the business infrastructure, and redevelopment of the walled city area, particularly its road and electrical lines. Traders also question the functioning of the

Municipal Corporation of Delhi and Delhi Police in this constituency. It lags behind in the health sector. Muslims dominate two to three Assembly constituencies. Local issues mattered the most in 2014.

Prior to 1977, the Congress won thrice from this constituency and the BJP once. After the 1977 elections, one of the highest winning margins was in 2004 when the Congress candidate Kapil Sibal defeated BJP's Smriti Irani with 71.17 percent of the votes, second highest after 1977 election when BLD candidate secured 71.91 percent of votes. The lowest winning margin was in the 1999 election when the BJP swept Delhi and its candidate Vijay Goel won by a margin of only 0.99 percent votes. In 1998 too, the BJP won this seat by a margin of less than 2 percent of votes. The Congress usually performed better than the BJP in Chandni Chowk with the support of significant Muslim voters.

BJP's Dr Harsh Vardhan won the 2014 election by a margin of 136,320 (13.9 percent) votes. In third place, Congress's Kapil Sibal secured a total of 176,206 votes, a figure that was even less than his previous victory margin.[14] Muslim voters, more than 20 percent of the total, split between the AAP and the Congress. The split, coupled with a Modi wave, made Chandni Chowk an easy win for the BJP. It won 44.6 percent of the total votes. The AAP despite having four MLAs received 30.7 percent. The BJP led in all Assembly segments.

Northeast Delhi Parliamentary Constituency

The politically active Northeast Delhi Constituency is one of Delhi's most populated regions, dominated by people from eastern Uttar Pradesh and Bihar, commonly known as *Purvanchali*. Their numeric strength has increased greatly in the past few decades and they have been demanding equal treatment and equal opportunities. This area is seeking colonies' regularization, and expansion of the metro, roads, and civic facilities. Many rural Assembly constituencies, like Burari, Karawal Nagar, and Ghoda, are demanding early regularization so they can be developed by the Municipal Corporation of Delhi. This constituency has Muslim-dominated assemblies of Seelampur, Mustafabad, and a SC-reserved constituency of Seemapuri. Northeast Delhi is one of the 90 minority districts in the country where a population of one minority community (mostly Muslims) is over 20 percent, for which the Center sanctioned a special component plan for their development.[15] All parties had promised better development of civic facilities, educational system, and health facilities, with special focus on women's safety.

Major promises made during campaigning include the setting up of an East Campus on the lines of the North and South campuses of Delhi University, establishing schools, and regularization of unauthorized colonies. The AAP slammed the Congress and the BJP for neglecting development. Its candidate, Prof. Anand Kumar, highlighted the neglect of this area by the Congress at the parliamentary and legislative levels on the one hand and by the BJP through its municipal corporation on the other. The AAP, BJP, and Congress candidates promised to prioritize the solutions for sewer, water-logging, and transport, along with the availability of government land for hospitals, road, transport, community hall, park, cemetery, mortuary, and places for cultural programs.

The BJP/JS had won this seat six times, the Congress eight, and the BLD once. From 1957 through 1971, this constituency had four parliamentary elections out of which BJS won only once in 1967. The Congress won the others. After the 1977 elections, the BJP and the Congress represented this seat five times each with BLD winning once. In the 2014 election, BJP winning vote share of 45.3 percent is the lowest after the 1977 election. The BLD candidate secured the highest percentage of votes, 66.25 percent, in 1977 when the winning margin was 36.68 percent. In 2014, the winning margin was comparatively low at 11 percent. A major reason was the AAP presence that made it a triangular contest. The lowest winning margin was of 0.54 percent was in 1996 when the BJP won. The Congress candidates' winning margins were better than those of BJP candidates. Even during the clean sweeps of 1971, 1984, and 2009, the Congress performed better than the BJP's clean sweeps of 1999 and 2014.

Bhojpuri movie actor and BJP candidate Manoj Tiwari won by a margin of over 1.40 lakh votes in the Northeast Delhi constituency with AAP candidate Anand Kumar finishing second and sitting Congress Member of Parliament (MP) J.P. Agarwal taking the third spot. Despite a massive vote swing in favor of the AAP, primarily owing to its increased popularity among the Muslims who constitute 21 percent of the electorate, the BJP won by a comfortable margin due to division of Muslim votes between the AAP and the Congress. Mr Tiwari polled 596,125 (45.3 percent) votes as against 452,041 (34.3 percent) of AAP's Professor Anand

Kumar. Mr Agarwal of the Congress could only manage to poll 214,792 (16.3 percent) votes.[16] The Assembly seats where the AAP secured the maximum number of votes were Seemapuri, Seelampur, and Burari. In the rest of the seven assemblies, the BJP secured more votes than the AAP and Congress. The Muslim community turned out in strength, and many admitted voting for the AAP, but middle-class voters, along with the youth, blunted their impact.

East Delhi Parliamentary Constituency

Delimitation strongly affected the East Delhi PC, which was divided between the East Delhi and Northwest Delhi PCs. The new East Delhi PC has a large presence of Group Housing societies and *Juggi Jhopdi* (slum) colonies. Housing a population of 1,707,725 people, the East Delhi PC is one of the most thickly populated regions of Delhi and is continuing to grow. Traversed by the Yamuna River, this PC also covers Shahadara, Gandhi Nagar, Preet Vihar, and Seelampur. The civic facilities here are not as good as in the South Delhi and New Delhi constituencies. It lacks enough planned areas for schools, playgrounds, and hospitals like Central Delhi. This PC has a Muslim-dominated Assembly constituency and two SC-reserved Assembly constituencies.

Out of 13 parliamentary elections in this constituency, the BJP/JS and Congress have won six times each and BLD once. BJS won the constituency in the first elections held in 1967 by a narrow margin of 600 votes, but in 1971, Congress candidate H.K.L. Bhagat won the election by more than 70,000 votes. Bhagat won thrice more. He set a record of 76.95 percent votes in 1984, while his Janata Party counterpart received only 14.74 percent votes. Bhagat's winning margin was 62.21 percent, which is the highest ever in all seven Delhi seats since 1977. The second highest winning margin was in 1977 election when the BLD candidate defeated Congress's Bhagat with a margin of 37.59 percent of votes. The lowest winning margin was in the 1998 election when the BJP won this seat by a margin of 3.94 percent against the Congress.

In 2014 election, East Delhi residents voted out two-time Congress MP Sandeep Dikshit and replaced him with BJP candidate and Art of Living leader Maheish Girri, who got 47.82 percent of the total votes. Girri, who won 572,202 votes, defeated AAP's Rajmohan Gandhi by 190,463 (15.92 percent) votes. Gandhi came in second with 381,739

(31.9 percent) votes and Dikshit polled 203,240 (17 percent) votes. In 2009, Mr Dikshit won by the highest margin of over 2.41 lakh in Delhi. In East Delhi, the BJP managed to lead in all Assembly segments represented by AAP MLAs. In Patparganj, a seat represented by senior AAP leader and former minister Manish Sisodia, BJP's Maheish Girri bagged 68,205 votes as compared to 41,872 votes by the AAP candidate. Because of its large Muslim and resettlement colony population, East Delhi was considered an AAP stronghold. Middle-class and upper-middle-class BJP voters, disillusioned with the AAP, countered the slum and split Muslim votes. Despite having won five Assembly seats in 2013, the AAP lost with the second highest margin among the seven Delhi seats.

New Delhi Parliamentary Constituency

The New Delhi Lok Sabha seat is one of the most prestigious constituencies in the national political scenario of India. Prominent political leaders such as former Prime Minister Atal Bihari Vajpayee and former Deputy Prime Minister Lal Krishna Advani of the BJP as well as other BJP and Congress leaders have been MPs from this seat. The radical leader Sucheta Kripalani, who began the Kisan Mazdoor Praja Party and later associated herself with the Congress, represented it for the first two terms. This constituency came into existence in 1951, and has become one of the main BJP bastions, although the Congress won it in 2004 and 2009.

It stretches across prominent regions of Delhi such as Rajpath, Janpath, and Connaught Place, besides housing the Parliament Houses and the Delhi Secretariat. Water is an important problem for this constituency. Roads and electricity are adequate. Most of the city's good schools and hospitals are located in this constituency, so the electorate has not demanded much in terms of infrastructure and civic facilities except for water. The upper and middle class also demanded a corruption-free system and effective governance.

Prior to 1977, the predecessor of BJP, the BJS/JS, managed to win this seat in 1967 and 1961. Vajpayee made history by winning this seat with a margin of 43.67 percent votes in the 1977 election on a BLD ticket. By contrast, Advani barely won with a margin of 0.74 percent in the 1991 election by defeating the film actor and Congress candidate Rajesh Khanna. He almost ended BJP veteran Advani's political career as Advani won the New Delhi seat by only 1,589 votes as a shocked

Khanna refused to accept the narrow defeat, rolling on the ground at the counting station insisting that he had been cheated of a win.[17] Khanna did win the seat eventually in a by-election after Advani vacated the constituency by keeping the Gandhinagar seat in Gujarat that he also won. However, unlike the other constituencies of Delhi, the winning margin of the BJP has always been better in this constituency except in 1991 and 1980 when Advani and Vajpayee won by 0.74 percent and 2.66 percent, respectively.

In the 2014 general elections, Meenakshi Lekhi of the BJP won the New Delhi constituency. She received a total of 453,350 (46.7 percent) votes, defeating her closest rival Ashish Khetan of the AAP by a huge margin of 162,708 (16.7 percent) votes. The AAP vote share stood at 30 percent. A large share of middle-class and lower-middle-class support went to the AAP in Delhi's urban villages and slums. Congress's Ajay Maken came third, although he did manage to get the highest percentage of votes among all the seven Congress candidates in Delhi.[18] In the last Lok Sabha elections, Maken had won this seat by 187,809 votes. Both Lekhi and Khetan have remained first-time candidates, taking on Congress General Secretary and spokesperson Maken who remained the MP from this constituency in the 14th and 15th Lok Sabha, respectively. Lekhi drew immense support of the masses in the constituency. At present, in the New Delhi constituency, the Congress has no sitting MLA. The AAP won eight and the BJP two seats in the Assembly elections held in December 2013, and this parliamentary seat sprung a surprise in December when the Congress lost in all 10 Assembly seats and AAP supremo Arvind Kejriwal defeated Sheila Dikshit, the longest-serving CM from Delhi. The BJP managed to win the Assembly segment represented by AAP chief Kejriwal by over 12,590 votes, considered to be one of the safest seats for the AAP.

Northwest Delhi Parliamentary Constituency

The important Northwest Delhi seat is reserved for the SCs. This constituency is one of the most densely populated regions of the capital with an estimated population density of 8,254 inhabitants per square kilometer and a population of 3,656,539. It covers the vast residential and commercial regions of Delhi, such as Saraswati Vihar, Rohini, Narela, Model Town, and Mangol Puri. Constituency issues include 24×7 electricity, better civic facilities, and increased connectivity to and extension of the metro rail. Most of the Assembly segments lack good schools and health infrastructure, especially hospitals. Many assemblies are expanding with the few remaining rural agricultural lands becoming urbanized. Institutional development has taken place in Bawana area. People here demanded jobs for villagers who sold their land or whose land has been acquired for various government projects. Women safety is also a major concern. There was also a tussle between local and outsider populations because the Purvanchali population is important and dominates the Kirari Assembly constituency.

This seat has had 14 Lok Sabha elections with the Congress winning eight times, the BJP five, and the BLD once. After the 1977 elections, the winner–loser margin was the highest (39.34 percent) in the 1984 election when the Congress swept Delhi. The lowest winning margin was in 1991 when the BJP won this seat by 0.99 percent votes. In all clean sweep elections of 1971, 1977, 1984, 1999, 2009, and 2014, the BJP's percentage of winning margin was comparatively lower, 4.83 percent in 1999 and 7.8 percent in 2014. While the same percentage was higher for the Congress, it was 39.34 percent and 21.49 percent in 1984 and 2009, respectively. In the lone clean sweep of BLD in 1977, the winning margin was 30.19 percent.

In 2014 election, BJP candidate Dr Udit Raj won by a margin of 106,802 votes against his nearest rival, AAP's Rakhi Birla. Dr Raj polled 629,860 (46.4 percent) votes while Ms Birla got 523,058 (38.6 percent) votes. Then Union Minister and two-time sitting MP Krishna Tirath had to settle for the third spot with 157,468 (11.6 percent) votes,[19] forfeiting her deposit. In the 2009 election, the Congress candidate's margin of victory over the BJP was 1.84 lakh. The Congress's biggest problem was the split in the Muslim and Dalit votes in the city between the Congress and the AAP. Some Muslim leaders mobilized the community to vote for the BJP. Even BSP workers took a collective decision to not vote against a party, but to vote for development and governance. Many of them have voted for the BJP by crossing the traditional boundaries of identity politics. They were buying cans of drinking water because the piped water was not fit for drinking. So many residents were eagerly looking for development of their area that they preferred Modi's agenda of development despite its various deficiencies. Birla has also secured the highest vote among AAP candidate but nothing stopped the BJP in winning this seat by a comfortable margin. A Modi wave and the constituency's Jat-dominated villages made all the difference.

West Delhi Parliamentary Constituency

This is a fairly new constituency but politically significant in Delhi. Before 2008, it was partially included in the Outer Delhi PC, and partially in the South Delhi constituency. It has been a Congress stronghold from the very beginning. One of the most densely populated regions in Delhi, housing a population of 2,543,243 people and a population density of 19,563 inhabitants per square kilometer, this constituency covers vast residential and commercial regions of Delhi such as Janakpuri, Tilak Nagar, Punjabi Bagh, and Patel Nagar. Water was the biggest issue in many areas. West Delhi also lacks in health facilities for the middle and lower middle classes. People were also demanding sports facilities like Central and East Delhi that were developed during the Commonwealth Games. Electorate also demanded regularization of colonies, particularly in Assembly segments like Uttam Nagar and Najafgarh. It has one reserved Assembly constituency and a marginal 4 percent of Muslim voters.

Out of 16 Lok Sabha elections, the BJP/BJS won only four times and the Congress 10 times. Janata Party won once in 1989, and BLD once in 1977. In 1977, the BLD candidate was the old-time Congress veteran B. Prakash who represented this seat in 1971, 1967, and 1962. In the first and second general elections, this outer Delhi constituency had twin Lok Sabha constituencies, and in both the elections and in both seats Congress candidates won. In 1984, the winning margin was the highest of all 16 Lok Sabha elections in this constituency when the Congress candidate secured 72.75 percent of votes and defeated his rival by a margin of 49.70 percent votes. The lowest winning margin was in 1989 when the same defeated candidate won this seat on a Janata Dal ticket and defeated his Congress rival by a margin of 6.74 percent. This constituency has decisive voting behavior as the margin never been below 5 percent.

In 2014, BJP's Pravesh Verma won the West Delhi seat by a margin of 268,586 (19.9 percent) votes, setting a new victory margin record, attributing his victory to the "Modi wave and his father's (Ex-chief minister S.S. Verma) legacy." His margin was also boosted by the votes garnered by the two namesakes of AAP candidate Jarnail Singh, who together polled over 90,000 votes. Mr Verma secured 651,395 (48.3 percent) votes and the official candidate of the AAP secured 382,809 (28.4 percent) votes. The BJP broke the previous victory record set by outgoing an East Delhi Congress MP, who won by a margin of 2.41 lakh votes in 2009.[20]

For AAP candidate from West Delhi Jarnail Singh, the main issue turned out to be his name rather than his rivals. One Jarnail Singh is the AAP MLA while the other is the journalist-turned AAP leader. He made headlines after he threw a shoe at Union Minister P. Chidambaram during a press conference in 2009 to protest against the clean chit given by the Central Bureau of Investigation to Congress leaders Bhagat and Sajjan Kumar in the 1984 anti-Sikh riots. Voters were unaware of a second Jarnail Singh. They mostly recognized the MLA Jarnail Singh. MLA Jarnail Singh said the confusion existed since the AAP's Delhi list was declared.[21] This constituency has a high percentage of Purvanchali voters and a significant percentage of voters from the Sikh community. That's why the BJP candidate promised to expedite the probe into the 1984 anti-Sikh riots while kicking off his campaign from the Bangla Sahib Gurdwara.[22] Congress candidate Mahabal Mishra got 193,266 (14.3 percent) votes in West Delhi.

South Delhi Parliamentary Constituency

The South Delhi constituency has been a BJP power center in Delhi. Some of its most popular leaders such as Sushma Swaraj and Madan Lal Khurana have been elected here. It came into existence in 1966. As per the 2011 Census of India, with its population of 2,733,752, it is one of the most densely populated regions of Delhi with an estimated 10,935 inhabitants per square kilometer. Covering vast regions such as Munirka, Begumpur, Jia Sarai, Katwaria Sarai, Badarpur, Mandi Village, Hauz Khas Village, Lado Sarai, Ber Sarai, C.R. Park, and Badarpur, this seat from its inception in 1966 to 1993 consisted of eight Metropolitan Council segments. From 1993 to 2008, it encompassed 13 segments. After the Delimitation, two Assembly constituencies were reserved. Slum resettlement, water problem, and women safety were the major concerns raised by voters. Community feeling has been strong as the voters are believers of traditional values. Community elders are important, with the BJP candidate claiming that community leaders from across the spectrum pledged their support to the BJP. "We met the leaders of communities such as the Jats, Khatik and Prajapati and also got support from various village elders in Raj Nagar, Palam and Kishangarh," Bidhuri said.[23] AAP candidate Colonel Devinder Sehrawat, on the other hand, said his support base is not limited to any caste or community groups, but includes supporters across the spectrum including street vendors and auto-rickshaw drivers. The BJP won this seat eight times since 1967, the Congress four, and the BLD once in 13 parliamentary elections. The highest vote secured by a winning candidate was in the 1977 election when BLD's V.K. Malhotra secured 69.81 percent defeating the Congress candidate by a margin of 40.82 percent. Subsequently, Malhotra joined the BJP. The winning margin was more than 10 percent in all elections since 1977.

In the 2014 Lok Sabha polls, nearly 50 percent votes went to BJP's Ramesh Bidhuri.[24] While Bidhuri polled 497,980 (45.2 percent), Sehrawat's vote total was 390,980 (35.2 percent). As many as 17 of the 19 candidates including the Congress's Ramesh Kumar with 125,213 (11.4 percent) votes forfeited their security deposits lacking more than one-sixth of the total votes. Of the 10 independents, Ruby Yadav outperformed all of them with 56,749 votes. Despite the AAP retaining the three Assembly segments of Deoli (SC), Ambedkar Nagar (SC), and Sangam Vihar it won during the 2013 Delhi Assembly elections, the BJP led by significant numbers across the other seven Assembly segments. The AAP, however, recorded gains in Palam, Chhattarpur, Badarpur, and, most interestingly, Bidhuri's stronghold of Tughlakabad. In BJP's assessment, the party could not win Muslim votes that either went to the Congress or the AAP.

Local Considerations: Issues and Promises of the 2014 Delhi Elections

Civic Amenities and Social Welfare

Delhi voted over the same age-old civic issues of water, electricity, better roads, and education facilities, apart from the generic issues of price rise and corruption. Numerous issues also include slum resettlement, civic facilities, efficient mass transport, hospitals, and waste management.

People want everything fixed by the next government.[25] Various media reports on the expectations of the capital's voters suggest that routine local issues swayed the votes. CSDS National Election Study (NES) data on housing, rural employment guarantee, health, and pension (old aged, widows, and disabled) schemes explored the voters' reaction to government welfare schemes in the 2014 election. The percentage of voters who reported to have benefitted from a scheme varied from 15 to 21 percent of the entire electorate and about three-fourths of the beneficiaries of these central schemes voted for an opponent to the ruling party or alliance.

During the 2014 election, a large majority of the voters across caste, class, religions, and the rural–urban divide credited their respective state governments for the benefit. Even then, there is no correspondence between the perception as to who the benefactor is and what the vote preference is. The Congress's claiming ownership of many welfare schemes did not succeed either in the Assembly or in the parliamentary elections. In Delhi, like other states, the benefits of welfare schemes had only a marginal impact on voter decisions. A large proportion of the beneficiaries preferred the BJP or its allies rather than the UPA in Delhi.

Corruption and Price Rise

The AAP's overwhelming victory in the Delhi Assembly election in 2013 highlighted corruption as the focus of electoral politics for the 2014 general election. There was a consensus among commentators that Congress-led UPA performed poorly in this election owing to charges of massive corruption at the highest level, besides lack of leadership and the government's inability to control price rise. Repeated references were made during the election campaign to scams involving coal, the 2G spectrum allocation, the Commonwealth Games, Adarsh Housing scam, and the Gujarat government favoring the Adani group. However, the political importance of corruption is debatable.[26] There is a crucial difference in how voters think about corruption and how political parties and leaders represent this issue in their campaigns. Voters care more about the corruption they encounter on an everyday basis, whereas parties make the issue a spectacle. Since most local-level corruption cases are directly linked to state officials, and state institutions like the police are not directly linked to any particular party, corruption was not an issue on which voters discriminate while exercising their franchise. CSDS NES data indicates that big-ticket corruption does not determine electoral outcomes in India.

Women Safety and Representation

After the December 2012 Nirbhaya rape and murder case, women safety became a key election issue for Delhi. Thomson Reuters Foundation reports that crimes against women in India, such as rape, dowry deaths, abduction, and molestation, increased by 26.7 percent in 2013 compared to the previous year. According to the National Crime Records Bureau, there were 309,546 crimes against women reported to the police in 2013 against 244,270 in 2012. The National Crime Records Bureau said the number of rapes in the country rose by 35.2 percent with Delhi reporting 1,441 rapes in 2013, making it the city with the highest number of rapes and confirming its reputation as India's 'rape capital'.[27] It also forced the Indian parliament to enact stiffer penalties for crimes against women, including death for repeat rape offenders, criminalizing stalking, making acid attacks, and human trafficking specific offences. Therefore, women issues and women representation was an important agenda that figured in the manifestos of all three major parties of Delhi; however, all parties nominated only one woman candidate for the Delhi 2014 election.

There has not been more than one woman representative from Delhi in Parliament in most of the elections. The BJP and the Congress have not nominated many women candidates. Even the radically different AAP nominated only one woman candidate. Other than Meenakshi Lekhi and Krishna Tirath, Sushma Swaraj, Sucheta Kripalani, Meera Kumar, and Anita Arya have previously represented Delhi women in the Lok Sabha. In Parliament, parties constantly demand women reservation but they are not ready to field more women candidates. Meenakshi Lekhi, the only woman representative from Delhi in the 16th Lok Sabha, polled fewer votes, 453,350, than AAP's Rakhi Birla of Northwest constituency, 523,058, among the women candidates who contested from the national capital.[28] The maximum numbers of female candidates were in the New Delhi seat, five women out of a total of 29 candidates. There were two constituencies, West Delhi and Northwest Delhi, which did not provide a single woman candidate.

Crime and Law and Order

Delhi's crime rate has risen in the past few years. Five out of seven BJP candidates in the 2014 Delhi elections have criminal cases against them with four of them even facing serious charges like kidnapping, criminal intimidation and extortion. According to the report of the Association of Democratic Reforms and Delhi Election Watch, after analyzing the self-sworn affidavits of all the 150 candidates who contested in Delhi, 23 candidates (15 percent) have criminal cases against them while 13 (9 percent) are facing serious criminal charges.[29] "Five (71 percent) of the seven BJP candidates, two (29 percent) candidates each from the Congress and the BSP out of the seven candidates have criminal charges cases against them," states the report, while two (67 percent) out of the three candidates fielded by Shiv Sena, one (14 percent) out of the seven candidates of the AAP, one candidate each from Agar Jan Party and Rashtriya Ekta Party, and nine (16 percent) out of 58 independent candidates have declared criminal cases against themselves in their affidavits. A few candidates were also facing charges of crimes against women. Despite civil society pressure, political parties continue fielding such candidates.

Networked Election: Media and Money Impact on 2014 Delhi Election

Delhi's 2014 parliamentary election was one of the most watched general elections in recent times and the role of the media was crucial. Mass media served as a system for communicating messages and symbols, not only entertaining but also inculcating individuals with values, beliefs, and codes of behavior that carry out a system-supportive propaganda function. They rely on market forces, internalized assumptions, and self-censorship of the larger society without overt coercion.[30] The use of vitriolic language during campaigning in Delhi manifested feelings of exclusion. All parties personalized their attacks on each other. As the *Indian Express* defined it:

> Speech crosses the line when it involves the defamation of vulnerable individuals by means of defamation of group characteristics. It carries a different

charge from the swagger of a minority leader trying to convey fearlessness to his constituency, even when they are all motivated by electoral gain.[31]

In this election, neutrality was never really there in reality. Journalists were frank in the run-up to 2014. Just as newspapers in the United States formally endorse one candidate or the other in state and federal elections, this is beginning to happen in India too.

Delhi has a large electorate residing in slums and resettlements colonies where money and services have become an important aspect of bargaining between the inhabitants and the party. Reports stated that whoever gives money and/or other considerations gets the vote. Electricity supply was constant during this time, there were no inspections or evictions, and the drive to close down unauthorized businesses ceased. For people in the slums, this was a routine associated with all elections, a business opportunity that arrived with the election period and would soon pass. Delhi's voting trend shows that slum dwellers have a very big participation in elections and often decide who wins.

That's why, in the December 2013 elections, the AAP suggested that cameras be placed at each slum colony to check the use of money and liquor to buy votes. Despite Election Commission claims on checking the misuse of money, candidates have exceeded their limits although they manage the ledger books according to existing rules. No party is ready to put a list of contributors and their expenditure on a website. The AAP took the lead, but by the end of campaign, it seems they lost the thread. Indian elections are becoming a money and media show. Many independent candidates also contested, but coverage was poor. These candidates lack funds to make them visible, which is why many smaller and regional parties have been demanding state-sponsored elections.

Delhi Moved from a Two-party to a Three-party System

For many decades, Delhi has witnessed a two-party rivalry between the Congress and the BJP including its JS predecessor. However, in 2014, Delhi faced a three-way contest for the first time. The 2014 election results

Figure 8.1

Vote Share of Different Parties in 2014 Lok Sabha Election

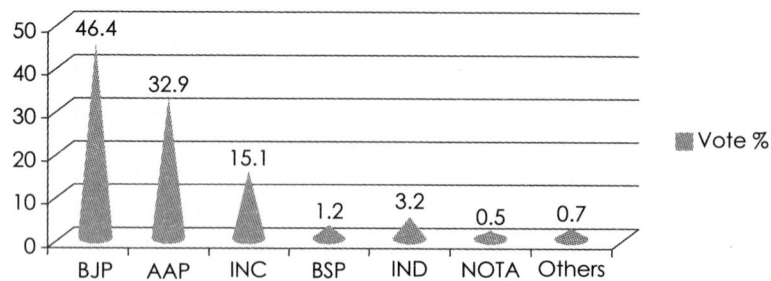

Source: Election Commission of India, General Elections 2014. Data on May 17, 2014. http://eci.nic.in (Party-wise trends and result).

show that BJP won all seven Lok Sabha seats by more than 100,000 votes over the AAP. A total of 133 of the 150 candidates in Delhi forfeited their security deposit after failing to poll at least one-sixth of the valid votes, including four from the Congress. BJP's vote share in the Delhi Lok Sabha polls jumped to 46.1 percent from 33.07 percent in the Assembly polls (Figure 8.1).

In the elections held in 1983, the Congress came to power defeating its BJP rival in the Metropolitan Council. In 1993, under the newly set-up Assembly with 70 members, the BJP won the elections with more than a three-fourths majority. In the 1998 Assembly elections, the Congress defeated the incumbent BJP by winning 52 out of 70 seats. However, while losing at the state level, the BJP continued to hold its ground at the parliamentary level in Delhi, winning six seats in the 1998 elections and all seven seats in 1999. The Congress won the 2003 Assembly elections overcoming the incumbency factor in Delhi where the pattern of national biparty rivalry is reflected in the electoral politics of the state. But in the 2004 parliamentary elections, the electorate replaced the BJP by the Congress, which won six out of seven seats in Delhi. Again in the 2008 Assembly election, Delhi established a record by electing a Congress government for the third time in a row. Most importantly, in the 2009 general election, the Congress won all seven parliamentary seats, establishing the same party in power at both the Center and state governments.

Advantage BJP, Disappointed AAP, and Decimated Congress

The spectacular victory of the BJP in the national capital in 2014 has opened up fresh opportunities for the party, just short of just three members in the December 2013 Assembly election, to explore the formation of a state government or hold new Assembly elections. In the Lok Sabha elections, the BJP led in 60 of the 70 Assembly segments, the AAP in the remaining 10. The Congress, which ruled the capital for 15 years, drew a zero. One report suggests that the BJP could gain 29 Assembly seats based on their parliamentary results.[32]

Despite their aim to usher in an alternative brand of politics, the AAP failed to bag even a single seat from Delhi after spectacular success in the Assembly elections in 2013. The party was blamed by its own workers of taking the home turf 'for granted'.[33] The AAP nonetheless increased its vote share from 30 percent to 33 percent in Delhi even though a large part of the middle-class and upper-middle-class votes deserted the AAP in the 2014 election. The AAP began in November 2012 as a movement for clean government and administration, ending special privileges for the elected representatives, and good governance. It appealed to supporters disenchanted with the existing political class, attracting thousands of volunteers to work for the party full time.[34]

Nationally, the AAP gave a new turn to social activism of the Lok Satta Party in Andhra Pradesh and the Mazdoor Kisan Shakti Sanghatan in Rajasthan. It represented the first attempt to bring about radical political change at the national level and tried to transform the character of Indian politics. Due to the AAP's impact, the main contenders of Indian politics, including the BJP and the Congress, had to respond to the challenge it posed. Despite failure in the 2014 Delhi election, the national performance of the AAP, 2.0 percent of the national electorate with 11,325,635 votes, was at par with or much better than some of the established parties such as the Communist Party of India, which polled a mere 0.8 percent of the national vote, or that of the Nationalist Congress Party or the Janata Dal (United), which polled 1.6 and 1.1 percent votes, respectively.

More importantly, it received substantial support from diverse social sections, breaking the barriers of class, caste, religious, and regional identities, as voters from middle and poorer classes, Hindus, Muslims, and Sikhs, as well as upper castes, backward castes, and Dalits equally endorsed the AAP. Voters in urban areas and educated voters came forward in support of the AAP in greater numbers than in the rural areas. Kejriwal's resignation as Delhi's chief minister created an impression of him as a 'quitter' that led to erosion in AAP's support base, and people bought the BJP's propaganda against the AAP. However, an overestimation of people's support and fielding almost as many candidates as the two major political parties led to AAP's failure. Nationally, the BJP put up 428 candidates, the Congress 464 and the AAP 432.

AAP made significant gains among Muslim voters and retained its core voter base in poorer sections of the city. In the four Assembly segments of Okhla, Seelampur, Sultanpur Majra (SC), and Badli, AAP polled more votes than the Congress, whose legislators represent these constituencies in the Delhi Assembly. The party polled higher than the BJP and the Congress in Matia Mahal, and has recorded gains across Ballimaran, Gokulpur, and Seelampur. Even in the BJP stronghold of Kirari, the AAP polling more votes could be an indication of its growing reach in Delhi's unauthorized colonies.

Despite having two clean sweeps and winning more than a majority of seats in most of the past Lok Sabha elections, the Congress faced a rout in two back-to-back elections within six months. The Congress lost by 0–7 in the 2014 Lok Sabha elections and was thrown out of power after the Delhi Assembly elections in 2013. Given the prevailing anti-Congress sentiment in the Delhi electorate, it faces an uphill task in its efforts to recover.[35] Delhi may be becoming a BJP versus AAP battleground. Congress candidates in the Lok Sabha polls finished a poor third in all seven seats, with four of them forfeiting their security deposit. The AAP has, at least temporarily, filled the void created by the Congress decline. Before 2014, the worst Congress defeat was in 1977 when BLD swept Delhi and the winning margin percent was high in all seven seats. The major problem the Congress faces is not only of leadership but also of the erosion of the party's support base among traditional voters like Dalits and Muslims.

Muslim and Dalit Voters: Game-Changer in 2014 Election

The heavy turnout in Muslim-dominated areas of the capital in many ways became a game-changer for the three main parties in the capital. Disenchantment with the Congress led to straight fights between the BJP and the AAP. While the BJP pointed to the record turnout as "evidence of the Modi wave," AAP volunteers said they were encouraged by the "heavy turnout" in Muslim-majority areas of the city, especially in Central and South Delhi.[36] Muslims overwhelmingly cast their ballots against the BJP but their votes became divided between the AAP and the Congress. Muslims saw the AAP as better placed to counter the BJP, but conflicting loyalties prevented a clear consolidation. While election appeals of religious figures like Shahi Imam and Ahmed Bukhari have limited impact, they added to the high decibel competition for Muslim votes, and created some confusion. Muslims in the capital had voted for Congress for decades, but this time there was a clear split. The so-called 'en bloc' voting did not take place. The AAP's effort to reach out to Muslims was too little and too late. AAP touched upon community-specific issues like fast-tracking of cases of the riots-affected and speedy trails for those languishing in jails in terror-related cases, as well as the need for proper compensation if acquitted, but couldn't convince enough voters.

CSDS NES data clearly shows that in states where the Congress was in direct competition with the BJP, it got nearly three-fourths of the Muslim vote overall. On the other hand, in states in which there was a presence of strong regional parties (Uttar Pradesh, Bihar, Andhra Pradesh, Tamil Nadu, Orissa, West Bengal, Delhi, and Assam), the overall Muslim support for the Congress dropped to about one-third, as the community also voted for the non-Congress options. The BJP too saw its vote share among Muslims rise to about 8 percent at the national level compared to the 4 percent it had five years ago. While this undeniably indicates greater support for the BJP among Muslims, the increase in Hindu support, from 22 percent in 2009 to 36 percent in 2014 was proportionately much greater. Even as Muslims rallied behind non-BJP options, a counter-Hindu upper caste and OBC (Other Backward Castes) consolidation was much greater in magnitude.

Like India, Delhi too saw a shift among Dalit voters largely due to two reasons. First, pre-election alliances played an important role that include BJP's alliance with Dalit leaders like Ram Vilas Paswan's Lok Janshakti Party in Bihar, Ramdas Athavale's Republican Party of India (Athavale) in Maharashtra, and inducted Udit Raj in Delhi. Second, as evident from the CSDS NES survey data, Modi's popularity cuts across caste lines. The BJP's gain among Dalit voters came at the expense of the Congress and the BSP. AAP became the principal beneficiary of the losses incurred by the Congress and the BSP among Dalit voters in Delhi and Punjab. In this election, the AAP's core support base includes the Dalits as AAP polled 38 percent among Dalits and 63 percent among Balmikis. But it failed to attract many votes from the upper castes, middle class, and OBC.

In the CSDS post-poll survey, the BJP enjoys overwhelming support (61 percent) among the upper-caste voters. The rest was divided between the AAP (20 percent), the Congress (11 percent), and others. In addition to this, the Muslim vote share was split almost in equal proportion between the Congress and the AAP, which worked in favor of the BJP candidates this time in North Delhi, Chandni Chowk, North East, and East Delhi. In South, West, and Northwest Delhi, the winning combination for the BJP was the middle class, OBC, and the Sikhs. Jats, Gujjars, and the other OBC voters, mainly residing in outer Delhi, and influenced by politics in the neighboring States, gravitated toward the BJP. Despite the AAP's promise to probe the 1984 Sikh riots, it could not win the support of Sikh voters. In contrast, the BJP received an overwhelming support (68 percent) from the Sikh community.

To conclude, Delhi's clean sweep by the BJP along with other states indicates a northwest BJP wind. Some political commentators observe that the BJP's win in 2014 is the return of a one-party system. However, looking at Delhi's electoral past, it is too early to arrive at such a conclusion. Moreover, the BJP is still not in power in many states that are either governed by the Congress or by regional parties. Post general election, by-elections raise questions about the BJP's continuing popularity. Even in Delhi, it is unclear that people will vote again on a national election pattern. The AAP may be making inroads and consolidating its support base through efforts such as decentralized budgeting in MLAs' constituencies. Economic recovery is necessary to build India as a major power, but at the same time, it may be insufficient to strengthen its democracy without ensuring proper social justice, entitlement of rights, and redistribution of socioeconomic goods. Delhi's discerning electorates know how to use their voting power to achieve these goals. Therefore, deepening of democracy is only possible when "elections can not only determine who is in power but also determine how power is used."[37]

Notes and References

1. *Hindu*, May 17, 2014.
2. *India Today*, May 26, 2014, p. 16.
3. A crore is 10 million, a lakh is 100,000.
4. Report of Association for Democratic Reforms, Centre for Media Studies and National Election Watch, New Delhi, 2014.
5. For details, see Mukulika Banerjee, *Why India Votes?* (New Delhi: Routledge, 2014), p. 2.
6. "History of Delhi Legislative Assembly," http://delhiassembly.nic.in/history_assembly.htm (accessed on May 25, 2014).
7. *Economic Survey of Delhi 2012–2013* (New Delhi: Planning Department, Government of Delhi), Chapter 2.
8. Census of India, http://censusindia.gov.in/2011-prov results/data_files/india/Final_PPT_2011_chapter3.pdf (accessed on May 27, 2014).
9. http://articles.economictimes.indiatimes.com/2013-09-12/news/42011594_1_capita-income-2-28-lakh-sound-economic-situation (accessed on August 15, 2014).
10. "Brahm Prakash: Delhi's First CM. Ace Parliamentarian," *Hindustan Times*, September 27, 2013.
11. "Delimitation Will Make or Mar," *Times of India*, New Delhi, March 3, 2009.
12. "Election Results 2014: Clean Sweep for BJP in Delhi," *Times of India*, New Delhi edition, May 17, 2014.
13. http://www.thehindu.com/news/cities/Delhi/bjp-sweeps-all-7-seats-in-delhi/article6015679.ece (accessed on May 25, 2014).
14. "The Winner Is All Smile," *Hindu*, May 17, 2014.
15. "AAP Releases Manifesto for North East Delhi Constituency," http://indianexpress.com/article/cities/delhi/aap-releases-manifesto-for-north-east-delhi-constituency/99/ (accessed on April 10, 2014).
16. "Bhojpuri Star Shines in North-East Delhi," *Hindu*, May 17, 2014.
17. "How Rajesh Khanna Almost Ended Advani's Career in 1991," *Times of India*, July 19, 2012.
18. "Lekhi Writes a New Chapter," *Hindu*, May 17, 2014.
19. "Congress' Two-Time Sitting MP Krishna Tirath Settles for Third Spot," *Hindu*, May 17, 2014.
20. "Pravesh Verma Conquers West Delhi by Record Margin," *Hindu*, May 17, 2014.
21. "West Delhi Confused: Will the Real Jarnail Singh Stand Up?" http://indianexpress.com/article/cities/delhi/west-delhi-confused-will-the-real-jarnail-singh-stand-up/ (accessed on June 25, 2014).

22. "Will Expedite Probe into Anti-Sikh Riots, Says Pravesh," http://indianexpress.com/article/cities/delhi/will-expedite-probe-into-anti-sikh-riots-says-pravesh/ (accessed on June 25, 2014).

23. http://indianexpress.com/article/india/politics/candidates-of-south-delhi-keep-busy-with-poll-prep-cadre-interactions/ (accessed on May 10, 2014).

24. "Nearly 50% of Votes Polled Here Went to Bidhuri," *Hindu*, May 17, 2014.

25. "Civic Issues Will Decide Vote Pattern in Delhi," *Hindu*, April 9, 2014.

26. "Does Corruption Influence Voter Choice?," *Hindu*, May 28, 2014.

27. http://in.reuters.com/article/2014/07/08/india-rape-crime-stats-idINK-BN0FD0DF20140708 (accessed on July 2014).

28. "Delhi's Lone Woman MP Lekhi Got Less Votes than AAP's Birla," *New Indian Express*, http://m.newindianexpress.com/nation/310624 (accessed on June 25, 2014).

29. "Five Out of 7 BJP Candidates in Delhi Facing Criminal Charges," *Hindustan Times*, April 2, 2014.

30. Edward S. Herman and Noam Chomsky, *Manufacturing Consent: The Political Economy of the Mass Media* (New York: Pantheon, 2002), pp. 306–07.

31. "Crossing the Line," *Indian Express*, March 31, 2014.

32. "BJP Gains '29 Assembly Seats', Wrests 24 from AAP," http://indianexpress.com/article/india/politics/bjp-gains-29-Assembly-seats-wrests-24-from-aap/ (accessed on June 25, 2014).

33. "AAP Took Its Home Turf for Granted, Say Partymen," *Hindu*, May 19, 2014.

34. K.C. Suri, "AAP: A Fledgling Party in Indian Politics," *Hindu*, National Election Survey, May 28, 2014.

35. "Congress Despairs over Delhi Loss," http://www.newindianexpress.com/elections/news/Congress-Despairs-Over-Delhi-Loss/2014/05/18/article2231682.ece (accessed on May 22, 2014).

36. "BJP Rides Modi Wave, AAP Heavy Muslim Turnout," http://indianexpress.com/article/cities/delhi/bjp-rides-modi-wave-aap-heavy-muslim-turnout/99/ (accessed on April 15, 2014).

37. For details, see Paul Collier, *The Bottom Billion: Why the Poorest Countries Are Failing and What Can Be Done About It* (Delhi: Oxford University Press, 2008).

9

Decoding the Electoral Verdict in Punjab: The Future of Regional Parties?

Pramod Kumar

Elections are about winning and for some to make others lose. Elections in India are shorn of competitive ideological persuasions. For one set of political leadership, the language of power became legalistic, procedural, and threatening, while for the new breed of agitators or dissenters-turned politicians, it is theatrical, surgical, musical, and puritanical (with numerous entertainers, professionals and others taking the plunge), and, of course, divorced from ideological positioning. Another distinct articulation presented the face of politics that was decisive, concerned, and connected with a promise to perform in the realm of governance and development in the generic sense. These tendencies emanate from a common contextual structural base.

This invites attention to uncover a combination of factors to understand the 2014 elections through exceptions like Punjab. In Punjab, the persistence of anti-incumbencies of both the Congress-led UPA in the Center and the SAD–BJP coalition in the state neutralized the

'Modi Magic'. This election has also shown that voters' behavior is not guided by a wave, but a measured response to the available electoral choices. For instance, in Punjab, in two constituencies where choices were available from within the mainstream political parties, voters did not park their votes with the new political rookie party—the AAP. But where such choices were not available, they voted for the AAP, even though its candidates were political novices. Is this voting behavior in dissonance with the historical trends in a predominantly agrarian society like Punjab? Furthermore, this chapter also attempts to examine the validity of the hypothesis that 'Modi's phenomenon' has been largely shaped by semi-urban and urban aspiring classes and has to be understood through urban prisms. An inferential analysis may conclude that since Punjab is predominantly an agrarian society, therefore, it remained insulated from 'Modi's urban-centric' political discourse. Such a conclusion would lead to an empiricist trap. This chapter attempts to decode the electoral verdict in Punjab and shows that a form-centric reductionist analysis may help to describe a phenomenon, but it amounts to undermining the historical analytical approach to capture the long-term trends.

It may not be, therefore, correct to focus on these apparent changes or discontinuities as these are form-centric. Forms are descriptive categories—static in nature, reductionist in interpretation, and problem-centric in its approach. While acknowledging the discontinuities, it would be pertinent to analyze emerging politics in terms of system continuities that remain central and determining factors.

In this chapter, an attempt has been made to answer some of the questions as follows. Why the BJP along with its ally, the SAD, could not maintain its electoral position in Punjab? How did the AAP win only in Punjab? How come the so-called 'right wing shift relating to role of state' in the right-wing-ruled state of Punjab could not garner more votes for the BJP–Modi-led coalition? Why Narendra Modi's charisma as a leader could not win votes even for a stalwart like Arun Jaitley with an unblemished image in Punjab?

Let me preface focusing on these questions with four contextual postulates. These postulates define continuity and boundaries for electoral discourse in the country.

Consensus on Structural Issues: Harnessing Continuities

Given the consensus amongst the political parties on a neo-liberal path of development and in the absence of any alternate vision, electoral discourse conveniently located crony capitalism, unemployment, poverty, and inequalities in policy paralysis.

Overtly, the content of politics of consensus on economic reforms is to (i) reduce employment in the public sector and allow market forces to generate or curtail employment in the private sector, (ii) encourage people to participate in self-help groups and launch small businesses in the face of intense competition, (iii) tell people to mind their own health and give subsidies to private hospitals, and (iv) teach them to pay for life-saving services even if they do not have the opportunities to earn a livelihood. This contributed to a tension between the path of development and redistribution of income and citizens' capacity to access various resources.

Also, in Punjab there is a near consensus on neo-liberal economic reforms among all the major political parties. All the political parties are in favor of FDI. But the SAD and BJP qualified it with a rider that they are in opposition to FDI in retail. The Congress has decided to support the FDI in multibrand retail 'to transform agrarian economy and ensure better returns for farmers'.[1]

Notwithstanding the political rhetoric, it is worth noting that the process has already begun. FDI in the wholesale sector has already been allowed in Punjab. Walmart has opened 14 wholesale stores in four states in collaboration with Bharti Retail; the company also supplies backend assistance to Bharti Retail's 150-plus supermarkets and compact hypermarkets in nine states. Out of these 14 stores, one-third is in Punjab. Another global retailer, Metro Cash and Carry, has started the process of launching 15 outlets in India, of which six are in Punjab. These stores are functional in Ludhiana and Jalandhar, and are under construction in Bathinda, Patiala, Zirakpur, and Amritsar. These stores make their products available to local retailers and also procure produce from local farmers. The process of intermediation has now begun. According to an informal survey, 70 percent of customers in Zirakpur Bharti–Walmart are retailers. In electoral discourse, these issues have not been debated.[2] Is there a blueprint to make retailers, farmers and small manufacturers and small industrialists competitive? Are there the long- and short-term plans to make farmers produce globally competitive through new technologies and research innovations that enhance competitiveness?

No doubt, there is a consensus on the neo-liberal path, of course, with minor differences, but at the same time, political parties are proactive in moderating the callousness of the market and providing much needed legitimacy to the political system.

Politics of Moderation of Exclusion: Right-based Politics Laced with Doles

Politics is seen as a means to resolve the tension between the opposing claims of market, efficiency, and economic growth as against those of social equity and justice. It has guaranteed various rights to meet the challenges and experiences of exclusion. On the one hand, accumulation by dispossession and encroachments rather than through transparent institutional mechanisms has been practiced. "The state continued to work for speculators and rentiers in a highly unequal milieu. It took upon itself to encourage FDI, introduces user fees, withdraw subsidies, encourage privatization in social development."[3] The main feature of this has been values of the indiscriminate acquisition of material assets and overconsumption. Simultaneously, it has introduced a right-based regime providing transparency and deliverables, but not accountability.

A number of legislations ranging from Right to Information, Right to Employment (MNREGA) to Right to Food were passed. It has also introduced the Right to Fair Compensation and Transparency in Land Acquisition, Rehabilitation and Resettlement. This proposed Act clearly demonstrates the attempts to moderate the tension between opposing claims of market and social equity. To illustrate, the new proposed Act on land acquisition focused on pricing, compensation, resettlement, and rehabilitation. This is a shift from an earlier Act in which the main thrust was on the redistribution of land rather than on 'fair compensation'. It will replace the Land Acquisition Act of 1894.[4] The political parties promised to extend this right-based regime to other spheres of governance also. The

Congress Party in its manifesto promised the Right to Health and Right to Home to create an environment conducive to capital accumulation and to acquire legitimacy for politics.[5]

For instance, in Punjab, to moderate the impact of privatization and public sector, disinvestment parties continue to be in favor of power subsidies to the farmers. This was an outcome of the lesson learned by the Congress Party in the 2004 Parliamentary elections. After returning to power in the 2002 state elections, the Congress initiated the reduction of power subsidy to farmers, expenditure in government, and disinvestment of the public sector. As a consequence, it lost 53 percent of the seats in the 2004 Parliamentary elections as compared to the 2002 Assembly elections. Similarly, the SAD–BJP alliance that took an initiative to rationalize power subsidies to farmers by introducing a productive bonus suffered a setback in the 2009 Parliamentary elections.[6]

The Congress and the Akali Dal promised not only free electricity and water, but also sops ranging from free laptops, allowances for unemployed youth, and cable connection for ₹100 to *atta–dal* (food grains) at the subsidized rate. And all these were neatly packaged in market-driven governance in which subsidies were given and people were exhorted to pay user charges.

(De)constructing Vote Banks: Blurring Structural Inequalities

Along with the moderation of politics, electoral discourses tend to present voters as population and (de)construct them in electoral discourse as homogeneous groups and collectivities locating 'Hindu civilizational symbolism' in ethnic particularism and linking these with universal categories like citizens. The manner in which the process of globalization has claimed to be undifferentiated, similarly in elections politics, is being presented as universal. It attempts to blur the distinction between the Center and periphery and the hierarchical system of power, exchange, and benefits. In a way, it is blurring of structural inequalities at the manifest level. For instance, 'development for all, along with all' and Punjabi, Punjabiat, and Punjabi identity slogans claim to be universal, more pure, and unadulterated underplaying structural inequalities located in caste, religion, gender, and ethnicity. In other words, from a conglomeration of identities to catch-all categories to maximize votes.[7]

This kind of electoral discourse has not only taken away politics from people, but also blurred their structural position for them. And the use of symbols including Ganges (river), Geeta (Scripture), and Navratras (ritual), as well as national icons, such as Madan Mohan Malviya, Deen Dayal Upadhyay, Sardar Vallabh Bhai Patel, have been appropriated to provide content to 'Hindu' and Indian nationalism.

The Modi-led BJP campaign selectively appropriated symbols and icons from Indian history and invoked ideology to make these sound inclusive. Martyrdom and national pride were evoked against "an untrustworthy 'Delhi Empire' that tolerated gruesome acts against Indian soldiers by Pakistan."[8] A rally was addressed with two minutes of silence for martyred soldiers in Tamil Nadu. Collectivities were identified for appreciation, "Biharis are hardworking and very inspirational";[9] "Tamilians are sincere and above all, they are royal and loyal people! For Tamil people, workplace is worship place."[10] Rousing of cultural idioms and regional symbols of pride and group values were activised to seek the reinforcement of the slogan 'Welfare of all'. The national icons were located in diverse regions in the country to establish their link with Indian culture. Whether it was farmers in anguish over their grain rotting, while citizens starved or the Tamilian to whom work is worship. If Gandhiji is from Gujarat, his conscious keeper Rajaji is from Tamil Nadu.[11]

The symbols so selected interlocked the religions with the cultural terrain. For instance, 'Muslim' symbols were linked with national pride and 'Hindu' symbols treated as synonymous with Indian civilization. The Taj Mahal as a tourist destination was projected as an 'Indian Brand' icon.[12] Colonel Nizamuddin was acknowledged with reverence in his capacity as a colleague of Subhash Chandra Bose.[13] Sufi poets such as Azan Fakir in Assam were acknowledged as legends.[14] In contrast, certain values were labeled as 'Hindu' values and were located in Indian culture.

Haryana is the land of Kurukshetra, and Lord Krishna provides the message of Geeta to the world.[15] Assam is the land of Maa Kamakhya, and Jammu crowds into the rally attributed to Maa Vaishno Devi blessings.[16] Respects are paid to the Goddess of Basta Aradhya Devi and Mata Dhantswar in Chhattisgarh.[17] Bengal is renowned for Durga Puja,

Rosgulla, and drum beats (*dhaak*), and songs (*saankh*) as an integral part of Durga Puja.[18] Gujarat became the 'land of Somnatha', while Bihar's historic and glorious role was hailed during the Ramayana, Mahabharta, Buddhist, and Mauryan era, and during the British period.[19] Uttar Pradesh as the land of *Ram Rajya* was evoked with the strength, traditions, and cultural heritage. "People of this land, your own ancestors realized the idea of Ram Rajya."[20]

Furthermore, 'Hindu' symbols were identified with purity. "Uttar Pradesh the holy land of mother Ganga."[21] It was not the cleanliness of Ganges that was promised, but its 'purification'. Similarly, the Yamuna river was not to provide safe drinking water, the development terminology, but 'pure water'.[22] Funds sanctioned for cleaning Ganges were accused of being flushed down the river Ganges. Corruption and non-performance were linked to the vilification of 'Hindu' symbols "who have sinned even in the holy name of Ganges." The people who cannot take care of Ganges, how will they take care of the nation?[23]

And above all, Modi and Gujarat were presented as synonymous with religious, traditional connections drawn to rally locations. Yadavs in Bihar were reminded that the king of Yadavs, Lord Krishna, resided in Dwarka, Gujarat, the home of Modi.[24] Speaking at a rally in Muzaffarpur in Bihar on March 3, 2014, Narendra Modi emphasized his own lower caste origins, and said: "The next decade will belong to the Dalits and the backwards." In South India, inaugurating the centenary meet organized by the Kerala Pulayar Mahasabha in Kochi, Modi said that the saints and social reformers in the past century had belonged to either the Dalit or backward sections of the society. He wondered why a memorial honoring the contribution of Ayyankali was not built in Kerala.[25] No doubt, he identified himself humbly as a small man, but from the land of Mahatma Gandhi and Sardar Patel.

Historically, a number of leaders and political parties used religious and national symbols and spaces. They argued that the bifurcation of politics among Muslims, Sikhs, and Hindus shall help to represent the secular interests of religious groups in politics. This is nothing but communalism.

The protagonists of the BJP–Modi (Hindu) civilizational approach argue that labeling this type of politics as religious or communal is wrong. The correct approach is to find out whether this politics has a vision, a clearly defined ideology, and an alternate political mode of reaching out to people. This politics has brought a shift in BJP's pronouncements from communal to 'Hindu civilizational'. It has put all issues such as Article 370, Ram Mandir, Ram Setu, religious conversions, and population stabilization into the back burner.

However, the question remains: Under what conditions and political contexts this nuanced use of 'Hindu civilizational' symbolisms will degenerate into a 'clash of civilizations'? Is it not a fact that the blurring effect of this cocktail of symbolisms saps the will of the people to transform the system; in other words, the civilizational reservoir is being used to make individuals more humane, moral, and honest without addressing the basis of their miseries. Commercial interests would be the main beneficiaries of this morality of austerity, thrift, and healthy life for the poor, as it would facilitate them to multiply and accumulate wealth.

These articulations blur the multicultural dimensions of Indian society and politics. For example, in Punjab, all the political parties vacillated between religious identity to Punjabiat as per the electoral and political needs. Consequently, religious, linguistic, and regional factors became so mixed up that none of these emerged as a single factor in electoral mobilization. And it has weakened the struggle for people's survival. Punjab has the highest percentage of Dalits in the country, and poverty among them is more than double as compared to non-Dalits. In addition, there is no engagement of Dalits to bring about transformation in their social conditions and build their capacities to have access to resources. One of the reasons is that contemporary politics is reproducing itself within a broad range of bounded and unbounded seriality, Center with periphery or without and historical (in terms of symbolism) and ahistorical (in ideological persuasions). This brings us to another level, that is, how this cocktail of symbolisms facilitates a catch-all approach?

Convergence of 'Deficient' Citizens with Electoral Democracy

Having blurred structural inequalities, commonalities of experience of the (deficient) citizen interaction with the state are captured for providing access to the so-called good governance.

There are certain commonalities of experience of the citizen inter-action with the state between various segments of society. The claims to identity, dignity, productivity, and democratic engagement with the institutions have also become the part of electoral discourse not only at the national level, but in Punjab as well. Nonrealization of these claims for a large section of the population results into an experience of exclusion in their interaction with the state. It is this dimension of 'deficient citizenship' that is appropriated in electoral discourse, that is, fight against corruption, governance reforms, simplification of procedures, etc. Because it is a common deficient experience and, therefore, becomes consistent with the 'welfare of all' thrust of electoral mobilizations, it is this experience of exclusion that has been made central to political discourse and not the exclusion of marginalized sections from market and the dominant politics.

Connects and Disconnects in Post-1997 Phase

These contextual postulates in the interaction with three axes related to identity politics have produced distinct results in 2014 elections. The three axes in Punjab are 'dwarfed' identity assertions, majoritarian assertion, and minority aspiration, and intermeshed caste and class social categories. The perusal of history shows that in Punjab, the religious, communal, and secular articulations have all remained deficient. Both Hindus and Sikhs suffered from a majority–minority persecution complex.[26,27] A large section of Hindus suffered from a majority–minority complex as they perceived themselves to be a majority in India and a minority in reorganized Punjab. Similarly, Sikhs are in a majority in the state and in a minority in India; thus, they also suffer from a minority–majority complex.

At the political level, Sikhs as a minority find expression in anti-centrism and demand for strengthening of federal polity, while urban Hindus look toward the Center for protection for their perceived insecurities. In the socio-political domain, the caste and class are intermeshed, and religion as a category in political discourse remains dominant. These characteristic features in their interaction with the catch-all politics produced electoral volatility. This process is an outcome of 10 years of turmoil in Punjab. Emerging out of terrorism, the democratic resurgence in Punjab proved to be a panacea and was impregnated with lessons for political parties. Put simply, it took Punjab out of the 'teach a lesson approach' to learn lessons for strengthening democracy. It was widely believed that this was the only insurance against the reemergence of terrorism.

Having learnt lessons from the 10 years of turmoil in the state, political parties shifted their agenda—in the religio-cultural domain—from a competitive religious identity to a composite Punjabi identity, and in the political sphere from intermeshed religious demographic categories (i.e., urban Hindu traders seen as BJP's support base and the rural Jat peasants as SAD's support base) to citizens unbounded by religion, caste, and demographic location. In 2014 elections, this discourse found articulation in the Modi-led BJP campaign. The traditional categories having been blurred, the citizen as a voter became unbound and footloose. The major parties, that is, the Congress and the Akali increased their vote share in other parties' strongholds.

Post 1997, people's agenda for peace over that of political parties' sectional interests characterized this phase.[28] There was also a shift from the politico-religious identity confined to the Sikh identity to the agenda of Punjabiat with the adoption of Moga Declaration 1995. To quote, "The spirit of Punjabiat would be strengthened so that these matters get projected as common problems of the entire Punjabis rather than a section thereof."[29] Political parties that had been historically articulating the language question on communal lines also shifted their stance. For instance, the Akali Dal and BJP in their Common Minimum Programme (1997) asserted, "Punjabi being our mother tongue is the state language of Punjab. Every Punjabi is proud of the richness of the Punjabi language and culture."[30] In addition, the Akali Dal in its policy program, adopted on April 14, 1995, emphasized disputes over the apportionment of river waters, allocation of Punjabi-speaking territories as a discrimination against Punjab rather than the Sikhs (as it used to be in pre-1992 resolutions), and linking the prices of agricultural products with the price index.[31]

Another shift has been on issues related to greater autonomy for states. The BJP changed its stance from a strong Center to a greater autonomy for states, and the SAD changed its position from anti-centrism to cooperative federalism. BJP's 1997 election manifesto reinforced this shift. To quote,

> We [BJP] shall pursue with the centre for the implementation of the main recommendations of the Sarkaria Commission, to restore the balance of resources in favour of the states, for ending the misuse of Article 356 of the Indian Constitution, and consulting states on the choice of governors.[32,33]

All these issues were incorporated in the Common Minimum Programme of 1997 evolved by the Akali Dal–BJP alliance with the thrust of the Akali Dal agenda changed from anti-centrism to cooperative federalism.[34,35]

This shift in agenda converged with people's quest for peace and survival and paid dividend to its main proponents, the SAD and the BJP. In 1997, it elected them to power in the state legislature. In the 1998 Parliamentary elections, the SAD won the largest number of seats, that is, 8 and polled 33 percent of the votes. The BJP won three seats and polled 12 percent of the votes (see Table 9.1).

The Congress, BSP, and Communists entered into a pre-election alliance and could not win even a single seat. The Akali Dal–BJP alliance performed better because it provided the Akali Dal with the much needed political space at the national level to shed its antinational image, and to the BJP it gave a political plank to counter the Congress and the Left propaganda that its politics is anti-minorities. But its performance in state politics remained dismal as it failed to provide corruption and harassment-free governance.

As a consequence, in the 1999 Lok Sabha elections, the pre-election alliance of the SAD–BJP failed miserably with the Congress–CPI alliance winning nine seats with a 42.18 percent vote share. This election witnessed the BSP and the Akali Dal (Tohra) in the role of spoilers. The SAD (B) secured 28.5 percent of the votes. The Akali Dal (Tohra) acted as a spoiler for the SAD (B) with around 4.6 percent votes and the BSP acted as a spoiler against the Congress in nearly 27 assembly segments in the 1999 Lok Sabha elections. This was followed by the Congress victory in the 2002 Assembly elections, winning 62 seats with 36 percent vote share (see Table 9.1).

The BJP and the Akali Dal after winning the 1997 elections on Punjabiat as reflected in the Moga Declaration of 1995 subsequently started

Table 9.1

Punjab Elections 1992–2014

		Parliament				Assembly		
Year	Party	Contested	Won	Vote %	Party	Contested	Won	Vote %
1992	BJP	9	0	16.51	BJP	66	6	16.48
	SAD	3	0	2.58	SAD	58	3	5.2
	CPI	1	0	1.57	CPI	20	4	3.64
	CPM	3	0	3.98	CPM	17	1	2.4
	INC	13	12	49.27	INC	116	87	43.83
	BSP	12	1	19.71	BSP	105	9	16.32
	JD	4	0	1.3	JD	37	1	2.15
	JP	1	0	0.93	Others	9	2	0.74
	Others	3	0	0.13	IND	151	4	9.24
	IND	32	0	4.01				
1996	BJP	6	0	6.48				
	SAD(M)	7	0	3.85				
	SAD	9	8	28.72				
	BSP	4	3	9.35				
	CPI	3	0	1.6				
	CPM	3	0	2.68				
	INC	13	2	35.1				
	JD	1	0	2.66				
	JP	1	0	0.03				
	Others	31	0	2.01				
	IND	181	0	7.51				
1997					BJP	22	18	8.33
					SAD	92	75	37.64
					CPM	25	0	1.79
					CPI	15	2	2.98
					INC	105	14	26.59
					BSP	67	1	7.48

(Table 9.1 Continued)

(Table 9.1 Continued)

	Parliament				Assembly		
Year	*Party*	*Contested*	*Won*	*Vote %*	*Party*	*Contested*	*Won*	*Vote %*
					JD	27	0	0.56
					JP	1	0	0.01
					SAD(M)	30	1	3.1
					Others	65	0	0.65
					IND	244	6	10.87
1998	BJP	3	3	11.67				
	SAD	8	8	32.93				
	JD	1	1	4.18				
	CPI	1		3.4				
	CPM	3		1.06				
	INC	8		25.85				
	BSP	4		12.65				
	SAD(M)	4		2.73				
	Others	21	0	0.64				
	IND	49	1	4.91				
1999	BJP	3	1	9.16				
	SAD	9	2	28.59				
	DBSM	1		2.71				
	SAD(M)	1	1	3.41				
	CPI	1	1	3.74				
	CPM	1		2.18				
	INC	11	8	38.44				
	BSP	3		3.84				
	JD(S)	2		0.03				
	JD(U)	2		0.1				
	Others	29	0	5.34				
	IND	57		2.45				

(Table 9.1 Continued)

(Table 9.1 Continued)

Year	Party	Parliament			Party	Assembly		
		Contested	Won	Vote %		Contested	Won	Vote %
					BJP	23	3	5.67
					SAD	92	41	31.08
					DBSM	2	0	0.33
					SAD(M)	84	0	4.65
					CPM	13	0	0.36
2002					CPI	11	2	2.15
					INC	105	62	35.81
					BSP	100	0	5.69
					JD(S)	4	0	0.03
					JD(U)	2	0	0.01
					Others	213	0	2.94
					IND	274	9	11.27
	BJP	3	3	10.48				
	SAD	10	8	34.28				
	SAD(M)	6	0	3.79				
	CPI	1	0	2.55				
2004	CPM	1	0	1.81				
	INC	11	2	34.17				
	BSP	13	0	7.67				
	JD(S)	1	0	0.01				
	Others	26	0	2.5				
	IND	70	0	2.75				
					BJP	23	19	8.21
					SAD	94	49	37.19
					CPI	25	0	0.75
2007					CPM	14	0	0.28
					BSP	116	0	4.1
					INC	117	44	40.94
					SAD(M)	37	0	0.51

(Table 9.1 Continued)

(Table 9.1 Continued)

Year	Party	Parliament			Party	Assembly		
		Contested	Won	Vote %		Contested	Won	Vote %
					Others	191	0	1.23
					IND	438	5	6.79
	BJP	3	1	10.06				
	SAD	10	4	33.85				
	SAD(M)	3	0	0.36				
	CPI	2	0	0.33				
2009	CPM	1	0	0.14				
	INC	13	8	45.23				
	BSP	13	0	5.75				
	Others	59	0	1.94				
	IND	114	0	2.33				
					BJP	23	12	7.18
					SAD	94	56	34.73
					CPI	14		0.82
2012					CPM	9		0.16
					BSP	117		4.29
					INC	117	46	40.09
					PPOP	92		5.16
					Others	612	3	7.56
	BJP	3	2	8.77				
	SAD	10	4	26.37				
	CPI	5	0	0.4				
	CPM	3	0	0.13				
2014	INC	13	3	33.19				
	BSP	13	0	1.91				
	AAP	13	4	24.47				
	Others	75	0	1.15				
	IND	118	0	3.61				

Source: Election Commission of India Reports 1992–2014.

operating in the Sikh religious domain. This was mainly due to the competition for 'Sikh Jat votes' between the two Akali Dal factions. The outcome of this approach led to the alienation of a large section of urban Hindus, the moderate Sikhs, and the Dalits, whereas the vote share of the Congress Party in the 2002 elections in semi-urban constituencies increased from 26 percent to 35 percent and in the urban constituencies from 31 percent to 46 percent as compared to the 1997 Assembly elections (see Table 9.2).

But after winning the 2002 elections, the Congress Party led by Captain Amarinder Singh, a former Akali, focused more on the rural Jat peasantry and the Sikh identity by repealing the Punjab agreement on sharing of river waters and overactive participation in religious celebrations of the Sikh and Shiromani Gurdwara Prabandhak Committee (SGPC) elections. The purpose of these mobilizations was to weaken S. Prakash Singh Badal's hold over the rural Jat Sikh vote bank. Much needed urban renewal was neglected, and urban Hindus being minority in the state could not find articulation in the state policy and an adequate representation in the decision-making institutions. Consequently, the vote share from largely Hindu voters in the 2004 Parliamentary elections in semi-urban constituencies decreased from 40 percent to 35 percent and in urban constituencies from 54 percent to 48 percent as compared to the 1999 Parliamentary elections (see Table 9.3).

Having learnt their lessons, the SAD–BJP alliance promised to shift the development visibly from a *Panthic* (religious) to a *non-Panthic* (nonreligious) agenda in their election manifesto and public pronouncements. The alliance won the 2007 Assembly elections and formed the government.

The Congress did not learn anything from the Akali Dal–BJP alliance in 2002 and its own defeat in the 2004 Parliamentary elections. It continued to cater to identity-based sectional interests to make inroads into the Akali bastion, but suffered a major loss within its own support base of Dalits, urban traders, slum dwellers, etc. The Congress suffered a defeat in the semi-urban areas and was routed in the urban constituencies. To illustrate, the SAD elected only 25 Sikh Jats in 2007 as compared to 41 in the 1997 elections. In 2007, the Congress elected almost an equal number of Sikh Jats as compared to the SAD. It is clear that Sikh Jats are not exclusive supporters of the SAD. This shift is especially significant in the post-Blue Star phase. On the contrary, the number of Dalit Members of

Table 9.2

Punjab Assembly Elections Party Results 1997–2012: Votes Polled and Number of Constituencies Contested and Won

	Location	BJS/BJP	CPI	CPM	PPOP	INC	SAD/ADS	ADM	JP/JD	BSP	Others	Total
1997	Rural											
	Won	4	2	0		7	53		0	1	3	70
	Contested constituencies	6	9	17		62	62		10	41	155	362
	Poll %	3.65	3.13	2.09		26.34	42.87		0.28	8.27	13.37	100
	Semi urban											
	Won	9	0	0		4	19		0	0	3	35
	Contested constituencies	9	5	8		32	26		10	18	112	220
	Poll %	12.25	2.69	1.71		25.77	33.44		1.02	6.48	16.64	100
	Urban											
	Won	5	0	0		3	3		0	0	1	12
	Contested constituencies	7	1	0		11	4		8	8	72	111
	Poll %	26.81	3.01	0.00		31.44	16.30		0.86	5.55	16.02	100
2002	Rural											
	Won	1	1	0		32	32			0	4	70
	Contested constituencies	6	8	11		61	62			61	298	507
	Poll %	2.76	2.22	0.45		34.63	35.99			6.26	17.69	100

(Table 9.2 Continued)

(Table 9.2 Continued)

	Location	BJS/BJP	CPI	CPM	PPOP	INC	SAD/ADS	ADM	JP/JD	BSP	Others	Total
Semi urban	Won	2	1	0		19	9			0	4	35
	Contested constituencies	9	2	2		33	26			29	210	311
	Poll %	8.16	1.86	0.27		35.46	27.16			4.65	22.45	100
Urban	Won	0	0	0		11	0			0	1	12
	Contested constituencies	8	1	0		11	4			10	71	105
	Poll %	18.41	2.75	0.00		46.51	8.57			5.52	18.25	100
Rural	Won	5				25	35				5	70
	Contested constituencies	6	15	8		70	64			69	336	568
	Poll %	3.74	0.69	0.31		39.99	41.99			4.54	8.74	100.00
2007	Won	7	9	5		17	11			0		35
Semi urban	Contested constituencies	9	9	5		35	26			35	235	354
	Poll %	10.98	0.77	0.27		42.85	33.38			3.67	8.08	100.00
Urban	Won	7				2	3			0	0	12

	1	2	3	4	5	6	7	8	Total
	Contested constituencies	8	1	1	12	4	12		95	133
	Poll %	29.94	1.09	0.07	40.29	17.14	2.64		8.83	100.00
	Won	3			19	38			1	61
Rural	Contested constituencies	5	6	6	61	56	61	47	266	508
	Poll %	3.38	0.61	0.21	39.40	41.14	4.57	4.77	5.92	100.00
	Won	4			2	34			1	41
2012 Semi urban	Contested constituencies	8			41		41		251	415
	Poll %	6.47	0.09	6.88	40.08	31.83	4.25	1.00	9.40	100.00
	Won	3			6				1	15
Urban	Contested constituencies	10			15		15		95	155
	Poll %	27.93	1.32	0.08	43.45	12.69	3.10	1.66	9.76	100.00

Source: Election Commission of India Reports Punjab, 1997–2012.

Table 9.3

Votes Polled in Parliament Elections: Assembly Segment-wise, Party-wise, and Location-wise (1999–2014)

		AAP	INC	SAD	BJP	CPM	CPI	BSP	SAD(M)	Others	Total Valid Votes
1999	Rural	Vote %		35.73	34.53	3.36	2.79	3.80	4.51		15.27	100.00
		Seats contested		57	58	6	7	6	18		449	601
		Won		34	23			5	1		7	70
2004	Rural	Vote %		31.84	41.18	3.67	2.28	2.59	7.86	4.43	6.16	100.00
		Seats contested		57	64	6	7	6	70	31	507	748
		Won		13	52	4				1	0	70
2009	Rural	Vote %		41.98	43.09	4.08	0.15	0.38	6.11	0.24	3.97	100.00
		Seats contested		61	55	6	4	11	61	12	766	976
		Won		20	39	2					0	61
2014	Rural	Vote %	22.33	32.48	34.87	3.63	0.11	0.39	2.15	0.32	3.72	100.00
		Seats contested	61	61	56	5	8	19	61	44	860	1175
		Won	17	11	28	5					0	61

Year	Category											Total
1999	Semi Urban	Vote %		40.12	29.09	8.15	1.50	4.46	3.44		13.25	100.00
		Seats contested		30	24	8	2	3	9		268	344
		Won		22	6						2	35
2004	Semi Urban	Vote %		35.18	34.11	10.86	1.37	3.12	8.05	3.49	3.82	100.00
		Seats contested		30	26	9	2	3	35	22	247	374
		Won		8	18					1	2	35
2009	Semi Urban	Vote %		46.55	32.25	8.48	0.18	0.34	6.23	0.68	5.29	100.00
		Seats contested		41	32	9	5	6	41	15	536	685
		Won		31	9	1					0	41
2014	Semi Urban	Vote %	29.89	30.67	25.78	7.28	0.18	0.43	1.91	0.24	3.62	100.00
		Seats contested	41	41	33	8	14	20	41	35	523	756
		Won	15	13	9	3					1	41
1999	Urban	Vote %		53.99	15.93	22.81	0.00	0.00	0.00		7.27	100.00
		Seats contested		12	5	7	0	0	0		111	135

(Table 9.3 Continued)

(Table 9.3 Continued)

		AAP	INC	SAD	BJP	CPM	CPI	BSP	SAD(M)	Others	Total Valid Votes
2004	Urban										
	won		10		2					0	12
	Vote %		48.03	14.76	28.49	0.00	0.00	4.72	0.04	3.96	100.00
	Seats contested		12	4	8	0	0	12	1	119	156
	Won		8	1	3					0	12
2009	Urban										
	Vote %		56.93	17.05	20.94	0.00	0.11	2.48	0.00	2.49	100.00
	Seats contested		15	7	8	0	1	15	0	255	301
	Won		14	1						0	15
2014	Urban										
	Vote %	17.94	43.64	8.05	18.60	0.07	0.35	0.86	0.03	273.00	100.00
	Seats contested	15	15	5	10	5	6	15	2	1	74
	Won	1	13							1	15
1999	Total										
	Vote %		38.44	31.46	6.28	2.18	3.74	3.84		14.05	100.00
	Seats contested		99	87	21	9	9	27		828	1,080

											Total
2004	Total	Won		66	29	4	0	8	1		9	117
		Vote %		34.17	36.87	7.89	1.81	2.55	7.67	3.79	5.25	100.00
		Seats contested		99	94	23	9	9	117	54	873	1,278
2009	Total	Won		29	71	13	1	1	1	2	0	117
		Vote %		45.23	36.43	7.48	0.14	0.33	5.75	0.36	4.26	100.00
		Seats contested		117	94	23	9	18	117	27	1,557	1,962
2014	Total	Won		65	49	3			1		0	117
		Vote %	24.46	33.19	28.41	6.73	0.13	0.40	1.91	0.26	4.50	100.00
		Seats contested	117	117	94	23	27	45	117	81	1,656	2,277
		Won		33	37	8					2	117

Source: Election of India Commission Reports Punjab, 1999–2014.

Note: Seats adjusted between BJP and SAD according to their previous assembly seats.

the Legislative Assemblies (MLAs) in the Congress was reduced from 14 in 2002 to 7 in 2007. And the BJP could maintain in 2007 its 1997 tally of four Dalits. The number of Dalit MLAs in the SAD was 16 as compared to 23 in the 1997 elections.[36]

In the 2009 Parliamentary elections, the SAD–BJP alliance performed poorly due to intra-alliance differences over sharing the spoils of power. The SAD won four seats as compared to eight seats in 2004, and the BJP secured one seat as compared to three seats in 2004. However, the SAD could win in 49 assembly segments in the 2009 Parliamentary elections as it did in the 2007 Assembly elections (see Tables 9.1 and 9.3). The BJP attributed their defeat to the indifferent attitude of the SAD leadership toward their urban support base and party activists.

Another major shift in electoral politics took place in giving representation to all the existing fault-lines of religion and caste by the competing political parties. For instance, the SAD, which has been mainly a party of Jat-Sikh peasants, gave representation to Punjabi Hindus with 11 out of 94 SAD candidates for the 2012 Assembly elections. The BJP party that largely represents urban Hindu traders in Punjab politics gave representation to Sikhs. Similarly, the Congress made inroads into the SAD support base of rural Jat Sikhs by fielding an equal number of rural Jat Sikhs with the SAD. Dalits who constitute around 32 percent of the population were represented in all the political formations. Thus, Punjab's electoral politics showed the signs of blurring religious and caste fault-lines.

In the post-terrorism phase, in the 2012 Assembly elections, for the first time in Punjab, the incumbent party was voted back to power. This was mainly because of the promise of development and good governance. However, in the 2014 Parliamentary elections, despite the Modi wave in the North and West India, the BJP–SAD alliance performed miserably in Punjab. The SAD could win four seats with 26 percent votes and the BJP could win only two seats with 9 percent votes. The Congress Party could survive because of strong anti-incumbency faced by the SAD–BJP alliance, winning three seats with 33 percent votes (see Table 9.1). It fielded its top leadership in the electoral contests including the former Chief Minister Captain Amarinder Singh, Punjab State Congress Party President Pratap Bajwa, Leader of Opposition in state legislature Sunil Jakhar, and Central Ministers Ms Ambika Soni and Ms Praneet Kaur.[37] All of them lost the elections except Captain Amarinder Singh. The AAP was a surprise winner with four seats and 24 percent vote share.

Electoral Outcomes: From Bound to Footloose Voters

Historically, in Punjab, political power is altered between the SAD–BJP alliance and the Congress due to the presence of a spoiler to work to the disadvantage of a particular party as per the prevalent political context. But in 2014 parliament elections, the combined vote share of the SAD–BJP alliance and the Congress Party was 68 percent as compared to 89 percent in the 2009 Parliamentary elections. This decline has been reflected in an increase in the number of parties by votes, which, in turn, signifies effective competition for every seat.

Let us briefly summarize the outcomes of the 2014 Parliamentary elections. This election marked the closure of consequences of the deadlier politics of the 1980s and 1990s, a complete reversal of the voters turnout (24 percent) in 1992 elections to 71 percent in 2014 (see Table 9.4).

This election has also shown an increase in urban voter turnout from 63 percent to 67 percent, for semi-urban from 70 percent to 72 percent in the 2009 and 2014 Parliamentary elections, respectively. And there is a decline in the rural vote share from 72 percent in 2009 to 71 percent in 2014 elections (see Table 9.5).

Table 9.4
Voter Turnout in Parliament Elections

Constituencies	1998	1999	2004	2009	2014
Total	60.07	56.11	61.59	70.04	70.89

Source: Election Commission Reports Punjab, 1998–2014.

Table 9.5
Location-wise Voter Turnout

Constituencies	2009	2014
Urban	62.87	67.15
Semi urban	69.61	71.63
Rural	72.02	71.32
Total	70.04	70.89

Source: Election Commission Reports Punjab, 2009 and 2014.

Decline in the Vote Share of Main Political Parties

All the main political parties registered a decline in vote share. As compared to the 2009 Parliamentary elections, the SAD, BJP, and Congress lost 7.4 percent, 1.3 percent, and 12 percent votes, respectively. These parties lost their support base in the urban, semi-urban, and rural constituencies.

The SAD in the rural, semi-urban, and urban constituencies had a reduced vote share of 8.2 percent, 6.5 percent, and 9 percent, respectively, as compared to the 2009 Parliamentary elections. The BJP vote share in the semi-urban and urban constituencies declined by 1 percent and 2.3 percent, respectively (see Tables 9.1 and 9.3). The SAD lead in Scheduled Caste reserved constituencies also decreased from 21 in 2012 to 6 in the 2014 Parliamentary elections.

The Congress like the SAD has a reduced vote share in the rural, semi-urban, and urban constituencies by 9.5 percent, 16 percent, and 13 percent, respectively, as compared to the 2009 elections. The Congress Party decline in the semi-urban segment as compared to the SAD is almost double. The decline in the vote share of the SAD, the BJP, and the Congress is in all regions, locations, and religio-caste groups.

Electorally Volatile Elections

This election was also significant in terms of electoral competition and coalition politics. In 2014, the effective number of parties by votes was 3.76 and the effective number of parties by seats was 4.02, whereas in 2009, the effective number of parties by votes was 2.09 and the effective number of parties by seats was 3.0. This clearly shows that the number of parties by seats that could make a difference increased from 3.0 in the 2009 elections to 4.02 in the 2014 elections[38] (see Table 9.6).

A contrary trend took place at the national level, "the effective number of parties by seats used to be five to six, this time it was 3.45 ... the number of parties that matter in the conduct of the 16th Lok Sabha has declined in this elections."[39]

Table 9.6
Taagepara and Shugart Index for Parliamentary Elections in
Punjab 2004–14

Election Year	Effective Number of Parties by Votes	Effective Number of Parties by Seats
2004	2.19	3.93
2009	2.09	3.00
2014	3.76	4.02

Source: Calculated from Election Commission of India Reports Punjab, 2004,
2009, and 2014.

However, there has been a significant shift in electoral support from
one party to the other—both at the national level as well as in Punjab.
The electoral competition can be captured from the rate of movement of
electoral votes from one party to another.

The electoral volatility multiplied from 11 between 2004 and 2009
to 25 between 2009 and 2014[40] (see Table 9.7). This shows a shift in
party preference in Punjab. At the national level, the shift worked to the
advantage of the BJP, whereas in Punjab, the new political formation AAP

Table 9.7
Pedersen Index of Electoral Volatility

	BJP	AAP	SAD (B)	SAD (M)	CPI	CPM	INC	BSP	Others	Total Net Change (TNC)	Pedersen Index of Electoral Volatility
2004 to 2009	0.42	0	0.43	3.43	2.22	1.67	11.06	1.92	0.99	22.14	11.07
2009 to 2014	1.29	24.47	7.48	0.1	0.07	0.01	12.04	3.84	0.23	49.53	24.77

Source: Calculated from Election Commission of India Reports Punjab, 2004,
2009, and 2014.

took maximum advantage of the electoral instability. Another change witnessed in this election was the AAP surge in Punjab's political scene. It took maximum advantage of the asymmetry between the seats and vote share as compared to both the SAD and the Congress. But this was less than the BJP.

The BJP won more seats for each percentage of votes polled in the 2009 and 2014 Parliamentary elections (with a multiplier of 0.76 and 1.75, respectively) as compared to the SAD (with a multiplier of 0.91 and 1.17, respectively), and the Congress (with a multiplier of 1.36 and 0.70, respectively).[41] The Congress Party even with a higher percentage of votes polled than the AAP in 2014 could win fewer seats. The AAP won four seats with a multiplier of 1.26 as compared to the Congress (with a multiplier of 0.70, see Table 9.8).

Thus, the BJP, as the Congress and SAD, also had a greater capacity to translate the vote share into seats as compared to the AAP.

The moot question, however, is: Will the SAD–BJP alliance be able to improve their performance in the forthcoming Assembly elections in 2017 as compared to their performance in the 2014 Parliamentary elections? Another related question is: Will the BJP with a greater capacity to translate votes into seats be able to capture on its own space occupied by the AAP in the 2017 Assembly elections, or will the AAP in the Assembly elections without much ideological support be able to hold on to the space it occupied in the 2014 Parliamentary elections?

The early signs emerging out of two assembly by-elections in Patiala and Talwandi Sabu showed that the AAP may not be able to consolidate its support. The AAP won the Patiala Lok Sabha seat, and in the Patiala

Table 9.8

Seat–Vote Multiplier for Different Parties in Previous Parliament Elections

	BJP	AAP	SAD (B)	Congress
2004	2.20		1.80	0.45
2009	0.76		0.91	1.36
2014	1.75	1.26	1.17	0.70

Source: Calculated from Election Commission of India Reports Punjab, 2004, 2009, and 2014.

assembly segment, it secured more than 36 percent votes. But in the assembly by-election, caused by the seat vacated by Captain Amarinder Singh, it could secure merely 6 percent votes. It will be interesting to see that whether this shift in electoral completion and vote share from a dominant party to other parties will bring an electoral transformation in terms of electoral alliances in the state.

Implications for Coalition Politics

Punjab has a history of electoral alliances and merges. After independence, between 1947 and the mid-1960s, the SAD and the Congress merged in 1948 and 1956. Politics of merger between these two parties is a pointer toward a fact that even diametrically opposed political parties can enter into alliances. The mergers were followed by four post-election coalitions. The first post-election coalition government was formed under the leadership of Gurnam Singh consisting of a United Front of parties opposed to the Congress. The second post-election coalition government was formed under the leadership of Lachhman Singh Gill's breakaway Akali group with the support of the Congress Party in 1967. The third post-election coalition government was formed in 1969 led by Gurnam Singh. Its main alliance partner was Bharatiya Jana Sangh (BJS). Prakash Singh Badal led the fourth coalition government with the support of BJS. Both these post-election coalitions were marriages of convenience of the leadership with the sole aim of capturing power with their ranks regarding each other with suspicion and a clash of ideologies.

The pre-election alliances between the SAD and the BJP in the post-1990 phase were formed in the background of the triumph of democracy and assertion of people's agenda for peace over that of political party's sectional interests like in the post-election coalition of the 1970s. The Congress and the Communists, on the other hand, also entered into an alliance for the 1997 elections. However, this alliance could not last for the 2002 Assembly elections. The SAD and the BJP continued their alliance in subsequent elections for both the assembly and Parliamentary elections.

The mergers, post-election coalitions, and pre-election alliances have their own dynamics. The outcome of the 2014 elections also has implications for coalition politics in the state. The election outcome at the national level and the performance of the SAD in Punjab have weakened the alliance. For the first time, the BJP has emerged as the dominant party at the national level and has shown an inclination to emerge as the main player in Punjab.

A number of developments such as the defeat of BJP's national-level strategist, Arun Jaitley, in Amritsar and the assertion of the state-level BJP leadership for a greater share in the decision-making processes have strained the relationship between the SAD and the BJP. There are signs that this alliance may become unsustainable ideologically in the context of the changing political idiom in the country. At the pragmatic level also, an analysis of seat sharing between the SAD and the BJP has shown that in the 2009 Parliamentary elections, there was a change in the bargaining power of the alliance partners. As compared to the 2009 Parliamentary elections, the BJP got 15 percent less than its quota and the SAD got 4 percent more than its quota in the 2012 Assembly elections (see Table 9.9).

The emergence of the BJP in the dominant position at the national level and change in their bargaining power at the state level has brought exclusive support bases, that is, rural Jat Sikhs of the SAD and urban traders of the BJP, into the competitive spectrum. The BJP earlier underplayed its ideological thrust as it could not make policy interventions for the consolidation of its urban support base such as the slashing of urban property taxes, waste management, renewal of urban spaces, and subsidies

Table 9.9
Bargaining Power of Alliance Partners: Proportions of Seats Allocated to Alliance Partners beyond Normal Quota, 2012 Assembly Election Based on 2009 Lok Sabha Election

Alliance in 2012 Assembly Election	No. of Seats Contested in 2012 Assembly Election	Performance in 2009 in Assembly Segments of Parliamentary Election		
		Winner	Runner	Seat Managed to Get Beyond Quota
BJP	23	11	16	−4 (−15%)
SAD	94	41	49	4 (4%)

Source: Election Commission of India Reports, 2009–2012.

for industries. The SAD undoubtedly pursued its agenda for the rural population with decisions like free electricity and water, but without pursuing Sikh minority politics. Its catch-all approach has brought it into competition with its alliance partner BJP.

After the 2014 elections, BJP has signaled that it would expand its support base in the state. It has nationalized the regional agenda by raising issues such as the transfer of Chandigarh to Punjab, resolution of river water disputes and social issues such as drug addiction, female feticide, and more powers for the states. This has made its alliance partner the SAD on a weak wicket and may push it further to look back and revive ideological persuasions for survival, that is, the rejuvenation of Sikh identity and anti-centrism. The 2017 elections may witness a radical change in Punjab politics.

Why Punjab Went the Other Way?

Electoral politics has taken a new shift in Punjab. Outcomes of 2014 elections in the state are diametrically opposed to the national trend. The voters have voted against the corruption and incapacity of leadership to deliver justice. They have negated the popular notion that doles, subsidies, bribes, and caste can influence their preference. A relevant question is: What values do voters prefer in selecting their representatives? If 'Aam Aadmi' is to be believed, it is 'good people who can do good'. A majority of the voters as recorded in Table 9.10, that is, 68 percent mentioned honesty, 30 percent decisive leadership, and 27 percent nationalist, whereas only 12 percent mentioned secular and pro-people leader.

Different politicians and would-be-politicians use this moral space to pull different strings; therefore, what is bad and good is situational and contingent. Corruption is bad and honesty is good. Personal honesty has a higher value because it has the markings of scarcity. In popular political parlance, individual honesty on its own has been marketed as a superior value than even the fight against hunger, poverty, inequality, greed, conspicuous consumption, or even corruption.

This situation, defined by the public recognition of the circumscribed value of honesty, acts as an invitation to those who have proved their

Table 9.10
Preferred Attributes in Elected Representative

	Frequency	*Percent*
Honest	286	67.77
Decisive and determined	126	29.86
Nationalist	112	26.54
Secular	52	12.32
Not applicable	1	0.24
Total	422	100.00

Source: Institute of Development and Communications (IDC), Chandigarh. Field Survey in Punjab, March–April 2014. The total number of respondents was 422. Due to multiple responses, the sum of all is not equal to the total number.

worth in their respective professions ranging from cinema to sports to social activism. These 'celebrities', with their reservoir of social credit, drift into politics. The 'celebrities' mortality rate in politics is alarming, but there are exceptions, particularly in South India.

AAP's recent emergence in politics is a commentary on this political culture and the absence of political ideology. The AAP has the dual advantage of being an outcome of a protest movement and an aggressive appropriator of the space created by the propagation of 'honesty' as a supreme value rather than a historical struggle against capital accumulation, inequalities, hunger, and poverty. The AAP has successfully used a popular screen to make their concerns appear pro-people, and it provided legitimacy to these by using civilizational and national freedom movement symbols. People voted for the AAP, but a negligible number of voters believed that it can emerge as an alternative in Indian politics. They argued that the AAP has forced political parties to adopt corruption, Jan Lokpal Bill, etc. as agendas and provided a platform to the common people. It has also introduced some changes for common people's engagement with politics (see Table 9.11).

There were other voters who believed that they were inexperienced in state craft and had introduced instability in politics, and that their approach to politics was guided more by demand side consideration

Table 9.11
Will AAP Make a Difference in Politics?

	Frequency	Percent
Set the national agenda on corruption, Jan Lokpal, women issue, etc.	134	31.75
Provided platform to common people	16	3.79
Honest educated and secular leadership	39	9.24
Changed approach to Indian politics	37	8.77
Merely a group of social activists	10	2.37
Inexperienced in politics	71	16.82
Failed in politics (Delhi)	28	6.64
Instability in politics	22	5.21
Don't know/no response	90	21.33
Total	422	100.00

Source: Institute of Development and Communications (IDC), Chandigarh. Field Survey in Punjab, March–April 2014. The total number of respondents was 422. Due to multiple responses, the sum of all is not equal to the total number.

without appreciating supply side constraints. It is more agitational than reformist. Notwithstanding with this, people in Punjab who voted for the AAP did not anticipate that it would capture power in the Parliament, but they voted the AAP to warn the dominant political parties to reform or perish. In other words, they parked their votes for the AAP hoping that other parties would learn the lessons.

A majority of voters, that is, 66 percent in the Institute for Development and Communication (IDC) Election Survey in Punjab observed that the main factor in this election was corruption, followed by inflationary price rises. Government performance on other issues such as infrastructure development, power generation, subsidies, and social security was referred to by only 20 percent of voters (see Table 9.12).

A large majority of young voters mentioned corruption as the main factor. From amongst those who mentioned the price rise as one of the main factors, a sizeable lot were from the higher age group. From those who referred to anti-incumbency, the majority was from the middle-age group.

Table 9.12
Factors in Parliament Election 2014

Age Category	Anti-incumbency	Corruption	Inflation	Don't Know/ no Response	Total
18–26	17	79	51		116
	14.60%	68.00%	43.90%		100.00%
27–49	48	121	75	1	182
	26.30%	66.50%	41.20%	0.50%	100.00%
50 and plus	22	77	63		124
	17.80%	62.20%	50.90%		100.00%
Total	87	277	189	1	422
	20.60%	65.70%	44.80%	0.20%	100.00%

Source: Institute of Development and Communications (IDC), Chandigarh. Field Survey in Punjab. March–April 2014. The total number of respondents was 422. Due to multiple responses, the sum of all is not equal to the total number.

It is, therefore, not surprising that a majority of young voters, that is, 55 percent, in Punjab, preferred the AAP leader Arvind Kejriwal as their choice (see Table 19.13).

Anti-incumbency was so strong that the people of Punjab did not cast their votes on the leadership issue, but on performance, whereas in centrally administered Chandigarh, the capital city of Punjab and Haryana, people voted for the leadership of Modi as anti-incumbency was a factor against the Congress and not the BJP. In Punjab, people were of the view that a change in the central leadership was needed. Neither the Congress nor the BJP will be able to transform their conditions in the state. They voted against corruption, price rise, and dismal performance in the justice delivery of the SAD–BJP alliance. A woman voter decoded anti-incumbency as "the incidents of snatching, drug peddling and petty crime are on the rise. The police have neither a sense of responsibility nor do they talk to women properly." A farmer concluded, "the highhandedness of Akali workers and the police" are the main factors.[42]

As a consequence, Mr Modi's leadership as a factor became secondary to anti-incumbency. This can be inferred from the results of

Table 9.13
Voters' Preference for Leader

Age Category	Narendra Modi	Rahul Gandhi	Sonia Gandhi	Kejriwal	Prakash Krat	Mayawati	Don't Know/ no Response	Total
18–26	32	16		64		1	3	116
	27.59%	13.79%		55.17%		0.86%	2.59%	100.00%
27–49	56	40	6	70		1	7	180
	31.11%	22.22%	3.33%	38.89%		0.56%	3.89%	100.00%
50 and plus	38	14	30	33	2	3	6	126
	30.16%	11.11%	23.81%	26.19%	1.59%	2.38%	4.76%	100.00%
Total	126	70	36	167	2	5	16	422
	29.86%	16.59%	8.53%	39.57%	0.47%	1.18%	3.79%	100.00%

Source: Institute of Development and Communications (IDC), Chandigarh. Field Survey in Punjab. March–April 2014. The total number of respondents was 422. Due to multiple responses, the sum of all is not equal to the total number.

two constituencies, Bathinda from where Harsimrat Kaur Badal (Chief Minister Prakash Singh Badal's daughter-in-law) was pitted against the Chief Minister's nephew Manpreet Badal, and in Amritsar where Captain Amarinder Singh was pitted against the BJP stalwart Arun Jaitley. In both these constituencies, people did not vote for the AAP as they found an alternative in Captain Amarinder Singh in Amritsar and Harsimrat Badal in Bathinda.

In these two constituencies, to overcome the anti-incumbency suffered by the Congress Party in terms of corruption scams, rising prices, violation of rule of law, and above all policy paralysis on account of indecisive political leadership, the Congress followed a different strategy. Its main feature was to regionalize the national elections and nationalize the regional agenda. This helped Congress to overcome its anti-incumbency of 10 years of rule at the Center; its victory from Amritsar is a testimony to this strategy. Its former Chief Minister Captain Amarinder Singh defeated the BJP stalwart Arun Jaitley. Captain Amarinder Singh raised regional issues and activized the anti-incumbency issue against the SAD–BJP government in the state. Arun Jaitley lamented that he could not have a dialogue with Amarinder Singh on municipal issues. He raised issues relating to India's foreign policy, relations with India's neighbors, and food policy, whereas Amarinder Singh raised issues relating to drug abuse in Punjab, the prices of sand and gravel that are allegedly controlled by people close to the ruling establishment, and cleanliness and sanitation in Amritsar city. He successfully nationalized the regional agendas.

Another factor that influenced peoples' verdict was their perception regarding the role of regional parties. Around 53 percent preferred national parties, that is, the BJP and the Congress, and 40 percent preferred the AAP. Only 7 percent favored regional parties to rule at the national level (see Table 9.14).

To sum up, the competing anti-incumbencies of the SAD–BJP coalition in the state and the Congress in the Center was one of the major factors for the electoral volatility in the 2014 elections. In addition, the election outcomes were influenced by the change in political agenda from identity politics to catch them all, from government hubris to dignified access to government services and from rotational corruption among the political class to fight against corruption. This agenda was activized by

Table 9.14
Relevance of Regional Parties in Indian Politics

	Frequency	Percent
Regional parties	29	6.8
National parties	225	53.4
Newly emerged parties like AAP	168	39.8
Total	422	100

Source: Institute of Development and Communications (IDC), Chandigarh. Field Survey in Punjab. March–April 2014. The total number of respondents was 422. Due to multiple responses, the sum of all is not equal to the total number.

the SAD–BJP alliance in the 2007 elections and votes were cast on their dismal performance in this domain.

Within three months of coming to power in 2014, the BJP changed its electoral strategy. In Assembly elections in Haryana and Maharashtra, the BJP did not enter into alliance with its traditional allies. This may have implications for the SAD–BJP alliance in Punjab. In an election rally in Tasgaon, Sangli district, Maharashtra, Prime Minister Modi appealed to the voters to give a clear majority to the BJP. To quote, "Alliances did you no good.... No party takes responsibility in alliance. The BJP will take responsibility if you vote it to power."[43]

The BJP is following a two-pronged strategy, that is, consolidation and expansion to emerge as a national alternative. This entails the regionalization of its leadership and symbolism. It has undertaken social engineering at the micro level by recruiting leaders from diverse social groups and articulating local issues in convergence with national politics. It is reconstructing federal polity not through alliances with regional parties, but appropriating regional politics at the national level.

This may pose a challenge to the survival of regional parties, as the BJP has regionalized its politics, electoral discourse, co-option of leaders representing regional diversities, and propounding decentralization and federal principles. It has appropriated regional discourse leading to the marginalization of regional parties. In Punjab, the only rider is the pragmatic relevance of the SAD as a 'Sikh party' to attest to the BJP not being against minorities. This is a challenge for the SAD either to go back to the

Panthic (religious) agenda to maintain its alliance or perform in the secular domain to deliver just corruption- and harassment-free governance. For the Congress, there is an urgent need to regionalize its organization, agenda, and leadership.

Notes and References

1. Indian National Congress (INC), "Your Voice: Our Pledge." Lok Sabha Election Manifesto, 2014, p. 32.
2. Pramod Kumar, "It Can Be Delayed, but Not Stopped." *Hindustan Times*, September 29, 2012, p. 4.
3. Atul Sood, "State, Neo Liberal Economic Reforms and Public Policy in India." Paper presented at the World International Studies Conference, *Frankfurt*, August 6, 2014.
4. Ibid.
5. See note 1, p. 10.
6. There are divergent views on this issue. It has been argued by followers of the neoliberal path of development that price distorting subsidies must be eliminated or drastically reduced. But there are others who argue that agriculture subsidies have to be given to provide survival to the poor. Furthermore, the developed countries subsidize their agriculture by labeling it as green or blue box subsidies. The free electricity and water given in Punjab is not in convergence with the WTO framework and, therefore, it must be rationalized and given as productivity bonus. To provide food security and ensure food sovereignty, agriculture must be subsidized to keep food grains globally competitive.
7. Pramod Kumar, "Coalition Politics in Punjab: From Communal Polarisation to Catchall Parties?" In E. Sridharan (ed.), *Coalition Politics in India: Selected Issues at the Centre and the State* (New Delhi: Academic Foundation, 2014), p. 276.
8. Narendra Modi, "Mega Public Rally Nava Bharat Yuva Bheri," Hyderabad, August 11, 2013.
9. Narendra Modi, "Hunkar Rally," Patna, Bihar, October 27, 2013.
10. Narendra Modi, "BJP Youth Conference," Trichy, Tamil Nadu, September 26, 2013.
11. Ibid.
12. Narendra Modi, "Bhartiya Upjay Rally," Hardoi, Uttar Pradesh, April 21, 2014.
13. Narendra Modi, "Mission 272+," Rohania, Uttar Pradesh, May 8, 2014.
14. Narendra Modi, "Maha Jagran Rally," Guwahati, Assam, February 8, 2014.
15. Narendra Modi, "Purv Sainik Rally," Rewari, Haryana, September 16, 2013.
16. Narendra Modi, "Lalkar Rally," Jammu, Jammu and Kashmir, December 1, 2013.
17. Narendra Modi, "Public Meeting," Jogdalpur, Chhattisgarh, November 7, 2013.
18. Narendra Modi, "Mega Rally," Kolkata, West Bengal, February 5, 2014.
19. See note 9.
20. Narendra Modi, "Vijay Shankhnaad Rally," Kashi, Uttar Pradesh, December 20, 2013.
21. Ibid.
22. Narendra Modi, "Vijay Shankhnad Rally," Agra, Uttar Pradesh, November 21, 2013.
23. See note 20.
24. See note 9.

25. Suhas Palshikar and K.C. Suri, "India's 2014 Lok Sabha Elections: Critical Shifts in the Long Term, Caution in the Short Term," *Economic and Political Weekly*, XLIX, 39 (September 27, 2014).
26. Pramod Kumar, "Communalisation of Hindus in Punjab," *Secular Democracy*, XI, IX(1982), p. 27.
27. Paul Wallace, "The Sikhs as a Minority in a Sikh Majority State in India," *Asian Survey*, XXVII, 3(1986), pp. 363–77.
28. There is a qualitative shift in the support bases of the political parties in Punjab; see note 7, p. 277.
29. Kanwaljit Singh, *The Policy Programme of Shiromani Akali Dal*, April 14, 1995, p. 4.
30. See note 7, p. 277.
31. To quote,

> Over the decades, Punjab has continually been a victim of the discriminatory and repressive policies of the Centre, in particular the rights of Punjab in respect of its left-out territories and the river waters have been ruthlessly suppressed and undermined.... For pursuance of the above objectives, the spirit of Punjabiat would be strengthened so that these matters get projected as common problems of the entire Punjabis rather than a section thereof. (See note 29.)

32. National Democratic Alliance (NDA). 1999. Manifesto Lok Sabha Elections.
33. The Sarkaria Commission was set up on June 9, 1983 to restructure India's Center–state relations. Article 356 of the Indian Constitution deals with this provision in the case of the failure of the states' constitutional machinery.
34. The Akali–BJP government has opened a new chapter in the Center–state relations, ushering in the age of co-operative federalism in the country. The era of confrontation has been effectively ended and replaced with a forward looking thrust on working together for the overall good of the state and the nation (see note 35).
35. Shiromani Akali Dal (SAD). 1998. Manifesto, Lok Sabha Elections.
36. See note 7, pp. 219–316.
37. Accidents in history sometimes change the course of history. This has precisely what has happened in the electoral competition amongst the parties and the leadership in the state. Had the SAD, in order to oust Navjot Singh Sidhu, a former BJP Member of Parliament from Amritsar, not wooed the BJP national leader Arun Jaitley to contest from Amritsar (who subsequently suffered defeat), the relationship between alliance partners may not have deteriorated so soon. Similarly, in the Congress Party, the fall of its state-level President P. Bajwa may not have happened had he not forced the former Chief Minister Captain Amarinder Singh to fight against Arun Jaitley from Amritsar.
38. *Taagepera and Shugart index.* The effective number of parties, in terms of the percentage of votes and seats secured by parties in elections to the directly elected chamber of parliament, is calculated for all the general elections using the Taagepera and Shugart procedure ($N = 1/\sum Pi^2$, where Pi is the fractional share of the ith party and $\sum$ stands for the summation of overall components).
39. See note 25.
40. *Pedersen index of electoral volatility.* It is computed by adding the absolute value of change in percentage of votes gained and lost by each party from one election to the next, then dividing the sum by 2. Thus, in a party system with "*n*" parties, the electoral volatility is = TNC/2, where TNC is the total net change in party support. The electoral volatility, thus, has a range of "0" (perfect stability of electoral support to parties,

where no party gained or lost votes) to 100 (perfect instability, where there is a total shift of voters from one party to the other).

41. *Seat–vote multiplier.* It is a ratio of the proportion of seats won by a party to the proportion of votes won by it. It is the expression of the relationship between the percentage of votes a party secures in an election and the seats it secures in the legislature. It is given by 1/[(vote share of a party/100)/(numbers of seats secured by the party/total number of seats in the legislature)].

42. Perneet Singh, "Anti-incumbency against Both Centre State Govt." *Tribune*, April 30, 2014, Chandigarh, p. 2. Also see, *Tribune*, April 26, 2014, p. 14.

43. Narendra Modi, Tasgaon, Maharashtra, October 4, 2014.

B. Kashmir and Western Cluster

10

Kashmir's Contentious Politics: The More Things Change, the More They Stay the Same

Reeta Chowdhari Tremblay and Mohita Bhatia

On the surface of it, the 2014 election results for the six parliamentary constituencies of the state of Jammu and Kashmir would appear to follow the trends in the rest of India—high voter turnout, the Modi factor, frustration with the incumbent regime regarding its inability to push development, its tolerance of corruption, and generally, its poor governance. Indeed, the voter turnout in the state went up by approximately 9.7 percent. The two coalition partners of the Omar Abdullah-led government, namely the National Conference (NC) and the Congress, were unsuccessful in all contests. The main opposition party, the People's Democratic Party (PDP), representing largely Kashmiri Muslims and contesting on a platform of good governance, won all three Valley seats. The BJP won in the remaining three constituencies in Jammu and Ladakh. The PDP and BJP victories, wiping out the National Conference and Congress, were the first ever event of its kind in the state of Jammu and Kashmir.

A careful study of the election results will show that the Jammu and Kashmir story is complex and that the responses of the population of the state's three regions—Jammu, the Kashmir Valley, and Ladakh—are quite distinctive. The higher voter turnout in the 2014 elections was not consistent across regions. Once again the Valley's three constituencies followed a post-insurgency trend of poor voter turnout. Like previous elections, Kashmiri Muslim citizens stayed away from the polling booth for reasons ranging from political alienation, adherence to the separatist election boycott call, fear of militant violence, to sheer indifference. Ladakh showed a slight downward change in voter participation but it is the Hindu majority in Jammu's two constituencies which made a break with the past and recorded the highest participation.

In the state of Jammu and Kashmir, each region has a distinct linguistic and religious identity: the Kashmiri-speaking Valley with a 97.16 percent Muslim population and less than 2 percent Hindus, predominately Dogra areas of Jammu with 65.2 percent Hindus and 31 percent Muslim, and Ladakhi-speaking Ladakh with a 47.4 percent Muslim and 46.9 percent Buddhist population. As a result of this demographic heterogeneity, the decision criteria of the citizens of each region emerge as the distinct products of their unique perceptions and experiences relating to a number of dimensions. These consist of their collective identity issues, the regional and religious nationalist dynamic, their perception of inclusion and exclusion in relation to Kashmiri identity, the Valley's nationalist/secessionist demands, and their satisfaction or dissatisfaction with governance. Jammu's Hindu population voting in such a large number for the BJP does not hold true for the Ladakhis who for the first time elected a BJP member of parliament. Similarly, the victory of the PDP in the Valley is less because of its soft nationalist agenda than because of Chief Minister Omar Abdullah's poor governance.

This chapter is divided into three sections. The first section begins with Narendra Modi's campaign in the state. With great passion, he introduced two prominent issues: Article 370 and "gender discriminatory" Permanent Residence provisions for citizenship status in the state. In the second section, in order to understand the relevance of these two issues for this election and Kashmiri politics, we will look into the constitutional history of these provisions in some detail. Our analysis of the Jammu and Kashmir elections will show that despite a great hype about these issues, they actually played a very marginal role during the elections, although they did gain prominence after Modi's government came into power. In the third section, the three distinct regional electoral responses from Jammu, the Valley, and Ladakh are explored along with the efficacy of political campaigns, particularly that of Modi.

Modi's Campaign Trail[1]

During his campaign, Narendra Modi's message was both strategic and targeted. First was the promise of the reactivation of Vajpayee's roadmap for resolving the India–Pakistan conflict. This was an appeal, particularly, to the Muslim population of the Valley and to court the main opposition party of the Valley, the PDP along with the moderate nationalist groups. Atal Bihari Vajpayee's discourse of 'humanity' remains to this day most appreciated by the Kashmiri population. In his Udhampur rally, Modi articulated publicly, "It is our duty to carry forward the roadmap and take to logical conclusion Atal Bihari Vajpayee's plan of 'Insaniyat', Jumhuriyat' and 'Kashmiriyat'."

Indeed, this message was to resonate well with both the PDP and some of the separatist groups. Mehbooba Mufti, the leader of the PDP, clearly stated the Valley's appreciation for Vajpayee: "We have always praised Atal Bihari Vajpayee, because whatever changes we see in Jammu and Kashmir today, were because of him—whether his going to Lahore or inviting Pervez Musharraf after Kargil." As early as November 2013, the Hurriyat Conference Chairman Mirwaiz Umar Farooq suggested that his group "would cooperate in case government of India followed the Vajpayee initiative," praising Vajpayee's sentiments of taking "everybody forward within the ambit of humanity."[2]

The second message brought by Modi was related to progress and economic and technological advancement of the state. He suggested that the present label of 'beggar state' must be converted into 'better state'. Addressing the secessionist/nationalist groups in the Valley, he suggested that instead of demanding a separate state, "their demand should have been for a super state." To tackle the problems of unemployment and to forge ahead with a development-'progress' program, he pointed to several missed opportunities, such as creating very first rate education institutions (IITs and IIMs) and advancing the film and tourism industries.

Third, one of the most important and controversial messages of Modi's campaign, dealt with Article 370 that grants special status to Jammu and Kashmir. However, Modi placed it on the campaign agenda with a strategic nuance. While the BJP and its cultural parent body RSS have traditionally been adamant in its demand for the abrogation of Article 370, the party leaders are also cognizant of politically sensitivity around this issue. Astutely, Modi shifted the discussion during his campaign from abrogation toward the question of rationally debating the value of the special status and its contribution to the development of the state. Modi spoke the language of citizenship rights. He interwove his views on Article 370 with the permanent residency requirements in the state of Jammu and Kashmir and its gendered implications suggesting that married women did not have the same rights in the state to acquire property and seek employment as their counterparts in the rest of India. Using the example of the state's chief minister's own family, Modi asked, "If Omar (Abdullah) married outside Kashmir, his rights of being a citizen remain whereas his sister Sara loses the right for the same. Is this not discrimination against the women in the state?"

This discourse on citizenship rights was also extended, on the one hand, to the Pakistani refugees of 1947, 1965, and 1971, who are settled in the state (mostly in Jammu) but do not have permanent resident status and, thus, cannot benefit from the citizenship rights of acquiring property or seeking government employment, and on the other hand, to the Kashmiri Pandit community who have suffered internal exile within the state. In his two rallies, Modi also referred to other backward communities of the state including the Scheduled Castes and Scheduled Tribes, several times alluding to the neglect of the Gujjars and the Shias of Kargil.

Modi's reference to Article 370 drew immediate responses from both NC and the PDP. Omar Abdullah and his father Farooq Abdullah, an NC candidate from the Srinagar constituency, were the most vocal critics of Modi's speech. In an emotional tweet, Omar suggested, "(Modi) very conveniently used me and my sister as examples to illustrate a point that has no bearing on truth. Either he lies or is ill informed." In another tweet, he questioned Modi's facts on tourism. He reminded Modi that the exodus of Kashmir Pandits took place under the BJP appointed Governor Jag Mohan.

Both father and son pointed to the historic role played by the National Conference in defending Article 370 and *Kashmiryat*.[3] Both Farooq and Omar accused Modi of threatening secularism in India. Farooq also suggested that if India becomes a communal country, Kashmir would not remain its part and "those who vote for Modi should drown themselves in a river."[4] Given the sensitivity around Article 370, the PDP leader Mufti Mohammad Sayeed also criticized Modi for seeking a debate on the special status under Article 370. "Scrap this bridge with rest of the country and the entire gamut of accession and related issues stare in your face. Modi's raking up of Article 370 is a very disturbing indicator of his approach to sensitivities of the people of Jammu and Kashmir."[5] However, the party President Mehbooba Mufti, while ruling out an alliance with the BJP, did suggest PDP's support for Modi only if he takes forward the Kashmir issue from where Atal Bihari Vajpayee had left it.

The Context

Historical-Political Context: Article 370

After the conditional acceptance of Kashmir's accession to India and liberation of two-thirds of the state from the tribal aggression, the Indian Constituent Assembly approved Article 370, determining Jammu and Kashmir's political relationship with India. This constitutional provision was intended to be temporary. During his presentation of the Article to the Constituent Assembly, N. Gopalaswami Ayyangar elaborated upon the 'temporary' nature of this provision, "We are entangled with the United Nations in regard to Jammu and Kashmir and it is not possible to say now when we shall be free from this entanglement."[6] Amitabh Mattoo expands on the unique circumstances giving rise to the temporary nature of this provision,

> Ayyangar argued that for a variety of reasons Kashmir, unlike other princely states, was not yet ripe for integration. India had been at war with Pakistan over Jammu and Kashmir and while there was a ceasefire, the conditions were still 'unusual and abnormal'. Part of the State's territory was in the hands of 'rebels and enemies'.[7]

Kham Hausing points to the different intent of the Constituent Assembly behind Article 370 and the Article 371. He maintains that first the Sixth Schedule and then later Article 371 give constitutionally and legally 'a differential constitutional status and powers' to the Naga tribes and others in the North East region. The difference, however, remained that whereas in the matter of Jammu and Kashmir, the genesis of federal asymmetry is due to 'the unique circumstances' pertaining to the accession of the state to India, the special powers given to the North East were an acknowledgment of the distinct tribal culture and practices.[8]

However, under Article 370, the threshold to exercise internal autonomy is higher for Jammu and Kashmir as compared to any other state in the Indian federation. It empowers the state by enshrining the condition that any constitutional amendments approved by the Parliament, applicable to all states, is not automatically applicable to the state of Jammu and Kashmir and must be approved by the state government and its Legislative Assembly.

Article 370 also lays out a process for its own revocation (reiterated in Article 368(2)). It empowers:

> the President to declare, by public notification, that Article 370 shall cease to be operative or shall be operative only with such exceptions and from such date as he may specify; Provided that the recommendation of the Constituent Assembly of the State shall be necessary before the President issues such notification.[9]

What is the present status of Article 370? The original Article 370 and the first Presidential Order of 1950 have been amended several times, with the concurrence of the Jammu and Kashmir Legislature, so as to make most of the provisions of the Indian Constitution applicable to the state. Starting with the Presidential Order of 1954 and continuing till the mid-1970s, the state's integration has taken the form of a slow but steady abrogation of Article 370, with one exception relating to the privileges of the permanent residents—a topic which we are going to discuss below.[10] According to the State Autonomy Committee, appointed by the Jammu and Kashmir government in 1996 to examine the question of restoration of autonomy to the state of Jammu and Kashmir, out of 97 Union list entries in the Indian Constitution, 94 have been applied to the state; out of 47 entries in the concurrent list, 26 have been applied and out of total

12 Schedules 7 have been extended to the state. The report concludes, "the special status of the State in the Indian Union was emptied of its substantive content."[11]

Article 370 evokes strong reactions both within and outside the state. Within Kashmir, there are three divergent opinions, all strongly held. The mainstream political leadership of Jammu and Kashmir (the NC and the PDP) views Article 370 as the only link or bridge between the state and India assuring a distinct status to the state. Moreover, Article 370 is not seen as a temporary measure but a clear articulation of the special status of the state within Indian federation. Thus, all autonomy demands (reverting to the 1953 status) emanate from this particular context.

At the other extreme stand the secessionist groups of the Valley who consider Article 370 as conditional and provisional. For them, this provision was included in the Indian Constitution due to the conditional acceptance of the state's accession to India. For them, the accession is not final and Kashmiris' wishes regarding their political association must be ascertained through a plebiscite, a promise made by Indian leadership and confirmed by the United Nations. Then there are the pro-India integrationists, mostly based in Jammu and Ladakh regions (including the Kashmiri Hindu Brahmin community displaced from the Valley after 1989), who consider that despite various integrative measures, Article 370 still contains very important exceptions and it has, moreover, become a symbol for secession-inducing tendencies in the Valley.[12]

Citizenship: The Permanent Resident Provisions

While there is no direct relation between the Kashmiri citizenship privileges as underlined in the Permanent Resident provisions of the Jammu and Kashmir Constitution of 1957, on the one hand, and Article 370, on the other, these have, nevertheless, become symbolically and emotionally intertwined with the special status and distinct identity of the state. The citizenship requirements to acquire property and seek employment in the state have their origins in the constitutional history of the state. They are referred to in the 1952 Delhi Agreement, a political agreement between the two levels of government. It is the 1954 Presidential Order (The Constitution [Application to Jammu and Kashmir] Order, 1954) and the exceptionality Article 35A, and its concurrence by the Jammu and Kashmir Constituent Assembly through its enshrinement as Section 6 of the state's constitution which give the legal legitimacy to the state-determined citizenship provisions. Following is the constitutional chronology of the present Permanent Resident provision:

1. The genesis of Kashmiri citizenship and the property and employment privileges associated lie in the 1927 and 1932 promulgations by Maharaja Hari Singh defining 'state-subjects'.

2. These provisions were relabeled as 'Permanent Resident' by the 1957 Jammu and Kashmir Constitution, giving citizenship privileges their legal basis in the state constitution.

3. In February 1954, the Jammu and Kashmir's Constituent Assembly accepted the report of its Drafting Committee. One of the provisions is related to citizenship. It stated that by virtue of the accession treaty, all citizens of the state were citizens of India. It also qualified that "it is, however, recognized by the Government of India that this position would not affect the existing State Subject definition". The 1954 Presidential Order reiterated Kashmir's Constituent Assembly's provisions regarding Permanent Residenceship.

4. The 1954 Presidential Order added a new article 35A (an exception to the universal application of fundamental Rights guaranteed to all citizens in the Indian Constitution). This provision grants the state legislature to define special rights and privileges with regard to the employment and acquisition of property in the state as well as the grant of scholarship to its state subjects.[13]

5. Meanwhile the Jammu and Kashmir Constituent Assembly (convened and popularly elected in 1951)[14] approved the state's new constitution in November 1956, officially promulgated on January 26, 1957. One of its features included a provision with regard to the citizenship of the people of Kashmir and their classification into a special category of 'Permanent Residents'. While respecting Article 5 and its application of Indian citizenship to the people of the state and the criteria for citizenship as defined by the Maharaja promulgations of 1927 and 1932, the Constituent Assembly made a single modification pertaining to the nomenclature. State Subjects were reclassified into a 'uniform class of Permanent Residents'.[15]

During the campaign, as mentioned above, Modi raised the issue of discrimination against the women of the state who do not possess the same rights to acquire property and seek employment as their counterparts do in the rest of India, nor as do male permanent residents of the state. Is Modi correct in his interpretation? It was indeed correct that until 2002, the state of Jammu and Kashmir interpreted the permanent resident requirements in such a way that female permanent residents who married a nonpermanent resident lost their status as citizens of the states. An administrative practice was initiated in the state to stamp all unmarried girls' permanent residency certificate as 'Valid till Marriage'. No one is sure when this practice began, but a good guess would be after the promulgation of the Constitution. In 2002, Jammu and Kashmir High Court reversed this administrative practice and declared that a daughter of a permanent resident marrying a nonpermanent resident will not lose the status of the permanent resident of the state of Jammu and Kashmir.

The 2002 High Court judgment is an exemplary document which outlines the historical and constitutional chronology of the Permanent Resident provisions, the initial intent of these provisions, and the rationale for the gender-based discriminatory administrative interpretation. It points to the invalidity of interpretation and to the constitutional authority vested in the state legislature to define or amend the provisions of Permanent Residency. In the first place, Chief Justice V.K. Jhanji noted that the Maharaja's promulgation of 1927 was gender neutral.[16] Second, this principle came to be reinterpreted in terms of the married girl's new 'domicile'—the domicile of her husband, thus connecting a married woman's citizenship status to the domicile of her husband if the latter happened to be a non-permanent resident.[17] Justice Jhanji was to explain that this interpretation of the domicile of a married woman was based on an old 1914 British Common Law. But since the laws had subsequently changed Jhanji asserted that "the domicile of a married woman is to be ascertained the same way as the domicile of an independent person is ascertained."

Third, the government's case for stripping away a married girl's permanent residence status were she to marry a non-State Subject was based on Note III of the 1927 promulgation which pertained to the wife or a widow of the State Subject. The majority opinion of the High Court argued that Note III cannot be applied to those citizens who already possess the status of a permanent resident.[18]

Fourth, the state legislature has neither modified the definition nor made any provision to limit the rights of a female state subject in an event like marriage with a non-state subject. Therefore, the majority opinion of the Court was: "We hold that a daughter of a permanent resident marrying a non-permanent resident will not lose the status of permanent resident of the state of Jammu and Kashmir."

In response to this judgment, the PDP-led government initially appealed to the Supreme Court. However, in 2004, it withdrew its appeal and introduced the J&K Women's Permanent Resident (Disqualification) in the Legislative Assembly. The bill was passed with the support of all Kashmir-based parties including the NC. There was a huge vocal opposition to it from the Congress, the BJP, and the Panthers Party. Due to Sonia Gandhi's alleged intervention,[19] the bill was blocked at the Legislative Council, the upper house, when the Council Chairman Abdur Rashid Dar adjourned the session without permitting a vote. A PDP member reintroduced the bill in the upper house in March 2010. The bill was once again dropped by the Legislative Council on constitutional grounds stating that, "given that this was a constitutional bill, it should be introduced in the Assembly." As there have been no further attempts to reintroduce the legislation, the High Court decision stands and permanent resident women marrying a non-state subject do retain their status. Thus, Sara Abdullah remains a permanent resident of the state. What remains still problematic is that the permanent resident status of these married women does not pass on to their descendants.

One of the issues raised by Modi was providing equal rights to the Sikhs and Hindus who settled in the state after partition and after the two Indo-Pakistan wars. These refugees came from outside the undivided pre-partition state and do not fulfill State Subject requirements. They cannot own property, are not able to seek governmental employment, and cannot participate in state elections. While the Congress Party has supported seeking a solution to the rehabilitation of these refugees, all Valley–based groups, and parties radically oppose granting permanent residence status to them fearing a demographic shift in the state.

At the other spectrum of the discussion are those state subjects who migrated to Pakistan after 1947. The Jammu and Kashmir Constitution recognizes all those state subjects who went to Pakistan on account of the communal disturbances of 1947. In order to assert Kashmir's distinctness and its autonomy, one of Sheikh Abdullah's last acts before his death in 1982 was to legislate the Resettlement Bill to allow Kashmiri citizens settled in 'Azad' Kashmir to return freely to the state and allow them to reclaim property. The bill was vigorously opposed by Jammu's Hindus. The then Governor B.K. Nehru sent it back to the Assembly citing inconsistencies and later referred to the Supreme Court. In 2001, after nearly 20 years, with no word from the Supreme Court, the state government decided to implement the Act. In 2002, in response to a petition by Bhim Singh of Jammu Kashmir National Panthers Party (JKNPP), the Supreme Court stayed operation of the controversial Jammu and Kashmir Migrants Resettlement Act. Just recently, 12 years after Bhim Singh's filing his petition, the Supreme Court has agreed to list the petition against the 1982 Resettlement Bill approved by the Jammu and Kashmir Legislature.

Elections and Regional Responses

Jammu: The Unforeseen BJP's Massive Victory

In a surprising result, the BJP effortlessly won both the Parliamentary constituencies of Jammu that have traditionally been the stronghold of the Congress Party. Since the 1967 Parliamentary elections, the Congress Party has won both seats eight times. The BJP could manage to capture these seats only during the elections of 1996, 1998, and 1999 when secessionist/nationalist movement was at its peak by mobilizing Hindu voters on religious/regional lines. Leaving aside the politically sensitive period of political strife in the state, the Congress has remained the dominant party in Jammu. The 2014 election results were both surprising and unforeseen. Although riding on an exuberant Modi wave, the BJP was indeed considered a strong contestant against the Congress; however, its seamless victory with huge margins from both the constituencies was not anticipated. Before commenting on Jammu's electoral scenario, in general, and BJP's victory, in particular, it is pertinent to briefly sketch the electoral history of Jammu.

Table 10.1

Winning Parties in Lok Sabha Elections in Jammu

PC	1967	1971	1977	1980	1984	1989	1996	1998	1999	2004	2009	2014
JP	INC	INC	IND	INC	INC	INC	INC	BJP	BJP	INC	INC	BJP
UD	INC	INC	INC	INC	INC	INC	BJP	BJP	BJP	INC	INC	BJP

Source: Election Commission of India.

Note: PC = Parliamentary constituency; JP = Jammu constituency; UD = Udhampur constituency; INC = Indian National Congress; BJP = Bharatiya Janata Party.

In Jammu, till this election, the most preferred choice of a large majority of Hindu and Muslim voters was the Congress Party. Since the 1989 secessionist/nationalist movement, the BJP was steadily increasing its share of the vote particularly in the Hindu majority assembly constituencies, though not consistently. It has done so through a successful consolidation of its Hindu constituency as well as by attracting a bulk of Dalit votes (see Table 10.3). Until the 2014 elections, this strategy of communal polarization of voters and consolidation of Hindu votes had remained a partial phenomenon witnessed only during politically heightened periods. Whenever political tensions and the Valley's secessionist demands did subside, the consolidation of Hindu voters weakened, resulting in a large section of Hindu voters shifting away from the BJP toward the Congress or other political parties. Tables 10.1 through 10.4 reveal these trends.

In the Jammu constituency, BJP's share of votes came down to 36.80 percent and 30.98 percent, respectively, in the subsequent 2004 and 2009 Parliamentary elections (see Tables 10.2 and 10.4). A similar trend of enormous rise in voter share during militancy periods followed by a steep decline was witnessed in the Udhampur constituency as well, albeit not always consistently. Again, in both the constituencies, BJP's loss in terms of voter share synchronized with Congress's gain. The Amarnath agitation in 2008 is illustrative of this trend.[20] Spearheading the agitation and attempting to evoke religious sentiments, the BJP managed to perform remarkably well in the 2008 Assembly elections when it won 11 assembly seats. Although BJP's expectations were quite high for the 2009 Parliamentary elections, it did not manage to win any of the two

Table 10.2
Voter Share Percentage of BJP and INC in Jammu Region
(Udhampur and Jammu Constituencies) in Lok Sabha Elections

| | Udhampur | | Jammu | |
	INC	BJP/BJS	INC	BJP/BJS
1967	54.88	31.70	48.42	28.27
1971	60.97	25.82	60.04	29.91
1977	56.69	–	–	–
1980	53.37	–	62.46	–
1984	56.98	10.29	46.50	–
1989	40.65	12.63	41.81	6.16
1996	21.73	37.57	34.23	25.99
1998	7.13	48.67	18.11	43.25
1999	19.09	49.01	18.97	43.46
2004	39.61	31.85	38.94	36.80
2009	37.91	35.72	45.39	30.98

Source: Election Commission of India.

Table 10.3
Parties That Got Most Votes in Assembly Segments (Reserved) of
the Parliamentary Constituencies

	1999	2004	2009	2014
Bhaderwah	BJP	INC	INC	INC
Ramban	BJP	BJP	BJP	INC
Chenani	BJP	INC	INC	BJP
Ramnagar	BJP	JKPP	JKPP	BJP
Kathua	BJP	INC	BJP	BJP
Hiranagar	BJP	INC	BJP	BJP
Samba	BJP	BJP	BJP	BJP
Bishnah	BJP	BJP	BJP	BJP

(Table 10.3 Continued)

(Table 10.3 Continued)

	1999	2004	2009	2014
R S Pura	BJP	INC	INC	BJP
Marh	BJP	BJP	INC	BJP
Raipur-Domana	BJP	BJP	BJP	BJP
Chhamb	BJP	INC	INC	BJP

Source: Election Commission of India.
Note: JKPP = Jammu and Kashmir Panther's Party.

Table 10.4
Parties That Got Most Votes in Hindu Majority Assembly Segments
of the Parliamentary Constituencies

	1999	2004	2009	2014
Reasi	BJP	INC	BJP	BJP
Udhampur	BJP	INC	BJP	BJP
Kathua	BJP	BJP	BJP	BJP
Vijaypur	BJP	JKN	INC	BJP
Nagrota	BJP	BJP	INC	BJP
Gandhinagar	BJP	BJP	INC	BJP
Jammu East	BJP	BJP	BJP	BJP
Jammu West	BJP	BJP	BJP	BJP
Akhnoor	BJP	INC	INC	BJP

Source: Election Commission of India.
Note: JKN = Jammu and Kashmir National Conference.

constituencies. The easing of tensions in 2009 had weakened the electoral cohesiveness of Hindu voters to some extent.

What changed in 2014 reversing the historical trend? No significant
regional situation was available for the BJP to mobilize the Hindu population. The 2013 Afzal Guru hanging protests had remained confined
to the Valley with no accompanying tensions in the Jammu region.
Modi's two prominent campaign issues, Article 370 and the gender

discrimination of Permanent Residents remained marginal. Yet, Jammu witnessed a clear polarization of voters.

What struck a resonating chord with the voters was the critique of the incumbent government, both at the national and the regional levels. At the regional level, the factor that worked against the Congress was its alliance with the NC. Anti-alliance sentiment was, however, shared by both the regions. It was indeed Modi's campaign for 'development', 'efficient governance', 'removal of corruption', support and dignity for the 'backward' communities, and Jammu's 'proper place within the state' that were to resonate with the voters.

From a broader perspective, it is the conjunction of two complementary factors that explains the consolidation of the Hindu vote and the massive victory by the BJP in the Jammu region. First, following the national trend, it was a vote for Modi and his campaign for 'development' and 'efficient governance'. It was not simply a vote for the BJP. Second, instead of invoking a polarized politics, 'Jammu versus Kashmir' or 'Jammu Hindus versus Kashmiri Muslim' sentiments, Modi projected a wider developmental agenda for India, the state, and Jammu.

It is important to note that while the BJP was able to mobilize a large majority of Hindus irrespective of their caste, class or subregion, Muslims, on the other hand, largely voted for the Congress. This is evident from the fact that BJP won all 15 Hindu majority segments in the Jammu constituency and most of the Hindu majority segments in the Udhampur constituency. The Congress was able to register victories only in the few assembly segments that had majority Muslim populations. Indeed, Muslims voted en masse for the Congress, except for three Muslim majority segments—Poonch-Haveli, Mendhar, and Surankote—won by the PDP. The BJP managed to cut into the vote share of the Congress even from the traditional strongholds of the latter such as Akhnoor, Chaamb, Doda, Bhaderwah, and Kishtawar, indicating a shift of Hindu votes away from the Congress. That polarization, with Hindus voting for the BJP and Muslims for the Congress, together, given the consolidation of Hindu votes in the Hindu-majority Jammu regions, explains much of the outstanding performance of the BJP.

What also was to help the BJP candidates in winning their respective seats was the notable increase in the voter turnout in both Parliamentary constituencies. In the Jammu constituency, the voter turnout stood at around 70 percent, which is 21 percentage more than the 2009 Parliamentary elections. While the Muslim majority assembly segments such as Rajouri and Poonch also recorded a high voter turnout, the polling percentage in 14 out of 20 Hindu majority segments taken together was significantly greater. The polling percentage in the Udhampur constituency was a bit more intricate. Voter turnout in this constituency was around 72 percent, which is 27 percent more than the previous Parliamentary elections. Although this constituency has a few Muslim majority areas, some of these regions such as Kishtwar or Bhaderwah also have a noticeable Hindu population—of more than 40 percent. While witnessing a huge voter turnout in both Hindu and Muslim majority areas, the polling percentage of Hindus seemed to have greatly surpassed that of Muslims in this constituency, thus leading to BJP's success. A clear polarization of votes along with a higher voter turnout in favor of the BJP, thus, marked the 2014 elections.

To summarize, although the role of religion as one of the factors in shaping people's choice cannot be denied, many who voted for the BJP were convinced by Modi's campaign for an 'inclusive development'. The secular Hindu population was to join hands with the staunch and loyal Hindu supporters of the Hindu *parivar*. For the former, the development of the country and the state, Jammu's place in the state, and an anti-incumbency momentum were the motivating factors for shifting their support from the Congress to the BJP. For the hardcore Hindu nationalist minority, the motivating factors were Article 370, one nation-one state, return of the exiled Kashmir Pandit community, and citizenship rights for the Western Pakistani refugees. What cemented the unity at the polls of these two groups was Narendra Modi. The BJP was able to sell its prime ministerial candidate as a leader who could provide a positive thrust to India's economy and offer developmental solutions to all sections of society.

Ladakh

Like Jammu, Ladakh also elected for the first time a BJP candidate. In a close contest, BJP's Thupstan Chhewang, the founding father of the Ladakh Union Territory Front (LUTF), eked out a slim victory in the Ladakh Lok Sabha constituency with a razor thin margin of only 36 votes.

LUTF is a consortium of political parties formed in 2002 to carry out a unified regional struggle for the Union territory status for Ladakh. LUTF merged with the BJP in 2010. Chhewang defeated independent candidate Ghulam Raza, a senior Congress leader who decided to run as an independent when he was denied the party ticket.

Until 1996, the Congress Party held this seat except in 1989 when an independent candidate, Mohamad Hassan Commander, was elected. From 1998 through 2004, NC represented the Ladakh Lok Sabha constituency. Since 2004, this seat has only returned independent candidates. Chhewang had won in 2004 but as an independent leader. Ladakhis have once again expressed their discontent with the state administration and their historical demand for a closer association with the central administration in India; no less than Union Territory status for the region. Fearing their assimilation into a Muslim-dominated state, the Buddhists began their first agitation in 1969 and have insisted upon the protection of their distinct region and culture, which they feel is not possible within the existing Jammu and Kashmir governance structures. The BJP did promise the Union Territory status for Ladakh if it were to form the next government. And even though the Congress manifesto had similarly backed the Union Territory status, the Jammu and Kashmir Congress President Saif-ud-din Soz refused to include the demand for the Union Territory status to the frontier Ladakh region saying, "It is not the manifesto of Congress but a local demand."[21] Mehbooba Mufti, the PDP leader, accused the Congress of creating another partition. For her, "such a move will not only divide Jammu and Kashmir, but will also dilute the special status that the state enjoys under Article 370 of the constitution."[22] The upshot is that the BJP was the only party to categorically support the Union Territory demand. It was, therefore, not a surprise to see Thupstan Chhewang's victory, albeit with a very narrow margin.

The PDP Victory in the Valley

In the Valley, elections are a tricky business: the electoral arena has come to be occupied by two mainstream regional parties, the NC and the PDP. Each has carved out its own political space with their distinct agendas of governance, autonomy and India—Pakistan equation with regard to the Kashmir issue. The scope of electoral and democratic politics in the

Valley, however, remains circumscribed by the serious concerns of a larger alienated citizenry who continue to be mobilized in favor of *azadi* (freedom) by the nationalist/secessionist groups. The electoral success of either party, the NC or the PDP, largely depends upon the broader context of issues permeating the Valley that generate protest politics and consequent responses by the state government. The 2014 elections were held against the recent background of a politically charged atmosphere in the Kashmir Valley that had characterized the four-year period starting in 2009 with the Shopian incident and ending with the Afzal Guru hanging in 2013.

Generally, the Valley's Parliamentary voter turnout has been lower as compared to that of the Legislative Assembly elections, but it has yet to match the 1996 participation rate of 45.9 percent. The Valley is divided into two camps: voters and nonvoters. The former have consciously compartmentalized governance issues from their ethno-nationalist demands and participate in the electoral process with the aim of ensuring that their minimum daily needs will be met. The other group stays away from the polling booth respecting election boycott calls given by the separatist leaders. The latter reject the elections in the Valley pointing out that 'elections are no alternative to self-determination'. The separatist groups such as the different factions of the Hurriyat Conference, the Jammu and Kashmir Liberation Front, and jihadi outfits like the United Jihad Council have all painted elections as a meaningless farce. They did call for 'civil curfew' on April 24, 30, and May 7, three days of voting in Anantnag, Srinagar, and Baramulla, respectively. A large contingent of Indian police and paramilitary personnel were deployed in the Valley to prevent protests and to thwart any attempt by militants to disrupt the polling.

Protests and violence marred polls in the Kashmir Valley (Table 10.5). Police detained more than 500 people including most of the separatist leaders before the first round of voting in the Kashmir region. A poll official, a school teacher, was killed in the Shopian district by the militants and four others were wounded in an attack on a bus. A protest followed castigating the government for not providing foolproof security to its polling officers. In another incident, in Pulwama, two village heads were killed by local militants with the intent to frighten the voters away from polling. The death of a civilian youth by police firing affected voter turnout in Srinagar. There were numerous reports of protesters pelting stones at police and election officials in the Valley. Several police and security force stations and their vehicles were attacked. At least two dozen people were killed in election-related violence.

Poll boycott calls have greater resonance in urban areas resulting in low turnout. Table 10.6 shows that neighborhoods in and surrounding Srinagar such as Amirakadal, Hazartbal, Idgah, Khanyar, and Batmaloo have witnessed a much lower voter participation in Assembly elections. As compared to the rural constituencies, regular protests and complete shut downs are a common feature in these towns causes ranging from simple governance issues to *azadi* demands including protests against the abuses of police and the security forces. While the overall 2014 voter turnout remained very close to the last Lok Sabha elections, the usual separatist-supported urban constituencies recorded from very low

Table 10.5
Kashmir Region: Lok Sabha Turnout Percentage and the Winning Party

	Anantang	Srinagar	Baramulla
1967	NC-INC	35.9 JKN	49.8 INC
1971	63.5 INC	56.2 IND	49.2 INC
1977	52.8 INC	67.1 INC	54.5 JKN
1980	57.9 JKN	IND	54.0 JKN
1984	67.3 JKN	67.3 INC	58.9 JKN
1989	5.0 JKN	IND	5.4 JKN
1996	50.2 JD	40.9 INC	46.6 INC
1998	28.1 INC	30.1 JKN	41.8 JKN
1999	14.3 JKN	11.9 JKN	27.8 JKN
2004	15.0 PDP	18.6 JKN	35.7 JKN
2009	27.1 JKN	25.5 JKN	41.8 JKN
2014	28.0 PDP	26.0 PDP	39.1 PDP

Source: Election Commission of India from 1996 to 2009 results; 2014 voter turnout is based on newspaper reports.
Note: JD = Janata Dal.

Table 10.6
*Militant-support-based Constituencies in Kashmir Valley and Voter
Turnout Percentage in Assembly Elections*

	1996	2002	2008
Sopore	38.36	8.9	19.96
Hazratbal	23.78	7.12	28.19
Zadibal	12.71	4.78	17.31
Idgah	22.44	4.75	22.07
Khanyar	12.79	4.22	17.41
Habbakadal	17.17	3.21	11.62
Amirakadal	12.65	3.06	14.97
Batmaloo	19.72	4.01	19.97
Kashmir Region	52.3	29.7	51.6

Source: Election Commission of India.

to low voter participation. These include Habbakadal (1.75 percent),
Amirakadal (4.96 percent), Khanyar (7.3 percent), Idgah (7.5 percent),
Hazratbal (14.05 percent), Zadibal (12.84 percent), and Batmaloo
(12.87 percent).[23] The Sopore constituency recorded the lowest turnout at 1.02 percent. Not even a single vote was cast in many of the
polling stations in the town of Sopore. While its voter participation
record was low in the 2009 Parliamentary elections, merely 12 percent,
this time the area which had strongly resented the fact that Guru was
hanged out of turn and was not even allowed a last meeting with his
family, decided to boycott the elections. The situation after the election
day got worse in Sopore and other towns in the Baramulla constituency
when a group of young men, armed with *lathis*, took those people to
task who had voted.

PDP won all three seats in the Kashmir region with huge margins over
its close competitor, the NC. Its vote share was to remain almost the
same as compared to the 2009 Parliamentary elections. PDP's successes
can be largely explained by the poor performance of the NC. NC's share
of the electoral vote went down from 19.13 percent to 11.1 percent.
Thus, the PDP victory is fundamentally a vote against the incumbent
government and is not necessarily an endorsement of the PDP agenda.

Since forming the government in 2008 with the support of the Congress, Omar Abdullah's government has faced a very uncongenial regional environment. Despite his emphasis on good governance and change, his active positioning of the NC as a Kashmir-centric party, frank talk about militancy, Kashmir's autonomous and distinct status within the Indian federation, and the geopolitical reality of India and Pakistan, his government has been perceived as ineffective by the Valley in dealing with human rights violations and the abuse of power by security and police forces. The breakdown of the NC–Congress coalition on issues such as the Armed Forces (Special Powers) Act, a 2008 campaign promise which Omar pursued with no results, and the Guru hanging were to further reduce his internal legitimacy.

What also did not help Omar was his 2014 campaign strategy. He chose to campaign against Modi and the 'alleged' PDP/BJP partnership rather than speaking about the regional issues and using the Lok Sabha elections as a preparatory step toward winning the October Assembly elections, a mistake which Omar was to acknowledge after the PDP victory. The PDP, on the other hand, used these elections as a campaign against the incumbent government, its ineffectiveness, and as a step toward removing it from power in the upcoming Assembly elections (Table 10.7).

Four major events in the Kashmir Valley have proven the most damaging for Omar putting into question the effectiveness of his government. In May 2009, in the town of Shopian, the case of rape and murder of two women was mishandled initially by Omar Abdullah. After several mishaps, the Jammu and Kashmir government finally handed over the Shopian rape and murder case to the Central Bureau of Investigation. This action was too late for the government and damage had already been done. For more than three months, angry residents of Shopian

Table 10.7
Performance of NC and PDP: Voter Share Percentage in Lok Sabha Elections

Party	2014	2009
JKN	11.1	19.13
PDP	20.5	20.06

Source: Election Commission of India.

resorted to large-scale protests against the administration. There was much anger within the state. In December 2009, it was revealed that that across 55 villages, there were 2,700 unknown, unmarked mass graves containing almost 3,000 bodies, believed to be of missing civilians. In August 2011, the State Human Rights Commission confirmed the presence of mass graves in Kupwara, Baramulla, and Bandipora districts of the Valley. This was the first official acknowledgment of the disappeared civilians and that some of them might have been buried in mass graves in the Valley.[24] Not much progress has been made to identify the unmarked graves. The four-month-long 2010 protests in the form of stone-pelting in the Valley that ultimately resulted in the loss of 112 lives (mostly young men under the age of 34) started when it became known that the Indian army had killed three young men in a staged encounter in the Baramulla district, claiming that these young men were 'Pakistani infiltrators'. The unrest spread throughout the Valley resulting in a constant curfew for several days, which was to be defied by the protestors.

The February 2014 hanging of Afzal Guru involved the central government informing the family by mail and not handing over the body to the family. This was another controversial issue which was to mar Omar Abdullah's reputation and a further evidence of his inability to handle the Central government. Omar Abdullah criticized the government of India for using the death penalty on a selective basis and for not having had the courtesy to inform the family personally prior to Guru's execution. In light of his earlier record, Omar Abdullah's statements were not to have much resonance amongst the Valley's population who once again reacted with anger. And the final act was to vote against the NC in this election.

Concluding Reflections

Although Article 370 and Permanent Residence requirements did not figure at all in the Valley during the elections, these did become significant issues immediately after the Modi government assumed power, once again showing the huge potential for political volatility in Kashmir. Soon after taking his oath as a Minister of State, Jitendra Singh, the newly elected BJP member from Jammu, told a private news channel: "The process of repealing Article 370 has started. We are speaking to the stakeholders." This led to sharp reactions from three mainstream parties within the Valley, the NC, PDP, and Congress. Ghulam Nabi Azad, a veteran Congress leader from the state, asked the BJP to exercise caution and warned it about the sensitivity of these issues surrounding state politics.[25] Omar Abdullah tweeted, "Mark my words and save this tweet—long after Modi Govt is a distant memory either J&K won't be part of India or Articles 370 will still exist."

Omar Abdullah reminded the BJP minister that in order to revoke Article 370, the Constitutional Committee would need to be recalled and that cannot be done without questioning Kashmir's accession to India. He asked whether the BJP was willing to go in that direction. The PDP leader Mehbooba Mufti said in a statement that "The PMO must clarify the (Singh) statement to reassure the people of J&K that no mischief is on its way."[26] She also echoed Omar Abdullah's views on the relationship between the state's accession to India and Article 370. The BJP took immediate steps to undertake damage control. The law minister Ravishankar Prasad ensured everyone by stating that, "The government will take a structured view."[27] Singh also issued a clarification, "The reports in the media about my statement on Article 370 are misquoted."

During his first visit to Jammu and Kashmir after becoming the Prime Minister, Modi stayed away from the controversy generated by his minister on Article 370 and ensured the people that his priority was to win the hearts of the people of Jammu and Kashmir which can only be achieved through development and their welfare and that "the journey started by Atal Bihari Vajpayee in the state will be taken to its logical conclusion." BJP's 44 plus mission for the upcoming Assembly elections would certainly not be realizable if the Prime Minister Modi and the BJP do not tread carefully around Article 370. The Permanent Resident rules also remain sacrosanct and within the purview of the state government's jurisdiction. The Resettlement Bill remains explosive and one will have to wait for the Supreme Court's response to see how it is going to get played out. It will be interesting to see how the new Prime Minister handles, on the one hand, the Valley's strong commitment to Article

370 and citizenship regulations embedded in the Permanent Residence requirements, and on the other hand, the BJP and the RSS historical and traditional approach of one unified India and the abrogation of Article 370. This group also does not favor the Resettlement Bill and has been pushing for equal rights of citizenship for the Western Pakistani refugees settled in Jammu. Both of these do not find favor with any Kashmir-based political party.

As it has been for any other preceding central government, the twin-fold task which lies ahead for the Modi government is: first, to ensure that a distinct Kashmiri identity is reconciled within the larger frame-work of an Indian identity, neither one superseding the other; and, second, to maintain a delicate balance between the aspirations of Jammu and Kashmir's three distinct regions. The Valley's demand for autonomy and distinct identity ought to be taken seriously. Their participation in the electoral process remains limited. There is still a very large proportion of the population who remain outside the regular democratic political process. Those who participate in the elections are interested in pursuing their short-term economic/daily needs. They have continued their demands for *azadi* outside the institutional political framework. And those who do not participate in the elections need to be convinced of their association with both the regional and the national political agendas. For this group, the relaxation of AFSPA and protection of human rights remain central to their demands.

Although there is a general consensus that the state should actively support the safe return of Kashmiri Pandits to the Valley, any plan for their rehabilitation will have to be politically managed with the support of both the state government and the separatist element in the Valley. At the same time, Jammu will have to be managed carefully. The communal polarization of voters (Hindus voting for the BJP and the Muslims for the Congress) will further alienate the Valley's Muslims. In the past, Jammu's secular Hindus have maintained the political equilibrium in the state and the consolidation of Hindu votes in Jammu has remained only a partial phenomenon witnessed only during politically heightened periods.

What must be avoided at all costs is the adverse, negative impact of the symbiotic politics of the two regions. The more the Hindu popu-lation of Jammu and Udhampur raise the integrationist cry, the more defensive the Valley becomes in asserting its nationalism, which, in turn, further alienates the Jammu population. Like all its predecessors, the Modi government now faces a complex and challenging task. The election results of 2014 might appear to be both unanticipated and surprising, the ground reality has not shifted much. As the French would say: *plus ça change, plus c'est la même chose.*

Notes and References

1. For Modi's campaign speeches, see "Shri Narendra Modi addressing 'Lalkar Rally' in Jammu—Speech," http://www.youtube.com/watch?v=JHO-H4rERhQ and "Narendra Modi in Udhampur: AK47, AK Antony, and AK49 are praised in Pakistan," March 26, 2014 by *India 272 Campaign,* http://www.india272.com/2014/03/26/udhampur/ (accessed on July 10, 2014). All quotes are directly from Modi's speeches.

2. "Mirwaiz hails Vajpayee's stand on Kashmir," *Rediff News,* November 6, 2013, http://www.rediff.com/news/report/mirwaiz-hails-vajpayees-stand-on-kashmir/20131106.htm (accessed on July 15, 2014).

3. "Dr Farooq addresses public meetings in Khanyar-Magam/'Mufti Sayeed anti-Kashmir by conviction'/'Every single vote for NC will be vote against Modi–Mufti Alliance' *Kashmir Dispatch,* April 27, 2014, http://www.kashmirdespatch.com/news/dr-farooq-addresses-public-meetings-in-khanyar-magam-mufti-sayeed-anti-kashmir-by-conviction-every-single-vote-for-nc-will-be-vote-against-modi-mufti-alliance/ (accessed on July 10, 2014).

4. "Kashmir Will not Remain Part of a 'Communal' India, Farooq Abdullah Says," *Times of India,* April 27, 2014, http://timesofindia.indiatimes.com/news/Kashmir-will-not-remain-part-of-a-communal-India-Farooq-Abdullah-says/articleshow/34303011.cms (accessed on July 10, 2014).

5. "As Mehbooba Talks Kindly of Modi, Is PDP Sidling towards the BJP?" *F. India,* January 1, 2014, http://www.firstpost.com/india/as-mehbooba-talks-kindly-of-modi-is-pdp-sidling-towards-the-bjp-1317935 (accessed on July 11, 2014).

6. Quoted in P.L. Lakhanpal, *Essential Documents and Notes on Kashmir Dispute* (New Delhi: International Books, 1965), p. 311.

7. Amitabh Mattoo, "Understanding Article 370," *The Hindu,* December 3, 2013, http://www.thehindu.com/opinion/lead/understanding-article-370/article5426473.ece (accessed on July 31, 2014).

8. For a detailed analysis of Article 371A and the Nagaland tribal identity, see Kham Khan Suan Hausing, "Asymmetric Federalism and the Question of Democratic Justice in Northeast India," *India Review* 13, 2(2014), pp. 87–111.

9. Part Xll, Temporary, transitional and special provisions: Article 370. The Constitution of India, http://www.constitution.org/cons/india/p21370.html (accessed on July 31, 2014).

10. See, in particular, The Constitutional (Application to the Jammu and Kashmir Order) 1962, 1966, and 1985, and various amendments accompanying these Presidential orders, www.archive.india.gov.in/govt/documents/english/coi_appendix.pdf. For a detailed list (and a discussion) of all Presidential Orders and the accompanying amendments, see *Report of the State Autonomy Committee,* pp. 64–90.

11. Report of the State Autonomy Committee, p. 88.
12. One of the prominent voices of the opposition has been that of the Kashmiri Pandit community. See Mohan Kishen Teng, "Kashmir Article 370" in Kashmiri Pandit Network, http://www.koausa.org/article370/preface.html (accessed on July 10, 2014).
13. This part of the 1954 Presidential Order reads as follows:
    35A. Saving of laws with respect to permanent residents and their rights. Notwithstanding anything contained in this Constitution, no existing law in force in the State of Jammu and Kashmir, and no law hereafter enacted by the Legislature of the State,

    (a) defining the classes of persons who are, or shall be permanent residents of the State of Jammu and Kashmir; or
    (b) conferring on such permanent residents any special rights and privileges or imposing upon other persons any restrictions as respects,

       (i) employment under the State Government;
       (ii) acquisition of immovable property in the State;
       (iii) settlement in the State; or
       (iv) right to scholarships and such other forms of aid as the State Government may provide,

    shall be void on the ground that it is inconsistent with or takes away or abridges any rights conferred on the other citizens of India by any provision of this Part.". The Constitution (Application to Jammu and Kashmir) Order, 1954, http://www.jklaw.nic.in/constitution_jk.pdf (accessed on July 15, 2014)
14. In September 1951, a general election was held for 75 constituent assembly seats. Jammu's Hindu Nationalist party, the Praja Parishad (later to merge with Bharatiya Jan Sangh), which protested the limited integration of the state into the Indian union, boycotted the election. Consequently, all 75 seats were won without contest by the National Conference. For a detailed discussion, see Reeta Chowdhari Tremblay "Jammu: Autonomy within an Autonomous Kashmir" in Raju G.C. Thomas (ed.) Perspectives on Kashmir: The Roots of Conflict in South Asia (Boulder, CO: Westview Press, 1992), pp. 153–67.
15. Mohan Kishen Teng, Ram Kishen Bhat, and Santosh Kaul, Kashmir: Constitutional History and Documents (New Delhi: Light and Life Publishers, 2006), p. 210.
16. 2002 JKJ 21990 High Court of Jammu and Kashmir at Jammu, Full Bench, Before Muzaffar Jan, T.S. Doabia, V.K. Jhanji, JJJ; State of Jammu and Kashmir vs. Susheela Sawhney (Dr) Date of Decision: 10 July,2002; Paragraphs 40 and 41. We would like to extend our thanks to H.L. Chowdhari, Advocate Jammu and Kashmir High Court, for making the full judgment available to us.
17. 2002 JKJ 21990 High Court of Jammu and Kashmir at Jammu, Paragraph 48.
18. 2002 JKJ 21990 High Court of Jammu and Kashmir at Jammu, Paragraph 43.
19. The PDP was a minority government and held power with the support of the Congress Party.
20. For details, see Reeta Chowdahri Tremblay, "Kashmir's Secessionist Movement Resurfaces: Ethnic Identity, Community Competition, and the State," Asian Survey XLIX, 6(November/December 2009), pp. 924–50.
21. "Ladakh Union Territory status row: Mehbooba Mufti lashes out at Cong," Oneindia News, Srinagar Lok Sabha Election 2014 Special Coverage, April 20, 2014, http://news.oneindia.in/srinagar/ladakh-union-territory-status-row-mehbooba-mufti-lashes-out-at-cong-lse-1431268.html (accessed on July 30, 2014).

22. Ibid.

23. As detailed statistics have not been published by the Election Commission, these figures are based on newspaper reports and their exit polls.

24. Thousands of young men have disappeared in Kashmir. Some went to be trained as militants in Azad Kashmir, while the others were killed or detained by the security forces in the Valley. The wives they left behind are known as half-widows, because the fates of their husbands are unknown. Parents keep vigil for sons who were arrested two decades ago.

25. "BJP using Article 370 to garner votes for Jammu and Kashmir polls: Congress," *Economic Times*, June 23, 2014, http://articles.economictimes.indiatimes.com/2014-06-23/news/50798511_1_article-370-office-jitendra-singh-kashmiri-pandits (accessed on July 30, 2014).

26. "Modi's minister talks of Article 370 debate; Omar, Mehbooba fume," *Rediff News*, May 27, 2014, http://www.rediff.com/news/report/modis-minister-talks-of-article-370-debate-omar-mehbooba-fume/20140527.htm (accessed on July 30, 2014).

27. Ibid.

11

Mega Marketing and Management: Gujarat's 2014 Elections

*Ghanshyam Shah**

For Narendra Modi, the 2012 Gujarat State Assembly elections was a prelude to the 2014 Lok Sabha polls. Assuming himself to be BJP's prime ministerial candidate in the forthcoming elections, he launched his campaign on the very day of the assembly result. He delivered a 'thanks giving' speech to his electorate in Hindi and not Gujarati, as if he was addressing the people of India. Though BJP did not do as well in the state assembly as it did in 2007, he set a target of 100 percent of the 26 Lok Sabha seats from Gujarat in 2014. And, he did succeed. The party surpassed its earlier record by securing more than 59 percent votes.

Congress was completely routed although it came close to its 1991 position in vote share. But, in terms of seats, it was the worst since the state was formed in 1961. In fact, after its debacle in 1991, Congress was slowly catching up with BJP. The gap between the two was only

*I thank Loknit, CSDS for permitting me to use election survey data, Himanshu Bhattacharya for generating tables, Shama Desai for introducing me to digital social network media, and Paul Wallace and Achyut Yagnik for their comments on the earlier draft of the paper and several friends who shared their observations of the election with me.

Figure 11.1
Vote Share between BJP and Congress in Parliament Elections in Gujarat

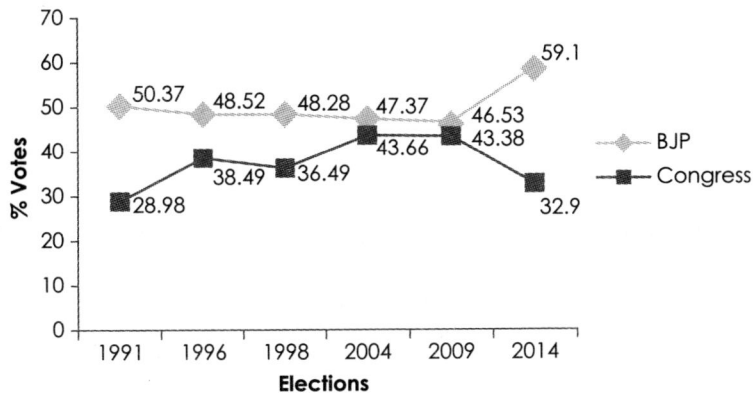

Source: Statistical report on general elections.

3.15 percent of votes in the 2009 elections (Figure 11.1). But instead of consolidating its strength, Congress declined rapidly. Within six months of the 2012 polls, the party lost its four seats to BJP in the June 2013 by-poll. That reinforced Congress' depression, while stimulating Modi's tactical moves to conquer all the Lok Sabha seats.

In my earlier analysis of the 2009 elections, I argued that despite the relatively better performance of the Congress-led UPA as perceived by Gujarati voters, BJP still could win 15 out of 26 seats due to Narendra Modi's political craft. He mesmerized people with his superior propaganda and management skills, euphonically called governance.[1] My argument remains the same in this chapter.

Modi was anointed as the BJP Prime Ministerial candidate in September 2013. Before that, in his Independence Day speech, he essentially asked the nation to compare his speech delivered at Lalan College Bhuj with Prime Minister Manomohan Singh's speech from Lal Quila, Delhi. The Gujarat chief minister (CM) presented himself as an alternative national leader for 'development' and 'security'. In fact, in the previous Lok Sabha elections, though Advani was BJP's Prime Ministerial candidate, Modi asserted in his campaign speeches that Gujarat's model would be followed for the country's development if the BJP-led NDA came to power at the Center. On the polling day, the BJP advertisement declared: *Gujaratna Gauravvanta* (For whom Gujarat is proud) CM Narendra Modi appeals to the people of Gujarat, "Gujarat's uninterrupted (*avirat*) path for development with the clearly laid down policy of my government has continued with a mantra, 'For the *vikas* (development) of Bharat, *vikas* of Gujarat'."[2] Be it noted that a majority of BJP voters in Gujarat preferred Modi to Advani in their choice for prime minister in 2009.

Party Organization

During his 10-year tenure, he successfully converted Gujarat's BJP into Modi's party. Slowly, he eliminated or silenced all dissident voices from the party. He decided who gets when, how much, and what share in power. In his view, none of his party members had the imagination to run the party and the state with 'efficiency'. As a brilliant strategist he changed his tactics from time to time and region-to-region to select political aspirants. At one time he followed a 'no repeat' policy for sitting members, another time he favored most of the sitting members as candidates. For a long period, he did not appoint political leaders as chairpersons of several Government Corporations/Boards. Then, in October 2013 for the first time in the 10 years, he appointed chairpersons for 11 Boards/Corporations to appease disgruntled and aspiring party colleagues.

As in the past elections, Modi had the major say in the selection of the BJP Gujarat candidates in 2014. While selecting candidates, he took into account a combination of factors: first and foremost personal loyalty, then caste identity and money power of the aspirants. This time 10 sitting MPs were repeated and nine sitting MLAs including three ministers were selected. The party fielded six new faces, including three former Congressmen who joined the party on the eve of elections, one industrialist and one noted film actor.

The Congress Party, the only rival of the BJP in the state, was faction ridden. Three major factions are: the erstwhile members of the Rashtriya Janata Party (RJP) led by the former BJP leader Shankersinh Vaghela, the former Janata Dal members, and the remaining 'original' Congressmen. A tug of war among the state leaders discouraged and generated cynicism in the rank and file. Each faction attempted to please 'the High command', that is, the central Congress leadership, to favor his or her loyalists. Ahmed Patel, the political secretary of Sonia Gandhi, the party president, functioned as an intermediary between her and the aspirants. Patel, the former MP and a minister in the Gujarat government in the 1980s, lacked a base in the state. He enjoyed power mainly because of his closeness to Gandhi.

"Congress also has centralized authority like the Gujarat BJP but our centralized authority has no roots and political understanding of ground reality like that of Modi," a senior Congressman said.[3] Moreover, as an average Congress person perceived very little ideological difference between both the parties s/he was susceptible of any opportunity to gain power. Modi is aware of this. He used all tactics to win over important local Congress functionaries with a local patronage network. On the eve of the Assembly elections, a few other important state and local Congress leaders joined BJP. Narhari Amin, former Deputy CM, in the early 1990s was a prominent defector. The process escalated as 2014 approached. Defectors include MLAS Jasa Barad, Bavku, Kotadia from Saurashtra, and Chavada from north Gujarat. Around 1,000 Congress workers of National Students Union (NSU) deserted the party and joined BJP in May 2013.

Similar to the BJP, major considerations for the Congress in selection of candidates were winnability coupled with money power and caste networking. On the whole, the dispirited state Congress leaders had almost given up any hope to win. Even some of the sitting Congress MPs including a minister in the UPA government was reluctant to contest. As late as January, on the eve of the election campaign the party introduced on an experimental basis the system of 'primaries' for selection of candidates through local party workers in 15 Lok Sabha constituencies in the country. Two of them were from Gujarat—Vadodara and Bhavnagar. However, the party changed the Vadodara candidate who was not sufficiently confident to contest against Modi.

Gujarat Parivartan (transformation) Party, a BJP off-shoot was formed in August 2012. It had a one-point program to oppose Narendra Modi. With a Patidar brotherhood and disgruntled BJP elements, it gained 3.63 percent votes with only two seats in the assembly. Soon after the assembly poll, Modi skillfully managed to win over the spoilers, mainly Patidars, and the party merged with BJP in February 2014. AAP came into existence in 2013, but its party structure remained ad hoc. Initially, the party appeared to pose a threat to the BJP by focusing on the mobilization of the urban middle class, but it could not succeed. AAP contested all the seats but lacked an effective organizational network.

Party Structures

Both BJP and Congress have party structures extending from the village/city level to the state level (Figure 11.2). At each level they have executive committees and office bearers. Before the poll, election committees were formed at each level to organize public meetings, contact voters,

Figure 11.2
BJP Election Party Structure

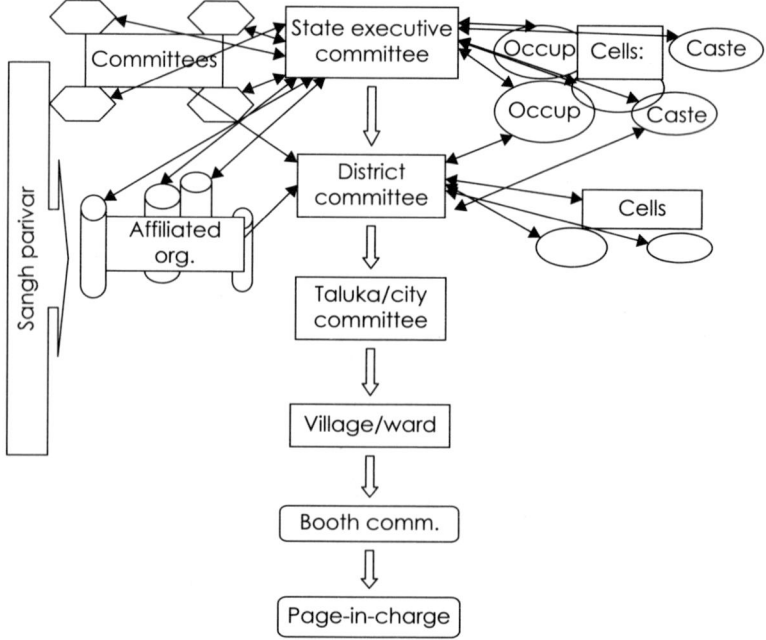

Source: Author.

and mobilize people for meetings and voting. Moreover, both parties have committees for women, Scheduled Castes, Scheduled Tribes, Backward Castes, and minorities. BJP is more organized than Congress in activating these committees. BJP also formed caste- and occupation-based cells at the state as well as local levels. Occupations-based cells included doctors, Chartered accountants, lawyers, fishermen, unorganized workers, and migrants. In Vadodara, the party formed a *Jyotish* (astrologer) cell which besides conducting *pujas* and *yagnas* for the party, was used to "promote religion and spirituality according to party lines and spread message of the party."[4]

On paper, both parties formed polling booth committees. Most of the Congress committees during the Assembly elections remained dormant in contrast to those of the BJP. It was more so during the 2014 Lok Sabha elections. BJP claimed it constituted 42,000 booth committees out of 44,000 booths in Gujarat. In order to secure all seats with impressive margins, BJP's strategy was to mobilize all voters so as to achieve a 100 percent voting turnout. With this view, each booth was divided into a cluster of 100 voters listed on an electoral roll page. Responsibility of each cluster was assigned to a worker designated as Page-in-Charge (Figure 11.2). This was specifically done in Vadodara from where Modi was contesting. To encourage grass roots workers, the party announced that Modi himself would felicitate those who could achieve 100 percent voting. The BJP had better booth management than the Congress.[5]

According to legal provisions, each candidate has a right to appoint a representative for each booth to oversee impartial functioning of voting. In our observations of a few booths, we found that each booth had a committed BJP agent, well versed with procedures. This was not the case with many Congress agents. In two booths in Vadodara, we noticed that Congress agents were mute spectators where local BJP municipal councilors entered the polling booth in the afternoon, and sought information from their representative regarding those who had not voted. And from the premise itself the absentee individual was called on a mobile to come to vote. Neither the Congress agent nor the presiding officer objected. Moreover, there were quite a few booths both in urban and rural areas where Congress agents were absent. AAP also did not have their agents in many booths.[6]

Both parties have affiliated organizations working in between and during the elections to mobilize public opinion; for example, students, labor, and women. Unlike Congress, BJP has close ties with kisan (farmer) organizations and close links with numerous religious and cultural organizations called Sangh Parivar that includes RSS, Swadeshi Jagran Manch (SJM), VHP, Bajrang Dal, Hindu Milan Mandir, and others. Though Gujarat VHP and also Kisan Sangh as well as SJM were lukewarm to support Modi in the 2012 Assembly elections, all of them actively canvassed for BJP and enthusiastically mobilized their supporters to vote for BJP in 2014. For them it was a war for righteousness in which Modi was Krishna as well Arjun—a strategist and warrior to build 'Akhand Bharat', that is, undivided India that includes Pakistan and Bangladesh. While analyzing the election outcome, Gujarat VHP's journal *Viswa Hindu Samachar* observed that a 'Hindu undercurrent' was more dominant in the 2014 election campaign than that during the Ram Janmabhomi movement of the late 1980s. According to the editor of the journal, various moves by Modi, his and/or his companions' direct or indirect pro-Hindutva statements were enough to boost the morale of Hindutva proponents in Gujarat as well as elsewhere.[7]

Campaign

Modi has been an election campaign manager for himself and the party much before the task was assigned to him in 2013 by BJP.[8] His drive to project himself as a visionary and a strong leader for development as well as a savior of India was implicit after his second time victory in the Gujarat Assembly poll in 2007. According to some observers, he undertook a systematic campaign, projecting himself at a national level after the fall of the NDA government.[9] It was more so in the 2009 elections. Business and other summits in Gandhinagar, Gujarat's capital between 2011 and 2013 reinforced his goal. Reaching out to rural India, particularly rich peasants, the Government of Gujarat (GoG) organized the 'Vibrant Gujarat Global Agriculture summit 2013' in the first week of September. Around 4,000 farmers from 542 districts attended the function. He felicitated 'progressive' farmers of different states.

Similarly, to attract youths, the state government organized 'Vibrant Gujarat National Education Summit 2014' in February. Moreover, in the business/investors summit in January 2013, a few leading industrial tycoons from Gujarat not only praised his ability but also expressed the opinion that he was the best person for India's economic development. On August 3, *The Times of India* published an advertorial and promotional feature on the 'Most Influential Gujaratis'. It highlighted some industrial tycoons and Narendra Modi as 'son of the soil'. Newspaper advertisements of GoG's August 15, 2013 declared, "Gujarat leading the way for a brighter tomorrow." On the next day (14 September) of the party's official announcement about BJP's Prime Ministerial candidate, in full-page newspaper advertisements several infrastructure entrepreneurs congratulated him and wished him success. The advertisements also declared: "Gujarat has been transformed (under his leadership)," "the country will see true nature of development," "One who has provided successful leadership to Gujarat will take the country to new height of development," "Now India awaits to shine under the visionary, vibrant and valiant leadership of Shri Narendra Modi," "Gujarat's pride, India's icon," etc.

After 2007, Modi focused all his election campaigns—state assembly and Parliament—on 'development'.[10] In 2014, the Gujarat model of development was the central theme. At the same time in subtle ways, a Hindutva plank was also well entrenched. Under his leadership, Gujarat Pavitra Yathradham Vikas (Holy Pilgrimage Development) Board spent 38 crore between 2003 and 2011 for 'development and organizing fairs' at Hindu temples.[11] None of the non-Hindu pilgrimages, except one Jain holy town, received any finances for their 'development'. This financial support was over and above infrastructure development in and around the temple towns.[12]

Among all places the state government promoted Ambaji temples more than others. One of the reasons for this favor according to the media's interpretation is that the CM is a strong believer in Goddess Amba. The temple organized *yatras* (processions) with 10 vehicles covering 10,000 km that travelled across the state in the first week of February 2014. The exterior of the decorated vans featured Modi who was "more visible than the temple'." The Tourism Department of GoG spent two crore rupees for the Shakti Pith Pran Prathistha Mahottsav (inauguration of replica of 50 Shakti Piths located across the Indian subcontinent) and other publicity. In a way, with this function a full-fledged election campaign was launched.[13]

During the Assembly elections, he posed himself as the primary candidate on behalf of all the party candidates. The party and/or others contestants were made almost irrelevant. Realizing that the BJP could suffer if a local incumbency became a deciding factor, he upped the stakes saying "I am your candidate on all 182 assembly seats. Every vote you cast for local BJP candidate is a vote for me."[14] The same strategy was followed in the 2014 Lok Sabha campaign in the country replacing 'Gujarat' with India. He told voters of the country, "*Aaj khud apne liye vote maang raha hoon ... meri appeal hai har gaali aur kuche se, aap ka vote seedhe, seedhe mujhe milega* (Today I am seeking a vote for myself. I want to tell all voters that your vote will reach me directly)."[15]

Gujarat Pride: Our Gujarati Prime Minister

In February, BJP floated a slogan appealing to Gujaratis to vote for a Gujarati, Narendra Modi to make him the country's Prime Minister. The main slogan told people that all Gujaratis would rejoice and take pride when "a Gujarati would become Prime Minister as we have witnessed progress under his leadership (in Gujarat)."[16] The state was projected as a model of development for the country. In the earlier election, the BJP repeatedly accused the Congress of being anti-Gujarat, jealous of Gujarat's development, obstructing it, and other accusations. The BJP repeatedly harped in the campaign that "Gujarat will get justice instead of a stepmotherly attitude and injustice when a Gujarati will become a Prime Minister (*Ormaya vartan ne badale have malse 'nyay'*)". During the campaign many more messages such as the following were frequently circulated through SMS and BJP's advertisements in Gujarati newspapers:

1. Ideals of Gandhi and Sardar Patel would realize when a Gujarati wins (*Gandhi ane Sardar na adarsho ni hayati jyare jitshe Gujarati*).
2. Let us not miss an opportunity to make a Gujarati as Prime Minister (*Tak rahi na jaya baki, banao vadapradhan Gujarati*).

3. Each and every Gujarati believes that a Gujarati (Modi) will fulfill dreams (*Ek-Ek Gujaratina dil ni vat, ek Gujarati karshe sapana sakar*).
4. For throne of justice, for felicitation of a lion of Gujarat (*Nayana sinhasan mate, Gujaratna sinhna sanamn mate*).

Congress was dumbfounded and did not know how to counter BJP's call for Gujarat identity and pride, symbolizing Modi. Furthermore, Modi announced a project to construct the world's tallest statue of Sardar Patel, symbolizing India's unity. This was a move to win over the peasantry in general and Patidars of Gujarat in particular, and to counter Nehru's idea of secularism and socialism as well as denigrate Sonia Gandhi. Perhaps most important, Gujarat Congress candidates were facing a funding shortage for advertising their campaigns. According to some estimates, funding differences between BJP and Congress candidates were as much as 9:1.[17] This was evident even to a casual observer while moving around the state in urban and rural areas seeing billboards, bus stand shelters, kiosks, and local newspaper advertisements. I also heard stories from pro-Congress activists that some of their candidates were most interested to save money. They were so demoralized that they accepted their defeat even before the campaign started.

Social Media

Nearly 80 percent households both in rural and urban Gujarat have cell phones.[18] Modi very effectively tapped this network plus social media, particularly, to reach out to the rural population. Modi, technologically savvy, had formed a team of digital experts in Gandhinagar in 2000. The team carefully watched Senator Barack Obama's United States presidential campaign in 2008. They also studied Mayavati's campaign in 2007–08 using a mobile phone network for booth management and interaction with voters in UP.[19] During the 2012 Assembly elections, Modi homologated himself to new social media 'language'. An interactive phone line was set up so that people from remote areas could listen to Modi's voice on a handset.

He repeated the use of various types of technology on a very large scale in the Lok Sabha campaign. Immediately taking charge of the BJP

campaign committee, he launched the digital India 272+ mission, refer-
ring to the number of seats he needed for a majority in Parliament. The
target was to mobilize young middle-class voters, enrolling and enthus-
ing them to spread Modi's messages; and also enlist others via mobile
phones. SMS and WhatsApp also were used to circulate jokes and tidbits
in Gujarati about Rahul and Congress; and messages around "Abb ki bar
Modi sarkar" (Now this time Modi will form the government). Congress
also used this strategy but it was late and slow to integrate social media
platforms like Twitter and Facebook. The party could not match BJP's
aggressive campaign.

Who Voted for Whom?

Both for the assembly and Lok Sabha elections, BJP tried its level best to
achieve a maximum turnout of voters. The party assumed that upper and
middle castes/classes were anti-Congress and apathetic to cast their vote.
Hence, it concentrated on these classes to generate a maximum vote. Its
polling booth management was geared for 100 percent voting particularly in urban areas. Incentives were offered to party workers to mobilize
voters in large numbers. The election commission and civil society organizations also extensively campaigned asking citizens to exercise their
voting rights for strengthening democratic participation.

All civil society organizations, including religious organizations,
were not straight forward in their messages. Some organizations, without naming Modi, appealed to their followers to vote for a 'corruption
free India', 'development', 'patriot', efficient management, etc. Though
seemingly non-political messages, they implicitly favored Modi. But
despite the intensive campaign for 100 percent voting, 36 percent did
not exercise their right. Though voting turnout in Gujarat was higher
(63.60 percent) than 2009 (47.90 percent), it was lower than the all
India average which was 66.40 percent. It is important to note that
among those who voted, 4,54,880 (1.8 percent) expressed their opinion that none of the candidates was their preference. They pushed the
NOTA 'None of the Above' button. In 17 constituencies out of 26 in
Gujarat, NOTA remained the third preferred choice of electors, after
BJP and Congress.

According to the National Election Survey (NES), though as many as three-fourth of the voters from Gujarat expressed their satisfaction with the performance of the UPA government in the 2009 elections, a majority of them did not vote for Congress. Instead they preferred the BJP/NDA because of their satisfaction with the state government.[20] In 2014, the proportion of the voters expressing satisfaction with the UPA government declined by 10 points. On the other hand, their satisfaction with Modi's government continued to remain high across the electorate. Hence, the outcome in favor of Modi was obvious. However perception about satisfaction is also colored with received and/or expected tangible benefits in one's socio-economic context and aspirations.

Though caste is not the determinant factor in voting, it is not unimportant either. Granting that all castes and communities are socially and economically stratified, both the parties consider that caste of a candidate matters in mobilization of voters. Therefore, social identity of an aspirant together with social composition of a constituency remains their major consideration in selecting party candidates. Moreover, caste/community organizations also build pressures on the parties to have more party candidates from their castes. Out of 26 constituencies, three are reserved for STs and two for SCs. Among the remaining seats, middle-caste majority candidates of both parties belonged to OBCs and Patidars. One Congress candidate was a Muslim, while the BJP had none. From upper castes, BJP had three and Congress had only one. In most of the constituencies, candidates of the same caste fought against each other, expecting to nullify the caste effect.

Socially and Economically Upper Strata

BJP and Congress do not have any substantial difference in their economic policy. Both subscribe to a neo-liberal path of development. With economic growth a 'new' middle class has emerged to some extent cutting across social boundaries.[21] In terms of size and number, upper and middle castes have a very larger proportion of growth benefits than lower castes, Dalits, tribals, and Muslims. Aspirations of this class, shaken with rising inflation and economic uncertainties coupled with published scams involving UPA leaders, tilted toward Modi's promises.

Figure 11.3

Voting by Economic Status in Different Elections

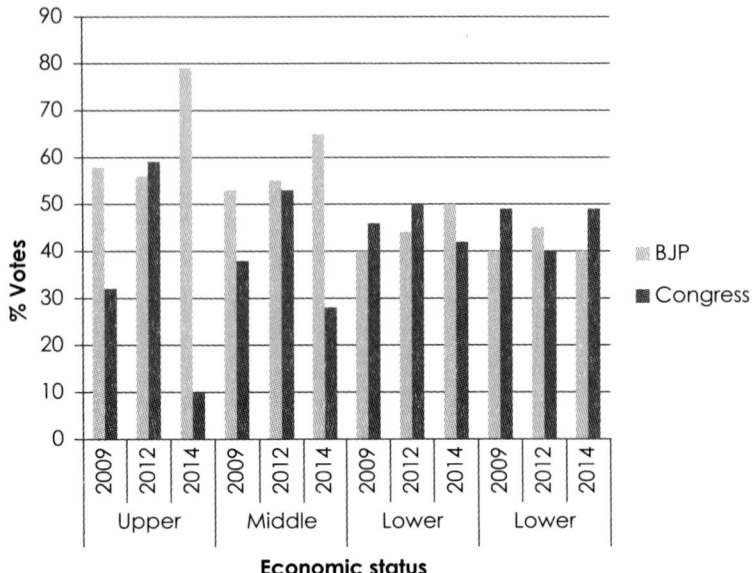

Source: National Election Study, Centre for the Study of Developing Societies, Delhi (NES), 2014.

In fact, Gujarati's middle class had already shifted to BJP since the mid-1980s with the Advani-led Ram Janmabhoomi movement.

Since 2007, Modi consolidated BJP's middle-class support base by focusing his governance and campaign to woo them further. Majority of the youths, below 25 years and school–college studied voted for BJP. Only one out of four preferred Congress. A large section of upper- and middle-class voters in Gujarat have been with the BJP since the 1990s. Their proportion, however, has increased at a phenomenal level from 58 to 79 percent of the upper class, and from 53 to 65 percent of the middle class between 2009 and 2014 (Figure 11.3). A similar pattern among the upper and middle caste voters is observed. Their proportion has also increased from 63 to 68 percent between 2009 and 2014. Nevertheless, their proportion had gone down to an all time low since 1995 (57 percent) in the 2012 Assembly polls. But the Congress was not its beneficiary (Figure 11.3). Upper caste/class BJP votes had gone to GPP which merged with BJP on the eve of elections.

Deprived Castes/Communities and Poor

Since 1970s, the Gujarat Congress has carved out its image as 'pro-poor'. Earlier, it had a band of active pro-poor leaders at the state as well as local levels. They lobbied for the interests of the deprived communities, worked for them, and actively engaged in delivering the benefits of welfare programs. The number of such committed workers has shrunk during the last two decades. Their involvement in implementation of or building pressure on local administration to translate welfare programs launched by the UPA government was almost invisible. At the most they complained to the media that the "Modi government was for industrialists."

BJP also have a few volunteers who have been working to help the poor through philanthropic activities. Their number however is not only smaller than the Congress workers but their patronizing attitude with religio-centered Hindutva reinforcing traditional hierarchical values could not sustain the confidence of the poor. Moreover, in the last 10 years, a few of the vocal pro-poor BJP/RSS workers have been marginalized within the party. However, Modi's government used UPA sponsored central welfare schemes to penetrate among the poor. GoG organized 642 garib mela (fair for BPL people) in the different parts of the state during 2010–12 in which the CM disbursed dole money to beneficiaries.[22] With all these efforts BJP succeeded in making a crack in the Congress share among lower income groups aspiring for middle-class position, what Modi called 'neo-middle' class (Figure 11.3). But its vote share among poor has not improved. Congress continues to have an edge over BJP.

Other Backward Classes

Socially and educationally backward castes/communities, called OBCs constitute more than one-fourth of Gujarat's population. OBC is an amorphous category with several jatis competing among themselves for social status. At a collective level, they hardly share an identity of being OBC. Kolis of the coastal area and Kshatriyas of the plain together constitute the single largest OBC. Efforts to unite them for social and political purposes have so far failed because of historical and cultural reasons.[23]

Figure 11.4
BJP Voters by Castes/Communities

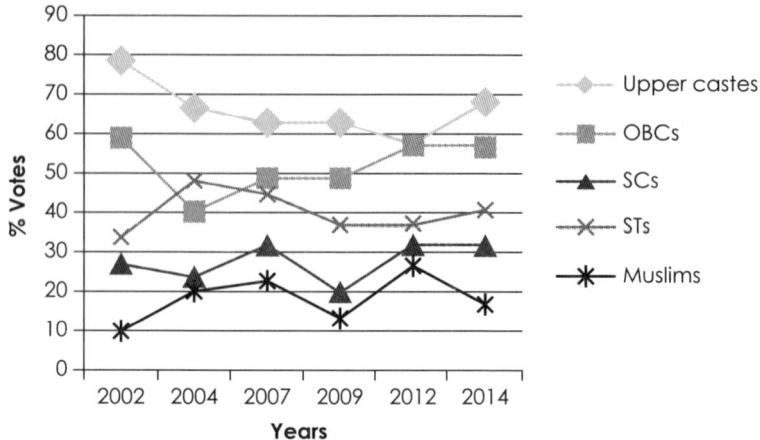

Source: National Election Study.

The rest of the OBC castes are scattered and fragmented. Wide gaps prevail in the economic condition among OBCs and within a few castes. A few OBC castes like artisans and middle peasants have somewhat improved their economic position and come closer to middle castes. Till the 1980s, Congress enjoyed their support, but the situation changed with BJP's Hindutva card. In different elections support of various segments of OBCs vacillate between the BJP and Congress. Narendra Modi for the first time explicitly revealed his identity of being an OBC. Majority (57 percent) of the OBC voters voted for BJP. A declining trend of OBC support to Congress began in 2007 reaching its lowest in 2014 (Figures 11.4 and 11.5).

Dalits

Scheduled Castes, that is, Dalits constitute seven percent of the population. Though BJP captured both the SC-reserved seats in parliament and three of 12 SC-reserved seats in the 2012 Assembly elections, a majority of Dalits does not support the party. Numerically, they are insignificant in any of the parliament constituencies, and none of the assembly constituencies has more than 15 percent SC voters. By and large they

Figure 11.5
Congress Voters by Castes/Communities

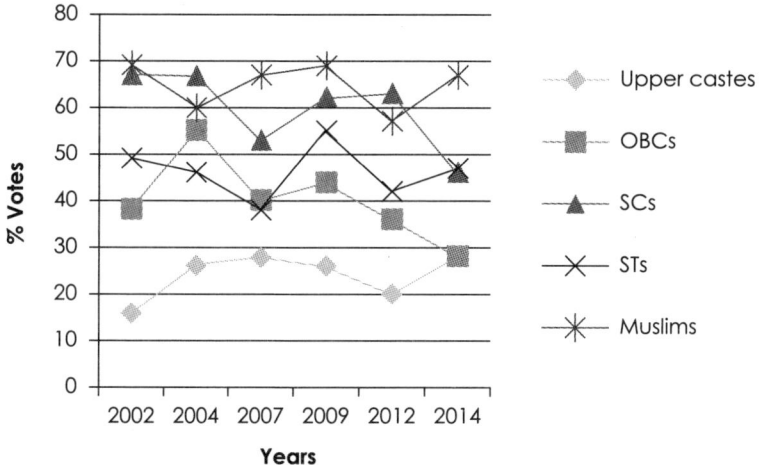

Source: National Election Study.

have continued to remain Congress supporters, though in 2014 its share declined significantly from 63 percent in 2009 to 46 percent in 2014 (Figure 11.5).

But loss of Congress was not BJP's gain. SC Congress voters have shifted to AAP or Independents. Only one-third of SCs voted for BJP. The party did try to woo them by co-opting a few Dalit litterateurs as well as political aspirants and hijacking Dr Ambedkar by celebrating his birthday as 'samrasata' (harmony) day. Non-party Dalit activists have often questioned the party on ideological grounds. They opposed the notion of 'samrasata' which hegemonies dominant Brahmanical ideology. In 2013, large number of Dalits celebrated Dr Ambedkar's birthday as 'samanta', that is, equality day as against the 'samrasta' day.

To counter Modi's project to build Sardar's statue, activists campaigned for Dr Ambedkar's statue. They argued that he united the country with his role in drafting India's Constitution. The activists organized village-to-village processions spreading Ambedkar's vision for an egalitarian society from December 25, 2013 to January 26, 2014. Moreover, Modi's government failed to take effective measures against an unabated rise in cases of atrocities against Dalits. GoG ignored the evidence related to the practice of untouchability in rural Gujarat.[24] BJP was caught in a dilemma between its core constituency of upper/middle castes, perpetrators of untouchability, and the Dalit victims.

Adivasis

ST constitutes 14 percent of the state population. Among the poor they are the largest in number residing in the most 'backward' blocks of the state. They are the victims of expansionist hegemonic culture and capitalist development. In the course of time, however, a small middle class of tribals has emerged. Most of them willy-nilly follow the footsteps of non-tribal upper castes in their aspirations and world view.

For years, Congress enjoyed their support in elections, thanks to a wide spread institutional network of Gandhians engaged in the field of education and so-called 'social reform', albeit Hinduization. Hindutva forces with education and socio-cultural reform entered the area from the 1960s and gradually expanded their base with the Ram Janambhumi movement. Congress' support base began to get shaken as dissatisfaction against its rule was mounting coupled with the marginalization of pro-tribal leaders with the party. Congress tribal leaders tended to block the entry of new leadership. For the first time in 1990, BJP won six out of 26 state Assembly ST reserved seats. Congress secured seven and a majority of the seats went to 'others' who were projecting themselves as 'radical' fighting against their exploitation by non-tribals.

BJP had successfully fractured these 'others' in the following elections and won 14 seats. Hindutva forces skillfully mobilized tribals in the 2002 anti-Muslim carnage. Soon after, BJP captured a majority of ST seats. But once emotions receded, it could not sustain its hold. BJP realized that mere mobilization around culture would not help beyond a point to win tribals. Hence, the mission for Hinduization through construction of temples as pilgrimage/tourist places was incorporated with a 'development' agenda.[25]

Vanbandhu Kalyan Yojana (VKY), a 10-point scheme with a total of ₹150 billion for the period of 2007–12 was launched.[26] Under VKY the government implemented several schemes to improve their livelihood. Except for high pitch publicity there was nothing new in the approach and method of implementation of these schemes as compared with the earlier Integrated Rural Development Programme (IRDP). As in the past, these programs lacked integration and forward and backward linkages. A positive impact on the life of tribals is not visible.[27-29] As they are on the receiving end of the capitalist market, there is not only "an increase in poverty risk, but also an increase in the incidence of poor" in the tribal region.[30]

To absorb young tribals in the market economy, the GoG opened Industrial Training Institutes (ITI) in most of the tribal talukas to provide short-term skill development. For school educated youth, 30 new Kaushalya Vardhan Kendra (skilled development centers) to impart professional skills were created in tribal areas in 2014. Modi launched the 'the first of its kind' Kaushalya Raths to train youth. The government announced that these *rathas* (vans) would move in interior parts of the state where ITI training centers were not available.[31] Having been disappointed with his party's performance in assembly polls in tribal areas, Modi geared up his administration to reach out to tribals. Besides appointing his trusted bureaucrats as *prabhari*, that is, monitor for each of the tribal districts, the GoG centralized monitoring of VKY programs. Implementation of Forest Rights Act (2006)[32] also was expedited. Till 2010, the government gave land rights to only eight percent of the applicants.[33] Enforcement of the Act was prioritized further after assembly results. Claims of 35 percent of the applicants were granted by March 2014. In October 2013, the CM distributed letters of their right to 15,000 tribal farmers in a public function.[34]

All these efforts did help BJP to somewhat improve its vote share of the tribals but could not make much dent in Congress votes. Anti-Congress votes of other parties or independent candidates had gone to BJP. It won all the three reserved ST seats, and swept more votes than Congress from 17 assembly segments through its election management. The Congress also improved its vote share of tribals. However at the aggregate level, its majority in vote share was reduced from 17 to merely 7 assembly segments (Figure 11.6). This was possible because BJP extensively mobilized non-tribal voters in the ST reserved segments and also used all resources so as to have a maximum voting turnout. Sixteen assembly segments out of 182 had a higher voting turnout than 2012. Of them only six had one or more percent difference than the past. Four of the six were from the Vadodara constituency from where Modi contested. One is Dangs, a ST-reserved constituency where the voting turn

Figure 11.6
*Number of Reserved ST Assembly Segments Won by Parties in
Different Elections*

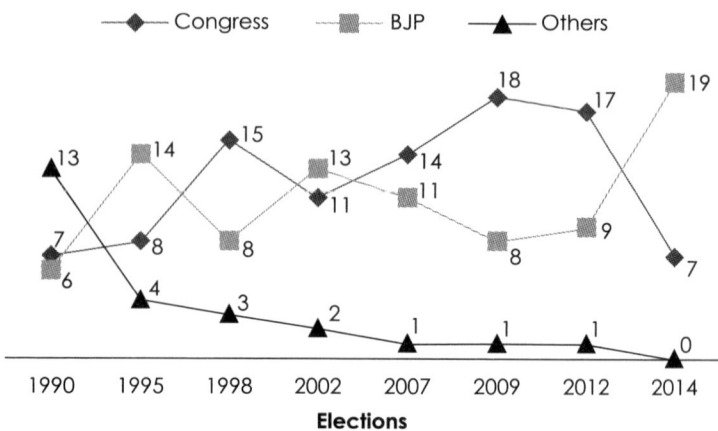

Source: Statistical report on general elections.

out was 81.32 percent as against 69.79 percent in 2012, nearly 12 percent higher. It may also be noted that highest preference for NOTA was in five numerically tribal dominated districts: Dahod (32,305), Chhota Udepur (28,815), Valsad (26,606), Panchamahal (25,871), and Bharuch (23,615).

Muslims

Muslims constitute 9.5 percent of the state's population. Like all major religious communities sect, caste and class also stratify them. Though the 2002 anti-Muslim carnage was spread in all parts of the state, the worse affected areas were Ahmedabad and Vadodara cities, urban and rural areas of central, and north Gujarat and the tribal belt in the east. The carnage, experiences of discrimination in public life, indiscriminate harassment and detention by police, published 'encounter' of Muslim detainees, and occasionally humiliating public statements by the CM Narendra Modi between 2002 and 2005 constantly keep Muslims in tension and insecurity. They have been pushed to be more community centric to support each other in business, education, health, and other needs.[35,36]

The Gujarat Congress Party treated Muslims as a mere 'vote bank' and used their anti-Modi sentiments for their political advantage without providing protection and offering any tangible benefits. The average Congress individual is not free from prejudice against Muslims. Most of the party leaders at all levels were onlookers in the 2002 anti-Muslim carnage. In fact, a few were a part of mobs involved in looting Muslim property during the massacre. The BJP and Modi realized limitations of its Hindutva plank and their anti-Muslim image if he and the party were to compete nationally. In the 2007 Gujarat Assembly elections, Modi mellowed somewhat in publicly ridiculing Muslims. From 2008, he made conscious efforts to win their support. The BJP announced its readiness to welcome 'nationalist Muslims' calling themselves a 'pro-Hindu but not anti-Muslim party'.[37] On the other hand, a section of Muslim elite also recognized that they could not afford to oppose or keep distant from the government.

Godhara provides an example. Muslims, 45 percent of the population, of the town faced constant harassment by the state alleging their involvement in the burning of the train. In the city's municipal elections of 2010, BJP won 18 of the total 48 seats, 20 were won by Independents, and 4 went to Congress. Most of the Independent candidates were Muslims. BJP won over seven of them so as to control the municipality. Their rationale for extending support to BJP was to obtain basic amenities like garbage collection, roads, and drainage in their localities as they had been neglected. By supporting BJP, Muslim councilors expected to have 'development and peace'.

Similarly, another town with a large Muslim population, Salaya in Jamangar district, governed by the Congress until 2010 and unaffected by the riots also experienced neglected infrastructure development. A few Muslim leaders moved to the BJP after the 2007 Assembly election. In 2008, for the first time, four Muslims contested municipal elections as BJP candidates and won. Then, the town started receiving state government funds for infrastructure development. Such tangible benefits convinced other Muslims to join the party. In 2013, BJP won 24 of 27 municipal seats.

"Honestly, joining the BJP was a tough decision for me…. But I was confident about myself, about my decision. I knew if I joined hands with Mr. Modi, it will mean more benefits for the town and more development.... It was like Narendra Modi opened the government coffers for us. Whatever money we wanted for development came flowing in. And it hasn't stopped," one of the leaders said.[38] Between 2009 and 2013, BJP fielded 51 Muslims in five municipal elections in the state. Of them 25 won. In 2010 among 2742 local bodies' seats in the state, BJP sponsored 256 (3.7 percent) Muslims. Of them 117 won. When one BJP Muslim candidate won against a Congress Hindu candidate in Rajkot in 2010, Modi claimed that Muslims were not against BJP. He announced that over 30 percent of them 'have voted for us' in Gujarat.[39]

Aspirant Muslims joined BJP for political or economic reasons. Suraiyya, a victim of the 2002 riots, joined BJP in 2012. She lives in a slum situated contiguous to the city's official municipal sewage farm in eastern Ahmedabad. "Do we have a choice? We have knocked on the Congress (Municipal) Corporators' doors so many times but they shoo us away. How long do we keep drinking yellow water and die of dengue?" A former CPI(M) member joined BJP because he believes that, "BJP is in power and will continue to remain in power for the next 15 years ... I cannot work with a dead party like the Congress or the CPM. Both Congress and BJP have killed Muslims but the Congress has given nothing in return. At least the BJP intends to do something now for Muslims too. I can only be able to work with a party that can do something."[40]

Business entrepreneurs extend support to BJP for similar reasons. Zafar Yunus Sareshwala was a Muslim icon in Modi's pro-Muslim campaign during the 2012 Assembly and 2014 Lok Sabha elections. His property and factory were destroyed in the 2002 riots and he wanted to prosecute Modi in the International Court of Justice. His views on 'justice' changed after meeting Modi in London in 2003. He believes "The idea of justice is meaningless in a vacuum of isolation within society. If we needed to solve our issues, with whom should we talk? We had no option, but to talk to (Modi) the Gujarat government."[41]

According to Sareshwala, the biggest damage is inflicted not during the riots, but thereafter. The curfews and inactivity brought misery to survivors of the riots. He emphasized that there has not been a riot in Gujarat in the last decade, thanks to Modi. According to him, Gujarat development was 'inclusive' and Modi and Gujarat "are development symbols for the nation."[42] With support from the state government, he and a few Muslims (around 30 auto dealers, estate builders, etc.) organized a

Muslim business conclave for three days in February. While inaugurating the function, Modi asked Muslim entrepreneurs to be job creators rather than job seekers.[43]

On the eve of Assembly elections, Modi launched a Sadbahana (Compassion) mission in different parts of Gujarat and observed one-day fasts. Without compromising his Hindutva ideology, he managed to mobilize a section of the elite Muslims at every district headquarters of the function. For the first time, BJP's Gujarat and now India manifesto expressed concern about 'development of Muslims'. It promised to "modernize *madrassas* to improve the quality of education." Further, the Gujarat party announced it would establish a 'skill development' university for making kites, incense sticks, *rakhi* (holy thread), and fire crackers; occupations in which a large number of Muslims are self-employed.

These measures as well as the persuasion of local pro-BJP Muslim elite seem to have influenced a small section (27 percent) of Muslim voters in 2012. But it did not work to that extent in the Lok Sabha poll. By and large, Muslims in Gujarat were guided by their experiences in the state and continue to suspect Modi and BJP's bona fides. On the basis on booth-wise voting turnout, it seems that Muslims were lukewarm in elections. In several predominant Muslim Assembly constituencies, percentage of turnout was lower than the 2012 Assembly elections (Table 11.1). On the basis of my observations (2010) and Dhattiwala's ethnographic study less than 10 percent Muslims voted for BJP from the 2002 carnage affected areas. I tend to agree with her that they displayed far greater public support to BJP than actual voting.[44] According to National Election Survey by CSDS (NES), only 17 percent voted for BJP in the Lok Sabha polls.

Muzzfarnagar riots in Uttar Pradesh alarmed those who voted for BJP in 2012. They viewed these riots as part of Modi's Lieutenant Amit Shah's political plan like that of the 2002 Gujarat riots.[45] They were frightened by VHP leader Pravin Togadia's speech in Bhavangar announcing the forcible eviction of a Muslim family from a Hindu locality.[46] Modi however disapproved of Togadia's statement.[47] "I am frightened by this and fear that what will happen to us if Modi becomes prime Minister?" one of the Muslim petty traders, otherwise towing Zafar's thinking told me.[48] Moreover, the discriminating approach of the Gujarat state toward Muslims evidently has not changed. The GoG refused to implement the

Table 11.1
Voting Turnout of Muslims in Minority-dominated Assembly
Constituencies

Assembly Segment	Lok Sabha Constituency	Minority % of Total Votes	Turnout %		
			2012	2014	Decrease
Siddhapur	Patan	20.98	77.42	57.71	19.71
Jamalpur-Khadia	Ahmedabad West	61.28	68.39	57.23	10.96
Wakaner	Rajkot	23.24	74.48	64.15	10.33
Mandvi	Kutch	20.10	72.07	63.85	8.22
Dariapur	Ahmedabad West	46.23	70.66	62.70	7.96
Godhara	Panchmahal	22.52	72.54	65.39	7.15
Danilimda	Ahmedabad West	48.00	68.47	61.98	6.49
Bapunagar	Ahmedabad East	28.49	67.56	61.50	6.06
Vejalpur	Gandhinagar	35.33	71.38	65.74	5.64
Jambusar	Bharuch	31.25	72.58	62.59	4.99

Source: Hemanshu Kaushik, "Did Fewer Minority Members Vote?" *Times of India*,
    May 6, 2014.

post-metric scholarship scheme of the central government for minorities.
Less than two percent of BPL dole recipients in garib Kalyan mela were
Muslims between 2010 and 2012.[49]

Conclusion

For political elite and parties in contemporary India, an election is a market place. Like investors and producers, they are engaged with gaining
power, and by selling their ideas and promises to voters. The latter have
been reduced to consumers who have no other option but to opt for one
among the available choices. Effective marketing propaganda to voters not
only requires it to be rooted in a socio-cultural milieu but also in a real or
imaginary performance in delivering some tangible material benefits.

In Gujarat, Narendra Modi had an edge over the Congress both in
marketing skill and delivery. His propaganda worked effectively because
he did deliver some tangible benefits to the upper middle class that is

vocal, controls the media and hence is influential in shaping public opinion. Since the Congress was not in power for nearly two decades in Gujarat, it had few achievements, particularly for younger voters. Though the party workers occasionally launch agitations involving mobilization of people on certain issues, they are by and large alien to mass politics. The party is fragmented and lacks any ideological direction except to defeat Modi. In electoral engineering, its earlier successful formulas and tactics have now become obsolete. Congress has been unable to evolve new strategies to win over new constituencies and also is losing ground among its traditional voters from the lower strata of society.

On the other hand, BJP under Modi in Gujarat provided a missionary spirit to win power. It was more so in 2014 in which all the Sangh Parivar groups and several religious organizations closed their ranks to elect Modi as India's Prime Minister. The party consolidated voters from upper and middle castes and classes to whom Modi government provided some benefits in the last decade. But marketing tactics and lollipops had not effectively worked on the lower strata of society and more so on minorities irrespective of class. They kept their fingers crossed. Despite the sluggish functioning of the Congress, a majority of them continued to vote for the Congress.

Notes and References

1. Ghanshyam Shah, "Goebbel's Propaganda and Governance: The 2009 Lok Sabha Elections in Gujarat." in Paul Wallace and Ramashray Roy (eds), *India's 2009 Elections* (New Delhi: SAGE Publications, 2011), pp. 167–91. For analysis on Gujarat governance, see Ghanshyam Shah, "Politics of Governance: A Study of Gujarat," *Studies in Indian Politics* I, 1(2013), 65–77. Also see, Ghanshyam Shah and Mahashweta Jani, "Modi's Political Craft and the Limping Congress," in Palshikar, Suhas, K.C. Suri and Yogendra Yadav (eds), *Party Competition in Indian States: Electoral Politics in Post-Congress Polity* (Delhi: Oxford University Press, 2014), pp. 100–22.
2. Ghanshyam Shah, "Goebbel's Propaganda and Governance: The 2009 Lok Sabha Elections in Gujarat."
3. Personal interview on January 10, 2011.
4. *Indian Express*, March 22, 2014.
5. Lancy Lobo and Jayesh Shah, "Extent of Individual Voting Patterns: The Case Study from Gujarat Local Elections 2010," (unpublished paper). Baroda: Centre for the Study of Culture, 2011.
6. Our observation is based on experiences on the polling day of a few friends including some who were on official duty in Ahmedabad, Vadodara, Surat and Rajkot; and also three rural areas.

7. Editorial of the journal observes, "… The model of Ram Mandir in the holding put up at Modi's rally in Faizabad, Amit Shah's statement of 'Apamanno badlo levano avasar aavyao che (Time has come to take revenge)', not giving ticket to Muslim candidate … Modi's statement. "Lakhi rakho … Baglaadeshi yo ne kadhi mukish (note it down … will send Bangladeshi nationals back)" Vol. 45, No. 6, June 2014 and see also *Indian Express*, June 7, 2014, 3.

8. On June 10, 2013, Modi was selected to head the poll campaign for the elections at the national level executive meeting of BJP in Goa.

9. Literature on Modi had been in circulation in different Indian languages in various parts of the country regarding his achievements/governance, and how he won elections since 2004. During his visits in southern states in 2003–05, full-page ads were placed in the main south Indian news dailies and his speeches translated into local languages.

10. See note 2.

11. *Times of India*. 2014, February 12.

12. Ghanshyam Shah, "Construction of Cultural Nationalism: A Case of Gujarat", paper presented in workshop on "*Israel, Palestine and South Asia: Seen Through the Prisms of Religious Nationalisms,*" at the Centre for Comparative Politics and Political Theory, School of International Studies, JNU, Delhi, 14th and 15th February, 2014.

13. *Indian Express*, February 4, 2014.

14. *Times of India* (Ahmedabad), November 11, 2012.

15. Deshpande, Rajeev and Mehta Harit (2014), "Modi bypasses party, tells electorate 'vote for me'", *Times of India*, April 6.

16. *Diya Bhasakr*, February 7, 2014.

17. Subodh Ghildiyal, "Congress Candidates Face Cash Crunch," *Times of India*, April 9, 2014, p. 1.

18. *Times of India*, November 17, 2013.

19. Robin Jeffrey and Doron Assa, *The Great Indian Phone Book: How Cheap Mobile Phones Change Business Politics and Daily Life* (London: Hurst & Company, 2013).

20. See note 2.

21. Leela Fernandes, *India's New Middle Class* (Minneapolis: University of Minnesota Press, 2006).

22. Ghanshyam Shah, "Governance of Gujarat: Good Governance for Who and for What," in Hirway Indira, Amita Shah and Ghanshyam Shah (eds), *Growth or Development: Which Way Is Gujarat Going?* (Delhi: Oxford University Press, 2014), pp. 517–56.

23. Ghanshyam Shah, *Caste Association and Political Process in Gujarat: A Study of Gujarat Kshatriya Sabha* (Bombay: Popular Prakashan, 1975).

24. Ghanshyam Shah, "Understanding or Ignoring Untouchability," https://www.academia.edu/5280139/Understanding_or_ignoring_Untouchability (accessed on June 20, 2014).

25. Pralay Kanungo and Satyakam Joshi, "Carving out a White Marble Deity from a Rugged Black Stone?: Hindutva Rehabilitates Ramayan's Shabari in a Temple," *International Journal of Hindu Studies* 13, 3(2009), 279–99.

26. Archana Dholakia and Yogesh Yadav, "Fiscal Financing for Tribal Development," in in Amita Shah and Jharna Pathak (eds), *Tribal Development in Western India* (Delhi: Routledge, 2014), pp. 259–84.

27. Tara Nair and Bhavani Shankar, "Livelihoods and Financial Behaviour of Tribal Households; Linking experience and Strategies," in Amita Shah and Jharna Pathak (eds), *Tribal Development in Western India* (Delhi: Routledge, 2014), pp. 241–58.

28. Jharna Pathak, "Agroforestry in Tribal Areas: Moving towards Sustainable Agriculture?" in Amita Shah and Jharna Pathak (eds),*Tribal Development in Western India* (Delhi: Routledge, 2014), pp. 161–201.

29. Rudra Narayan Mishra, "Dairy Farming as an Opinion for Strengthening Livelihoods: A Case of Poor and Landless Tribal Households," in Shah Amita and Jharna Pathak (eds), *Tribal Development in Western India* (Delhi: Routledge, 2014), pp. 202–40.

30. Y.K. Alagh, "Models and Realities," *Indian Express*, May 29, 2014. Also see note 28.

31. *Indian Express*, February 25, 2014.

32. The UPA government enacted "The Scheduled Tribes and Other Traditional Forest Dwellers (Recognition of Forest Rights) Act, 2006". The Act recognizes the rights of forest and tribal communities to the land and forest resources that they used (not to any new resources), which were not recorded when the forest laws were put into force.

33. Himanshu Bhatt, "Gujarat at Bottom in Allotting Land to Tribals," *Times of India*, February 10, 2010.

34. *Indian Express*, October 22, 2013.

35. Laurent Gayer and Christophe Jaffrelot, *Muslims in Indian Cities: Trajectories of Marginalisation* (New Delhi: HarperCollins Publishers, 2012).

36. Christophe Jaffrelot, "The Juhapura Model," *Indian Express*, April 25, 2014.

37. *Tehelka*, October 16, 2010.

38. http://www.ndtv.com/article/india/why-this-muslim-majority-town-in-gujarat-voted-for-narendra-modi-s-bjp-330383 (accessed on July 8, 2014).

39. *Times of India*, October 12, 2010.

40. Raheel Dhattiwala, , *The Puzzle of the BJP's Muslim Supporters in Gujarat* (Chennai: The Hindu Centre for Politics & Public Policy, 2014).

41. See note 33.

42. http://ibnlive.in.com/group-blog/the-india-blog/3581/why-gujarati-muslims-are-with-modi/64627.html (accessed on July 14, 2014).

43. Avinash Nair, "Stand on Your Own Feet, Modi Tells Muslims," *Indian Express*, February 8, 2014.

44. See note 41.

45. Ghanshyam Shah, "Gujarat after Godhara," in Ramashray Roy and Paul Wallace (eds), *India's 2004 Elections: Grass-roots and National Perspectives* (New Delhi: SAGE Publications, 2007), pp. 151–79.

46. *Times of India*, April 12, 2014.

47. Narendra Modi said on Twitter: "Petty statements by those claiming to be BJP's well wishers are deviating the campaign from the issues of development & good governance.... I disapprove any such irresponsible statement." http://www.ndtv.com/elections/article/cheat-sheet/narendra-modi-raps-vhp-s-pravin-togadia-for-alleged-hate-speech-10-developments-511889 (accessed on August 3, 2014).

48. Personal interview on April 30, 2014.

49. *Times of India*, February 3, 2012.

12

Maharashtra: Congress' Dramatic Decline

Suhas Palshikar and Nitin Birmal

In the excitement over BJP's victory in UP, Maharashtra's contribution to the party's overall performance has been somewhat ignored. With 42 seats for the NDA, Maharashtra played a crucial role in the return of NDA with a clear majority. The outcome of the 16th Lok sabha elections from Maharashtra signaled two major developments. First, the state now appears to be a part of the BJP sweep in north and west India. Second, the resilience of the Congress Party has almost reached its final stage.

In 1977, when the north and west voted for the Janata Party, the state followed that regional trend only half-heartedly. Again, Maharashtra partially resisted the Congress decline in 1989. The result was that when state after state was moving away from the Congress, the party still managed to win Assembly elections of 1990—to fall only in 1995. Even after that, and in spite of a vertical split in the state Congress caused by formation of the NCP in 1999, the two halves of the Congress still managed to wrest power from the Shiv Sena–BJP alliance in 1999 in a repeat of what happened in 1978. In 1978, two Congress parties, one proclaiming loyalty to Indira Gandhi and another opposed to her, contested Assembly elections separately and came together to form a post-election government. From 1999, the coalition of the two Congress parties, occasionally with the help of some other groups and

Independents, continued to rule the state by winning a majority in 2004 and 2009.

Finally, the steepest fall came in 2014. The Congress dipped to its lowest ever seat share in the state, winning only two Lok Sabha seats on its own, while its NCP partner won four seats. How did this happen and what are the implications of this drastic fall in terms of party competition in the long run? In this chapter, we attempt to answer these two questions.

The Long Shadow of Congress Decline

Politics in Maharashtra is characterized by the resilience of the Congress Party in the backdrop of Congress domination for a very long time. In 2009, the alliance of Congress and NCP retained power at the state level for the third term in a row—something rather dramatic in the times of overall decline of the Congress Party at the all-India level. However, in spite of this Congress–NCP victory organizationally, the party remained weak and fragmented. Besides, the third term of the state government unfolded in the backdrop of leadership changes in the state and the overall negative publicity the Congress-led UPA received at the national level from 2011 onwards. In other words, the entire third term of the state government and the edge received by the Congress in 2009 parliamentary election remained shadowed by the larger atmosphere of Congress' decline.

In 2009, Congress performed rather well in the Lok Sabha election and in the subsequent Assembly election as well. NCP and Congress improved their position in the Assembly while returning to power for the third term in a row. However, this by no means indicated a recovery of the Congress Party. Its performance in 2009 has therefore been described as "survival amidst decline."[1] At this time there was considerable goodwill for the central government led by Manmohan Singh. While the state government's performance was not seen as exceptional, its economy had gained momentum between 2001 and 2007–08. Additionally, the BJP–Shiv Sena coalition was marked by fatigue and internal unease[2] besides the fact that Shiv Sena had split and Shiv Sena chief Bal Thackeray was unable to campaign due to old age.

A few months before the 2009 Lok Sabha elections, the then chief minister, Vilasrao Deshmukh was inducted into the central cabinet. His successor Ashok Chavan also came from the same Marathwada region. Ashok Chavan retained his position after the Congress–NCP came back to power in the Assembly election of 2009. However, he had to resign under a cloud over the Adarsh scam[3] in November 2010 and Prithviraj Chavan became the chief minister. Prithviraj Chavan lacked experience at the state level since most of his political career was in Delhi. He belongs to the western Maharashtra region.

Ever since he became the chief minister, despite his clean image and arduous efforts to retain that image, Prithviraj Chavan ran into trouble with his party MLAs for his alleged indecision. Yet, the Congress Party (and NCP) fared well in the 2012 elections to local bodies in the state. In the district level Zilla Parishad elections, the Congress and NCP together won more than 60 percent seats across the state. The Shiv Sena and BJP could get a majority only in five of the 27 Zilla Parishads: Ratnagiri, Jalgaon, Jalna, Hingoli, and Nagpur.[4]

It would not be an exaggeration if the entire five-year period from 2009 is described as the period during which the ruling parties in the state were involved in one corruption scandal after the other. Within one year after the Assembly elections, Ashok Chavan, the then Chief Minister had to resign because of the strictures passed against him by an enquiry commission looking into irregularities involving the Adarsh Building Scheme in Mumbai. Soon after that, the Pune MP of the Congress Party, Suresh Kalmadi, was charged in corruption cases involving the Commonwealth games. Subsequently, the Deputy CM, Ajit Pawar, belonging to the NCP became the target of charges involving the irrigation department under his charge.[5] On the other hand, in an attempt to retain his clean image, the new Chief Minister, Prithviraj Chavan, came under criticism from his own party-men and also by his NCP alliance partner for delaying decisions and insufficient initiative. Thus, corruption charges and alleged inaction haunted the state government.

Throughout this period, the economy of the state was stable but marked by agricultural stagnation. While many infrastructure projects were begun, the image of the state government remained somewhat negative. This was in part due to the negative image of the UPA government at the Center and also because of the lack of coordination between the two parties ruling the state. The state government, and NCP in particular, also received very negative press coverage leading to a public impression that the state is on the verge of ruin.

Ironically, during this period, the main opposition parties, the Shiv Sena and BJP, were not very active in mobilizing protests. Popular protests, however, occurred at Jaitapur in the Konkan region over its nuclear plant.[6] This project, like the Enron project of the 1990s, deeply divided the region over matters of development and destabilization of local livelihood patterns. Shiv Sena took a strong stand against the project though BJP had not joined its partner in these protests.

Shiv Sena announced that it would continue its protest immediately after its victory as an alliance partner with the BJP in the 2014 parliamentary elections as the local people opposed it.[7] Besides this agitation, local unrest in western Maharashtra kept recurring during the five-year period mainly on the issue of sugar cane prices payable from the cooperative factories in the region.[8] These factories being mostly under the control of the Congress and NCP leaders, such agitations created an atmosphere against the local elite from ruling parties. So, the failure of the ruling parties in maintaining a close connect with the rural population helped in creating a negative impression.

The Outcome

Table 12.1 summarizes the results of the 16th Lok Sabha election from Maharashtra. It was clearly a one-sided affair. Of the 48 seats, the BJP-dominant NDA won 42 seats leaving only six for the Congress-led UPA. Just as the seat tally tells a one-sided story, the vote shares too intimate the one-sided nature of the outcome.

For the Congress, this was probably one of its most humiliating defeats. Maharashtra is traditionally seen as a party stronghold, but it dipped to its lowest ever seat tally. Even the two seats that the Congress won did not give it much comfort. The victory at Nanded was not only narrow, it also put the party in an awkward situation. Its winning candidate, Ashok Chavan (ex-CM), was an accused in the "Adarsh scam" giving the opposition additional leverage to criticize the Congress for shielding corruption.

Table 12.1
Maharashtra Lok Sabha Result, 2014

	Seats Contested	Changeover from 2009	Won	Changeover from 2009	Votes (%)	Changeover from 2009
BJP	24	−1	23	14	27.3	9.2
Shiv Sena	20	−2	18	7	20.6	3.6
NDA Allies	4	3	1	1	3.4	3.4
Congress	26	1	2	−15	18.1	−1.5
NCP	21	–	4	−4	15.9	−3.3
UPA Allies	1	−1	–	–	0.6	−0.7
MNS	10	−1	–	–	1.5	−3.4
BSP	48	1	–	–	2.6	−2.8
Others & Independents	743	79	–	−3	10.0	−3.9

Source: Compiled from official source by Data Unit, Centre for the Study of Developing Societies (CSDS).
Note: Total number of candidates: 897; Independents: 446; Turnout: 60.5 percent; Changeover from 2009: 9.8 percent.

Moreover, just when the elections were under way Ashok Chavan also came under a cloud over the pending case of "paid news" arising from the 2009 Assembly election! Besides being an embarrassment, this episode also meant that the election of Ashok Chavan would be in danger if he was found guilty of corrupt practices during the previous election.[9] The other seat won by the Congress, also from the Marathwada region, Hingoli, was wrested by the party from its partner NCP, after much haggling, for a candidate close to Rahul Gandhi, Rajeev Satav. While he did win the seat, the victory margin was a paltry 1,632, whereas elsewhere the Shiv Sena and BJP won with huge margins.

The four seats won by NCP also did not convey a message of the party's strength; rather, they intimate the story of its weakness and lack of organization. More than the Congress, NCP has become a party of autonomous chieftains as is evidenced from the election outcomes as well. Its candidate from Satara in western Maharashtra has been known for his personal stranglehold over the constituency and the party has practically no control over him. The Satara victory, thus, is his personal victory rather than the party's victory.

Another "personal" victory came in Baramati, the home constituency of Sharad Pawar, where his daughter Supriya Sule was contesting as a sitting MP. What made her victory humiliating to her party was the fact that she won with a margin of only 69,719 votes in contrast to her victory by over three lakh votes in the previous election. The third seat, Kolhapur, too, was not much to the credit of the party. Like Satara, this was the victory of its candidate who has a stronghold over the city independent of the party. In 2004, he contested on a Shiv Sena ticket and lost. In 2009, though he had joined NCP briefly, he contested against the party as an Independent and lost, but also ensured the loss of the NCP candidate.

Sharad Pawar won Madha, the fourth seat also in western Maharashtra, in the previous election. This time, another senior party leader, Vijaysinh Mohite Patil, contested it amidst reports of internal factionalism against Mohite-Patil,[10] but won only by 25,000 votes. In other words, the four seats won by NCP in no way suggest its organizational strength over the western region despite having a network of institutions over which the party leaders have had a long history of control.

While the Congress Party had already become weak due to its Assembly defeat in 1995 and subsequent split in the party in 1999, both Congress parties had retained their stronghold in the region of western Maharashtra. Therefore, the performance of Congress and its breakaway NCP faction in the western region was the most stunning aspect of the 2014 outcome. This feature probably capped the party's overall decline in the state. The NCP and the Congress did have some weak partners. The Bahujan Vikas Aghadi has a personalistic and limited following in the Vasai-Virar constituencies near Mumbai, while the Republican Party of India (Kawade faction) has support among Dalits of Marathwada. However, for all practical purposes, the election was fought only by the NCP and Congress against the larger alliance named *mahayuti* (grand or larger alliance; the Shiv Sena–BJP alliance was called as "yuti" and with the addition of new partners, it was described by "maha"yuti, i.e., grand alliance) led by the BJP.

In contrast to the Congress and NCP, the BJP and Shiv Sena moved more adroitly to register their handsome victory. In the first place, they were successful in expanding the NDA by bringing in not only the Republican Party of India (RPI-Athavale faction), but also Raju Shetty's Swabhiman Party. It has a following in parts of western and southern Maharashtra, particularly among farmers. NDA also included the Rashtriya Samaj Party of Mahadev Jankar with his following among the Dhangar community in the same region who contested against Supriya Sule. This strategy ensured that NDA could take on the Congress and NCP in their bastion of western Maharashtra.

As Table 12.2 shows, the outcome of 2014 practically did not have a regional variation. Traditionally, Vidarbha and western Maharashtra have been strongholds of the Congress and NCP. In Marathwada, since 1995, Shiv Sena has been in close competition against the NCP and Congress. However, the victory of BJP and Shiv Sena this time was by large margins in all regions. Not only did the NDA win seats in all regions, but the coalition also registered a high vote share in each of the regions of the state. The clean sweep that the NDA made is also evident if we look at the results in terms of urban and rural divisions. Maharashtra is a relatively highly urbanized state with more than 40 percent of its population living in urban localities.

Tables 12.3 and 12.4 report the result by level of urbanization for 2014 and 2009, respectively. It shows that while the distinction between urban and rural is not very drastic, the NDA is very well placed in urban localities. Furthermore, the NDA also performed well in constituencies reserved for Scheduled Tribes and Scheduled Castes (Table 12.5). It also had done well earlier, particularly in 1995–96. Thus, the 2014 elections signal an overall domination of the NDA in all parts and social sections of the state.

This feature of the election outcome is also seen from the huge victory margins of the NDA candidate as against the small margins with which the Congress and NCP won with the exception of Satara. Table 12.5 shows the grouping of constituencies in terms of margins of victory. The victory margins are linked to three features of the 2014 elections. First, it is indicative of the overall domination established by the NDA. These victory margins indicate that the NDA victories were not merely due to the vagaries of the first past the post electoral system. Second, this also indicates a fundamental shift in the structure of competition. This is also borne out by the fact that the effective number of parties by seats and

Table 12.2
Region-wise Result, 2014

Region	Seats	Turnout	Congress+		BJP+		MNS		AAP		Others	
			Won	*Vote*	*Won*	*Vote*	*Won*	*Vote*	*Won*	*Vote*	*Won*	*Vote*
N. Maharashtra	6	61.6	0	33.7	6	56.6	0	1.0	0	0.6	0	8.0
Vidarbha	10	63.2	0	31.6	10	49.7	0	0.3	0	3.8	0	14.7
Marathwada	8	64.5	2	39.1	6	51.0	0	0.0	0	0.5	0	9.4
Mumbai-Thane	10	51.6	0	29.3	10	55.0	0	5.5	0	4.0	0	6.2
W. Maharashtra	11	62.3	4	40.1	7	48.8	0	1.1	0	1.8	0	8.2
Konkan	3	63.4	0	30.1	3	45.8	0	0.0	0	1.6	0	22.5
Total	48	60.5	6	34.7	42	51.3	0	1.5	0	2.2	0	10.3

Source: Compiled from Official results by Data Unit, CSDS.

Table 12.3

Maharashtra Result by Locality, 2014

Locality	Total Seats	Turn-out	Cong+ Won	Vote	BJP+ Won	Vote	MNS Won	Vote	AAP Won	Vote	Others Won	Vote
Urban above 75%	10	51.6	0	28.2	10	56.1	0	5.4	0	4.7	0	5.6
Rural above 75%	21	64.2	4	38.2	17	49.5	0	0.1	0	1.3	0	11.0
Mixed	17	61.7	2	33.8	15	51.1	0	1.1	0	2.2	0	11.9
Total	**48**	**60.5**	**6**	**34.7**	**42**	**51.3**	**0**	**1.5**	**0**	**2.2**	**0**	**10.3**

Source: Data Unit, CSDS.

Table 12.4

Maharashtra Result by Locality, 2009

Locality	Total Seats	Turnout	Cong+ Won	Vote	BJP+ Won	Vote	MNS Won	Vote	Others Won	Vote
Urban above 75%	10	51.6	9	39.4	1	32.2	0	17.5	0	11.0
Rural above 75%	21	64.2	10	41.8	11	40.9	0	0.0	0	17.3
Mixed	17	61.7	7	36.5	9	36.2	0	2.5	1	24.9
Total	**48**	**60.5**	**26**	**39.5**	**21**	**37.6**	**0**	**4.1**	**1**	**18.8**

Source: Data Unit, CSDS; Proportion of urban and rural populations for Tables
      12.3 and 12.4 is based on data collected by CSDS through its project on
      Delimitation of Constituencies.

votes came down this time compared to the last parliamentary elections. Political competition is often better understood in terms of number of relevant or really effective parties in a system. Rein Taagepera and Mathew Shugart developed a measure of "effective parties." In their calculation, the number of effective parties is calculated separately for their relevance in terms of votes—ENP/v—and seats—ENP/s.[11] In 2009, the ENP/v was 7.03 and ENP/s was 4.1. These came down this time, respectively, to 5.6 and 2.6. This means that the de facto players were only about six or three if we consider the dispersal of votes or seats, respectively, in the 2014 election. Third, electoral arithmetic played only a limited role in the

Table 12.5
Result for Reserved Constituencies (SC/ST), 2014

Category	Seats	Turn-out	Cong+		BJP+		MNS		AAP		Others	
			Won	Vote	Won	Vote	Won	Vote	Won	Vote	Won	Vote
Reserved (SC)	5	61.5	0	34.8	5	53.1	0	0.0	0	1.3	0	10.8
Reserved (ST)	4	65.7	0	33.1	4	53.4	0	0.0	0	1.7	0	11.8
General	39	59.9	6	34.9	33	50.8	0	1.8	0	2.4	0	10.1
Total	**48**	**60.5**	**6**	**34.7**	**42**	**51.3**	**0**	**1.5**	**0**	**2.2**	**0**	**10.3**

Source: Data Unit, CSDS.

victory of the NDA. Usually, multiparty competition and factionalism do play a role in shaping the outcome in many constituencies. While that did happen this time around also, as we discuss later, the vote share of NDA candidates and their victory margins suggest that such contingent factors attendant on multiparty competition had only a limited role this time in the victories of the BJP and Shiv Sena.

Explaining the Outcome

It is not possible to fully explain the outcome of the Lok Sabha elections from Maharashtra primarily in terms of electoral arithmetic, though it did play a role in the impressive NDA victory. For instance, in the Mumbai-Thane belt, the weak performance of the Maharashtra Navnirman Sena (MNS) helped Sena-BJP, while in the Vidarbha region the near-absence of the BSP proved critical. If we compare this election with the 2009 Lok Sabha election, MNS which polled four percent votes in 2009 and practically spoiled Shiv Sena chances in the Mumbai-Thane urban region[12] also failed to make much impact this time, polling barely 1.5 percent votes.

Raj Thackeray, leader of the MNS, had much earlier praised Modi.[13] He also had a good equation with the Gadkari faction within the BJP and hoped to have some role to play in the expanded NDA. But Shiv Sena ensured that MNS did not become an NDA partner.[14] Even then, MNS declared its intention to not only contest but also to support Modi in case MNS candidates won the election.[15] This was clearly intended to create confusion for the NDA and among voters. It did have some effect on NDA as Nitin Gadkari made an attempt to ally with the MNS when the campaign was to begin with the NDA without consulting Shiv Sena.[16] At least for the voters, this ploy did not work. Similarly, the BSP, which was a significant player in the previous election polling nearly five percent votes did not campaign strongly almost anywhere in the state. As a result, it polled only three percent votes this time and this did make a difference in the Vidarbha region.

Thus, the political arithmetic stayed in favor of the NDA. Not only did it not lose votes to MNS, but it gained from an ineffective BSP campaign and also gained reasonably from its alliance with the RPI Athavale faction. NDA gave it only one seat at Satara, while the Swabhiman Party and the Rashtriya Samaj Party helped the NDA in defeating the Congress–NCP in the western region. At the same time, the AAP could have split anti-Congress votes, but failed to make an impact. Spreading its resources thin, the new entrant contested all 48 seats and ended up polling only about two percent votes. The vote share of the AAP did not make an impact on the outcome anywhere in the state.

In Maharashtra, as in many other states, Congress Party politics tends to be mired in factionalism and revolts by party leaders. This factor often leads to a few victories for the non-Congress opposition. This election also was not an exception. In Latur and Hingoli, there were reports that Congress factions did not cooperate with the official candidates of the party.[17] Moreover, the two UPA partners, Congress and NCP, also did not help each other in many places. Thus, newspaper reports kept listing instances of how the Congress–NCP alliance was internally weakened due to the recalcitrance of their workers in Thane, Kalyan, Bhivandi, Ratnagiri, Sidhudurg, in the Mumbai-Konkan region to Akola, Buldhana, Amravati, in Vidarbha region as also Nandurbar in north Maharashtra, and so on.[18]

As alternative explanations, it is tempting to argue that anti-incumbency, lackluster performance of the state government, and negative campaign against UPA government caused this outcome. Since the Congress and NCP were in power both at the Center and the state, this "double-incumbency" became a burden for them. In the pre-election surveys conducted by Lokniti, we found that the popular dissatisfaction with both the governments kept increasing from July 2013 onwards. In July 2013, 29 percent respondents said they were dissatisfied with the UPA government in Delhi, and 17 percent were dissatisfied with the state government. As against this, in February 2014, 37 percent were dissatisfied with central government, and 39 percent with the state government.[19] This, however, also alerts us to the fact that dissatisfaction soared only in the run up to the election. In other words, the perceived dissatisfaction was only an external indication of the change in the public mood that did not necessarily originate in the anti-incumbency alone.

To appreciate this point, let us go back to the outcome of 2014 once again. Compared to 2009, the BJP and Shiv Sena added 21 more seats to their tally while NCP and Congress lost 19 seats. The two Congress parties together lost almost five percent votes compared to last time whereas the gains of the BJP and Shiv Sena amount to almost 13 percent; more than double the loss of the ruling parties. In other words, it is difficult to interpret the outcome merely in terms of the popular dissatisfaction with the UPA and the ruling parties in the state as also electoral arithmetic, although these factors must have definitely contributed to the loss of the UPA.

The combined vote share of the BJP and Shiv Sena is 14 percent higher than that of the Congress–NCP. Such a swing is not merely a function of the anti-incumbency factor. Similarly, the expansion of the NDA coalition is also not an adequate explanation. It is true that the expanded NDA gained in terms of social sections brought into the NDA through its coalition partners. The RPI (Athavale faction) has a following among the Buddhists in parts of the state and the Rashtriya Samaj Party has a following among an important OBC community, the Dhangars. However, such coalition strategies help only when the targeted social sections are already disappointed with the ruling party/alliance. So, in a sense, the expanded NDA was only a reiteration of the anti-incumbency of the Congress–NCP.

In order to understand the landslide victory of the NDA in the state, we must first remember that the Congress Party, though reelected to the state Assembly in 2009, has been on the decline in Maharashtra just as in many other places. Ever since the Assembly defeat of 1995, the Congress has never really recovered as a party. The 1995 defeat was primarily caused by the disintegration of the party into factions that could not be controlled by any single leader.[20] The return of the two Congress factions to power in 1999 artificially changed the political outcome. But even after that, neither the NCP nor the Congress could really improve its condition. This is borne out by the fact that the combined vote share of Congress and NCP has steadily declined from 1999 to 2009. The decline in 2014, though steep, only falls into this pattern. In this sense, the outcome has a state-specific dimension in that the process of decline of the Congress was already underway. However, such incipient processes often require an external push. The Congress and NCP were already sitting on a weak throne with declining legitimacy. Their earlier victories were products of contingent factors and as such, when the push came, they crumbled rather dramatically.

That push came in the form of the "national mood" or the overall drift away from the Congress everywhere.[21] In 2009, while the state level dynamics did matter, already the impact of national level factors was felt. First, in the parliamentary election, the satisfaction with national government played a role in helping the state Congress to post a decent electoral outcome. Then for the Assembly election, the goodwill of the reelected UPA government was a crucial factor. This process of national level factors outweighing the state level factors continued in 2014 too. Since the middle of 2013, the popular opinion started shifting away from the UPA and later that shift became very pronounced.

In Maharashtra, though the popular resentment against Congress and NCP was not quite visible, the national mood captured popular imagination. The role of Narendra Modi as a symbol expressing the mood for change must also be recognized. The "Tracker" polls measuring the public opinion consistently indicated that Modi was ahead of all other leaders in terms of popularity for becoming prime minister. In July 2013, 21 percent respondents from Maharashtra favored Modi as the future prime minister, while in February 2014 this proportion rose to 31 percent. Not surprisingly therefore, 16 percent BJP voters in the state said that they voted for BJP because Modi was its prime ministerial candidate.[22] This ability of Modi to decisively impact the electorate is also borne out by the response he received across the state during the campaign.

Congress and NCP did not have the leadership that could match Modi in his popularity, his public speaking skills and his ability to excite the electorate. While Rahul Gandhi had a limited appeal in rural areas, the state-level leadership of the Congress and NCP is traditionally more skillful at appropriating the networks of cooperative organizations, upcoming activists, and sitting MLAs. They rarely resort to demagoguery and as such, they did not have a matching response to Modi's management of the public mood. In this particular respect, this campaign was comparable to the campaign led by Bal Thackeray in 1995 during the Assembly election in which the Congress Party also found it impossible to match Thackeray's rhetorical skills.

However, a charismatic individual or demagogue can only exploit the disappointments with the existing regimes and anxieties arising out of the political uncertainties of a transitional period. In both these instances—1995 and 2014—these factors existed. Having lost its hegemony, the Congress Party in the state finds itself left with its local networks of power which are deeply resisted by not only the ordinary voter but also by the aspiring political activist who finds that the available opportunity structures are monopolized by the existing power holders mostly belonging to the Congress and NCP. This disappointment allows the voter and the aspiring entrants to politics to sway their preference in favor of the seemingly anti-establishment alternatives.

Conclusion

Following its defeat in 1995, the outcome of 2014 can be seen as the next blow to the fate of the Congress parties in the state. The implications of such a defeat are not confined only to subsequent outcomes in the immediate future. For the politics of Maharashtra, the all-round defeat of the Congress has two more long-term implications. One pertains to the structure of party competition. On the one hand, factions and leaders started gravitating toward the BJP in the aftermath of the parliamentary elections. At the same time, NDA in Maharashtra—labeled as Mahayuti—becomes overcrowded. Already, there have been problems between the BJP and Shiv Sena on the issue of leadership and seat sharing. With more partners, the intra-coalition competition becomes more strenuous. This situation forestalls the rise of a clear single-party dominance in the state in the near future.

The other implication for competitive politics is about the redistribution of political resources and space lost by the Congress. Should the Congress fail to reorganize itself, the critical question in state politics will be: who—which party and which forces—will gain control over the vast networks of resources built by the Congress factions? This in itself is likely to become a contentious and central factor in the politics of the state for the next decade.

The other issue relates to the role of Maratha leadership. There has been a long history of Maratha factionalism in the state leading to fragmentation of the Maratha community that constitutes roughly 30 percent of state's population. In 1995, that fragmentation was articulated in the form of large-scale rebellion within Congress and voters' readiness to vote for the "rebel" candidates.[23] This time around, the fragmentation of the Maratha community was not only expressed through some Maratha leaders joining BJP and Shiv Sena—e.g., a rebel Maratha leader of NCP, Vinayak Mete, joined the BJP Shiv Sena alliance[24]—but more than that, it was expressed through local activists' refusal to work for the NCP–Congress coalition resulting in full-fledged fragmentation of the community across parties. The fragmentation of the Maratha vote has already been noted in analyses of elections since 1995.[25] That process became much more visible this time around when more Marathas voted for the BJP–Shiv Sena than for the Congress–NCP.

This development was accompanied by a huge surge among OBCs and upper castes in favor of the BJP–Shiv Sena and a split in the SC vote.[26] With only Muslims and Adivasis to support it, and even the latter were divided between the two alliances, the Congress was resoundingly defeated because it could get only residual support from almost every community except the Muslims. Thus, the state is now on the threshold of a more historic reconfiguration of politics than ever before

If the Maratha community continues to be divided politically, that opens up possibilities for a new phase in the politics of the state wherein not only the dominance of the Congress Party would wither away, but the dominance of the Maratha elite over politics in the state would also become circumscribed. Given the entrenched interests of the Maratha elite both in agriculture and now more increasingly in non-agrarian sectors as well, it is unlikely that they would easily let go their hold over the Maratha community and state's politics. Thus, the defeat of the Congress has opened up a new phase in state's politics. One possible direction of the politics of this phase would be erosion of Maratha dominance and rise of new social configuration. However, given the numerical strength, historical role, and material compulsions facing the Maratha elite, they are more likely to devise new strategies of dominance over the Maratha community. But their real challenge would be to ensure electoral dominance by getting support from non-Maratha sections as well. It is this challenge that would in fact determine the shape of the new phase in coming decade.

Postscript

As this chapter goes to press, elections to the state assembly in October took place defeating the Congress and NCP. While the defeat of the Congress was not unexpected, these elections saw a four-cornered contest since both coalitions broke. The BJP emerged as the largest party with 122 seats in the 288-strong legislature. As the decimation of the Congress continued in these elections, the broad trends emerging from parliamentary elections remained intact and we expect that the broad conclusions drawn on that basis apply to the latest outcome as well. These pertain not only to the defeat of the party in power but the possibilities of further realignments of social forces in the state leading to a new configuration of political competition. (For detailed analyses, see our article in *Indian Express*, October 21, 2014. "How Maharashtra Voted: Behind BJP, Upper Castes, OBCs and Rich," and a commentary in *Economic and Political Weekly*[27]).

Notes and References

1. Suhas Palshikar, Rajeshwari Deshpande, and Nitin Birmal, "Survival in the Midst of Decline: A Decade of Congress Rule in Maharashtra, 1999–2009," in Suhas Palshikar, K.C. Suri and Yogendra Yadav (eds), *Party Competition in Indian States* (New Delhi: Oxford University Press, 2014), pp. 431–50.
2. Suhas Palshikar, Nitin Birmal, and Vivek Ghotale, "Coalitions in Maharashtra: Political Fragmentation or Social Reconfiguration?" in Sridharan E. (ed.), *Coalition Politics in India* (New Delhi: Academic Foundation, 2014), pp. 147–49.
3. The "Adarsh scam" refers to Adarsh Housing Society at a prime location in Mumbai where alleged misappropriation took place through bureaucratic and political connivance. The land belonging to military was supposed to be used for war widows

and other military personnel, but flats were allotted to relatives of politicians and bureaucrats. The scandal erupted in 2010 followed by appointment of an enquiry committee that indicted a number of political leaders including the then Chief Minister Ashok Chavan and many civil servants. *Hindustan Times*, Mumbai, April 22, 2013, http://paper.hindustantimes.com/epaper/viewer.aspx (accessed on July 19, 2014); see also report on the enquiry commission, *Indian Express*. Mumbai, December 22, 2013, http://archive.indianexpress.com/news/adarsh-panel-indicts-former-cms-maharashtra-cabinet-rejects-report/1209897/ (accessed on July 19, 2014).

4. https://docs.google.com/spreadsheet/pub?key=0AsTha_h2wXTSdHpXWXU1d2dDO DlGY1EwbTg5RVJrbkE&output=html (accessed on July 6, 2014).

5. *Business Standard*, September 25, 2012, http://www.business-standard.com/article/economy-policy/what-is-maharashtra-irrigation-scam-112092503026_1.html (accessed on July 8, 2014). The state government appointed a committee to inquire into the allegations under the Chairmanship of a retired expert and civil servant, Madhav Chitale. The report of this committee was tabled in the assembly in June 2014. It exonerated the minister for direct involvement; *Times of India*, Mumbai, June 14, 2014, http://timesofindia.indiatimes.com/city/mumbai/Irrigation-projects-initiated-without-proper-permissions-Chitale-committee-report/articleshow/36505180.cms (accessed on July 8, 2014).

6. *Hindu*, May 5, 2010, http://www.hindu.com/2010/12/05/stories/2010120562481000. htm (accessed on July 8, 2014).

7. *Economic Times*, Mumbai, June 18, 2014, http://articles.economictimes.indiatimes. com/2014-06-18/news/50678844_1_jaitapur-project-land-acquisition-nuclear-project (accessed on July 8, 2014).

8. *Indian Express*, Pune, November 8, 2013, http://archive.indianexpress.com/news/ sugarcane-farmers-begin-48hour-bandh-in-maharashtra/1200615/ (accessed on July 8, 2014).

9. *Times of India*, Mumbai, June 2, 2014, http://timesofindia.indiatimes.com/city/mumbai/Paid-news-case-Ex-Maharashtra-CM-Ashok-Chavan-fails-to-dodge-framing-of-charges-by-EC/articleshow/35858288.cms (accessed July 8, 2014).

10. *Daily Lokmat*, Pune, March 26 and April 3, 2014.

11. Rein Taagapera and Mathew Soberg Shugart, *Seats and Votes: The Effects and Determinants of Electoral Systems* (New York: Yale University Press, 1989), pp. 7–91.

12. In the 2009 Lok Sabha election, MNS polled 21 percent votes in the Mumbai-Thane region and thus adversely affected Shiv Sena. See Rajeshwari Deshpande and Nitin Birmal, "Maharashtra: Congress–NCP Manages Victory," *Economic and Political Weekly*, XLIV, 39(September 26, 2009), 137.

13. *Times of India*, Mumbai, August 4, 2011, http://timesofindia.indiatimes.com/india/Raj-Thackeray-praises-Narendra-Modi-says-his-govt-Indias-best/articleshow/9468326. cms (accessed on July 8, 2014).

14. Maharashtra Navnirman Sena (MNS) was formed in 2006 by Raj Thackeray, nephew of Bal Thackeray. Raj was a key leader of the Shiv Sena before he left Shiv Sena over differences with his cousin and son of Bal Thackeray, Uddhav. For more details on MNS, see Palshikar Suhas, "In the Midst of Sub-democratic Politics," *Economic and Political Weekly* XLV, 7(February 13, 2010), 12–16.

15. *Hindustan Times*, Mumbai, March 10, 2014, http://www.hindustantimes.com/elections2014/state-of-the-states/mns-to-support-narendra-modi-in-ls-polls-raj-thackeray/article1-1192762.aspx (accessed on July 8, 2014).

16. *Daily Lokmat*, Pune, March 25 and April 1, 2014.
17. *Daily Sakal*, Pune, March 19 and 20, 2014.
18. *Daily Loksatta*, Pune, April 1, 2014; *Daily Lokmat*, Pune, April 1, 2014.
19. Source: CSDS Data Unit.
20. Rajendra Vora and Suhas Palshikar, *Maharashtratil Sattantar* (Marathi) (Mumbai: Granthali, 1996), especially pp. 66–70.
21. For a more elaborate argument on these lines, see Rajeshwari Despande and Nitin Birmal, "Maharashtra: The last Fortress Falls," *Hindu*, Web edition, June 26, 2014, http://www.thehindu.com/opinion/op-ed/maharashtra-the-last-fortress-falls/article6151743.ece (accessed on July 19, 2014). Also see Nitin Birmal and Rajeshwari Deshpande, "Maharashtra: The End of the Congress System?", *Panjab University Research Journal-Social Sciences* 22, 2(2014), 152–61.
22. Source: CSDS Data Unit. Data for July 2013 and February 2014 was collected through the surveys conducted as part of the Lokniti Tracker Polls and data for post-poll survey was collected through National Election Study 2014. One of the authors, Nitin Birmal, was the coordinator for Maharashtra for conducting these surveys.
23. Vora and Palshikar, *op. cit.* and also Suhas Palshikar, "Capturing the Moment of Realignment: Maharashtra Assembly Elections; 1996," *Economic and Political Weekly* 31, 2 and 3(January 13–20, 1996), 174–78.
24. *Daily Lokmat*, Pune, March 20, 2014.
25. Palshikar, Deshpande and Birmal, 2014, op.cit, pp. 440–41.
26. Deshpande and Birmal, 2014, op.cit.
27. See note 1.

C. Eastern and Southern Cluster

13

TMC Dethrones the LF in West Bengal after 34 Years of Uninterrupted Rule

Amiya K. Chaudhuri

A major change has occurred in West Bengal politics with the replacement of the Left Front (LF) with the TMC led by Mamata Banerjee. It roughly parallels the replacement of the Congress Party-led successive United Front Alliance (UPA 1 and 2) coalition governments at the Center, except that the LF ruled for 34 years. With 34 of the 42 seats in Bengal, TMC's sweep validates its assembly victory in 2011 and parallels the BJP majority at the national level.

The present trend is tending toward vote bank politics comprising castes and religions in which the BJP is benefiting. The BJP won two Lok Sabha seats in 2014 as it did in 1999 in coalition with the TMC. Mamata Banerjee used the alliance with the BJP in 1999 to fight against the CPI(M) in the state and the Congress Party at the Center. At that point of time, it appeared as a beginning of a permanent coalition era. Nonetheless, until the Lok Sabha election of 2014, BJP's electoral performance in the state was insignificant. During its coalition period in the late 1980s and 1990s, BJP's vote percentage ranged between 4 percent and 6 percent.

Even refugees who crossed over to West Bengal following independence did not vote for the Rightist Jana Sangh, the earlier version of the present BJP. The refugees felt secure when the Congress was in power at both the national and state levels. Then they switched from the Congress to the Leftist coalition when it dominated the state. The Left parties stood against the Congress government policy of sending East Bengal's Bengali-speaking people to the Andaman Islands and the arid Dandakaranya, and assisted the pauperized refugees. That is why first they began supporting the two United Fronts in the late 1960s and thereafter the LF from 1977. They lost everything and suffered at the hands of the Ansar Brigade of East Bengal and then East Pakistanis.[1] Yet, they did not feel one with 'Hindutwabadi' or any Rightist party in this part of the country.

Until 2014, the BJP could not gain any foothold in West Bengal as it did in the Hindi heartland. Also important is to understand the dynamics of party politics in the state.[2] West Bengal and Bangladesh are having a common porous border on both land and sea, touching entire North Bengal districts. Infiltrations are rampant particularly through land borders including illegal cash payments for entry. Bangladeshis, mainly Muslim peasants, illegally cross over the border, take shelter with Muslim families and ultimately get voter identity and ration cards with the help of powerful local political party leaders. They become part of vote bank politics. Hindu family inflow also is regular with only 9 percent of Hindus still remaining in Bangladesh. Hindu refugees settling in colonies also did not support the BJP.

But in the 2014 parliamentary elections, there was a vote swing favoring the BJP even in West Bengal where it has not been significant. This time its vote share was 17 percent, an increase of 12 percent from its early 4–6 percent. Only twice during its coalition period did its vote share rise to 11 percent. West Bengal's politics is quite intricate and different from that of other Indian states. BJP, as data showed, did not have the capacity to compete electorally against the three most competitive parties: the LF led by the CPI(M), TMC, and Congress. The distinction is a key to see the moods of the electorates in the state.[3] Earlier, in the 1960s and 1970s when the Congress dominated, political appeals on the basis of caste and religion were less important.[4] Now, Schedule Castes, Tribes, and Muslims are significant in the electoral arithmetic of all parties. Earlier the BJP used to claim that it was a party with a difference and criticized the Congress and Left Parties as 'pseudo secular'.[5] They were of the opinion that too much pampering of the Muslims by other parties might jeopardize the national interests of the country. They follow quite a different agenda. All parties are to be treated as the central- and state-centric leaders of the party have been and continue to claim. On the other hand, all the political parties rose in a voice that the BJP led by a single leader Narandrabai Modi during his election campaign in 2014 was trying to polarize the voters between the Muslims and Hindus.

Leaving aside the example of other states, West Bengal legislative politics is always dominated by the elite sections of society. The composition of the West Bengal legislature was mostly elitist during the earlier Congress era, the long LF regime and even the new legislative assembly led by the Chief Minister Mamata Banerjee. Brahmin, Kayasth, Baidya, and other castes with a few upper echelons of Muslim communities dominated the assembly. Despite much rhetoric, the empowering of the subalterns is still a chimera. In the area of larger politics, the subalterns almost remain as they did till the mostly Muslim peasants land movement at Singur in the Hooghly district. The politics of West Bengal is still dominated by the elite sections of society.[6] This is crucial even to analyze the present day political dynamics of a truncated state.[7]

Particularly before the Singur and Nandigram movements, the elites could not believe that a Marxist-ruled state[8] like West Bengal—the cultural hub of the Leftist—is corrupt in any way and could persecute the poorer sections of people. So they simply followed their predecessors— earlier intellectuals, semi-intellectuals, and like-minded people.[9] Seeing the brutal incident perpetrated against poor peasants revised their position. But they were not ready to support the idea of TMC led by Mamata Banerjee taking over in place of the Leftists.[10] They wanted to have a modernist Leftism or a fully chastised Marxist regime of change. They were unwilling to leave their Marxist dogma even in a changed world of enormous technological development all over the world. Their definition of the Indian state was yet to be changed. Chief Minister Buddhadeb Bhattacharya and his Minister for Industry Nirupam Sen vociferously argued that unless the state of West Bengal became fully capitalist, socialism the ultimate aim of the CPI(M) would not be a reality. They argued thus while justifying the taking over of the fertile land from the peasants of Singur for the Tata's automobile plant in a meeting at Assansol sometime in October, 2006.[11]

West Bengal is mostly rural with the main sources of income coming from agriculture. Marginal workers, however, engage primarily in subsistence agriculture. That means if the marginal workers are dispossessed total agricultural production would not suffer. But now it is very difficult to build up heavy industries. Most of the big industries including jute became 'sick' during the LF's 34 years of rule. Approximately 55,000 industries closed over the years and there are continuing high levels of unemployment. These problems became an albatross that the LF regime left to the TMC under the leadership of Mamata Banerjee who needed to provide leadership to building new industries. But where is the land? The proprietors of closed big industries are absolutely unwilling to vacate their possession of land that could be utilized by the present government.

Most of the manufacturing industries in different districts including Howrah that once was regarded as the Manchester of West Bengal are closed. There also are the problems of the closed and struggling tea plantations, and the exorbitant debt left behind by the 34-year-old LF. It requires more time than the little more than three years of the present Mamata government. These programs are to be taken up immediately by the new TMC government. Here also the excess or marginal agricultural laborers can be absorbed, lowering the quantum of rural unemployment. It is really difficult to get rid of unemployment, of significant numbers of people, skilled, unskilled, and educated. The decennial increase of population has been ever increasing due to higher percentage of birth rate, importantly which is very high among the Muslims and the poorer castes and the economically depressed people. The politicians of all hues and their parties are often engaged to take advantages of the same. Muslim population and the under privileged castes and classes are in position to determine the seats each party would win from panchayat levels, and assembly and parliamentary elections.

Table 13.1 shows the population distribution in each of the 42 parliamentary constituencies. The Muslim population in West Bengal was 25.25 percent in the 2001 census report. Within a period of 10 years it becomes more than 31 percent (Census Report of India 2011). The party or coalition of parties that are able to effectively mobilize Muslim votes

Table 13.1
Caste, Religion, and Urban Distribution of Population in Parliamentary Constituencies in West Bengal

Const. Name	SC %	ST %	Urban %	Hindu %	Muslim %	Christian %	Sikh %
Cooch Behar	48.8	0.4	9.5	75.4	24.2	0.1	0
Alipurduars	29.1	25.2	17.8	83.3	10.9	4.3	0
Jalpaiguri	49.2	7.8	17.8	83.3	10.9	4.3	0
Darjeeling	16.1	11.7	32.3	76.9	5.3	6.2	0.1
Raiganj	29.5	4.6	12.1	51.7	47.4	0.5	0
Balurghat	28.5	14.9	13.1	74	24	1.5	0
Maldaha Uttar	22.5	10.4	7.3	49.3	49.7	0.3	0
Maldaha Dakshin	8.8	1.7	7.3	49.3	49.7	0.3	0
Jangipur	16	2.1	12.5	35.9	63.7	0.2	0
Baharampur	13.5	0.9	12.5	35.9	63.7	0.2	0
Murshidabad	8.2	1.1	12.5	35.9	63.7	0.2	0
Krishnanagar	21.7	1.6	21.3	73.8	25.4	0.6	0
Ranaghat	36.3	3.2	21.3	73.8	25.4	0.6	0
Bangaon	42.1	2.5	54.3	75.2	24.2	0.2	0.1
Barrackpore	15.2	1	54.3	75.2	24.2	0.2	0.1
Dum Dum	9.6	0.5	54.3	75.2	24.2	0.2	0.1
Barasat	16.8	1.1	54.3	75.2	24.2	0.2	0.1
Basirhat	25.3	6.4	54.3	75.2	24.2	0.2	0.1
Joynagar	40.8	3.3	15.7	65.9	33.2	0.8	0
Mathurapur	30.3	0.6	15.7	65.9	33.2	0.8	0
Diamond harbour	21.5	0.2	15.7	65.9	33.2	0.8	0
Jadavpur	27.3	0.5	15.7	65.9	33.2	0.8	0
Kolkata Dakshin	6.3	0.3	100	77.7	20.3	0.9	0.3
Kolkata Uttar	5.3	0.2	100	77.7	20.3	0.9	0.3
Howrah	10.2	0.4	50.4	75	24.4	0.1	0.1
Uluberia	19.6	0.3	50.4	75	24.4	0.1	0.1
Srerampur	15.5	1	33.5	83.6	15.1	0.1	0

(Table 13.1 Continued)

(Table 13.1 Continued)

Const. Name	SC %	ST %	Urban %	Hindu %	Muslim %	Christian %	Sikh %
Hooghly	25.9	7.5	33.5	83.6	15.1	0.1	0
Arambagh	29.7	3.1	33.5	83.6	15.1	0.1	0
Tamluk	14	0.3	10.2	85.6	11.3	0.2	0
Kanthi	15.7	0.3	10.2	85.6	11.3	0.2	0
Ghatal	16.6	7.9	10.2	85.6	11.3	0.2	0
Jhargram	16.8	26.2	10.2	85.6	11.3	0.2	0
Medinipur	14.6	12.4	10.2	85.6	11.3	0.2	0
Purulia	18.6	15.4	10.1	83.4	7.1	0.3	0
Bankura	27.7	17.4	7.4	84.3	7.5	0.1	0
Bishnupur	35.6	3.7	7.4	84.3	7.5	0.1	0
Bardhaman Purba	30.3	8.2	36.9	78.9	19.8	0.2	0.3
Burdwan-durgapur	26.3	6.6	36.9	78.9	19.8	0.2	0.3
Asansol	22.3	6	36.9	78.9	19.8	0.2	0.3
Bolpur	30.9	6.7	8.6	64.5	35.1	0.2	0
Birbhum	29.4	6.1	8.6	64.5	35.1	0.2	0

Source: Census report 2011, Electoral Roll, Personal Survey and help provided by Researcher Abhay Kumar stationed in a Research Institute in New Delhi.

are assisted in gaining and holding political power. In field studies by the present author in several of his articles and books it was shown that the LF were able to get 63 percent of Muslim votes and more than 56 percent of backward caste votes until the 2006 Assembly election. This was over and above the upper middle class and middle class votes accruing to the LF.[12] The poor and poorest persons voted for the TMC and Indian National Congress.[13] It was puzzling that the political party that claimed itself as the party of the poor did not get enough votes from the poorer section of the people. Majorities of unban and women voters were against the TMC.

This façade of the LF began to crack in the panchayat elections in 2008. Yet the LF was in a position to hold on, but gradually the CPI(M), the mainstay of the LF was losing ground.[14] Earlier from 1987 to 2006, some of the language dailies like the *Bartaman Patrika* quoting voting figures and trends in several booths attempted to prove the extent of rigging that the CPI(M) resorted to in each of the elections. Apparently nothing seemed to be wrong, but it was established as to how the CPI(M) resorted to political cleansing before the panchayat elections in 2008 and in the 2009 parliamentary elections[15] in many selected constituencies.

An initial jolt to a long-term LF dominance took place in 1984 when the LF led by the CPI(M) had to concede 16 seats to the undivided Congress Party. However, the LF recovered in the 1987 Assembly and subsequent Lok Sabha elections. In 2004, the CPI(M) alone won 26 out of the LF total of 35 seats. However, Table 13.2 registers a major jolt for the LF in the 2009 election. CPI(M) dropped to only 9 seats, while the TMC leaped ahead with 19 seats. It was not only in West Bengal, but elsewhere that the CPI(M) was gradually becoming irrelevant in India's parliamentary politics. The CPI(M) thought that it could rise again in the next national election. To the contrary, in West Bengal it has been reduced to only 2 seats and all its Left partners drew a blank. TMC now clearly dominates with 34 Lok Sabha seats. In the present Lok Sabha, the entire LF has been reduced to a new low of 10 seats.

The question that inevitably rises is how and why the CPI(M) with such a radical image and successful history deteriorated to such a low point in the 2014 elections. The CPI(M) had been a structured party with a chain of cadre at each level from the Zilla Parishad to the booths at each gram panchayat. But the party organization was almost in disarray and the cadres became demoralized beginning even before the 2009 parliamentary elections. A large number of CPI(M) supporters and sympathizers changed their political leanings. Many of the card holder members either resigned or did not renew their membership card. Many urban CPI(M) members also becoming disillusioned changed their political loyalties and did not go to the polling booths. After the panchayat elections in 2013, the CPI(M) and for that matter the LF after the 2014 elections realized that the politico-electoral process in the state at least for the near future was irretrievable. In this election, the seat share of the CPI(M) came down to two only. It was remarkable to note the downslide of the CPI(M) from 26 seats (2004) to 9 seats (2009) and then ultimately to only 2 seats (2014) with the other important partners CPI, FB, and

Table 13.2
Percentage of Votes Polled and Seats by Each Party in the 2009 West Bengal Lok Sabha Election

Party	CPI (M)	CPI	RSP	FB	INC	TMC	SUC	BJP	SP	JMM	NCP	BSP	MUL	Independent
Vote Share	33.1	3.6	3.6	3.1	13.5	31.2	1.6	6.1	0.1	0.26	.09	1.0	0.01	2.7
Seats	(9)	(2)	(2)	(2)	(6)	(19)	(1)	(1)	(0)	(0)	(0)	(0)	(0)	(0)

Source: Election Commission of India Report 2009.
Notes: Total numbers of Lok Sabha seats in West Bengal are 42.
Figure in the parenthesis indicates the number of seats captured by different parties.

RSP of the LF drawing a blank. Observing the election results of the LF, it appears that it is too late to retrieve its position.

CPI(M)'s Manifesto had characterized the TMC as a soft communal party. During the Atal Bihari Vajpayee-led NDA central government, the TMC was a coalition partner. Vajpayee's BJP according to the Manifesto was a soft communal party. Already the economic condition and the process of development in the state were in jeopardy.[16] If the TMC would come to power and would be a prominent partner of the central government, it would make a mess of the state. The manifestos of the CPI(M) dished out before any election, appeared to be essentially the same with only minor changes. They were copying their political and socio-economic planning and programs from a book *Twenty Years of Left Front* edited by Anil Biswas the then party secretary of the West Bengal state committee. He set forth the objectives for speedy growth, all-round development, and equity in distribution. But even after 34 years of their uninterrupted stay in power, the question still remained among the mass of people: development for whom and how much equity in the distribution chain had they achieved.

In the Manifesto of the TMC, the party claimed that they would go in for empowering women. They would never try to achieve jobless growth. The party gave up their ministerial berths from the Congress-led government to oppose FDI in retail and also to oppose the creation of special economic zones (SEZs) because these measures of the government would hamper the interest of the poorer sections of society. Social justice and special provisions for minorities were two other prime objectives of the party.[17]

The 2011 Assembly election was singularly remarkable for the TMC. From this point the party became dominant. The TMC and the state Congress like in the 2009 parliamentary election agreed to a seat adjustment formula. The Congress under the guidelines of the 'High Command' was compelled to have a seat adjustment and that it achieved good results. By fielding 66 candidates they won 40 seats as shown in Table 13.3, whereas the TMC by contesting in 226 constituencies won 185 seats. The CPI(M) captured only 42 seats, the lowest since 1967, excepting 1972 when they allegedly were 'forced' to have only 14 seats in a House of 280 seats. As a protest they boycotted the assembly for 5 years. It was an abnormal situation for the CPI(M).[18] Total Numbers of

Table 13.3

West Bengal 2011 Assembly Election Results: Number of Seats Contested, Seats Won, Votes, Percentage of Votes, and Vote Percentage in Seats Contested

Party	Seats Contested	Seats Won	Votes	% of Votes	Vote % in Seats Contested
BJP	289	0	1,934,650	4.06	4.14
BSP	150	0	291,602	0.61	1.22
CPI	14	2	876,578	1.84	38.71
CPI(M)	213	40	14,330,061	30.08	41.30
INC	66	42	4,330,580	9.09	42.67
NCP	1	0	13,093	0.03	7.15
FB	34	11	2,285,829	4.80	41.71
TMC	226	185	18,547,678	38.93	50.15
RSP	23	7	1,411,254	2.96	40.55
JMM	30	0	343,931	0.72	79.79
DSP	2	1	1,679,963	0.35	45.46
GMM	3	3	343,931	0.72	79.79
SUC	30	1	209,795	0.44	4.45
RJD	1	0	21,711	0.05	19.68
MUL	15	0	32,453	0.07	1/36
PDS	27	0	47,016	0.10	1.05
IND	401	2	1,491,944	3.13	4.68
Others	–	0	–	2.02	–
Grand total	–	294	47,638,132	100.00	–

Source: Election Commission Report of Assembly Election 2011.

seats for the LF were 62 only as shown in Table 13.3. The TMC and the Congress combine were ahead of the LF by more than 8 percent. It is remarkable that in the Lok Sabha election of 2009 the swing in favor of TMC was 4 percent. This was a fall from 235 in 2006 to 62 seats.

The LF led by the CPI(M) found that it was rapidly losing its sway over the rural hinterland in the panchayat elections in 2008. It appeared that because of a massive victory in 2006, the CPI(M) were not sensitive to the life and living conditions of the peasant communities who mostly belonged to the Muslim and Schedule caste categories. Land to the tillers was the most important issue ingrained in minds of the peasants. Without giving a thought to these aspects of rural people, Chief Minister Buddhadeb Bhattacharya and Nirupam Sen began taking over lands by applying an antiquated land acquisition Act of 1894 enacted by the British Indian government to build up communication systems like railways and create other needed infrastructure of that time.

The previous Chief Minister Jyoti Basu's formulation of an industrial policy in a 1994 document was not of much help. New investments were very necessary. The Chief Minister approached both indigenous and foreign investors. Beni Santosa of the Salem group of companies was invited to invest in road building from Dum Dum airport to Raichalk, a wide riverside five star hotel by the Ganges with numerous beautiful bungalows inside the complex. It was quite a long distance from Kolkata airport so to construct a very lengthy road large tract of lands was necessary. The government proposed to acquire the land, but was stubbornly opposed by the peasants. The movement started at Bhangar 24 Parganas was the first spark that culminated in the intense peasant movements first at Singur and then in Nandigram. Some local leaders of the TMC backed the movement at Bhangar. After Mamata Banerjee's intervention, Beni Santosa of the Salem Group temporarily withdrew and left the state. The pet project of Chief Minister Buddhadeb Bhattacharya was kept pending.

He and his colleagues also signed a contract with industrialist Ratan Tata to immediately build a small car factory for his projected 'Nano'. The government entered into a commercial contract with the Tata organization, the nature of which is still unknown to the people of West Bengal. In exchange for ₹1,500, the government leased out 997 acres of the most fertile lands. The mostly absentee landowners received a compensation that was much less than the market price. However, the government had to face a serious challenge from the peasants who were dependent on the land for their living, assisted by Mamata Banerjee and the TMC. So much land for producing small cars perhaps was not necessary. Tata allotted 397 acres for the companies that would make ancillaries. TMC led by Mamata Banerjee agitated on behalf of the peasants even though she faced obstruction by the police hierarchies.

The government's small payment from the Tatas for the upkeep of the land included the construct of elaborate fencing around the land. That led to repressing the unfortunate peasants so that they could not approach near the fence. The police lathi charged and dispersed the mob every day, and in firing killed Rajkumar Bhul, a very young boy, who died on the spot. A young girl who used to spearhead the movement in the wee hours of the morning was found dead with burn injuries in the lower part of her body. It is alleged that she was raped by the CPI(M)'s cadres and the case remains pending in the court with two important members of the party still on bail.

Mamata Banerjee first established a camp by one side of the Durgapur Highway staying there for several days. Civil society groups supporting the hapless peasants extending support to the movement joined her. Then, she camped in Metro channel and resorted to an indefinite fast that terminated on the 26th day. Important political leaders from the state and the Center came to visit Mamata Banerjee, except West Bengal government representatives, to request Mamata to break her fast. Civil society groups increased their support to the peasants. The peasants trusted Mamata Banerjee and her TMC because they thought that it was Mamata who would be able to dislodge the LF. They again would get back their lands.[19] They did not trust rival civil society groups who were supporting the Buddhadeb Bhattacharya government arguing for the uplift of the state's sagging industrial.[20] The governor tried to reconcile the parties, but Ratan Tata's representative did not turn up and attempts at reconciliation that included Mamata Banerjee and Chief Minister Buddhadeb Bhattacharya ultimately failed. Ratan Tata was not agreeable to part with any amount of leased land. The Buddhadeb Bhattacharya government fought a lost battle for a Nano small car factory in Singur. Ultimately, Ratan Tata left the state to produce the small car in Gujarat. Before leaving West Bengal, he issued a front-page advertisement aimed at the younger generation campaigning indirectly against the TMC and against Mamata Banerjee for her allegedly 'anti-industry'[21] movement at Singur.

Surprisingly, during the Singur movement, another severe peasant movement started at Nandigram on a much larger scale.[22] A CPI(M) MP Lakshman Seth, a very important state committee member and powerful leader of Tamluk, gave notice to the effect that 14,000 acres of mostly cultivable lands would be taken over by the government to start a chemical hub. There also would be a nuclear power project at Haripur, East Midnapur. This infuriated all classes and the villagers rose in revolt creating barricades at several places so that the police and unknown people might not enter the villages at Nandigram.[23] At the end of 2006, Binay Konar, Anil Bose, and Shymal Chakraborty abused the members of the civil society in the most gutter communist languages. Binay Konar stated, "The CPI(M) cadres would encircle Nandigram and make the life hell of obstructionists." Chief Minister Buddhadeb Bhattacharya threatened in a big meeting that he would crack the heads of the opposition TMC people if they continued obstructing the industrial policy of his government. These were reported in language dailies for several days and were properly documented.[24]

The police force to clear the roadways first opened fire on January 7 on the unarmed men and women, and killed seven people. A second firing took place on March 14, 2007 killing 10 people. Peasants more, determined than ever, rose in revolt and hounded the CPI(M)'s supporters so that they fled to Khejuri on the opposite side of Nandigram. By this time the Maoists were trying to eliminate people who acted against them at Jangal Mahal. They killed both the policemen and ordinary citizens. The LF government being unable to quell the disturbances at Jangal Mahal, without banning the Maoists as was done in other states, wanted central paramilitary and rapid action forces. They arrived in Howrah on November 5, 2007 but were kept idle for long five days.

The people who fled to Khejuri along with a large number of CPI(M) cadres formed a shield with 500 people of Nandigram who were abducted from different places. They approached Nandigram where a large number of men and women were offering Puja. Open indiscriminate firing took place. Biman Basu the secretary of the state committee showed unbounded elation exclaiming, "see the sun rise at Nandigram."[25] Then from November 11–12, the CPI(M) allowed the deployment of central forces.[26] More than 14 people were killed and many more fled. The fleeing women were chased by CPI(M) goons and allegedly raped. They used rape as a weapon both in the Singur and Nandigram operations. Many more human bodies were thrown in the nearby river. A CBI inquiry was ordered by the Calcutta High Court leading to the arrest of 10 miscreants. They were released on bail with their cases continuing to be unresolved. These CPI(M) atrocities weakened their almost permanent hold over Bengal. Gradually, the CPI(M) organization eroded resulting in the LF defeat in all subsequent elections in terms of both seat shares and the percentage points of votes.

Table 13.4 supports the decline of the LF in Lok Sabha and Assembly elections. Congress continues to decline, while BJP's vote share gain to 17 percent is remarkable. The outstanding performance of the BJP is credited to Narendra Modi and BJP president Amit Shah. Modi's strategy of sidelining senior BJP leaders and his tailor-made campaigning for each state succeeded. He knew that Bengal would not be much of help for him. That is why he made a scathing attack against both the Congress and CPI(M) in the Brigade parade ground in Kolkata, but appeared to be soft against Mamata Banerjee. He wanted to share the 'Delhi-laddu' with Mamata at the state and himself at the Center. Later in north Bengal, he raised the pitch of his voice against Mamata to a high level.

Mamata Banerjee felt that the CPI(M)'s organizational strength was in tatters and Congress would not be any factor in the 2014 election. Congress, without seat adjustments, suffered an electoral debacle in the

Table 13.4

Vote Share Percentage and Seats Won by the TMC, Congress, Left Front, and BJP in the 2009 and 2014 Lok Sabha and 2011 West Bengal Assembly Elections

Party	2009	2011	2014
TMC	31.39 (19)	41.05 (185)	39.02 (34)
Congress	13.46 (6)	8.91 (40)	9.70 (4)
LF = (CPM + CPI + RSP + FB)	43.28 (15)	30.10 (42)	29.60 (2)
BJP	6.15 (1)	4.06 (0)	17.00 (2)

Sources: Compiled from Election Commission and newspaper reports.

Note: Figure in parenthesis shows seats won. There were seat adjustments between TMC and the Congress in all three elections.

Municipal elections, particularly in the Kolkata Corporation in 2010. Mamata got 95 seats and the Congress only 10 out of a total of 141 wards. Perhaps Mamata instinctively felt that Modi would present greater problems than the Congress and the LF. She thought that Modi would get only the Darjeeling seat; she did not imagine that the TMC candidate would lose the Assansol constituency. Therefore she chose to make a vitriolic attack against Modi and the BJP rather than Congress and the LF. Both the Congress and the LF in their campaigning emphasized that Mamata might join the NDA alliance. However, Mamata's TMC bagged 34 seats in the 2014 Lok Sabha elections, which is the highest ever for any one party from Bengal.

Conclusion

For the last three years Mamata Banerjee and the Trinamool Congress Party have been in power during a period of reduced political volatility even though the three major groups in the state—Congress, CPI(M) and BJP—almost combine together in their attacks against TMC rule. The 2014 Lok Sabha election reinforces the continuing and now rapid decline of the LF following their dominance in state politics for 34 years. An important indicator of the decline in addition to the electoral results is the large number of CPI(M) members who have crossed over to the TMC. They are attempting to come close to the chief minister, and the new entrants are in competition with the original members of the TMC. Congress defections also have taken place. As a result, intra-party clashes in addition to inter-party rivalries are common.

Some more serious political clashes continued to occur in 2014, even evoking the Nandigram movement. Siddiqulla Chowdhury, a Muslim leader close to Mamata Banerjee and the TMC, invoked the Nandigram movement in warning that the police should not enter *madrassas* except under specified condition while investigating bomb blasts attributed to Muslim extremists from Bangladesh. He referred to the erstwhile LF "Government's attempts to set up industries by forcibly acquiring farm lands' as leading to 'Bhattacharya's downfall." But, he quickly reaffirmed his ties to Mamata Banerjee.[27] This is normal politics contrasting with the extreme violence of the Nandigram and Singur movements. TMC has established itself in place of the LF as the dominant party in West Bengal with Mamata Banerjee joining the other major regional leaders of India.

Importantly the one-point program Mamata has been following is all round economic development of the people of the state. The problems of minorities, the SC, ST, and other economically and educationally deprived classes are the priority in her government. Her two outstanding achievements that may be the hallmark of her style of governance are first, to solve the Maoist problems and the problems of poverty, malnutrition, ill health, and education throughout the Jangal Mahal areas.

Secondly, she is introducing a new administrative culture. Local problems are to be solved locally at the district level. For this purpose, she created a second and new Secretariat at Siliguri, in North Bengal. Within a few months of her taking office, she arranged a tri-partite agreement forming the Gorkhaland Territorial Administration (GTA). Thus, she went forward many steps in attempting to solve the more than two-decades-old intractable Gorkhaland problem. She visited Darjeeling hills at least 22 times establishing rapport with the several hill tribes.[28]

It is also instructive to note a comparative analysis of development indices of Bengal compared to all Indian averages. The average percentage growth rate in agriculture, industry and service sectors' contribution to the Gross State Domestic Product (GSDP) of Bengal is noteworthy during 2012–13.[29] India's GDP growth in the above period is 4.96 percent, whereas Bengal's GSDP growth rate for the same period is 7.60 percent; in agriculture it is 1.795 in India and Bengal's GDSP stood at 2.56 percent; India's growth rate in industry is 3.12 percent and in Bengal it is 6.24 percent. In the service sector, Bengal is far ahead with a growth rate of 9.48 percent and the all India average is 6.59 percent.

Mamata Banerjee and the TMC appear to be succeeding since replacing the three decades plus rule of the LF in 2011 in managing the political economy of West Bengal. There are positive beginning results and noteworthy goals in health, education, removing illiteracy, fighting against poverty, reestablishing industrialization, and above all to achieve good governance. Validation of its rule in the 2014 elections could assist these goals. Time will establish what will happen in the next few years.[30]

Notes and References

1. Hemchandra Chattapadhay, who was the headmaster in an English High School who came to India before 1956, told the author the story of his tragic experience in East Bengal.
2. Survey findings that were done in the early 2000s among the people in different colonies around Calcutta and North Bengal district in West Bengal.
3. A.K. Chaudhuri, "Mapping a Political Challenge: West Bengal 2009," in Paul Wallace and Ramashray Roy (eds), India's 2009 Elections: Coalition Politics, Party Competition and Congress Continuity (New Delhi: SAGE Publications, 2011), pp. 192–216.
4. Rajni Kothari, Politics in India. (New Delhi: Orient Longman Ltd, 1972).
5. BJP categorized them as "pseudo" secularists in public statements and their election manifestos.
6. John Broomfield, Elite Conflict in a Plural Society: Twentieth Century Bengal (Bombay: Oxford University Press, 1968).
7. Shankar Ghosh, 1974. The Truncated State. Calcutta.
8. Tom Nossitor, Marxist State Government in India: Politics, Economics and Society (London: Printer Publishers Limited, 1988).
9. Sumit Sarkar, Tania Sarkar and many other Left-minded intellectuals in various places in India brought out a statement condemning the killing spree of the CPI(M) at Nandigram in January 7, 2007; they were also supporting a change of regime in West Bengal.
10. Kaushik Sen, a thespian by profession and a few others held this opinion even before the 2009 Lok Sabha election, although they participated in the civil society movements for a change during the Singur and Nandigram uprising of the peasants.
11. Interview, Nirupam Sen at a seminar in Netajee Institute for Asian Studies, Kolkata November 13, 2006.
12. Amiya K. Chaudhuri, West Bengal in Perspective: Politics and Governance. (New Delhi: Shipra Publications, 2014).
13. UPIASI field Survey after 2004 parliamentary elections in West Bengal.
14. Paul Wallace and Ramashray Roy (eds), India's 2009 elections: Coalition Politics, Party Competition and Congress Continuity (New Delhi: SAGE Publications, 2011), pp. 192–214.
15. As a participant observer among many others like Aparna Sen, Kaushik Sen, Saoli Mitra, D. Bandyapadhyay, Sunanda Sanyal and others were debarred from entering Nandigram and other vulnerable places in the western part of the state before the 2009 Lok Sabha election. Outsiders like the above people were physically obstructed to enter Keshpur and other places in Midnapur district.
16. Manifesto of the CPI (M) 2014 in Bengali, "Shorash Lok Shabha Nirbachan 2014, Bamfront."
17. Election Manifesto of the All India Trinamool Congress of the 16th Lok Sabha, 2014.
18. Dr Asok Mitra the first finance minister in a large meeting in Calcutta Maidan as also in the house of the legislature called the House of 1972–77 as the house of the "thieves" (Choreder Bidhan Sabha). For reference see Amiya K. Chaudhuri, Legislative Control Administration: India, a revised version (New York: Wiley, 1998).
19. Amal Sarkar. 2011. Jamir Ulatpuran (Bengali). Kolkata: Anustup. This contains a compilation of literature in the form of articles and booklets since the very beginning of the 2006 Singur peasants movements from various newspapers.

20. A debate was held in Bardhaman between two rival civil society groups for and against the government policy of industry and agriculture, February 3, 2011. The proceedings were telecast live, particularly on channel 10.

21. Ratan Tata, statement after abandoning the Singur project in late November 2010.

22. Akramul Huq and Nemai, *Gano Abhyutaner Aaloke Nandigram*, Midnapur, West Bengal: Ashwamed, 2008.

23. Ibid.

24. Ibid.

25. All the newspapers including *The Statesman, Ananda Bazzar, Bartaman, Telegraph,* and *The Times of India,* Kolkata editions, November 11, 2007.

26. *The Daily Statesman.* November 12, 2007.

27. Arup Chanda, "Mamata Aide Incites Muslims against Blast Probe," *The New Indian Express,* October 23, 2014, http://www.newindianexpress.com/nation/Mamata-Aide-Incites-Muslims-against-Blast-Probe/2014/10/23/article2489866.ece (accessed on October 23, 2014).

28. For a detailed discussion of the Maoist Problems and GTA at Darjeeling, North Bengal. See, Amiya K. Chaudhuri, *West Bengal in Perspective: Politics and Governance* (New Delhi: Shipra Publications, 2014).

29. *Powering Progress Empowering People, Two Years An Authentic Document 2011 to March 2013.* Department of Culture, Government of West Bengal, 2013.

30. Ibid.

14

Tamil Nadu: Strategic Interaction and Alliance Choices*

Andrew Wyatt

The 2014 elections in Tamil Nadu were notable for the marginal positions of the national parties. The two main regional Dravidian parties—the AIADMK and the DMK—have dominated state politics since the 1970s. National parties gain a little more importance as alliance partners whenever national elections are held. Yet, the AIADMK and the DMK virtually ignored the Congress and the BJP in 2014. Indeed, this was the first Lok Sabha election since 1967 in which national parties were excluded from the alliances led by the Dravidian parties, an ironic outcome given the national focus imparted to this election by the BJP in most other parts of India. In many ways, Tamil Nadu did not participate in the nationalization of the 2014 election, and a regional pattern of politics characterized the state. However, important changes occurred within the state as the AIADMK broke from the established pattern of alliance politics and contested all the seats itself. The foundational

* I am very grateful to participants at the election workshops at King's College London and the University of Nottingham who commented on an earlier draft of this chapter. I am also very grateful to C. Manikandan of Pondicherry University for his help with interviewing in April 2014.

assumption that elections in Tamil Nadu cannot be won without an alliance was shattered. Even more remarkably the AIADMK won a landslide victory without allies.

In most recent elections in Tamil Nadu, competition has been bipolar with almost all parties joining one of two electoral alliances. This did not happen in 2014. Two viable alliances did form with the DMK leading one of them, and the BJP leading the other but they were opposed in every constituency by the AIADMK. The Congress Party did not join an alliance and the AAP put up candidates as well. In some constituencies, six credible candidates were competing with each other. In this chapter, I will show how Tamil Nadu deviated from the national trend that favored Narendra Modi and the BJP.

Regional parties and political entrepreneurs that concentrate on local issues dominate the state party system. The BJP has not been able to find a place in a crowded party system in which religious divisions are not seen to be important. I argue that a rational choice approach with a focus on calculation and strategic interaction provides an interesting way of interpreting the outcome. In the first section of the chapter, I outline how political entrepreneurs have shaped a party system dominated by regional parties. In the second section of the chapter, I discuss the calculations that determined the incomplete process of alliance formation ahead of the election. The third section of the chapter shows how the campaign reflected the priorities of the main parties in Tamil Nadu. In the fourth section, I assess how the results fit with longer term trends in the state. In the fifth and concluding part of the chapter, I analyze the different pattern of alliance politics in 2014 and consider the implications of the election for party politics in Tamil Nadu.

The Party System in Tamil Nadu

Tamil Nadu has a somewhat unusual party system in that regional parties dominate it and national parties only have small followings. The two main regional parties, the AIADMK and the DMK, are the only parties that have won power via Assembly elections since 1967, even though they face competition from many other regional parties that have formed in the state since the late 1980s. The party system in Tamil Nadu is highly fragmented.[1] Normally, this fragmentation is contained by a bipolar alliance system in which the two largest parties, the AIADMK and the DMK, share seats with allies and try to make sure that no more than two strong candidates contest a seat.[2] The conventional wisdom was that the AIADMK and the DMK lack the support needed to win outright and need junior allies to secure victory, though this assumption was severely questioned in 2014. A threefold classification helps sort the profusion of parties in the state; each can be said to fall into one of three groups: regional, national, and small, mostly caste-based parties.

The parties in the regional category are connected to a Tamil identity, which originated in the Dravidian movement. The Dravidian movement to promote the South Indian culture gained momentum in the first half of the 20th century and the DMK emerged as a political party from this movement. The DMK was formed under the leadership of C.N. Annadurai in 1949 and won control of the assembly for the first time in 1967. The party split in 1972 and the actor-politician M.G. Ramachandran (MGR) formed his own party the Anna DMK, later renamed the AIADMK. The AIADMK and the DMK are the leading regional parties, which between them have the support of about two-thirds of the electorate.

Another split in the DMK saw the formation of the Marumalarchi DMK (MDMK) or renaissance DMK in 1994. The MDMK alleges the DMK has given up Dravidian principles and offers the services of its well-known leader, Vaiko to the electorate. In 2005, another regional party, the Desiya Murpokku Dravida Kazhagam (DMDK), was formed by the actor-politician, Vijayakanth. The appeal of the DMDK again rests with the personality of its leader. It does not have a direct link to the Dravidian movement in the way that the AIADMK, DMK, and MDMK do, but DMDK party symbols still incorporate red and black colors used by the other Dravidian parties. The DMDK also imitates the populist approaches made familiar by the DMK and the AIADMK.[3] Vijayakanth presents himself as a generous protector of the poor, very much like MGR, and has the support of about a 10th of the electorate.

A number of national parties have a presence in Tamil Nadu. These parties were hostile to Dravidianism but ideological divisions have softened, and national and regional parties regularly ally in the state. None of the national parties are contenders for office in Tamil Nadu but they help link the state to national politics and swing some voters behind an alliance. Congress is the largest national party in Tamil Nadu. By allying with the regional parties in most national elections since 1971, Congress has been able to get Tamil MPs elected to the Lok Sabha in New Delhi. Some of these MPs, such as P. Chidambaram, have been nationally prominent. The CPI and the CPI-M are tied to trade unions but only have a marginal electoral presence in the state. Both parties depend totally on alliances to win elections. The BJP has the support of Hindu nationalist organizations in Tamil Nadu but is seen by many as an outsider. The party gained some influence when it led the national coalition government between 1998 and 2004 but since then has struggled to find allies. The BJP has shown little sign of growing popularity in the state and without the support of allies it gets roughly 2 percent of the vote in Tamil Nadu.

A third group of identity-based parties regionally confined to Tamil Nadu appeal to the caste or religious sentiments of their supporters. Since the late 1980s caste cleavages have become salient again. This system of social stratification has a peculiar pattern in Tamil Nadu with a very small upper caste stratum, Brahmans constituting approximately 2 percent of the population. Tamil Nadu has an unusually large middle segment, most of which are known as 'backward' classes or castes, which make up about 67 percent of the population.

The Dalits, a group of castes considered so ritually impure that they are excluded from the caste system, are another large minority (at least 19 percent of the state population). The Pattali Makkal Katchi (PMK), formed in 1989, exploited tensions within the backward caste segment arguing that affirmative action schemes for the Backward Classes were monopolized by prosperous groups and the 'most backward castes' are neglected by the state. The PMK gains support from the numerically strong Vanniar caste in northern Tamil Nadu. Its support, about 5 percent of the statewide vote, is geographically concentrated making the PMK a useful electoral ally. Parties representing Dalit groups are mobilized against social inequality and their caste oppressors. Thus, the Puthiya Thamizhagam (PT) made a mark in the 1998 Lok Sabha elections. A social movement named the Dalit Panthers, later renamed the Viduthalai Chiruthaigal Katchi (VCK), contested the 1999 elections. Initially, both parties were the object of violent attacks from higher status groups and police repression, but they have become an accepted part of state politics.[4]

The party system in Tamil Nadu has been shaped by social structure, institutions, and the agency of political entrepreneurs. Ambitious politicians have exploited political conflict and emphasized social divisions that work to their advantage. The electoral system and the federal nature of the India state, which Shepsle would describe as 'structured institutions',[5] create incentives for ambitious politicians. The plurality electoral system strongly encourages the formation of electoral alliances that are discussed in the next section.

The federal institutions of the Indian state create opportunities for politicians to seek office at the state and national levels. The state-level office is the most desirable for the two largest parties in Tamil Nadu. Yet seats in the national parliament offer sufficient prestige to attract some ambitious members of the larger regional parties and the period of coalition politics that began in 1989 opened up the possibility of cabinet posts.[6] The party system of Tamil Nadu, dominated as it is by regional parties, gives the state additional importance in national coalition formation. The regional parties do not face an electoral threat from either the BJP or Congress, and this makes it easier for Tamil parties to move from one national coalition partner to another. The smaller parties from Tamil Nadu are even more interested in the national elections. The AIADMK and the DMK have adamantly refused to form state-level coalitions. So, if members from the smaller parties want to hold ministerial office then the national level offers the most likely prospect.

Alliance Formation

Alliance formation is the keenly observed precursor to elections in Tamil Nadu. It is a period in which politicians act instrumentally to further their interests "making reasoned choices given the likely choices of others and the contextual and institutional constraints."[7] The DMK and the AIADMK do not ally with each other. Instead they seek out what they hope will be their own winning coalition. The two larger parties seek to optimize their chance of winning office. The junior parties seek to maximize the number of seats they can win. The process of alliance formation is highly pragmatic. Known rivals abruptly drop objections to each other and cooperate in spite of ideological differences. Each party is assumed to bring a core vote to the alliance it joins. The prediction of what the accumulation of allies will add to the vote share of an alliance is known as the 'election arithmetic'.

The strongest alliance gives the leading Dravidian party in that alliance a tactical advantage and increases its chances of holding office. The leading party in each alliance assesses what each additional party will bring to its coalition and works out how many seats to offer each junior ally. The calculation and negotiation have to be done carefully. An offer of too few seats might see the potential ally defecting to the other side. Offering too many seats to a junior ally might set a precedent for other allies to bid higher and all seats given to alliance partners mean fewer opportunities for ambitious members of the leading party in the alliance.

Alliance formation is a process of strategic interaction. Party leaders make decisions based on the expectations of what other parties will do.[8] They accumulate knowledge of the strengths of their potential allies and the constraints they face. Parties only willing or able to join one alliance have limited bargaining power. Decisions, or anticipated decisions, of an opposing alliance condition how generous the coordinating party needs to be. The iterations of the alliance game change its character, producing cooperation dividends.[9] Experience of previous alliances establishes the collegiality of an alliance partner and it gains credit for its ability to 'transfer' its vote to the alliance as a whole. Some parties, like the IUML and the VCK, have been very loyal to their allies and are easy to place in an alliance. The PMK has rarely settled into long-term cooperation and is known for switching sides at short notice. The PMK's robust negotiation strategy has altered expectations and made alliance negotiations more intricate. So for example, the DMK obliged some pre-commitment by the PMK when the two parties allied ahead of the 2011 Assembly election. The DMK offered the PMK assembly seats in 2011 and a seat in the Rajya Sabha, but the latter part of the deal would only be concluded *after* the Assembly election.

The trend in Tamil Nadu has been very much toward inclusive alliances, with most parties accommodated in one of two main blocs. The mechanics of the plurality voting system encourage bipolar competition. The third front in the 1999 Lok Sabha election was crushed between the two main alliances. Small parties left out of alliances know that they will almost certainly lose that election. The larger parties link up with smaller allies to gain a tactical advantage and deprive their opponent of potential support. In the 2011 Assembly election, the two main alliances took 90.9 percent of the vote. What was startling in 2014 was the breakdown of the bipolar alliances. The AIADMK declared in late 2012 that it would contest alone; plainly stating it was not interested in an alliance with the BJP or Congress. The AIADMK showed a little indecision, offering a few seats to the left parties, but ultimately decided to keep all the seats in Tamil Nadu for itself.

Counter-intuitively, the DMK decided to avoid the national parties and did not take up an opportunity to outflank the AIADMK. The DMK ended its nine-year alliance with the Congress in March 2013 claiming that the Congress policy on Sri Lanka was unacceptable. The decision was explicable given public hostility toward the Government of Sri Lanka expressed by ordinary people in Tamil Nadu, but somewhat inconsistent given the DMK stuck with the Congress during the traumatic end of the Eelam war in April and May 2009 when the UPA government did not take strong action. Congress leaders attempted to renew the alliance in 2014 but the DMK refused their entreaties. The DMK also ruled out an alliance with the BJP, and only shared seats with four small parties.

The BJP was able to link up with a number of small parties and form its own NDA front in the state. It announced an alliance with Vijayakanth's DMDK, the PMK, the MDMK, and three very small caste-based parties. The Congress Party, unable to find allies, put up candidates in all 39 seats. The CPI and the CPM, after their disappointment with the AIADMK contested outside of an alliance. The AAP also joined the contest. The presence of more than two serious candidates in each seat was a novelty.

The strategic interaction between parties in Tamil Nadu was influenced by the assumption that 2014 would produce a hung parliament in which the regional parties would be able to help make the new government. It was further assumed that the BJP and Congress would perform so poorly at the national level that regional parties would be more powerful than usual in the formation of the national government. Avoiding an alliance with a national party would allow the AIADMK and DMK to offer support to either national party after the election. The AIADMK leadership also thought they might be able to head the national government run by a federal front. Another good example of strategic interaction was the decision by the AIADMK to dispense with allies. The party calculated the DMK would perform poorly and so the AIADMK would not need allies to win. Abandoning allies meant the AIADMK might maximize the seats won, and with a block of 39 MPs be in a formidable bargaining position in a national coalition. The AIADMK decision gave the DMK more flexibility with its own alliance building, making more partners available. What is curious is that the DMK did not do more to bring more allies into its own alliance to increase its chances of winning seats. I offer an explanation for the DMK's caution in the concluding discussion.

The Campaign

The DMK used the 2014 Lok Sabha election as an opportunity to campaign against the incumbent state government led by the AIADMK. The DMK hoped the elections would draw attention away from the political difficulties it has experienced since it was voted out of office in May 2011. In that state Assembly election, the AIADMK campaigned vigorously alleging that the DMK was corrupt and abusing the powers of office. As well as losing that election the DMK was subsequently battered by police investigations into 'land grabbing' cases in which lower level leaders are said to have coercively acquired land. Furthermore, the DMK had long been divided over leadership questions. The Party President M. Karunanidhi expressed a wish to retire in 2009 but disagreement over who should succeed him prevented this from happening.

Two of his sons, M.K. Azhagiri and M.K. Stalin, covet the leadership. An amicable settlement could not be reached and more or less public feuding between the brothers did not improve the image of the party. Azhagiri lost ground in the party after the 2011 elections. Stalin's victory over his brother was confirmed when Azhagiri was suspended from the party in January 2014 and then expelled in late March. Azhagiri toured the southern districts of the state offering support to opponents of the official DMK candidates. Stalin remained a leading campaigner for the DMK, directing the campaign, touring the state, and speaking out against the AIADMK government.

The AIADMK began campaigning promptly. Party posters depicted Chief Minister Jayalalithaa against the background of the Lok Sabha building equating its party leader with national government. Party workers were enjoined to win all 39 seats to maximize their leader's influence in New Delhi. Jayalalithaa's speeches rehearsed some of the themes used before the 2011 election, and referenced a number of populist themes.[10] The DMK and Congress were said to have failed in New Delhi, betraying the interests of the Tamil people. Jayalalithaa claimed to have governed effectively since 2011, promising to promote the welfare of the Tamil people after the 2014 election.

Congress campaigned on its record hoping that it would get support by drawing attention to its record affecting Tamil Nadu. Sonia Gandhi and Rahul Gandhi both gave speeches in Tamil Nadu toward the end of the campaign but the party could not dispel the expectation that it would do badly in the state. The DMDK was especially important for the campaign of the BJP alliance given its statewide organization. The PMK concentrated its efforts in northern Tamil Nadu. The PMK is rarely far from controversy and after December 2012 it has been strongly criticized for exploiting caste tensions between Dalits and Vanniars in the Dharmapuri district. The BJP campaigned hard in the state. Narendra Modi visited the state before and during the campaign, managing to get the attention of the leading star of Tamil cinema, Rajnikanth during April.

The Results

The AIADMK won 37 out of 39 Lok Sabha seats in the state. The BJP alliance won the remaining two seats but this was by no means a breakthrough for the Hindu nationalist party. The outcome of the election is of longer term significance for two reasons. Firstly, it shows that the regional dynamic of politics was not transformed by the BJP's attempt to make this a national election. Secondly, the election showed the DMK has not recovered its popularity since its heavy defeat in the 2011 state Assembly election.

The AIADMK won a spectacular victory, the like of which has not been seen since 1980 in Tamil Nadu. The party did not win all 39 seats, a feat achieved by the DMK alliance in 2004, but the AIADMK gained nearly all its seats without the support of any significant allies. The AIADMK defied two opposition alliances and its victory resembled that of MGR in 1980. The actor-politicians faced down a supposedly superior alliance of the Congress and the DMK, and the voters returned the AIADMK to the state assembly with a majority of its own. In 2014, the AIADMK offered the voters an alternative, a chance to vote for a potential Prime Minister who was independent of the Congress and the BJP. Many voters consider the AIADMK has governed well since 2011. Electricity shortages have not been eliminated but manifesto promises are being implemented. The innovative Amma canteens and offering cheap meals for ordinary people have been noticed. The AIADMK also benefited from the ongoing difficulties of its main rival, the DMK.

The DMK did not win any seats even though it received the second largest vote share, 23.6 percent of the statewide vote. The DMK demonstrated it was still a major party in Tamil Nadu in 2014; its average vote was 27.2 percent in the seats it contested. The party secured its highest vote share in the Nilgiris (38.4 percent) and came closest to victory in Chennai central (where it still trailed the AIADMK by a 5.6 percent margin). The results were demoralizing for the DMK, and suggested the AIADMK is the favorite to win the 2016 Assembly election (Table 14.1).

The BJP alliance came third in terms of vote share (17.7 percent), and, unlike the DMK alliance, it managed to concentrate some of its vote. However, the result gave no indication that the BJP is on an improving

Table 14.1

The DMK Alliance in 2014: Seats Contested and Share of the Vote

Party	Statewide Vote Share(%)	Seats Contested
DMK	23.6	34
VCK	1.5	2
IUML	0.5	1
PT	0.6	1
MMK	0.6	1
Totals	26.8	39

Source: Calculated by the author from results posted by the Election Commission of India. http://eciresults.nic.in/.

trend in the state. The vote share of the alliance was slightly lower than one would expect given the number and caliber of parties in the alliance, and one would expect the share to have been higher given the BJP had a strong candidate for the Prime Minister. The two seats won by the alliance were unusual. The BJP victory in Kanniyakumari occurred in a district that is exceptional in the state for reasons given below. The BJP had already won 33 percent of the vote in 2009 and with its allies its share of the vote went up to 38 percent in 2014. The other alliance seat went to the PMK in the sensitive Dharmapuri constituency. The party made much of its caste allegiance and poured resources into the constituency. All said, however, the result did give BJP some representation in Tamil Nadu, where it has long struggled to win elections (Table 14.2).

The electoral geography of the election reflected some well-known patterns. The DMK tended to get a higher vote share in the northern seats around Chennai and in the Thanjavur delta region. Most of the southern seats, where the DMK usually tends to weaker support, recorded below average vote shares. Given that Azhagiri campaigned against the DMK in these seats one might have expected an even poorer result. The AIADMK performed well across the state but did especially well, exceeding its statewide average, in most seats in the west of the state and also in the delta region. It also did well in Madurai and Theni districts in the south.

Table 14.2
The BJP Alliance in 2014: Seats Contested and Share of the Vote

Party	Statewide Vote Share (%)	Seats Contested
BJP	3.4	6
DMDK	5.1	14
PMK	4.4	8
MDMK	3.5	7
KMDK	0.7	1
PNK	0.8	1
IJK	0.6	1
Totals	18.5	38

Source: Calculated by the author from results posted by the Election Commission of India. http://eciresults.nic.in/.

Table 14.3

Seats and Votes Won by the Main Alliances and Parties

Party	Statewide Vote Share(%)	Seats Won
Aam Aadmi Party	0.5	0
AIADMK	44.3	37
BJP alliance	17.7	2
Congress	4.3	0
DMK alliance	26.8	0
Left	1.0	0
Totals	94.6	39

Source: Calculated by the author from results posted by the Election Commission of India. http://eciresults.nic.in/.

The Congress recorded above average vote shares in most southern constituencies where the BJP alliance, including the MDMK, also exceeded its statewide average in a number of seats. The southern-most district of Kanniyakumari has a longstanding connection with the BJP. Hindu nationalist organizations have been very active there since the early 1980s.[11] The very visible presence of Christians in the district makes Hindu nationalist claims about minorities more plausible (Table 14.3).

The incompleteness of the electoral alliances gave several parties a chance to test their strength and get a clear sense of their core vote. For professional observers, the elections were an improvement on rather uneven opinion polls. The BJP alliance obscured the individual vote shares of its constituent parties, but as commented above these parties did less well than one would expect given estimates of their support based on earlier elections. The elections showed that the main Dravidian parties still dominate state politics with the AIADMK and the DMK together taking nearly 68 percent of the votes. The national parties, including Congress, CPI, CPM, and the AAP took just under 6 percent of the vote and it is unlikely that BJP support would take this figure over 10 percent. The smaller Dravidian parties and the caste-based parties account for around 20 percent.

One very clear conclusion from reading the results is that regional parties still dominate politics in Tamil Nadu. The state has a strong regional political culture. Voters do appreciate national issues but they respond most positively to parties with local origins.[12] Many find the Tamil-affirming populism of the DMK and the AIADMK reassuring. Those who dissent from the Dravidian mainstream have local champions as well. The lower caste groups represented by the PMK and the VCK often reject the national parties. The national parties are criticized for their indifference to caste inequality and their dominance by higher caste leaders within Tamil Nadu. Hence, the appeal of national parties remains limited and they can only win elections when they are integrated into alliances with regional parties.

Conclusions

The AIADMK hoped the 2014 election would be the springboard to national power and influence. The party aimed to win all 39 seats in the state and bargain its way into a national coalition. The ambitions of the party were partly achieved when it received 44.3 percent of the vote and won 37 seats. However the remarkable success nationally of the BJP thwarted Chief Minister Jayalalithaa's ambition to shape the new government, and even lead the new coalition government. The AIADMK, rather like the BJP state government in Gujarat, has a formula for governing which includes promoting the image of the incumbent chief minister. Successful implementation of certain high profile policies has been made a government priority, and their 'success' is advertised in the press and linked to the personality of the Chief Minister on roadside hoardings across the state. The AIADMK has also gained from the weakness of the DMK.

The DMK did not do enough to win the 2014 Lok Sabha elections in Tamil Nadu. Its main 'mistake' was leaving the Congress out of its alliance. The party was divided over the leadership question with a minority of the party opposing the steady rise of M.K. Stalin because they preferred M.K. Azhagiri. These omissions need to be understood in a broader context. Or as Tsebelis would put it the leadership of the DMK was engaged in a 'nested game'. The 2014 election was the 'primary arena',[13] but the DMK leadership were involved in another game: the 2016 state Assembly elections.

National elections are a secondary objective for the DMK. Some DMK politicians are keen to serve as MPs and DMK MPs have certainly enjoyed holding national cabinet posts since 1999. Yet, most leaders in the DMK consider control over the state government their priority and they hope the party will return to office in 2016. The main objective of the DMK leadership remains winning the 2016 Assembly election and the 2014 Lok Sabha election campaign was approached with that in mind. Thus, the DMK did not field its strongest candidates. Most of the powerful district secretaries of the DMK did not stand as MP candidates so they would be available for the state assembly and state cabinet posts in 2016. The Congress Party was disciplined for past misdemeanors to ensure that if needed it would join a DMK alliance on realistic terms in 2016.[14]

Likewise the thorny leadership issue moved toward resolution. Stalin was able to turn the DMK defeat to his advantage. The official introspection shifted the blame for the defeat to middle level leaders alleged to have worked against the party. In June 2014, a high-level committee recommended restructuring of the party. The number of district units of the party will nearly double, thus diluting the power of the current district secretaries and giving Stalin greater authority in the DMK. The DMK certainly did not win the 2014 election. However, it has prepared the way for its next major challenge. It enters that game with several issues having been resolved. Whether the DMK has done enough to enhance its public appeal remains to be seen. The 2014 elections reflected very well on the AIADMK leadership who will continue to exert pressure on the DMK. The AIADMK was not invited to join the BJP-dominated NDA coalition at the Center, but its presence in the Rajya Sabha means it has the ear of Prime Minister Modi for at least the next couple of years. The unprecedented victory of the BJP in 2014 will inform alliance calculations in future elections. National parties may well find it easier to ally with the AIADMK and the DMK in 2019.

Epilogue

Not long after the election, the confidence of the AIADMK was rudely disturbed by a verdict delivered by a special court in the state of Karnataka. On September 27, 2014, it found Jayalalithaa guilty of having acquired disproportionate assets in relation to her income and sentenced her to a four-year prison term that began that very day. The case has been running for years dating back to Jayalalithaa's period in office between 1991 and 1996 when she had declined to draw a salary and accepted a token payment of one rupee. The verdict had added significance because of a 2013 Supreme Court ruling that requires disqualification from office for 10 years of any elected politician who is convicted in a case serious enough to warrant a custodial sentence of two years or more.

Thus, Jayalalithaa ceased to be chief minister and a member of the Legislative Assembly. The outcome shocked the party and prompted speculation that the party might fall apart without her personal leadership. Mass protests ensued, including numerous reports of suicide attempts by distraught supporters. The legislative party elected state finance minister, O. Panneerselvam as chief minister, an individual known to be highly loyal to Jayalalithaa. If the sentence had run its course, the AIADMK would have been vulnerable, as the Assembly elections were less than two years away, and Jayalalithaa would have much less impact on the election campaign.

The longer term implications of the ruling are unclear. Jayalalithaa can only advise the incumbent chief minister while she remains convicted. This ruling by 'remote control', as it is popularly known, is difficult to do from prison. This problem was eased when the Supreme Court granted Jayalalithaa bail on condition that an appeal began by December 18, 2014. If the Karnataka High Court overrules the original court, she will be permitted to return as chief minister. Otherwise, Jayalalithaa may have to return to prison and it would be difficult for the AIADMK to contest the 2016 election with an incarcerated leader.

The DMK took some comfort from Jayalalithaa's disqualification but it too faces difficulties from a corruption trial. The party has been tainted by the '2G scam' in which it is alleged the Union Telecommunications minister and DMK MP A. Raja skewed the allocation of licenses for the 2G spectrum used by mobile telephone operators and that certain bidders were preferred in return for kickbacks. Raja was forced to resign from the cabinet in 2010 and the Central Bureau of Investigation (CBI) pressed charges against him.

Karunanidhi's daughter Kanimozhi was also charged in the case which has been underway since 2011. The 2G tag was used by the AIADMK to tarnish the image of the DMK and to taunt Karunanidhi during the 2011 Assembly election. The trial is expected to conclude in late 2014 or early 2015 and if it results in convictions for Raja and Kanimozhi, the image of the DMK will be further sullied, especially if Jayalalithaa is acquitted in her case.

The situation in Tamil Nadu is highly ironic and delicately poised. The AIADMK won a decisive victory in the 2014 elections with massive support that augured well for the party. The constraints of electoral alliances had lifted and the party appeared to have found a formula for governing which boosted its popularity. Yet ironically the strategy of the AIADMK may be undermined by decisions made in the courts on issues related to governance. The situation is delicately poised because the AIADMK may recover its confidence on the back of a successful appeal and the DMK be further demoralized by convictions in the 2G case. If both parties suffer setbacks in the courts, then the smaller parties in Tamil Nadu will be accorded more weight in the next round of alliance negotiations. Strategic interaction will be more open and difficult to predict. The outcome of the 2016 Assembly election looks much more uncertain than it did in the immediate aftermath of the AIADMK landslide in May 2014.

Notes and References

1. A. Wyatt, *Party System Change in South India: Political Entrepreneurs, Patterns and Processes* (Abingdon: Routledge, 2009).
2. In the 2011 Assembly election, the two main alliances led by the Dravidian parties included a total of 19 parties. Almost all parties of any consequence were members of an alliance.
3. N. Subramanian, *Ethnicity and Populist Mobilization: Political Parties, Citizens and Democracy in South India* (New Delhi: Oxford University Press, 1999).
4. H. Gorringe, "The New Caste Headmen? Dalit Movement Leadership in Tamil Nadu," in P. Price and A. Ruud (eds), *Power and Influence in India: Bosses, Lords and Captains* (New Delhi: Routledge, 2010).
5. K. Shepsle, "Rational Choice Institutionalism," in R.A.W. Rhodes, S. Binder and B. Rockman (eds), *The Oxford Handbook of Political Institutions* (Oxford: Oxford University Press, 2008), p. 28.
6. E. Sridharan, "Coalitions and Party Strategies in India's Parliamentary Federation." *Publius: The Journal of Federalism* 33, 4 (2003), pp. 146–47. K.K. Kailash, "Institutionalizing a Coalitional System and Games within Coalitions in India (1996–2014)." *Studies in Indian Politics* 2, 2 (2014), p. 197.

7. M. Levi, "Reconsiderations of Rational Choice in Comparative and Historical Analysis," in M. Lichbach and A. Zuckerman (eds), *Comparative Politics: Rationality, Culture, and Structure* (Cambridge: Cambridge University Press, 2009), p. 118.

8. M. Levi, "Reconsiderations of Rational Choice in Comparative and Historical Analysis," in M. Lichbach and A. Zuckerman (eds), *Comparative Politics: Rationality, Culture, and Structure* (Cambridge: Cambridge University Press, 2009), p. 129.

9. K. Shepsle, "Rational Choice Institutionalism," in R.A.W. Rhodes, S. Binder, and B. Rockman (eds), *The Oxford Handbook of Political Institutions* (Oxford: Oxford University Press, 2008), p. 31.

10. A. Wyatt, "Populism and Politics in Contemporary Tamil Nadu." *Contemporary South Asia*, 21, 4 (2013), pp. 365–81.

11. A. Wyatt, *Party System Change in South India: Political Entrepreneurs, Patterns and Processes* (Abingdon: Routledge, 2009), pp. 153–55.

12. A. Wyatt, "Caste and Vernacular Politics in Tamil Nadu, South India," in T. Neyazi, A. Tanabe, and S. Ishizaka (eds), *Democratic Transformation and the Vernacular Public Arena in India* (Abingdon: Routledge, 2014).

13. G. Tsebelis, *Nested Games: Rational Choice in Comparative Politics* (Berkeley: University of California Press, 1990), pp. 7–8.

14. The Congress Party upset many DMK members by making what were felt to be extravagant demands for assembly seats in the 2011 alliance negotiations. At the same time Kanimozhi, daughter of the DMK Party President was arrested and detained ahead of the trial in the 2G spectrum case. Many in the DMK assumed the case was politically motivated and felt that the Congress could have exerted pressure on the investigating authorities to avoid Kanimozhi's arrest.

15

Andhra Pradesh Bifurcation and Electoral Outcomes: Contextual Change, Social Coalitions, and Developmental Discourse

Karli Srinivasulu

The key marker of the 2014 elections in the Telugu state of Andhra Pradesh (AP) was its bifurcation into the states of Telangana and AP.[1] Elections were held within a couple of months after the passing of the Telangana State Formation Bill and with the appointed day[2] for the actual division coming much later.

Telangana's movement for statehood has been a significant issue since the late 1990s. The announcement in 2009 by the UPA government to initiate the process of the formation of the Telangana state constitutes a major turning point in the history of the state.[3] The December 9 announcement ignited a strong reaction against the bifurcation in coastal Andhra and Rayalaseema cutting across the political spectrum and social groups with the students and employees being most active.

The Andhra response to the Telangana movement which was subdued earlier, thus, became quite vocal and intense.

The negative reaction in coastal Andhra and Rayalaseema was quite dramatic with an element of surprise and disbelief. This is despite the fact that the Telangana demand has emerged as a major issue in the 2004[4] and 2009 elections with the Telangana Rashtra Samithi (TRS) as the electoral and political face of the Telangana movement. The alliance of the Congress and Telugu Desam Party (TDP), the two major parties in the state, with the novice TRS in the 2004 and 2009 elections clearly demonstrated their perception of the popular support to the Telangana state demand. It is true that the TRS due to its spatial and organizational limitations was not capable of winning a majority by itself in the region as evident in the successive by-elections that took place following the resignation of the TRS MLAs and MPs in 2006 and 2008. Nonetheless, despite its weaknesses, the TRS could decisively influence the electoral outcome through its adversarial position. In view of these weaknesses, it becomes necessary to examine how such a weak TRS could win the 2014 elections with a convincing majority on its own.

In the residuary AP state, the Congress both as a national party leading the central government and the state, and the TDP having its presence in both regions and having given its consent in writing for the bifurcation, were in a defensive position. The Yuvajana Shramika, Rythu Congress Party (YSRCP) had an especially bright electoral prospect. Led by Y.S. Rajasekhar Reddy's son, Y.S. Jaganmohan Reddy, it had reconciled to its presence in the residuary AP as an Andhra–Rayalaseema party. This optimism was supported by the pre-poll surveys conducted by various national channels and print media.[5] How that initial advantage was lost paving the way to TDP's success needs to be examined.

Neither the TRS in Telangana nor the TDP in AP were the unequivocal choices in 2014. What changes in the context of elections brought about by the reality of bifurcation made this election different if not unique? What strategy and social base contributed to their success? How were their agendas framed and communicated? This chapter attempts to answer these questions. It examines the context of the state's division and dynamics of electoral alliances, social coalitions and policy shifts that underlie the electoral outcome that resulted in the TRS and the TDP winning power in the new states of Telangana and AP, respectively.

The presentation here is divided into four sections. The first section attempts to map the context of the elections defined by the reality of the state's bifurcation. The second section examines the relative party positions and their changing social support. In the third section, we analyze the dynamics of development in both regions, how it impacted on the configuration of social forces and paved the way for the electoral success of the TRS and the TDP. The fourth section seeks to provide perspective and sum up the analysis.

Bifurcation of Andhra Pradesh

With the passing of the Telangana Bill in New Delhi after many years, bifurcation became a reality. This marked a decisive departure in the political discourse within both regions with attendants' concerns and anxieties resulting in real or imagined post-bifurcation blues. The focus in both Telangana and Andhra turned from struggle and resistance to reconciliation and preparation and to the question of which parties and leaders would represent the interests of the regions and new states best. The electoral scenario in both prospective states could be seen as evolving into a keen contest between major parties with the smaller ones and independents largely sidelined and rendered inconsequential.

In Telangana, the electoral competition was between the TRS, Congress, and TDP, whereas in Andhra it was between the TDP, YSRCP, and Congress. Congress, despite its earlier electoral dominance, clearly was in a disadvantageous position in both states. If earlier elections were fought on a variety of issues, this election was principally centered on the theme of development. Telangana's demand was premised on the issue of regional backwardness, thus legitimizing development as the objective of the new state. For an entirely different logic, development also became projected as the chief issue in Andhra as well. As a consequence of Hyderabad city going to Telangana, development centered on building a new capital city was projected to be the central electoral issue in Andhra.

In both regions, the Congress seemed to be politically marginalized in contrasting ways. In Andhra, the Congress has been perceived as the culprit that caused the bifurcation of the state and inflicted loss on the region. The major contentious issue in the debate on bifurcation had been the city of Hyderabad. It had grown rapidly since the mid-1990s as a result of the state-level economic reforms initiated and pursued vigorously in the TDP regime led by N. Chandrababu Naidu and continued by the Congress regime. Hyderabad became a center of local and global investments due to the state pro-liberalization policies. In the popular perception, it became the primary source of quality education and employment in the state for all the regions. The growth of institutions offering technical, engineering, and management education given the supportive role of the regime attracted youth seeking quality education.

The growing service sector, with the IT and IT-enabled services being the most prominent, boosted the employment opportunities in Hyderabad for the educated, while the growth of real estate and construction industry attracted labor, peasants, and artisans displaced and impoverished due to the decline of rural economy in the state. Thus, the city has seen a massive migration of different sections of society: the neo-rich and peasant proprietors as a destination of investment in big and small businesses and real estates, the middle class youth seeking quality education and jobs, and labor in search of work in the expanding urban economy, with the construction sector being the most prominent.

Hyderabad city's status was the most contentious issue in the debate on state division. The loss of the city in the event of bifurcation has been the crucial issue that influenced the mobilization of opposition to the Telangana demand in the Andhra region. The politics of the city's growth has to be understood in terms of the caste and class character of migration, with the process of accumulation and interest articulation being all along determined largely by the political power configuration. If it were the Kammas of coastal Andhra that benefitted during the TDP rule, then the Congress regime could be seen enriching the Reddys of Rayalaseema. The development of the city and its nature of accumulation clearly point to the party–power–caste symmetry.

The acceleration in Hyderabad's economic activity has largely been dominated by the neo-rich of Coastal Andhra and Rayalaseema, predominantly due to the political proximity of the Kamma and Reddy communities to the TDP and Congress, respectively. If the process of accumulation was slow and relatively low keyed earlier, in the post-reform scenario, then it has assumed an unparallel speed and scale. If a significant part of this was because of the so-called development projects of the state, related to real estate, township development, highways, SEZs, industry and tourism parks, then their impact on the speculative interest in these lands by the dominant castes contributed in a mutually supporting way to the expansion.

The scale of expansion could be gauged from the fact that four districts neighboring Hyderabad in a significant measure have been merged into the city affecting scores of villages, displacing their inhabitants, dispossessing them of their livelihood, assets, and habitat. If a small section of the landowning class of these districts have benefited, then several times more have been displaced and dispossessed.

This objective reality forms the background to both the Telangana movement and the opposition to it in Andhra and Rayalaseema. What is interesting is the spatial coalescence of caste and class interests along the regional demarcations. The dominant caste elite in Telangana have nurtured a grudge that the major chunk of the so-called development has been grabbed by the elite of the Andhra and Rayalaseema regions. Among the middle classes, there has been a sense of disgruntlement as most of the jobs and promotions have been perceived to have been snatched by those of the developed Andhra region largely because of the asymmetry of power relations. This was despite the safeguards provided at the time of the formation of the state of AP in 1956.[6] The earlier articulation of the violation of the safeguards was the Telangana movement in 1969. The withdrawal of the movement also led to certain concessions that also drew a blank in the process of implementation. The peasantry also suffered on account of the neglect of traditional irrigation following the TDP coming into power in 1983. In the place of policy support to the traditional irrigation, there was undue encouragement to micro irrigation. It is this history of nonimplementation and neglect that has provided ammunition to the present movement.[7]

The demand of Telangana has its contra echoes in the other two regions. The separation of Telangana could be seen as depriving speculators of the benefits of their investments. It is this class with its interests in real estate, construction, contracts, and other businesses relying on political patronage that saw its interests being harmed. Since the 1990s, this class has developed a direct interest in politics by investing its money in elections, thereby not only escalating the cost of fighting elections, but also transforming elections into a speculative venture. Candidate profiles across parties[8] show a secular increase in the number of those with a business background. Quite logically, once in politics and in power it would be probable that they would pursue their economic interests much more vigorously even compromising public interests. Thus, in AP, the line of demarcation between politics and business became largely blurred. The 2014 elections in both regions have shown the culmination of this trend.

Thus, the business and political elite of Andhra and Rayalaseema have developed a substantial economic interest in Telangana, in general, and in the Hyderabad city, in particular, which are largely linked to and determined by their access to political power. The formation of the state of Telangana with Hyderabad as a capital could be seen as a substantive injury to their interests. Their concerns have been the underlying reason for the demand to declare Hyderabad a Union Territory or joint capital.

For the middle classes and laborers who have migrated to Hyderabad rapidly growing into a major venue of employment and livelihood catalyzed by a reform process, the sudden shift in the status of the city heightened their anxieties. In addition, rumors emphasized that bifurcation would lead to increased water problems for the Andhra region. Telangana, the rumors maintained, being the upper riparian region would tap most of the Krishna and Godavari rivers. Andhra's farmers became unduly anxious when as a matter of fact the relevant water commissions determine the allocation of river waters. This misinformation spread by the influential elite led to the massive rural participation in the movement against the impending bifurcation in Andhra and Rayalaseema.

The scenario that unfolded after the December 9 announcement has witnessed a vertical division of political parties along regional lines. The undue indecisiveness and procrastination on the part of the Congress only deepened the fault-lines along the regional lines. The role of media in this imbroglio cannot be ignored. Largely owned and controlled by the coastal Andhra propertied class, the vernacular media both electronic and print played a clearly partisan role. They not only sided with the Andhra region by highlighting their concerns, but also incited their anxieties and insecurities. The role of media, thus, has largely been focused on the side of deepening divisions rather than on creating and spreading information, awareness, and understanding of the present and future of the issue. The Andhra neo-rich-dominated media has largely been viewed in a negative manner in Telangana.

The sharp polarization among the political parties, elite, and different sections of society only deepened the popular distrust of the political class in both regions. The political elites belonging to the Congress Party in both regions were the worst victims of the trust deficit. Their wavering stances—going in delegations to Delhi, threats of resignations, talk of convincing the party High Command—in the face of the High Command's indecisiveness only added to their disrepute in the popular mind. The inexplicable tolerance of the Congress High Command of Congress Chief Minister, Kiran Kumar Reddy's open defiance of the High Command only added to the growing unpopularity of the party in all the regions of the state and especially in Telangana. This state of the Congress contributed to its lack of support throughout the regions creating the conditions for its adversaries to take advantage of its political weakness.

Relative Party Positions and Their Changing Social Support

The fate of the Congress in Telangana makes a curious case. The quid pro quo understanding between the Congress and TRS, publicly admitted by the leadership of both the parties, was that, once the Telangana State Bill is passed, the TRS would merge with the Congress. Curiously enough, the TRS kept the Congress waiting for its merger decision until the end when it finally declined to even have an alliance let alone the merger. The Congress decision to form the Telangana state as expected did estrange it in the Andhra and Rayalaseema regions. Its political marginalization in Telangana despite its expected strategic advantage of having created the state was largely a making of its own. The indecisiveness, protracted procrastination, formation of committee after committee, holding of consultations and parleys with parties in the pretext of evolving consensus when the issue is a deeply divisive one, and the final decision taken on the eve of election have shown Congress in a poor light.

Thus, the only party which could project itself as a truly Telangana one was the TRS. The TRS could very soon realize it and its decision to go alone in the elections despite its limited spatial presence, fragile organizational structure, and unsure social support base as evident from its earlier electoral performance was based on the perceived weaknesses of its adversaries. A demoralized Congress nationally in the face of BJP's aggressive march found itself in a defensive mode in Telangana, and its Telangana leadership rudderless. The TDP also found itself in a disadvantageous position in Telangana. Its origin, leadership, and political dispensation were perceived to be from coastal Andhra.

In spite of its organizational strength, relatively stable backward class social base, and even electoral presence as evidenced in the local body elections held in the midst of the ongoing Telangana movement, TDP's vulnerability in 2014 was obvious as it was viewed as an Andhra party. The reality of the Telangana state imparted a strategic advantage to the TRS vis-à-vis the Congress and the TDP. The excitement and exuberance of the reality of Telangana achieved after a protracted struggle put the TRS in an incomparable advantage.

As in the case of Telangana, in AP as well the bifurcation of the state, in fact, set different social and political dynamics in motion. The Congress found itself marginalized and with little will to fight. Even those Congress leaders of the region who openly defied the High Command and took to the streets to protest could not muster enough support in the electoral sphere. A majority of the prominent and vocal leaders of the Congress either withdrew from the electoral fray or joined the TDP or YSRCP to contest the elections. The volatility of the situation was such that both parties openly invited those who still had some influence on voters in their constituencies. In the popular perception, the Congress as a party failed to live up to their expectations, but not leaders in their individual capacity.[9] Thus, in the electoral field, the competition was virtually reduced to the one between the TDP and YSRCP in Andhra.

The YSRCP star campaigners, comprising Jagan, his mother, and sister, literally were on the streets since the death of YS Rajasekhar Reddy in a helicopter crash in September 2009. Christened as 'Odarpu Yatra' (meaning consoling journey), it sought to console people in mourning at the death of YSR. The Yatra continued till the 2014 elections. It is the evidence of the tenacity of the family that in spite of the ordeal experienced on account of the CBI enquiry and Jagan's long jail term, the mother–sister duo leadership continued the Yatra. In fact, for the

YSRCP, it became a protracted election campaign; and so the people and their political adversaries saw it. This, in fact, accounted for the high ratings the party got in pre-election surveys, resulting in the people queuing up to join the party with an eye on the party ticket.

Chandrababu Naidu, being out of power for two successive terms and with almost an invisible prospect of comeback, was the most worried man. Despite his age and doctors' advice, the motivated Naidu launched a *padayatra* of his own throughout the undivided state that was almost reminiscent of YSR's *padayatra* before the 2004 elections. This was basically meant to keep himself connected to the people and to keep his party rank and file intact lest they be swept by the political tempest in the state. The 2014 elections showed the fragility of the party structure, ideology, and loyalty as horse-trading reached its peak *sans* qualms, reservations or guilt.

With the state bifurcation becoming a fait accompli and the uncertainty and unpredictability that characterized the political scenario in the state in the aftermath of YSR's death giving way to some clarity, Naidu could identify a strategy, which consisted of the following: one, forging the right social coalition; two, fielding candidates with winning as the principal criteria; three, voicing right slogans; and above all, regaining space and visibility in national politics through proper alliances.

The TDP in its three decades of existence has come to have a stable social support base among the Kammas, backward castes, and the Madigas. The Kapu, a major caste in terms of number and social presence who were initially with the TDP, moved away from it following the Kamma–Kapu riots in the late 1980s[10] and went first to the Congress and subsequently to the Praja Rajyam Party (PRP) floated by Chiranjeevi, their own popular cine actor. With the miserable performance of the PRP in the 2009 elections and its subsequent merger with the Congress, the Kapus found themselves in a state of disarray. The Kapus hope of coming to power in 2009 was premised on a comparison with 1983, with parallels drawn between Chiranjeevi and NTR—both popular cine actors. More curiously, it was also informed by a political Darwinian assumption propagated by Kapu and Dalit ideologues that viewed state politics in terms of the capture or transfer of political power in a descending order in the hierarchical structure of caste dominance.

AP, being ruled by Reddys since its formation in 1956, with the TDP coming to power in 1983, saw the political rise of the Kammas. The

2009 elections, with the promise of Chiranjeevi and PRP, were seen as signaling the rise of the Kapus in the state politics. The failure of Chiranjeevi in 2009 disproved the purported evolutionary logic and found the Kapus in disarray and made them to reconcile to playing a second fiddle to either Reddys in the Congress or Kammas in the TDP.

The ambition of political power has its attendant tensions and contradictions. Kapus' attempt at political ascendancy intensified their contradiction with the Dalits. In the aftermath of TDP's political rise in the 1980s, the dominant Kammas engineered a series of very violent attacks on Dalits.[11] This apparently eased with Kammas' move in a perceptible way from agriculture to urban vocations and a change in their *modus operandi*. The same dialectic could be seen operating in the relation of the Kapus with the Dalits. The relation between the Kapus who are a dominant community in Godavari districts and northern coastal Andhra and the Dalits has never been comfortable. Dalits increasingly assert themselves as part of the process of expansion and benefits of modernity like education and mobility. Urban exposure has impacted on their self-perception, self-identity, and politics, leading to the noncompliance if not frequent frontal challenges to the dominance of the upper castes, in this case, the Kapus. The most recent manifestation of this conflict is the Laxmipet massacre.[12]

The successful attempt on the part of the YSRCP to attract the Dalits, especially the Malas in coastal Andhra and Rayalaseema has to be appreciated against this backdrop. YSR's family identifying as a Christian Reddy has been politically instrumental in forming an alliance of Reddys including those of the Hindu community with Dalits, the majority of whom in these regions belong to the Christian faith. With the bifurcation of the state, the political potential of this social combination has assumed a greater significance and catalyzed regrouping of communities and castes. With the marginalization of the Congress in the electoral compass and the usurpation of its position by the YSRCP, the contra social coalition mobilized with urgency.

The result of this is the gravitation of the Kapus to the TDP deserting the sinking Congress. In 2014, resolve and determination on the part of the Kamma–Kapu combine was visible in the movement of the elite and cadre of these communities from Congress to the TDP against YSRCP and the tireless effort of Naidu to win the elections. With fairly stable support among the backward classes, the TDP could consolidate a winnable social coalition in AP. Apart from the social and symbolic resources of caste, this election saw the unparallel mobilization of the material resources as is evident in the candidate selection, the majority of whom are super rich with an election expenditure averaging above ₹100 million in the case of the Assembly and ₹250 million in the case of the Lok Sabha.[13]

Dynamics of Regional Development and Electoral Performance

The electoral campaign in both regions was conducted on similar ideological lines with similar slogans. Regional identity and protection of interests formed a solid issue during the elections happening in the context of strong regional identity movements and identity-based state bifurcation. Equally and perhaps more important became the question of development with all the parties focusing on it. In fact, the electoral campaign appeared as if it was a virtual parade of parties and candidates in a development show. Thus, the question was which party would ensure a proper development of the state? The people were to decide whom they could entrust with this task (Table 15.1).

The electoral history of the TRS has been quite volatile. In its first major electoral appearance in 2004, the TRS in an alliance with the Congress won five MP and 26 MLA seats registering a 16.9 percent popular vote. Subsequently, with dissidents moving out of the party, the TRS' strength became reduced to 16 MLAs and four MPs.[14] When the entire contingent of TRS MPs and MLAs resigned in 2008, in the by-election their number further reduced to only seven MLAs and two MPs. Congress and the TDP won five and four MLA seats and one MP seat each, respectively. Despite the continual presence of the movement and its active role in it, the TRS which contested the 2009 election in an alliance with the TDP could not improve its performance as it won only 10 assembly and two parliamentary seats. What is even more noteworthy is with 9.43 percentage point popular vote it found a further spatial shrinkage in its base in electoral terms since 2004. In 2009, far from expanding into the south Telangana districts, the TRS registered an electoral decline even in its north Telangana stronghold.

Table 15.1
Party Performance in Telangana and Andhra Pradesh

	Telangana			AP		
	Seats			Seats		
Party	Lok Sabha	Assembly	Vote (%)	Lok Sabha	Assembly	Vote (%)
Congress	2	21	24.5	0	–	2.8
TDP + BJP	1+1	15+5	22.6	15+2	102+4	47.7
TRS	11	63	34.7	–	–	–
YSRCP	1	3	4.5	8	67	45.4
AIMIM	1	7	3.5	–	–	–
Others		5	10.2		2	4.1
Total	**17**	**119**		**25**	**175**	

Source: Election Commission of India, General Elections 2014. Data on May 17, 2014. Available online at http://eci.nic.in (Party-wise trends and result).

In contrast to the TDP that has nurtured a strong pro-backward class base, the TRS leadership in sociological terms has continued to retain the dominant Velama and Reddy caste image.

The TRS' electoral performance in 2014 winning 63 MLA and 11 MP seats and 34.7 percentage point popular vote on its own marks a clear departure in its electoral history. It is seen as a convincing vindication of its popular perception of being the near proximate reflection of Telangana aspirations. Apart from the question of Telangana identity, the decade long movement in which a multiplicity of civil society and political forces participated and mobilized the people orchestrated the question of regional backwardness. Despite the ideological plurality and multi-expressions of the movement, one of its continually articulated common themes was the issue of development. Given the complex plurality of the movement, needless to say, the idea of development meant different things to different constituencies quite often with contradictory images and inferences.

In caste and class terms, the land owning agrarian classes were aiming at the expansion of irrigation and ensured power supply at an affordable cost. A large majority of them are dependent on ground water and the artisan castes have experienced a tremendous crisis leading to displacement, thus seeking state support. The youth's grievance focused on their marginalization in the emergent employment situation, while employees felt a sense of unjust treatment in promotions. The pro-Telangana discourse projected the starvation deaths and suicides among the weavers and farmers, and the neglect of youth and employees as symptomatic of the asymmetrical treatment of the Telangana region and its people due to the unjust governance of the Andhra rulers with the only solution being the formation of a separate state.

The TRS also promised an elaborate welfare agenda with schemes like a loan waiver of rupees one lakh to small landholders, two bedroom houses at the cost of rupees three lakhs to the homeless, and the distribution of three acres to the landless Scheduled Caste families with support of crop investment. The party also promised the continuation of the existing fee reimbursement scheme for students, an increment to the six lakh government employees as part of the Telangana state celebration, and the promise of a 1,000-bed state of the art hospital with advanced medical facilities in each distinct headquarters in the new Telangana state.

In the hustle and bustle of the electoral campaign, the finer differences in the pro-Telangana organizations were evened out by the aggressive TRS and it emerged as the champion of the Telangana cause. If its decade-long role in the movement put the TRS on a higher pedestal, then the diffident posture position and lackluster leadership of the Congress and TDP put them on the defensive. The BJP, consistently in an active mode throughout the protracted struggle, hoped to benefit from its role in the Telangana state formation[15] in the 2014 elections. In fact, it was handicapped by its alliance with the TDP winning only one MP seat in Telangana. The TDP won in the urban constituency of Malkajgiri only because of the large presence of Andhra settlers in it. While the BJP alliance with the TDP proved to be mutually advantageous in the residuary AP, it was to the contrary in Telangana.

In the residuary AP, the TDP emergence as the majority party is a result of an astute electoral game plan, mature political strategy, and aggressive campaign. The TDP toyed with the idea of a non-Congress and non-BJP Third Front, but realized its improbability as the national scenario became fast changing with Narendra Modi emerging as NDA's

PM candidate. The TDP had a long relationship with the BJP during the entire tenure of Atal Bihari Vajpayee's NDA government. In fact, Chandrababu Naidu as the TDP CM played a key role in the NDA-I government gaining the image of developing the state and building the brand image of the Hyderabad city during this period. He never tired of reminding anybody about his role in the making of Hyderabad into a global metropolis.

Both the NDA and the TDP as part of the alliance tasted defeat at the polls in the 2004 elections despite their 'India shining' claim. In the succeeding decade, they charted their own paths and remained out of power. By a curious turn of events they found an opportune moment to come together in 2014. If the BJP found it necessary to expand its alliance through the NDA, then the TDP motivation to join the BJP seems to be two-pronged. Firstly, it was clear that the BJP under Modi was clearly on ascendancy and there was a certain commonality with the BJP agenda as its central focus was also on development. Secondly, with a pre-poll alliance, the TDP aimed at assuring the people in AP that it alone would be able to provide solutions to the post-division problems.

The TDP tried to make the best of the emergent scenario by harping on the benefits of the alliance with the BJP and a friendly regime at the Center. It reminded how being part of the NDA-I in the 1990s, the TDP regime could develop the state and the city of Hyderabad. It was argued that the most important and urgent task before the residuary AP was to build a capital city that would be the pride of the Andhraites. For such a city to be built, two lakh crores would be required which would be forthcoming only with a friendly Center. The issue of the capital city and development was used almost synonymously. TDP built a campaign for a state-of-the-art capital city as the symbol of the region's self-respect, and tried to assuage the sense of hurt resulting from the state division and 'loss' of Hyderabad.[16] It is supposed to be an answer to all the problems related to development, health, education, and employment through IT and IT-enabled sectors.

It is sad to note the absence of any self-critical reflection on the part of Naidu that the Telangana demand in a significant sense was a result of the concentrated growth of the Hyderabad city. Perhaps, a more even growth would not have resulted in such heightened passions and reactions. A similar urban growth strategy could lead to comparable problems in the future as there are internal sub-regional differences in terms of development in the residual AP and an awareness of the historical unevenness. The development mantra of the TDP did have a strong impact on the electorate. There was a strong sense of *déjà vu* in TDP's campaign which was in tune with the BJP national election campaign for development predicated upon the so-called Gujarat model.

The YSRCP, in contrast, lost its initial élan. In spite of its aggressive pro-united AP stand, it was seen as an extension or a variant of the Congress Party. Jagan's indication of his preference for the UPA as against the NDA gave rise to speculation that there was already an agreement with the Congress and that after elections the YSRCP might merge in the Congress. The Congress which was in shambles cast its spell on the YSRCP because of this association.[17] YSRCP's social base as stated earlier consisted of the Reddys, Christian Malas, and the Muslim minorities. This accounted for its 45.4 percentage point popular vote. The Congress by garnering only 2.8 percentage points proved to be a poor shadow of its earlier self. It is quite likely that the YSRCP was the major beneficiary of Congress' loss. A mere 2.3 percentage point difference in the popular vote between the TDP and YSRCP made a huge difference in terms of seats. The TDP–BJP alliance won 17 MP and 106 MLA seats compared to the YSRCP winning only 8 MP and 67 MLA seats. In many constituencies, the difference between the winner and second place was slim. The huge disparity in the votes and seats is a serious comment on the first-past-post system.

There was a remarkable shift in the AP politics. The shift was visible in terms of the sagging enthusiasm for Jagan and his party. As the electoral campaign picked up momentum, the issue of his perceived corrupt deeds came to be discussed openly and widely in the media and on the street with a usual mix of fact, fiction, and fantasy. There were few ethical qualms about the electoral politics as huge amounts of money were spent that in popular perception resulted from corruption. With everyone targeting him, Jagan's alleged corruption became a critical theme.

Naidu's electoral campaign assumed inclusiveness and expansiveness in contrast to Jagan's isolation. Jagan harped on the restoration of *Rajanna Rajyam*, which basically meant the continuation of the populist schemes of the YSR regime like free electricity and input subsidies to farmers, a free health scheme (*Arogyasree*), housing for the poor, old age pensions, fee imbursement for poor students, and the implementation of the rural employment scheme. Naidu's emphasis on development did not deter him from promising schemes like loan waivers up to ₹1.5 lakh to farmers and up to ₹1 lakh to women self-help groups for fee reimbursement. Naidu brought in popular cine star and Congress campaign chief Chiranjeevi's younger brother Pawan Kalyan as one of the chief campaigners for the TDP–BJP alliance. Apart from the cine glamour, this added credibility to Naidu's campaign as an adversary's brother was with him. He also benefitted from the regular appearance of BJP national leaders including the PM candidate, Narendra Modi. Naidu put emphasis on the necessity for the new state to have an experienced leader, namely himself.

Summary and Conclusion

The bifurcation of the Telugu state formed on a linguistic basis in 1956 into Telangana and AP forms the backdrop of the 2014 elections. The discursive shift in the post-division states was marked by anxieties and concerns in the popular mind. One of the principal issues common to both the new states was concerned with the development of the region. In a significant sense, the commitment to each region and the ability to develop it emerged as the crucial criteria shaping the electoral choice. The clear mandate to the TRS in Telangana and the TDP in AP reflects not only their strong regionalist image but also a certain degree of popular trust in their commitment and ability to address the developmental anxieties of the new states. Congress, which had dominated state politics during the last decade, performed poorly in its campaign and electoral results. Its poor vote and seat share in AP demonstrates its strong popular distrust mainly because of its poor handling of the state bifurcation issue.

Development in the two regions presented contrasting images and meanings. In Telangana, the anxiety about development was motivated by the view that with the division of the state enterprising Andhra capital might migrate elsewhere. With Telangana's image of being backward projected during the movement, it feared that it would be difficult to attract investment. In the case of Andhra, the disadvantage of not inheriting Hyderabad and the urgency of building a new capital assumed major significance in the elections.

Votes for these parties significantly reflect the popular perception of uncertainty about the new state and need for a stable and firmly regionalist government that caters to the needs of the region. The social support that brought the TRS and TDP into power shows a broad spatial coalescence of forces that is indicative of its popular realization. It is not to suggest that these victories are unproblematic and unconditional. The TRS with 34.7 and the TDP with 47.7 percentage vote totals cannot afford the luxury of claiming to be the sole representative of the regional aspirations. With the critical vocal presence of the Opposition, ruling parties will be under pressure to be responsive and responsible.

The vote for the regional parties cannot be seen, as suggested by some, as a rejection of the national parties. The TDP alliance with the BJP, despite the initial hiccups and dissuasion from the local units of both parties, shows the realization of the need for healthy regional–national cooperation. The vote for the TDP–BJP alliance reflects the view that a friendly government at the Center would further the development of the state. The TRS going alone in Telangana cannot be seen as a rejection of national parties, but is largely a result of the specificities of the 2014 context. Thus, the vote for strong regional parties cannot be seen as a reflection of narrow regionalism, nor can the vote for the TDP–BJP alliance be seen as an indication of the ascendancy of the Hindutva agenda. The dialectic of major–minor among the NDA partners does not always weigh in favor of the BJP; it has to be understood in the context of regional spatial political specificities. If BJP's desire and ability to expand the NDA is an indication of its electoral strength, then it is also symptomatic of its ideological compromise and the limited nature of its Hindutva agenda. The BJP despite its long cherished southern ambition was forced to play the role of a minor alliance partner in AP. The AP experiment further shows the serious limitations of third front possibilities this time around.

Notes and References

1. The Telangana region, which was part of the Hyderabad State, comprises 10 districts. The coastal Andhra and Rayalaseema, which were part of the Madras Presidency, consist of nine and four districts, respectively. In terms of the total population, the three regions constitute 40.5, 41.5, and 18 percent, respectively (Census of India, Andhra Pradesh, 2001).

2. The Presidential notification fixed June 2, 2014 as the appointed date.
3. This was in response to the fast by the TRS leader KCR and the massive mobilization going beyond party and political lines.
4. For an analysis of the electoral discourse on the Telangana demand, see, K. Srinivasulu, "Political Articulation and Policy Discourse in Elections, Andhra Pradesh, 2004," *Economic and Political Weekly* XXXIX, 34(August 21, 2004).
5. See, for instance, the Lokniti-IBN National Tracker poll conducted in Andhra Pradesh in January 2014, available at http://www.lokniti.org//pdf/Findings%20%20%20 Andhra%20Pradesh.pdf.
   Also, the local NTV-Nielson pre-poll survey results telecast on the Telugu NTV channel on March 30, 2014.
6. This is referred to as the 'Gentlemen's Agreement'. For details, see, K.V. Narayana Rao, *The Emergence of Andhra Pradesh* (Mumbai: Popular Prakashan, 1973), pp. 301–03.
7. For a discussion on the discursive mapping of the Telangana question, see, K. Srinivasulu, "Discourses on Telangana and Critique of the Linguistic Nationality Principle," in Sudha Pai and A. Sarangi (eds), *Interrogating States Reorganization: Culture, Identity and Political Economy in Independent India* (Delhi: Routledge, 2011).
8. The media did not shy away from reporting on the candidates, parties and their spending in elections. For instance, see, *Hans India* (Hyderabad Edition), April 19, 2014; *Andhra Jyothi* (Hyderabad Edition), April 27, 2014; *Namaste Telangana* (Hyderabad Edition), April 29, 2014.
9. Field notes, April and June 2014.
10. For the background of the Vijayawada riots, see, "Political Economy of Vijayawada Riots," a report of the Andhra Pradesh Civil Liberties Committee, 1989.
11. K. Srinivasulu, "Caste, Class and Social Articulation in Andhra Pradesh: Mapping Differential Regional Trajectories," *Working Paper* 179, Overseas Development Institute, London.
12. In this village in Srikakulam district, the dominant caste Kapus attacked and killed five Malas and injured more than two dozen seriously, Hyderabad Political Economy Group, "Laxmipet Dalit Killings," *Economic and Political Weekly* XLVII, 47–48 (December 1, 2012).
13. Field notes: Interviews with political activists, NGO representatives, and journalists.
14. For an analysis of the 2009 elections, see, Karli Srinivasulu, "Andhra Pradesh: Political Mobilization, Competitive Populism, and Changing Party Dynamics in Andhra Pradesh," in Paul Wallace and Ramashray Roy (eds), *India's 2009 Elections: Coalition Politics, Party Competition, and Congress Continuity* (New Delhi: SAGE Publications, 2011).
15. BJP's support was crucial for the passage of the Telangana Bill in the Parliament.
16. The movement against state division in this region nurtured a sense of hurt and loss at Hyderabad city going to the Telangana state. There were different variations of this 'loss'. Field notes: Interviews with civil society activists and journalists, Guntur and Vijayawada, April 2014.
17. Field notes: Interviews with K. Rajendra of Kadali Network, Mangalagiri, April 2014.

16

Karnataka: Change and Continuity in 2014*

S.S. Patagundi and Prakash Desai

The most significant achievement of the research on elections "to date could well be described as the generation of vast amounts of information, primarily survey data."[1] One necessity is to understand India's general elections at the regional level. The performance of the Congress-led UPA II in terms of effective governance, issues of development, and its alleged corruption contrasted with the Narendra Modi wave constituted the context of the 2014 general elections in Karnataka. National politics is mostly a reflection of the politics of states in India. The Lok Sabha elections can be better understood by examining the Karnataka Assembly elections held one year earlier in 2013.

The 2013 Assembly Elections

The results of the 2013 Assembly elections of Karnataka registered an impressive performance by the Congress Party. It won 122 seats, whereas the BJP and JD(S) won 40 seats each. The five-year rule from 2008 to

* The authors gratefully acknowledge the suggestions and advice of Professor R.K. Hebsur, Professor K. Raghavendra Rao, and Professor A.A. Mutalik Desai in writing this chapter.

2013 by the BJP ridden with corruption, infighting, and a leadership crisis was seen as the inability of the BJP to provide good governance. The electorate of the state was not happy with BJP's governance or developmental programs. The five-year BJP rule evoked a poor image of its leaders being accused in cases of corruption, sexual and physical assault on young men and women "by goons owing allegiance to fringe Sangh Parivar outfits,[2]" and "of three BJP legislators watching pornographic clips on a cellular phone while the assembly was in session."[3]

The BJP on its part did not provide tough competition as a house united in this election, and one of the nodal leaders who had brought the party into power in South India for the first time, B.S. Yeddyurappa, had left the party. Because of rivalry over power in the party, he had to quit and form his own party–the Karnataka Janata Party (KJP). Although his party did not succeed in gaining many seats, its presence caused a huge loss to the BJP. Yeddyurappa's party "garnered 9.83 per cent of total votes and wrecked BJP's prospects. The fledgling party, besides playing a spoiler, won six seats but credibly finished second in 36 and third in 35 constituencies."[4]

One of the reasons for the Congress victory in the 2013 Assembly elections was its strategy of social engineering.[5] The party "adopted a formula that shifted the spotlight from the two dominant communities, Lingayats and the Vokkaligas to the OBCs, Dalits and minorities."[6] The Congress Party in Karnataka has been successful to a great extent in mobilizing backward class communities in its favor in electoral politics. This had happened in Karnataka in the 1970s. Credit for the successful mobilization of these communities to support the Congress Party in the past goes to Devaraj Urs, a former Chief Minister of Karnataka (1972–80) with the support of Indira Gandhi. It was he who enabled the backward communities to make their voice present in the devising of public policy.[7] Such support and encouragement from Urs' leadership enabled backward and marginal communities "to redefine their terms of social association with other castes and communities afresh."[8] It also paved the way for the emergence of promising leaders from these communities.

Siddaramaiah is one leader influenced by the era of Devaraj Urs in state politics. Twenty-five years after that era, it was Siddaramaiah who revived Urs' strategy and started mobilizing these communities. Today, in Karnataka politics, he is a prominent leader of the AHINDA[9] community.

AHINDA is an abbreviation for the backward section of the population "which is a combination of minorities (mainly Muslims) and Backward classes, which include the Kuruba (the caste to which Siddaramaiah belongs), Idiga"[10] and other non-Lingayat, non-Okkaliga, non-Brahmin backward castes, "and the entire population of the Scheduled Castes and the Scheduled Tribes."[11] The mobilization of AHINDA in the 2013 Assembly elections in favor of the Congress Party under the leadership of Siddaramaiah helped it to a considerable extent.

The BJP lost very heavily in coastal Karnataka and Malnad (hilly region) in the 2013 elections. These are the regions from where the Rashtriya Swayamsevak Sangh (RSS) and its affiliates have been working for many decades and have been "successful in cultivating a social base for its Hindutva ideology cutting across caste lines. Right from the 1990s, these two regions saw a polarization of Hindu votes in favor of the BJP, resulting in an assured Hindu vote bank for the party."[12] The reasons for the failure in maintaining this success might be the failure of the BJP in including more leaders from these regions in the Council of Ministers, the unpopular acts of some organizations like Sri Ram Sena which had indulged in moral, cultural policing, and the poor performance of the party as far as governance was concerned.

The dynamics of Hindutva politics in coastal Karnataka could be understood from the results of the 2013 elections. After "the BJP came to power in 2008, there emerged a conflict of interest within the Sangh Parivar. The authoritarian attitude of the Parivar and its inability to accommodate conflicting interests resulted in the moving away of substantial groups such as the Bunts and Mogaveera communities."[13] Many leaders from these communities who contested elections won in 2013 as candidates of the Congress Party. At least for a short period, the Hindutva agenda suffered.[14]

The 2014 General Elections

The BJP did well in the 2014 Lok Sabha elections by winning 17 out of 28 seats. The Congress and JD(S) got nine and two seats each:

> When one first looks at the Lok Sabha results from Karnataka, there is a temptation to conclude that the state witnessed a BJP victory. However,

a deeper analysis shows that while the BJP has done well in the State, the Congress did not face a humiliating defeat like it did in the rest of the country.[15]

The results of this election came as a disappointment for the ruling Congress government led by Siddaramaiah, but it did do well in winning more seats compared to the Congress in other states.[16] The Congress Party also did well in its vote share (see Table 16.1). It secured 40.8 percent votes, whereas BJP and JD(S) got 43 percent and 11 percent votes, respectively.[17]

The performance of the Congress Party "was far below the chief minister's own assessment and expectation."[18] He was "pitching for 18 to 20 seats in Karnataka, but the Congress managed to win just nine, three of which with less than 10,000 margin. Compared to 2009, the Congress' tally went up by three seats."[19] Even after having introduced several welfare programs, the Congress Party could not succeed in gaining success. Siddaramaiah did not focus much on achievements of his government.

Table 16.1
Party Position and Vote Share

Party	2004 Parliamentary Election		2009 Parliamentary Election		2014 Parliamentary Election	
	Seats	Vote Share (in %)	Seats	Vote Share (in %)	Seats	Vote Share (in %)
Congress	08	36.82	06	37.65	09(+3)	40.8
BJP	18	34.77	19	41.63	17(−1)	43.00
JD(S)	02	20.45	03	13.57	02(−1)	11.00
Others	−	7.96	−	7.15	−	05.20

Sources: Data for this table is collected from http://eci.nic.in/eci_main/archiveofge2009/Stats/VOLII/STATE_PARTYWISE SEATWON AND VOTES_Lok Sabha 2009_2401 2014.pdf, http://eciresults.nic.in/PartyWiseResultS10.htm?st=S10, and R.K. Hebsur, "The Surge of Saffron: Some Genuine and Some Imitation," in Paul Wallace and Ramashray Roy (eds), *India's 2009 Elections—Coalition Politics, Party Competition and Congress Continuity* (New Delhi, SAGE Publications, 2011), p. 279.

Note: Difference in seats compared to the 2009 Lok Sabha polls mentioned in parentheses.

Instead, he "went on the offensive against Narendra Modi, even calling him a 'Narahanthaka' (mass killer)."[20] Such rhetoric played a negative role and did not convince the voters. It simply failed to convince the voters about the performance of the government in one year of its rule in the state.[21]

There are some serious questions about poll surveys in India.[22] The history of earlier poll surveys "has been a mixed baggage of success as well as failure."[23] This applies to the 2014 elections in Karnataka because its predictions show discrepancies. Several agencies such as CVoter, AC Nielsen, Hansa, and CSDS provided predictions.[24] All but CSDS predicted that the BJP would win 15 seats.[25] CSDS predicted "just 10 seats for the BJP and 15 for the Congress."[26] Speculations emphasized that for the Congress and the BJP, the 2013 Assembly elections were "critical for adding the maximum numbers from the principal party to the UPA and NDA"[27] and victory in this election "would be a morale booster in the run-up to the Lok Sabha poll."[28] But the 2013 elections did turn out to be critical because the Congress could not repeat its assembly victory in the Lok Sabha elections.

The observation that the voter of "Karnataka has been unique and discerning"[29] remains true because the choice of Karnataka voters in 2014 again exhibited their capacity for making distinctions between a national and state election. One of the typical features of the Karnataka elections is that it generally goes against the ruling party at the Center. "After a long time, Karnataka went with the national trend in a Lok Sabha poll."[30]

The Modi wave or 'Namo' factor constituted one of the reasons for BJP's national success. But in Karnataka, the so-called Modi wave did not make a very significant difference to the outcome. Caste combinations and capability of the candidates took centre stage and the Modi wave was felt primarily in the urban areas.[31] Apart from Modi's campaign, Yeddyurappa and B. Sriramlu's entry propelled the BJP. Of the total 28 Lok Sabha seats, the Congress and Janata Dal (Secular) (Janata Dal[S]) managed to win 11 seats. So, the result was not a verdict against the Congress-led state government. This can be substantiated by the fact that the Congress not only won nine seats but also managed to get 40.8 percent of the total vote, just a few percent less than the BJP. However, both the BJP and the Congress increased their votes in 2014 as compared to the 2009 election.

Issues in the 2014 Elections

There were no dominant issues that were fiercely debated by the political parties in the state during these elections. Issues such as corruption, development model, and some local, however, were involved to a considerable extent in the campaigns. On the question of corruption in Karnataka, certain important checks and balances are more evident here than in many other states, because most politicians are aware "that excessive corruption damages their hopes of re-election. The successors of Gundu Rao and Bangarappa sharply curtailed their excesses because they were seen as politically suicidal."[32] Maintaining a clean public image on the part of the most of the politicians from the state from all political parties remained for many years after Bangarappa's government. No major corruption scams happened in these years. Maintaining a clean image, however, was neglected during BJP's rule.

Corruption had been one of the major issues for almost all parties in the 2014 elections. The BJP focused on corruption cases that happened during the UPA rule at the Center, whereas the Congress highlighted corruption cases that occurred during the BJP rule in the state. Janata Dal(S) targeted both the Congress and the BJP for their corruption cases. All these parties used corruption in other parties as a poll plank, but people remained immune to their rhetoric and criticism of each other. If we look at some prominent winners from the BJP, it was Yeddyurappa, who was linked to corruption charges and B. Sriramalu, a close aide of the Reddy brothers, who succeeded in these elections. Corruption charges against Yeddyurappa and Reddy brothers did not make much difference to the voters. It can be said that some of the BJP leaders did not try to maintain a clean public image.

During campaigning, parties highlighted some issues to woo voters which they thought would bring the electoral gain. Chief Minister Siddaramaiah "used every platform to lambast Modi and to project himself as the saviour of the backward classes."[33] He "wooed the electorate with his flagship *Anna Bhagya* (providing 30 kilograms of rice to below poverty line families at ₹1 a kg) and *Ksheera Bhagya* (free milk to children studying in government schools) programmes."[34] The BJP, "attempted to make the 'Gujarat model of governance/development' its plank,"[35] and "also highlighted corruption scandals that rocked the UPA government."[36]

Apart from the development model and corruption issues, some local issues pertaining to a few districts came up during the campaign. These include, support price for sugarcane farmers, diversion of water from some area to other dry areas, development of rail and road infrastructure projects, and a ban on arecanut production, etc.[37]

One of the issues that drew attention of people in this election was the role played by the leaders from the state at the Center. There was dissatisfaction among many that the state leaders had not played any significant role as central ministers in exerting greater influence and in bringing central resources to the state.[38] Kannada activists and the media were reminding people of the nature of the politicians, "holding up Mamata Banerjee or J. Jayalalithaa as more appropriate models to emulate."[39] The former Prime Minister and JD(S) supremo H.D. Devegowda had to justify "the political relevance of his party exactly on this issue, arguing that only an 'extortionist' regional party could protect the state's interests."[40] Such discussions did not enter in actual campaigning during the elections.

Comparison between the 2013 Assembly and the 2014 General Elections

Comparison of the 2014 general elections with that of the 2013 state Assembly elections gives a surprising picture of voters' behavior. A region-wise analysis of the electoral results of the 2013 assembly and the 2014 general elections with the focus on some Lok Sabha constituencies has been made to understand the shift in voters' choice. This comparison will also help in understanding the issues which made a different impact on the behavior of the voters in these elections.

In the 2013 Assembly elections, the BJP had done poorly in Malnad and the coastal regions. Within a year, however, the party rebounded from the heavy losses with the support of the Sangh Parivar. In 2013, Hindutva had been a nonissue, but the efforts of the Sangh Parivar helped the party to bounce back in the 2014 elections. The BJP won all the Lok Sabha seats from this region in 2014, but in 2013, it had managed only four assembly seats (see Table 16.2). It seems that the party convinced the people about its clean governance agenda or its

Table 16.2

Seats Won by the Parties in the 2013 and 2014 Elections from Different Regions of Karnataka

Party	Coastal and Malanad Region		Old Mysore Region		Mumbai Karnataka Region		Hyderabad Karnataka Region	
	2013 Assembly Elections (Total 32 Seats)	2014 Lok Sabha Election (Total 4 Seats)	2013 Assembly Elections (Total 104 Seats)	2014 Lok Sabha Election (Total 13 seats)	2013 Assembly Elections (Total 48 Seats)	2014 Lok Sabha Election (Total 06 Seats)	2013 Assembly Elections (of 40 Total Seats)	2014 Lok Sabha Election (05 Seats)
BJP	04	04	18	05	13	05	05	03
Congress	19	00	50	06	30	01	23	02
JD(S)	04	00	30	02	01	00	05	00
KJP*	01	00	00	00	02	00	03	00
Others	04	00	06	00	02	00	04	00

Sources: Data compiled from Election Commission of India, *Statistical Report On General Elections, 2013 To The Legislative Assembly of Karnataka, 2014.* http://eci.nic.in/eci_main/StatisticalReports/AE2013/StatReports2013.pdf, data on May 17, 2014 and from local newspapers.

Note: *In 2014 KJP, the party headed by Yeddyurappa merged with BJP.

commitment to the Gujarat model of development and ideology of cultural nationalism.

It should be emphasized that the regions have many cultural complexes of Hindu temples and maths. Most prominent are the Udupi Krishna temple, the Dharmasthala Manjunath temple, and the Sringeri Shankarcharya Math. All these institutions have a large number of followers and a very significant spiritual influence. These cultural complexes have been an inspiration for the party as well as the Sangh Parivar.

Congress' performance in the Old Mysore region was good. It won five seats, just one less than the BJP. As in the 2009 elections, the BJP repeated its comfortable victory in all the Bangalore city constituencies. The JD(S) won Hasan and Mandya constituencies salvaging its reputation, but it suffered humiliation at "Chikkaballapur, where former CM H.D. Kumaraswamy was relegated to the third position."[41] The result of the Mysore constituency was the biggest embarrassment for the Chief Minister Siddaramaiah "who couldn't ensure the victory of the party candidate A.H. Vishwanath, sitting MP, in his own home district."[42]

In the Mumbai–Karnataka region, the BJP retained its seats in Belgaum, Bijapur, Bagalkot, Haveri, and Dharwad constituencies but lost the Chikkodi constituency to the Congress. There was a good deal of speculation among many that the BJP would lose in Bijapur. This was the Congress hope because of Prakash Rathod, son of the former KPCC president, K.T. Rathod. Although the Congress had done very well in the Assembly elections, it had to be content with only one seat in the 2014 general elections from this region.

After its dismal performance in the last Assembly elections in the state, the BJP made a solid come back in the Hyderabad–Karnataka region. Had the Congress not won in Gulbarga and Raichur constituencies, it would have been a complete rout. The biggest blow for the Congress in this region was the defeat of the former Chief Minister Dharam Singh in the Bidar constituency. The BJP was a big gainer here because in the 2013 Assembly election, it had won only five seats, but in this election, it increased its strength by three parliamentary seats. The reason for BJP's good performance was not merely the Modi wave but also the return of leaders like B. Sriramlu to the party fold and the selection of appropriate candidates.

In contrast to the 2013 Assembly election, the AHINDA mobilization strategy did not work in favor of the Congress Party in the

2014 Lok Saba election. The Hindutva of the BJP became the overriding factor that reduced the appeal of AHINDA in this election. The other change in this election was the choice made by Lingayat voters.[43] Electoral results clearly indicate that they voted for the BJP as a community. These changes in electoral preference in the state happened just after one year from the previous election.

There is the matter of identity of Lingayats and their electoral choices. Being a distinct community in its social and spiritual philosophy, how does it as a community vote for or support Hindu nationalist parties? It does not adhere to the *Varna* or caste system associated with Hinduism. It also rejects the authority of the Vedas, central to Hinduism. But this distinctness has to be analyzed in the context of electoral politics and the struggle for wielding power in the state and national politics. Their distinctness or the consciousness of being different from the followers of Hinduism has not made Lingayats nonsympathetic to the Hindu Nationalist Party, the BJP, or even not associating with RSS, one of the frontal Hindu cultural organizations dreaming of a united Hindu nationhood.

There are significant numbers of persons from this community in both the BJP and RSS. There has been criticism from various corners about Lingayats taking part in these organizations. Vocal criticism has come from not only within the community but also from outside the community. Progressive academicians, the media personalities, religious leaders like heads of Lingayat maths and many others belonging to the community have reservations about Lingayats being associated with the BJP or RSS. Criticism from outside the community is that Lingayats by being an active part of sectarian nationalist organizations have subordinated their own identity. Such criticism comes from Dalit organizations and leaders in Karnataka.

Some inferences may be made regarding the Lingayat community's social identity and struggle for power. In an effort to gain power, time and again, the community has not shown any hesitation in aligning with conservative forces in Karnataka politics. There are even instances of some heads of maths openly coming in support of community leaders whenever their political position is in vulnerable situation. As has been frequently said and written, the BJP has been considered as a party widely supported by the Lingayat community. The results of this election reinforce this observation. Out of 17 seats won by the BJP, seven are from the Lingayat community.

An analysis of some select high-profile constituencies would explain the complexity of the electoral politics of the Karnataka state. The constituencies selected for this purpose are: Belgaum, Bangalore South, Gulbarga, and Shimoga. The rationale for selecting these constituencies is that they represent different regions and they are great sources for understanding issues such as leadership, caste, money, power, and the influence of the film industry.

Shimoga was considered as one of the high-profile parliamentary constituencies in this election. The former Chief Minister and a senior leader of BJP, Yeddyurappa, contested from here as a BJP candidate. Janata Dal(S) fielded Geetha Shivrajkumar, the daughter of the former Chief Minister Bangarappa and the daughter-in-law of the cine actor late Raj Kumar, as its candidate. The Congress candidate Bhandary lagged behind in the race. The contest in this constituency was termed as a cliff-hanger between the BJP and JD(S).[44] Caste, leadership, money, power, and family backgrounds are the factors which made the contest in this constituency very close. Caste-wise, Geetha Shivrajkumar belongs to the Idiga community, whereas Yeddyurappa belongs to the Lingayat community. The other candidate Bhandary is a Bunt, the community which does not have much presence in the constituency.

Many cine personalities campaigned in favor of the JD(S) candidate, and the candidate being a member of the Rajkumar and Bangarappa family was another advantage to the candidate. Yeddyurappa relied on Hindu votes and was not confident of getting support from any minority community. The electoral result in favor of Yeddyurappa conveys the message that it was caste and the leadership of Yeddyurappa that helped him to be successful in the election. The community profile of this constituency is that Idigas and Lingayats "hold the key in the constituency, given their numbers."[45] But it is "not the forte of any single community."[46] It was the role and contribution of Yeddyurappa as a prominent leader; the caste factor and the Hindutva card might be the reasons of his victory with a huge margin.

The Gulbarga constituency was another which thrown up a very interesting verdict. Mallikarjun Karge, one of the prominent Congress leaders from the state, contested from this for the second time as a candidate of the Congress Party. The BJP fielded Revu Naik Belmgi, a former minister, as its candidate. The AAP had B.T. Lalitha Naik as its candidate, but her influence was marginal in the constituency because she is originally from the Raichur district. Among Scheduled Caste candidates who belong to the Banjara community were Revu Naik and Lalitha Naik. Kharge belongs to Schedule Caste (Harijan) within this larger Scheduled Castes' category.

An informal interaction with media people from the constituency suggested that the soft and lenient nature of the BJP candidate and the Modi factor might have worked in favor of him. But the result went against such predictions. It was not candidates like Revu Naik who won the election as Kharge retained his seat. According to some writers from the district, the reasons for Kharge's victory in this election are as follows:

1. His contribution to the district in the previous five years as a minister in the central government in New Delhi; and
2. A conscious decision of the dominant Lingayat community to support him because of the possible leadership vacuum in the district in the case of his defeat.

These observations indeed look right because there was no other leader from the district who could be matched with the stature and experience of Kharge. He has been there in the district and Karnataka politics for more than 35 years. He has played a crucial role in bringing a number of developmental projects to the Hyderabad–Karnataka region in his stint as a minister in various governments at the state and at the Center in the last UPA government.

Bangalore South constituency had received attention because of the contest between powerful personalities such as Anantkumar and Nanadan Nilekani. The Congress had fielded Nandan Nilekeni because of his managerial and leadership skills in the information technology (IT) sector. Other reasons for the Congress to support his candidature might be the constituency profile. The south constituency of Bangalore is one of the most growth-oriented and upward-looking middle-class localities in which one could find professional classes and highly educated families. Campaigning by Kannada literary stalwarts like U.R. Anantmurthy and Girish Karnad for Nanadan Nilekani had been assumed as a plus point for all efforts to defeat Anantkumar, but even the presence of such stalwarts did not work.

In the Belgaum parliamentary constituency, the fight was between the Congress and the BJP. It was reported that there was anti-incumbency feeling against the BJP candidate Suresh Angadi, primarily due to the lack of satisfactory performance in terms of the development of the constituency. The BJP candidate was more dependent on the Modi wave and his campaigning was not so impressive. Except for the Arabhavi and Gokak assembly segments, the Congress was not so influential in mobilizing the electorate in other assembly segments of the Belgaum parliamentary constituency. The anti-Congressism and Modi wave in the 2014 elections helped the BJP candidate to win in Belgaum. Suresh Angadi was a beneficiary of the situation. The Congress candidate Lakshmi Hebbalkar visited almost all villages as a part of her election campaign. In spite of this, the popular perception of the Congress candidate was that she did not have substantial support base on the basis of her service to the common people.[47]

Response to the Aam Adami Party in the State

In Karnataka too, as in Delhi and elsewhere, the AAP received some support especially in the urban areas. The national pulse against corruption spearheaded by some activists made some impact on the educated middle class in urban areas like Bangalore in Karnataka. Prominent people from different spheres of life joined the AAP during the elections. A former top executive of the IT giant Infosys, V. Balakrishnan, supported the AAP and contested as its candidate from Bangalore central.[48] The former Karnataka Child Rights Commission Chief Nina P. Nayak also supported the AAP and contested as its candidate from the Bangalore south constituency.[49] Another prominent personality who joined and contested as a candidate of the AAP was B.T. Lalitha Naik. She is a Kannada writer and a former minister in the Janata Dal government. Others who were in the fray as the AAP candidates were Babu Mathew, Ravikrishna Reddy, the former police officer K. Arkesh, the retired director of Mangalore International Airport M.R. Nayak, and theatre personality Kotiganahalli Ramaiah.[50] The AAP did not deviate from its national electoral campaigning concerning transparency. The candidate from Bangalore central V. Balkrishnan declared assets worth ₹189 crore during his nomination,[51] but this asset did not get reflected in the election expenditure of his party in his constituency. As it did in the Delhi Assembly elections, the AAP did employ a low-cost campaign in all constituencies. In the Bangalore central constituency, the campaign of the AAP in contrast "to the other parties in terms of expenditure made an attempt to connect with people through a band of dedicated volunteers going around the constituency mostly on foot."[52] Simple campaigning was followed in other constituencies also.

The enthusiasm that was shown by the people toward the AAP did not get reflected in its electoral outcome. The AAP did not manage to win a single seat from the state. Several reasons can be elicited for the failure of the AAP in the state. The AAP was a new entrant into the electoral fray in the state and the way it appealed in Delhi did not work in the state. It focused on issues of corruption and governance, and these issues might have been well received by the people, but its severe criticism of the corporate sector during elections might have not made any impact because preference for corporate sector employment is a common phenomenon in India's urban places. The other reason for AAP's failure is the lack of strong local leadership to lead the electoral campaigns and convince the people about issues it highlighted. Also, it lacked good organizational resources.

The Outcome of the 2014 Elections and Its Implications for the State Politics

Outcome of the 2014 elections has a wider implications for the state politics, especially the politics of representation of generally underrepresented or unrepresented social groups.

Muslim minority representation in the Lok Sabha from Karnataka is very poor (see Table 16.3). Muslim population in the state is 12.5 percent, but when it comes to its electoral mobilizing capacity, it has failed to win or it has been made to fail in getting represented in the representative institutions. This election outcome further adds to the nonrepresentation of Muslim minority from the state.

The result of these elections implies that if two dominant communities come together with the support of some minor communities for electoral informal understanding, other minor communities have a little chance of achieving representation. This raises the question: Is

Table 16.3

Representation of Communities in Lok Sabha from Karnataka

Year	Religion			Caste/Sect						
	Hindus	Muslims	Christians	Brahmins	Lingayats	Vokkaligas	Kurubas	Scheduled Castes	Scheduled Tribes	Others
2004	26	01	01	03	07	04	01	04	02	07
2009	28	00	00	03	08	05	01	05	02	04
2014	28	00	00	03	08	07	00	05	02	03

Source: Data for representation of select communities in Lok Sabha for 2004 elections taken from Parvathi Menon and S. Bageshree, "Caste and Electoral Choice: The Karnataka Case," *Hindu*, May 13, 2009, http://www.thehindu.com/todays-paper/tp-opinion/caste-and-electoral-choice-the-karnataka-case/article281264.ece (accessed on June 17, 2014).

Karnataka moving toward majoritarianism or at least majoritarianism of politically amalgamated communities? Be that as it may, it would be a major challenge to political parties like the Congress to go ahead with their idea of inclusive politics at least in a representational sense. This result has an implication of Janata Dal(S) changing its traditional strategy of relying on traditional caste groups. To make itself a widely accepted party, it might have to shed its traditional strategy.

The same story is with respect to the representation of women from the state. As it happens at the national level, the general trend in the state is that women rarely get elected and if there is a participation of more women candidates, then their success rate in winning is marginal. The 2014 election data on women candidates show the reality with respect to their contests. Table 16.4 outlines the position of women candidates in the electoral politics of Karnataka.

Out of a total of nine women candidates, only three managed more than a 40 percent vote share. One other candidate managed to get more than 20 percent vote share and the rest received less than a three percent vote share. Among these nine candidates, only one emerged successful.

Table 16.4
Position of Women Candidates in 2014 General Elections in Karnataka

Candidate	Party	Votes Polled	Percentage of Vote Share
Shobha Karandlaje	BJP	581,168	56.29
Ramya	Congress	518,852	43.53
Lakshmi Hebbalkar	Congress	478,557	44.40
Geetha Shivaraj kumar	JD(S)	240,636	21.31
Ruth Manorama	JD(S)	25,677	2.30
Nandini Alva	JD(S)	20,387	1.89
Nina Naik	AAP	21,403	1.92
B.T. Lalitha Naik	AAP	9,074	0.91
Padmamma M.V.	AAP	5,650	0.49

Source: S. Bageshree, "A Lone Woman MP from State," http://www.thehindu. com/news/national/karnataka/a-lone-woman-mp-from-karnataka/ article6030272.ece (accessed on July 14, 2014).

With respect to non-Congress and non-BJP political forces like Janata Dal, the result of this election has come as a shocker. In the recent past, Janata Dal "seemed to be on the threshold of a long and successful run as the dominant political force"[53] in the state. But from 1999 onward, it has not been able to manage to win a considerable number of seats in the general elections. Its internal rivalry and splits can be cited as a reason for this debacle. Now, Janata Dal in the form of Janata Dal(S) also has not been able to retain the attraction of the Janata Dal as the larger political formation it had earlier achieved in Karnataka. The result of the 2014 elections further proved that Janata Dal(S) is losing its place in the political landscape of the state.

Conclusion

The 2014 elections reveal that there has been change as well as continuity in the electoral politics of Karnataka. Change could be seen on issues like the waning role of third forces in Karnataka politics. Another change is the presence of alternative political forces like AAP. The presence of such forces at least introduces the possibility of politics of performance, devoid of caste and religion. Karnataka as one federal unit like other southern states had opposed the dominating character of national parties like the Congress. But the 2014 elections have brought changes in such features of state politics. Features which are being continued are the role of caste and amalgamation of a few castes for electoral success, nonrepresentation of people belonging to social categories such as religious minorities, numerically minute caste groups, women, and the youth. And above all, the discourse on political campaigning was revolving around AHINDA and the upper or dominant caste groups.

As far as the internal dynamics of political parties and the defeat of the candidates of both the BJP and Congress is concerned, it has been witnessed mainly as a consequence of the factional politics within the party in a large number of cases. Obviously, consolidation of local leaders is a major decisive factor in any party. National issues including the Modi wave were not so influential in determining the outcome of the 2014 general elections in Karnataka. Except corruption and governance to a certain degree, none of the issues of national importance played a crucial role in the elections in the state. Again it was the local issues which played a vital role in the electoral outcome. The merger of the KJP with the BJP consolidated the support base which contributed significantly to the success of the BJP in Karnataka.

Notes and References

1. Ian Budge, "Election Research," in Bertrand Badie, Bertrang Badia, Dirk Berg–Schlosser and Leonardo Morlino (eds), *International Encyclopedia of Political Science,* Vol. 3 (London: SAGE Publications and IPSA, 2011), p. 729.
2. Ravi Sharma, 'Karnataka Chooses Southern Shock', *Frontline,* May 31, 2013, p. 127, http://www.frontline.in/politics/southern-shock/article4714168.ece (accessed on June 17, 2014).
3. Ibid.
4. Ibid.
5. Smita Gupta, 'Social Engineering Formula Helped Congress win Karnataka Elections', *Hindu,* May 13, 2013.
6. Ibid.
7. Valerian Rodrigues, "Political Power and Democratic Enablement: Devaraj Urs and Lower Caste Mobilisation in Karnataka," *Economic and Political Weekly* XLIX, 25 (June 21, 2014), p. 62.
8. Ibid.
9. AHINDA is an acronym constructed from a Kannada phrase: *Alpasankhyataru* (Minorities, i.e., Muslims) *Hindulidavaru* (the backward classes), and Dalits (the Scheduled Castes).
10. Vikhar Ahmed Sayeed, "Bouncing Back," *Frontline,* Vol. 27, September 11–24, 2010, http://www.frontline.in/static/html/fl2719/stories/20100924271910600.htm (accessed on June 20, 2014).
11. Ibid.
12. Shivsundar, "The Defeat of Saffron in Karnataka," *Economic and Political Weekly* XLVIII, 21 (May 25, 2013), p. 17, http://www.epw.in/web-exclusives/defeat-saffron-karnataka.html (accessed on July 12, 2014).
13. Ibid.
14. Ibid.
15. Sandeep Shastri and Veena Devi, "Congress Fails to Impress in Karnataka," *Hindu,* May 24, 2014, http://www.thehindu.com/opinion/op-ed/congress-fails-to-impress-in-karnataka/article6041704.ece (accessed on June 17, 2014).
16. "In State, BJP Wins 17 as Cong Settles for 9," *Deccan Herald,* May 17, 2014, http://www.deccanherald.com/content/407469/in-state-bjp-wins-17.html (accessed on June 17, 2014).
17. Ibid.
18. Editorial, "Below Par," *Deccan Herald,* May 19, 2014, http://www.deccanherald.com/content/407865/below-par.html (accessed on June 17, 2014).
19. Ibid.
20. Ibid.

21. Ibid.
22. Praveen Rai, "Status of Opinion Polls: Media Gimmick and Political Communication in India," *Economic and Political Weekly* XLIX, 16(April 19, 2014), http://www.epw.in/election-specials/status-opinion-polls.html (accessed on June 25, 2014).
23. Ibid.
24. Pranav Joshi, "BJP to Cross 200 Seats, Congress to Face Worst-ever Electoral Defeat: Pre-poll Surveys," *DNA* Monday, April 14, 2014, http://www.dnaindia.com/india/report-bjp-to-cross-200-seats-congress-to-face-worst-ever-electoral-defeat-pre-poll-surveys-1978244 (accessed on July 3, 2014).
25. Ibid.
26. Ibid.
27. "It's a Litmus Test for All: Sandeep Shastri," *Hindu*, March 24, 2013, http://www.thehindu.com/news/national/karnataka/its-a-litmus-test-for-all-sandeep-shastri/article4542493.ece (accessed on June 17, 2014).
28. Ibid.
29. Sandeep Shastri, *Karnataka Politics: The Road Taken ... The Journey Ahead* (Jakkasandra, Karnataka: Jain University Press, 2011), p. 257.
30. See note 15.
31. Arwind Gowda, "Elections 2014: No Sign of Modi Wave in Rural Karnataka," http://www.firstpost.com/politics/elections-2014-why-the-modi-wave-might-not-work-in-karnataka-1483751.html (accessed on June 17, 2014).
32. James Manor, "Change in Karnataka Over the Last Generation: Villages and the Wider Context," *Economic and Political Weekly* 42, 8(February 24–March 2, 2007), 654.
33. Ravi Sharma, "On Shaky Ground," *Frontline*, http://www.frontline.in/cover-story/on-shaky-ground/article5956313.ece (accessed on June 19, 2014).
34. Ibid.
35. Ibid.
36. Ibid.
37. Ibid.
38. Prithvi Datta Chandra Shobhi, "The Campaign about Nothing," *Indian Express,* April 15, 2014, http://indianexpress.com/article/opinion/columns/the-campaign-about-nothing/99/ (accessed on June 17, 2014).
39. Ibid.
40. Ibid.
41. N.D. Shiv Kumar, "Election Results 2014: BJP Sweeps North and Coastal Karnataka," http://timesofindia.indiatimes.com/news/Election-results-2014-BJP-sweeps-north-and-coastal-Karnataka/articleshow/35219436.cms (accessed on July 5, 2014).
42. Ibid.
43. See note 15.
44. S.K. Nrupathunga, "Shimoga may See Cliff-hanger between BJP, JD(S)," *Deccan Herald*, April 10, 2014. http://www.deccanherald.com/content/398254/shimoga-may-see-cliffhanger-bjp.html (accessed on March 17, 2015).
45. Ibid.
46. Ibid.
47. Interview with the Journalist Vijaykumar Patil, Belgaum.
48. "AAP Fields Ex-infoscion in Bangalore Central," *Deccan Herald*, March 11, 2014, http://www.deccanherald.com/election/content/391193/aap-fields-ex-infoscion-blore.html (accessed on June 25, 2014).

49. Ibid.
50. Ibid.
51. "AAP's Low-cost, High-impact Campaign in Karnataka," *Deccan Herald*, April 15, 2014.
52. Ibid.
53. Harold A. Gould, "The 12th General Election in Karnataka: The BJP Achieves its Southern Beachhead," in Ramashray Roy and Paul Wallace (eds), *Indian Politics and the 1998 Election: Regionalism, Hindutva and State Politics* (New Delhi: SAGE Publications, 1999), p. 183.

D. North East

17

BJP's Consolidation, AIUDF's Polarization, and Congress' Defeat in Assam

Akhil Ranjan Dutta

Introduction

Several important trends highlight the 2014 parliamentary elections in Assam.

- Firstly, the election that witnessed highest ever voter turnout (80.13 percent) in the state reflects the reaction against the incumbent government manifested through popular mobilization and resistance.
- Secondly, it was about the political pragmatism of BJP's Prime Ministerial candidate Narendra Modi, who restrained from blowing the illegal foreigner issues out of proportion. Rhetorically, however, he captured the peoples' pride as well as frustration in energizing them against the incumbent government.
- Thirdly, it was almost a one-sided campaign in which the local media and the intelligentsia projected Modi's Gujarat development model as the most credible and sustainable one, thereby leaving very little space for the scrutiny of the model itself.

- Fourthly, the incumbent Congress-led government was obsessively defensive concentrating more on rebuffing Modi than capitalizing on its achievements and projecting a the road map ahead.
- Fifthly, the violence in Bodo Territorial Area Districts (BTAD) proved to be beneficial both for the BJP and the All India United Democratic Front (AIUDF), which used it for the polarization of votes around religious identity and sensitivity.
- Finally, it was almost a deathblow to the hegemonic domination by the minority Bodo community in BTAD. It became divided around intrafactional fights, while the multicommunity non-Bodo majority united to defeat the decade long rule by the dominant minority.

The Verdict

With its victory on 7 out of the 14 Lok Sabha seats[1] in Assam, BJP's upsurge in Assam in the present elections has been spectacular. BJP recorded the highest ever percentage of votes (36.5 percent) in the 2014 general elections in the state, which is 20 percent higher than the party polled in the 2009 Lok Sabha elections. It also led in 69 assembly segments out of 126. The party far surpassed poll predictions possibly because of its previous election results; winning four seats in the 2009 Lok Sabha elections and only five seats in the 126-member Legislative Assembly elections in 2011, in which voting percentages were 16.62 percent and 11.47 percent, respectively.

The BJP has penetrated into the Congress strongholds in upper Assam for the first time winning all four constituencies: Tezpur, Jorhat, Dibrugarh, and Lakhimpur. BJP's only failure in the 2014 general elections has been in the two Barak valley constituencies where the party registered its first victories in 1991 and won both seats: Silchar and Karimganj, with Karimganj being the only Scheduled Caste (SC) reserved seat in the state. The BJP won Karimganj in the subsequent elections in 1996, whereas in Silchar it won in 1998 and 2009, while the Congress won the Silchar seat in 2014. The AIUDF that primarily represents East Bengal origin Muslims registered its first victory in the valley by winning the Karimganj seat in 2014. The BJP secured the second position in both constituencies.

The AIUDF won in a dominate manner in two constituencies in lower Assam, Dhubri and Barpeta, which witnessed the highest polling in the state, 88.49 percent and 84.50 percent, respectively. It registered its first victory in the Lok Sabha elections in Dhubri in 2009 and secured the highest number of assembly seats in this Lok Sabha constituency in the 2011 Assembly elections.

In the two other constituencies in lower Assam, Gauhati and Mangaldoi, the BJP won both as it did in the 2009 Lok Sabha elections. The Congress did not have a monopoly over these two constituencies, as non-Congress parties registered victories in them from time to time. The Praja Socialist Party (PSP) won the Gauhati Lok Sabha seat twice, in 1957 and 1962, with the Communist Party of India (CPI) then winning it in 1967. In 1977, Gauhati returned the Bharatiya Lok Dal (BLD) candidate to the Lok Sabha, while the Asom Gana Parishad (AGP) won it in 1985 and 1996. In 1999 and 2009, BJP's Bijoya Chakraborty won it, as she did for the third time in 2014. The Mangaldoi constituency, formed in 1967, elected a PSP candidate in 1967, BLD won in 1977, and AGP won in 1985 and 1996. The BJP has been winning this seat consecutively for the third time since 2004. The Nowgong constituency in middle Assam had elected the AGP candidates in 1985, 1991, and 1996, but it has consecutively been won by the BJP since 1999. This is the only constituency in Assam where the BJP has won four consecutive times. The history of these three constituencies shows that BJP's consolidation has both been faster and wider in those seats where either PSP or AGP could win in the past (Table 17.1).

The other seat in middle Assam is Kaliabor where the Congress has won since its formation in 1967, except in 1985 and 1996 when the AGP candidates were returned to the Lok Sabha. It is now known as the dynastic constituency as Kaliabor was won by the present Chief Minister Tarun Gogoi in 1991, 1998, and 1999, his brother Dip Gogoi in 2004 and 2009, and now has been won by his son Gourav Gogoi in 2014. However, in 2014, the BJP secured the second position and registered its lead in four assembly segments compared to three each both by the Congress and the AIUDF.

There are two Scheduled Tribe (ST) constituencies in the state: the Autonomous district since the first election in 1951 and Kokrajhar formed in 1967. Both are the centers of hill tribes' and plain tribes'

Table 17.1

Performance of Political Parties in Assam Lok Sabha Elections (1991–2014)

Election	Voter %	Party	Seats Won	% of Votes
1991	75.3	INC	8	28.5
		AGP	1	17.6
		BJP	2	09.6
1996	78.5	INC	5	31.6
		AGP	5	27.2
		BJP	1	15.9
1998	61.1	INC	10	38.97
		AGP	0	12.7
		BJP	1	24.47
1999	71.30	INC	10	38.42
		AGP	0	11.92
		BJP	2	29.84
2004	69.08	INC	9	35.07
		AGP	2	19.95
		BJP	2	22.94
2009	69.52	INC	7	34.9
		AGP	1	14.6
		BJP	4	16.62
		AUDF	1	16.1
2014	80.13	INC	3	29.6
		AGP	0	03.8
		BJP	7	36.5
		AUDF	3	14.8

Source: Nani Gopal Mahanta, "Lok Sabha Elections in Assam: Shifting of Traditional Vote Bases to BJP," *Economic and Political Weekly* XLIX, 35(August 30, 2014), 19–22. Compiled from the Election Commission of India Reports.

politics in the state, respectively. The All Party Hill Leaders Conference (APHLC) dominated the Autonomous district constituency before the reorganization of Northeast India in 1972, while subsequently it became the battle ground between the Autonomous State Demand Committee (ASDC) and Congress. The Congress won the seat in 1951, but in the subsequent four elections the APHLC candidates won them. In the next nine elections, Biren Singh Engti won it five times, and in the four elections from 1991 to 1999, it was won by Dr Jayanta Rongpi, the leader of ASDC and affiliated to CPI(ML). Rongpi fought the 1999 election under the CPI(ML) banner after the ASDC divided. In the 2014 elections, however, the BJP registered its presence by securing the second position. In Kokrajhar constituency, the Congress won only twice, 1967 and 1971. In all subsequent elections from 1977 to 2009, candidates engaged in Bodo political mobilization won the seat. The year 2014 has been a watershed as for the first time this constituency has returned a non-Bodo candidate Naba Kumar Sarania, a former commander of the United Liberation Front of Assam (ULFA).[2]

The decline of the left parties has been phenomenal. CPI won the Lok Sabha elections from Gauhati constituency in 1967 and the CPI(M) won from Barpeta constituency in 1991 and 1996. In the Autonomous district constituency, Rongpi, affiliated to CPIM(ML), but under the ASDC label won it in 1991, 1996, and 1998, and with the CPI(ML) ticket in 1999. Left parties together maintained 6–10 percent votes from 1957 to 1991 in the Legislative Assembly elections in Assam winning 2–16 seats. In the 1978 Assembly elections, it won the largest number of seats, 16, with a vote share of 9.71 percent. From 1996, Left's vote share declined, and in the 2011 Assembly elections, CPI and CPI(M) together polled 1.65 percent votes. The decline continued. In 2014, the CPI(M) polled 0.4 percent votes, and the CPI(ML) and SUCI polled only 0.3 percent votes each.

The Context and Dynamics

The 2011 State Legislative Assembly elections not only brought the Tarun Gogoi led the Congress government in the state to power consecutively for the third time, with a landslide majority of 78 seats out of 126 seats for the party. The election was perceived as a "mandate for peace and development."[3] In 2001, when the Tarun Gogoi-led Congress government assumed power for the first tenure, the state was in a state of despair both in terms of economic slowdown and the law-and-order situation. Tarun Gogoi-led Congress government was credited with bringing back normalcy to the state, and the economy too showed signs of resurgence. The government initiated dialogue with various ethnic insurgent outfits and brought them to the negotiation table. One of the important achievements was the signing of the Bodo Territorial Council (BTC) Accord in 2003, which helped control Bodo militancy and violence to a great extent.

It was against this background that the Congress government under Tarun Gogoi's leadership was returned to power in 2006, although with a reduced majority and the second consecutive government under Gogoi's leadership was formed with a post-poll alliance with the Bodo Peoples' Front (BPF). This government, assisted by a series of centrally sponsored popular initiatives such as MNREGA, NRHM, and JNNURM could reach out to the people with individual-oriented beneficiary schemes, which helped the government to sustain its popular bases. During the second tenure of the Congress government, however, corruption became a huge issue and the government came into direct confrontation with the peoples' movements, particularly one led by Krishak Mukti Sangram Samiti (KMSS) on the issue of the Lower Subansiri Hydroelectric Power Project (LSHEP).

Assam witnessed a series of social resistance movements against the government. With the help of the newly enacted Right to Information (RTI) Act, 2005, the corruption at different layers and levels of the government was exposed. The alleged ₹1,000 crore North Cachar Hills Autonomous Council scam elicited shocking waves of protest and the government was put into the dock. On various other issues too such as granting land entitlement to the forest dwellers and implementation of Forest Rights Act, 2006, various social groups continued to come into direct confrontation with the government. A series of conflicts in BTAD targeting primarily the Adivasis and Muslims also exposed the failure of the government in maintaining law and order.

Amidst these challenges, with the initiative of Sanmilita Jatiya Abhibarttan (SJA) steered by a group of leading intellectuals, academics, and social activists, the dialogue between United Liberation Front of Assam

(ULFA) and the Union Government took off. With P.C. Haldar (retired intelligence bureau chief) as the interlocutor, the initiative of dialogue and negotiation with a few other insurgent groups in the state including Dima Halam Daogah (Jewel) (DHD-J), United People's Democratic Solidarity (UPDS), and National Democratic Front of Bodoland (NDFB) was also undertaken.

It is against this background that the 2011 Assembly elections were held. The ruling Congress not only won the election but with a spectacular majority of 78 seats in the 126 member legislative assembly. The state, however, witnessed the consolidation of both ethnic and religious polarization in lower Assam during this election, which was already witnessed in the 2006 Assembly elections. The AIUDF, representing the interests of the East Bengal origin Muslims, secured 18 seats and the BPF, the political organization of the Bodos, secured 12 seats in the Assembly. AGP was reduced to a total of 10 seats and the BJP was reduced to 5. One of the factors behind Congress' victory in 2011 amidst challenges was the absence of a credible challenger apart from its much-publicized achievements toward development and peace in the state.

During 2011 and 2014, the country, in general, and Assam, in particular, witnessed many significant political developments. The Congress-led Union government was maligned with a number of scams and the infamous Nirbhaya case in Delhi in December 2012 provoked mass reaction across the country. The state government's failure on the National Register of Citizens (NRC) update; the detection, deletion, and deportation of foreigners; the land swap deal with Bangladesh (2011), and most importantly, government's failure to stop killing of one-horned rhinos in Kaziranga National Park evoked large-scale protests.[4] In addition, price hikes and corruption further weakened the government. The 2012 violence in BTAD which displaced 392,000 persons[5] invited all-round condemnation and wrath from the people. The non-Bodos in BTAD, who now constitute more than 70 percent of the total population,[6] were already challenging the BTC Accord that gives overriding powers to the Bodos in the Council. Once the violence against the non-Bodos increased, they became more assertive and resistive both against the BTAD authority and the state government. The Congress–BPF alliance came under severe criticism as the violence exposed the unstable law-and-order situation in the state.

The state government also confronted with the much energized peoples' resistance on a variety of issues, particularly related to the LSHEP, land entitlements, hike in the urban property tax, and proposed water privatization in urban areas. Importing Dr Sanjay Singh, a politician from Amethi, Uttar Pradesh, for the Rajya Sabha seat from the state Legislative Assembly, election for which was held in February 2014, brought forth severe criticism in the civil society domain. It exposed the government's gross indifference toward Assamese feelings feeding disillusionment with the party and the government.

While the government was almost dysfunctional in dealing with these challenges, the worst was yet to come. And it finally came in the form of dissidence from within the party when around 50 percent of the Congress legislators publicly revolted against the incumbent Chief Minister Tarun Gogoi and a few of his trusted colleagues. The powerful Health and Education Minister, Dr Himanta Biswa Sarmah, led the dissident group. He had been Tarun Gogoi's trusted colleague. In the run up to the Lok Sabha elections 2014, although the dissidence appeared to have disappeared, in reality it was intact. It is the dissidents within the government and the party who caused more harm to the government, maligned it publicly, and rendered it dysfunctional resulting in the unprecedented defeat of the Congress in Assam. The Congress ended winning only three seats in the Lok Sabha elections, its lowest ever.

Consolidation of BJP

The 2014 Lok Sabha elections were fought in the state of Assam at various levels and with various strategies by the BJP using all possible means and capturing both state and local dynamics. The ruling Congress was busy mostly in fighting the growing dissidents within the party, particularly the threat posed by almost half of the party legislators to the incumbent Chief Minister Tarun Gogoi and a few of his trusted colleagues. While the public grievances against the government were growing, both the media and the intelligentsia at large played a pro-BJP role and indulged in projecting the Gujarat development model as truly people-oriented and toward high growth and inclusive development.

The RSS that was penetrating into the social dynamics at various levels including the educational network called Sankardeva Shishu Nikentan/Vidya Niketan,[7] which has over the years emerged almost as an alternative to the chaotic and discredited public school education system in the state, played an important role in social engineering for the political advantage of the BJP. Penetration of the Vanavasi Kalyan Ashram, an RSS affiliate, which has been working for the economic and educational developments of the tribal communities, particularly among the tea tribes in Assam, also helped the BJP to gain political mileage.[8] Violence in BTAD was not only a conflict between Hindus and Muslims, but it also affected both Adivasis and other non-Bodo non-Muslim communities. BJP, however, was successful in projecting violence in 2012 as a symbol and symptom of attack on indigenous communities by illegal Muslim Bangladeshis (Table 17.2).

Table 17.2
Performance of Political Parties in Legislative Assembly Elections (1985–2011)

Election	Voter %	Party	Seats Won	% of Votes
1985	79.21	INC	25	23.23
		AGP*	63	34.54
		BJP	0	1.07
1991		INC	66	29.35
		AGP	19	17.93
		NAGP	5	5.45
		BJP	10	6.55
1996	78.92	INC	34	30.56
		AGP	59	29.70
		BJP	4	10.41
2001	75.05	INC	71	39.75
		AGP	20	20.02
		BJP	8	9.35

(Table 17.2 Continued)

(*Table 17.2 Continued*)

Election	Voter %	Party	Seats Won	% of Votes
2006	75.77	INC	53	31.08
		AGP	24	20.39
		BJP	10	11.98
		AIUDF	10	9.03
		BPF**	11	—
2011	75.92	INC	78	39.39
		AGP	10	16.29
		BJP	5	11.47
		AIUDF	18	12.57
		BPF	12	6.13

Source: Election Commission of India.

Notes: *AGP's number of seats and poll percentage in 1985 have some confusion as the party candidates fought as independents and it supported a few candidates who later joined the party after the election.

**In case of BPF too in 2006, the Election Commission does not provide the poll percentage for the party as its candidates fought as independents.

BJP's emergence and consolidation in the state of Assam have been slow and steady. In 2014, it became spectacular. BJP's consolidation in the state has a parallel to that of the decline of the AGP in the state. Bharatiya Jana Sangh (BJS), the predecessor of BJP, was present in Assam's electoral politics since 1951, although with an insignificant impact. The BJP for the first time contested both in the Assam Assembly and Lok Sabha elections in 1985. In the Legislative Assembly elections, the party fielded 37 candidates and did not win a seat, registering 1.07 percent votes. For the Lok Sabha elections, it contested two seats, forfeited deposits in both and registered 0.37 percent votes. This election was fought after the six-year-long Assam agitation (1979–85) on the illegal foreigners' issue. The BJP supported the movement and its leaders. Atal Bihari Vajpayee also visited the state and held discussions with the movement leaders. Among those who campaigned for the cause of the movement at the national level was Arun Shourie, a journalist by profession and presently a BJP leader. It has been alleged that the RSS was instrumental in giving a communal face to the movement.

After the Assam agitation came to an end in 1985 with the conclusion of the Assam Accord on 15 August 1985, the movement leaders formed a regional political party, the AGP. The party came to power in fresh elections held to the Legislative Assembly in December 1985. It won 63 seats in the 126-member Assembly and registered 34.5 percent votes. The AGP also won 7 out of 14 seats in the Lok Sabha elections held in the same year. In the next Assembly elections held in 1991, the BJP contested 48 seats winning 10 with 6.55 percent votes against the Congress and the AGP registering 29.35 percent and 20 percent votes and winning 66 and 19 seats, respectively. In the Lok Sabha elections held in the same year, the BJP won two seats with 09.6 percent votes. Table 17.3 reveals that the BJP maintained a steady growth and the AGP experienced a decline after the 1996 elections. However, there is a difference in votes polled by the BJP in the assembly and Lok Sabha elections. While the votes polled by the BJP in Assembly elections was around 10 percent from 1996 to 2011, the tally in the Lok Sabha election was relatively high. BJP's vote surge to 36.5 percent in the 2014 elections, of course, was unprecedented. There are two possible explanations. One is the increase in total poll percentage (80.3 percent), and the other is an all time low of votes for the AGP—only 3.8 percent. The BJP has benefitted from both.

The BJP, with the help of the RSS network, penetrated into Northeast India in, general, and Assam, in particular, both through religious and educational institutions. The BJP reorganized itself in the run up to the Lok Sabha elections. One of the important initiatives in this regard was the appointment of Sarbananda Sonowal as the President of the state BJP unit. Sonowal, the former president of All Assam Students Union (AASU), 1992–99, joined the AGP after relinquishing his position in AASU, was elected as an Assembly member in 2001 and then to the Lok Sabha in 2004. One of the most important initiatives and achievements of Sarbananda Sonowal was to challenge the Illegal Migrants (Determination by Tribunals) Act, 1983, in the Supreme Court of India. It was condemned as an infamous and discriminatory Act that allegedly gave protection to foreigners in the state. The Supreme Court through its verdict in July 2012 struck down the Act. This achievement of Sonowal gave him a status of national hero (*Jatiya Nayak*) in the state. In 2011, Sonowal joined the BJP, became a national executive committee member of the BJP, and also the state's spokesperson. Sonowal was appointed as the president of the state BJP in 2012. Sonowal, then with the AGP,

Table 17.3
AGP–BJP Comparison in Lok Sabha and Legislative Assembly Elections in Assam

	Legislative Assembly Elections				Lok Sabha Elections		
Year	Voter %	AGP Seats and % of Votes	BJP Seats and % of Votes	Year	Vote %	AGP Seats and % of Votes	BJP Seats and % of Votes
1985	79.21	64 (34.54%)	0 (1.07%)	1985	77.40	7 (…)	0 (0.37%)
1991	—	19 (17.93%)	10 (6.55%)	1991	75.3	1 (17.6%)	2 (09.6%)
1996	78.92	54 (29.70%)	4 (10.41)	1996	78.5	5 (27.2%)	1 (15.9%)
2001	75.05	20 (20.02%)	8 (9.35%)	1998	61.1	0 (12.7%)	1 (24.47%)
2006	75.77	24 (20.39%)	10 (11.98)	1999	71.30	0 (11.92%)	2 (29.84%)
2011	75.92	10 (16.29%)	5 (11.47%)	2004	69.08	2 (19.95%)	2 (22.94%)
				2009	69.52	1 (14.6%)	4 (16.62%)
				2014	80.13	0 (03.8%)	7 (36.5%)

Source: Computed from Tables 17.1 and 17.2.

was the first leader to defeat the Congress in the Dibrugarh Lok Sabha constituency in 2004, which had been successively won by the Congress since 1951.

It was, however, the new political wave in the country generated by Narendra Modi's new *avatar* (incarnation), which added energy and vibrancy to BJP's electoral consolidation in Assam. Modi, a pragmatist, did not blow the illegal migration issue in the state out of proportion. Rather, he used all rhetoric possible to mobilize the people against the Congress government both in the state and at the Center. One-horned rhinos are Assam's pride. The state government failed to protect the rhinos over the years and hundreds of them were killed. There were condemnations against the state government for its failure to protect Assam's pride. The government remained steadfast not to rise to the occasion. Modi, in a pragmatic manner took it as the *Brahmastra* against the state government and linked the state government's indifference toward the protection of the one-horned rhinos to that of the government's pro-Bangladeshi attitude.

In his electoral rally on March 31, 2014 at Gogamukh,[9] Modi "accused the Congress led state government of trying to settle cheap Bangladeshi labourers in the forests of Assam by killing the endangered rhinos to clear the jungles."[10] It was a mass appealing argument. Linking the issue of endangered Assam's pride with the incumbent government's plan to settle Bangladeshis re-energized peoples' distrust against the Congress regime. He was playing his communal card too by stating that the indigenous Muslims and East Bengali Hindu immigrants should take a unified stand against the Bangladeshi problem in Assam.[11]

On his first visit to Assam on February 8, 2014, after he was declared NDA's prime ministerial candidate, Narendra Modi addressed the *Maha Jagaran* rally in Guwahati, where he regretted that,

> [D]espite Assam being endowed with immense natural resources the industrial growth rate of the State was pathetic. He lambasted the Congress governments in the State and at the Centre for the sorry state of affairs in Assam and held Prime Minister Manmohan Singh particularly responsible for the development bottlenecks that had been perennial to the State.[12]

He questioned Prime Minister Dr Singh's commitment to the state from where he has been a Rajya Sabha member for the past 23 years. Calling

Assam a peace-loving state, Modi attributed the state of conflict and violence in the Assam to the failure of the government.

With his political imagination and rhetoric, Modi touched the hearts of Assamese pride by citing the heroes of Assam's culture and politics. Praising the Assamese tradition in his hour-long speech, Modi said: "Assam has a great tradition. It can boast personalities like Srimanta Sankardeva, Madhavdeva, Ajan Fakir, Joimoti, Bhaskar Barman, Sati Radhika, Naranarayan, Lachit Borphukan, Bishnu Rabha, Bhupen Hazarika, etc. Under the Congress rule the tradition has been demolished."[13]

Modi's maturity had grown in capturing the popular imagination and agony. This is evident from the advertisements published on the first day of polling on April 7, 2014, the day five Parliamentary Constituencies went to the polls: Tezpur, Kaliabor, Jorhat, Dibrugarh, and Lakhimpur. These constituencies have strong presence of tea tribes[14] and also of communities who were struggling for the status of STs. These two issues had become very crucial in Assam's politics. The BJP unveiled its vision in the last page of its advertisement, which was in the form of a Manifesto and commitment. It assured that "For BJP, its Manifesto shall be the basis of its governance agenda for a powerful, secure and insurgent India and Assam."[15] The first commitment assured its initiative to accord ST status to the Ahoms, Konch Rajbongshis, Morans, Motoks, Chutiyas, and tea tribes.

All these communities, except for Konch Rajbonshis, have strong presence in these constituencies. Except for Kaliabor, in four other constituencies, the visibility of illegal Bangladeshis is not very strong. All the political outfits of the communities struggling for ST status are strong in those constituencies. Both small tea growers and tea tribes are concentrated in those areas. A number of incidents were reported over the years where tea laborers resorted to violence on the issues of bonus and wages. Therefore, it was critical to focus on their problems. The BJP prioritized it very well and made it the second issue in its list of commitments. Both the issues of updating NRC and detection, deletion, and deportation of illegal migrants were placed in the middle of the list of commitment. It, of course, promised that while updating NRC, it will take 1951 as the base year, as has been demanded by various nationality organizations in the state.

BJP's most important success was in the three Lok Sabha constituencies in upper Assam: Jorhat, Dibrugarh, and Lakhimpur, all of which have concentrations of tea tribe populations and tea estates. The Congress dominated all these constituencies from the time of their formation. BJP candidates in these constituencies not only registered victories, but they also won the majority of votes in almost all assembly segments. In the Jorhat constituency, the BJP candidate Kamakhya Prasad Tasa registered 49 percent votes and defeated the Congress veteran Bijoy Krishna Handique, a six-time MP from the constituency, by a margin of 1.02 lakh votes. He also secured a majority of votes in eight out of ten assembly segments.

The Dibrugarh constituency was one of the strongholds of the Congress. The Congress MP, Paban Singh Ghatowar, the former state Congress president and also the Minister of State in the UPA II, represented it five times. Since 1951, only in 2004 did the seat go to another party, the AGP. In 2014, not only did the Congress veteran Ghatowar lost the election, but the BJP candidate Rameswar Teli secured 55.5 percent votes and defeated Ghatowar by a margin of 1.85 lakh votes and registered a lead in all nine assembly segments. In Lakhimpur, Sarbananda Sonowal defeated his Congress rival Ranee Narah, a three-time Congress MP from the constituency and a state minister in UPA II, by a margin of 2.92 lakh votes. While Sonowal secured 55 percent votes, he led in 9 out of 10 assembly segments where the BJP has only one member in the present Legislative Assembly. In Lakhimpur, the political dynamics changed with an electoral understanding between the BJP and Gana Shakti, the political outfit of the Mising community in the constituency that registered a landslide victory in the Mising Autonomous Council election held in October 2013.

AIUDF: Polarization of the East Bengal Origin Muslim Votes

Perceived to be a party that primarily represents the interests of the East Bengal origin Muslims, the AIUDF, however, projects itself as a truly secular, democratic, and socially inclusive party. Its election manifesto[16] for the 2014 general elections highlights how the discriminatory policies of the governments both at the Center and in the state during the 66 years after independence ignored the issues of the STs, SCs, Other

Backward Classes, the Dalits, and particularly the religious minorities. It asserts that the aggression by the fascist, communal, and the authoritarian political tendencies, by which it primarily refers to the BJP, although without naming it, poses serious challenges to the democratic polity in the country.

The AIUDF considered corruption and price rise to be real challenges before the people. It made a reference to the Ranganath Mishra Commission Report, which recommended the reservation of 15 percent seats for minorities of which 10 percent would be for the Muslim minorities. It also asserted that there were a number of Lok Sabha and Legislative Assembly constituencies where the Muslim minorities constituted 35–40 percent and in some instances even more than 50 percent of the total population. Many of these constituencies were reserved for the SCs. The AIUDF demanded that these constituencies along with others where the Muslims had dominance be immediately declared as reserved constituencies for Muslim minorities.

AIUDF's emergence has a few parallels. One is the growing victimization of the East Bengal origin Muslims in the BTAD and in its surroundings who are often alleged to be Bangladeshis without discrimination. One of the worst affected communities by poverty, they are also alleged to be conspirators against indigenous communities of Assam. Violence in the present-day BTAD in 1993, 2008, and 2012 made lakhs of East Bengal origin Muslims displaced and homeless.[17] The United Minority Front (UMF) politically represented Muslim minorities, particularly of East Bengal origin. However, it had limited impact and achievements in electoral politics. It is only in 2006 that minority politics became completely changed with the emergence of the AIUDF. One of the significant factors behind AIUDF's emergence was the scrapping of the IMDT Act, 1983, by the Supreme Court of India in 2005, which made the immigrant Muslim community more apprehensive about their security and it forced the community to switch their loyalty to the AIUDF, 'a more radical' Muslim political organization.[18]

The BJP–AGP alliance in the 2004 Lok Sabha elections also contributed toward the polarization of East Bengal Muslim politics around the AIUDF. In its first attempt, the AIUDF contested 69 seats in the Legislative Assembly elections 2006, won 10 seats and 9.03 percent of votes. In the 2011 Assembly elections, the party contested 78 seats, won 18 becoming the second largest party in the Assembly and registered 12.57 percent of votes. It contested the 2009 Parliamentary election and fielded nine candidates, won one and registered 16.1 percent of votes. The party secured the second position in two and the third position in six constituencies. In the 2014 general elections, the party fielded ten candidates, won three, secured the third position in four constituencies, and registered 14.8 percent votes. In the 2014 general elections, it secured majority votes in a total number of 24 Legislative Assembly segments.

Waning of Bodo Politics: Verdict in Kokrajhar Constituency

Bodo politics became competitive, conflict-ridden, and fragmented after the signing of the BTC Accord and the formation of the Council. While the Bodo people now constitute around 26 percent of the total population within the Council area, it has overriding representation in the Council. According to the provisions of the Accord, out of the 46 members, 30 are reserved for the STs, 5 for non-Tribal communities, 5 open for all communities, and 6 to be nominated by the Governor from the unrepresented communities for the BTC area of which at least two should be women.[19] With 30 seats reserved for the STs, which primarily are secured by the Bodos, the community exercises its dominance in the council.

Kokrajhar constituency is a reserved constituency for the ST. Since the formation of the constituency in 1967, a Bodo member represented it. However, in the first two general elections held under the constituency, the Congress represented it. In all subsequent elections till 2009, candidates from Bodo political organizations have represented it. After the signing of the BTC Accord in 2003 which led to the formation of BTAD under the amended provisions of the Sixth Schedule of the Constitution of India, the constituency was represented by the BPF in the 2004 and 2009 general elections. BPF is the political front of the former extremist outfit Bodo Liberation Tigers (BLT), which signed the BTC Accord in 2003. The front has been in power in the BTAD since its inception. There are ten assembly segments under the Kokrajhar constituency out of which six are reserved for the ST. In the 2006 Assembly elections, BPF won seven out of those ten constituencies and registered victory in five ST segments. In 2006, it won eight seats including six ST seats. BPF won a total of 11 and 12 Assembly seats in 2006 and 2009 Assembly elections respectively. In the 2009 Lok Sabha elections, the BPF registered a lead in seven out of the ten assembly segments.

BPF was in alliance with the ruling Congress in the state, and therefore had Cabinet berths from 2006 till after the 2014 general elections. BTAD is a multi-ethnic homeland, but Bodos are the dominant minority as described above. With its overriding representation and power, BTC and other Bodo outfits, particularly the NDFB, have been alleged to have indulged in oppressions against the other ethnic communities and also attempts at ethnic cleansing against the Adivasis and the East Bengal origin Muslims living within BTC. Conflicts between Bodos and Adivasis as well as Bodos and Muslims since 1993 have assumed greater intensity. Conflicts of 1993, 1996, 1998, 2008, and 2012 are testimonies to it.[20]

The violence and killings in BTC have affected all communities including the Bodos. The sectarian Council and its activities led to the formation of *Sanmilita Janagosthiya Eikyamancha* in 2014, a conglomerate of non-Bodo communities. The important organizations that fall under the banner of The *Eikya Mancha* are All Konch Rajbongshi Students' Union (AKRASU), All Assam Minorities Students' Union (AAMSU), All BTC Minority Students Union (ABMSU), Bengali Yuva Chatra Federation, BTAD Citizens Rights Forum, Konch Rajbonshi Sanmilani, Non-Bodo Suraksha Samiti (NBSS), Citizens Justice Forum, Chilarai Sena, and Kalita Sanmilani. Another organization, *Sanmilita Janagoshthiya Sangram Samiti*, formed in the early 1990s, has also been mobilizing people against the sectarian provisions of the Accord and atrocities under the Council. Both the organizations are working in coordination with each other. The *Mancha* has been demanding the scrapping of the sectarian BTC Accord. Such an outrage against the Bodo dominance and suppression culminated in returning a non-Bodo candidate from the Kokrajhar constituency to the Lok Sabha in the 2014 general elections who was sponsored by the *Eikya Mancha*.

In the 2014 general elections, the independent non-Bodo candidate Naba Kumar Sarania (Hira) won the election with 51.83 percent votes in his favor.[21] He established his lead in a total of nine out of ten assembly segments including in five segments reserved for the ST. This election also revealed the competitive politics and polarization within the Bodo community. Just after the signing of the BTC Accord in 2003, two important factions of Bodo politics—BLT, the signatory to the Accord and the All Bodo Students Union (ABSU), signatory to the erstwhile BAC Accord signed in 1992—came together and formed a political front, the Bodo Progressive Political Front (BPPF). However, the front collapsed not long after its formation and the two factions became worst enemies of each other.

The faction that succeeded the ABSU retained the original name of the Front, that is, the BPPF and the BLT faction renamed itself as the BPF and subsequently formed an alliance with the ruling Congress in the state. Two prominent leaders of both factions contested the election in 2014. Chandan Brahma of BPF, the former deputy chief in the BTC and subsequently the cabinet minister in the Congress–BPF alliance government, is one of the leaders. The other is Urkhaw Gwra Brahma, the former president of the ABSU and also the former member in the Rajya Sabha. Two other prominent Bodo leaders Sansuma Khunggur Bwiswmuthiary and Ranjit Shekhar Mooshahary also contested the election as independent candidates. Bwiswmuthiary, the former president of the ABSU was also the signatory to the BAC Accord in 1992 as well as the first chief executive member of erstwhile BAC who represented the Kokrajhar Lok Sabha constituency for last four times, twice as a member of the BPF. In the 2014 elections, he was denied the BPF candidature. Mooshahary, the former Director General of Border Security Force (BSF) was also the Governor of Meghalaya. All four leaders lost the election to Naba Kumar Sarania, a former member of ULFA. The state of affairs in the Council could be gauged from the fact that even before the election result was declared, there were barbarous attacks on the Muslim minorities on May 1 and 2, 2014 that killed more than 50 people including children and infants allegedly in the pretext of these people not casting votes in favor of the BPF candidate (Table 17.4).[22]

Table 17.4

Performance in Legislative Assembly Elections 2006 and 2011 and Lead in Assembly Segments in 2014 Lok Sabha Elections

Party	Assembly Election 2006	Assembly Election 2011	Lead in Assembly Segments in General Election 2014
INC	53	78	23
AGP	24	10	00
BJP	10	05	69
AIUDF	10	18	24
BPF	12	12	01
Others	17	03	09
Total	126	126	126

Source: Data for 2006 and 2011 from the Election Commission of India, www. eci.nic.in. 2014 data computed from the results declared by the Returning Officers of respective Lok Sabha constituencies on May 16, 2014.

Conclusion

It will be politically unwise to write the epitaph of the Congress due to its debacle in the present elections. Although the party won only three seats, it secured 29.6 percent votes. In 1991 with 29.35 percent votes in the Legislative Assembly election, the Congress won 66 seats and with 28.5 percent votes it won eight Lok Sabha seats. In the 2014 general elections, the BJP was benefited by the higher percentage of voter turn-out and also due to the decline in AGP votes. Much will depend on how political pragmatism manifested by Narendra Modi in the election campaign is turned into political outcomes toward realizing peoples' aspirations. In the Legislative Assembly by-elections held in September 2014, following the Lok Sabha election results, the Congress, BJP, and AIUDF won seats according to their leads in their respective Assembly segments in the 2014 general elections.

Disillusionment with the BJP government may be on the rise. The role of the Minster of Department of Northeast Region, General V.K. Singh, has been both controversial and disappointing. On the issue of the Lower

Subansiri Hydroelectric Project, the government has been noncommittal; rather, they are in favor of constructing the dam as can be read from the reactions of both the power and water resource ministers. BJP's state manifesto released on April 3, 2014 promised that it will "oppose big dams that pose a threat to the state and will initiate dialogue with Bhutan on the issue of flood caused in lower Assam on account of release of water from the Kuruchi dam in the country."[23] KMSS, the pioneer in anti-large-dam movement in Assam indeed supported BJP's select candidates in the state on its commitment for opposing large dams. NDA government's u-turn has already invited strong and adverse reactions.

In September 2014, Jammu and Kashmir as well as Assam suffered from heavy floods that caused loss of lives and property in both states. While both Prime Minister Narendra Modi and Home Minister Rajnath Singh were prompt in responding to the woes of Jammu and Kashmir, the Union Government has appeared to be indifferent to the woes of Assam. It caused adverse reactions in the state. If the same attitude continues and Assam is seen only as a stock of resources for the development of 'India', the forces of political resistance will take no time to consolidate themselves against the Modi regime.

Notes and References

1. The Parliamentary Constituencies (PCs) in Assam were redrawn both in 1962 and 1967. Assam started with ten PCs in 1951 and 1957. Out of this, eight were single-member constituencies and the rest two were two-member constituencies. In 1951, all were General-member constituencies, but in 1957 one single-member constituency was reserved for ST. In 1962, all were converted into single-member constituencies and the number increased to 12, out of which one was reserved for SC and two for ST. In 1967, the number of constituencies was increased to 14 out of which 11 were General, one is SC, and two are ST constituencies. This arrangement continues till date.
2. Naba Kumar Sarania belongs to the community called Sarania Kachari, which was a part of the Bodo Kachari community. The community enjoys the ST status. However, prior to the elections, an organization called Janajati Suraksha Samity challenged the credibility of the ST certificate of Sarania. The Samity pointed out that "All Assam Tribal Sangha, which had issued the ST certificate to the Sarania Kachari community, was not a competent authority to do so." The members who issued the statement are Bodos. *Telegraph*, April 22, 2014, www.telegraphindia.com/ (accessed on October 6, 2014).
3. Sandhya Goswami, 'Assam: Mandate for Peace and Development', *Economic and Political Weekly*, Vol. XLVI, No. 23, June 4, 2011, pp. 20–22.

4. Quoting government sources, it was reported by *The Assam Tribune*, Guwahati, on January 9, 2014 that since 2001 around 170 rhinos had been killed in the state, mostly in the Kaziranga National Park, and in 2013 alone 43 rhinos were killed.
5. For details, see Dola Mitra et al., 'A Bridge Too Far', *Outlook India* (online version) dated August 13, 2012, http://www.outlookindia.com/article/A-Bridge-Too-Far/281840.
6. According to the 2011 census, the ST population constitutes 31 percent in four districts under BTAD. Zamser Ali, the president of BTAD Citizens Rights Forum and chief spokesperson of Sanmilita Janagoshthiya Eikya Mancha asserts that the non-Bodo ST population in BTAD is not less than 5 percent. Therefore, the Bodos constitutes only 26 percent of the total population in BTAD. Information is based on the personal discussion with Ali on October 5, 2014.
7. Sankardeva, a *Vaishnavite*, is a social and religious reformer of 15th and 16th century Assam who is perceived as the most important cultural architect of the greater Assamese identity across communities. Hindutva ideologues appropriate Sankardeva for its own mileage, and in the Brahmaputra valley alone there are 477 Sankardeva Shishu/Vidya Niketans. Affiliated to Vidya Bharati, these schools introduce students to the Hindutva ideology both through discipline and prayer. Information is based on interaction with Sada Dutta, Guwahati, a functionary of the school network on October 1, 2014.
8. Based on discussion with Indibar Deori, Guwhati on October 1, 2014, who is an authority on ethnic and tribal politics in Northeast India.
9. Gogamukh is around 400 kilometers from Assam's capital city, Guwahati, located in the Lakhimpur Parliamentary constituency from where the then BJP State President Sarbananda Sonowal was contesting.
10. Farhana Ahmed, 'Rhinos killed to settle Bangladeshis', *The Assam Tribune*, Guwahati, April 1, 2014.
11. Ibid.
12. *The Assam Tribune*, Guwahati, February 9, 2014.
13. 'Modi gives a clarion call, blames Congress for its "narrow mindset"', 2014, *The Sentinel*, Guwahati, February 9, 2014.
14. Tea tribes or tea tribe community is a composite group in Assam whose ancestors were brought to Assam from Central and Eastern India by the colonial authority as tea plantation migrant laborers. One of the most exploited communities in the state; the tea tribes lost their connection with their natives and became permanent settlers in the state. In their ancestors' place, these communities enjoy ST status. In Assam, they have been struggling for it.
15. 'Our Manifesto, Our Commitment', 2014, *The Assam Tribune*, Guwahati, April 7, 2014.
16. *16th Lok Sabha Nibarchani Istahar*, AIUDF, the Election Manifesto of the Party, Hojai, Assam.
17. See note 5 and also Subhash Barman, 'Conflict-induced Internal Displaces and their Security' in Akhil Ranjan Dutta (Ed.), *Human Security in Northeast India: Issues and Policies*, Anwesha, Guwahati, 2009, pp. 219–33.
18. Nani Gopal Mahanta, 'Lok Sabha Elections in Assam: Shifting of Traditional Vote Bases to BJP', *Economic and Political Weekly*, Vol. VLIX, No. 35, August 30, 2014, pp. 19–22.
19. *Bodo Territorial Council (BTC) Accord* at: cdpsindia.org/btc_accord.asp, accessed on October 2, 2014.

20. See note 17.

21. The *Times of India* reporter Prabin Kalita on May 17, 2014 while reporting on election outcomes in the Kokrajhar constituency wrote: 'Sarania was the only candidate in the state to hold the confidence of Hindus and Muslims alike and he was also the common choice of Bengali, Hindi and Assamese speaking people.' timesofindia.indiatimes.com>Lok Sabha Elections 2014, May 17, 2014 (accessed on October 6, 2014).

22. For details about the May 2014 killing in BTAD see *Balichanda*, July–September 2014 issue, edited by Hafiz Ahmed and published from Guwahati.

23. *The Assam Tribune*, Guwahati, April 4, 2014.

About the Editor and Contributors

Editor

Paul Wallace (PhD, University of California, Berkeley) is Professor Emeritus of Political Science at the University of Missouri, Columbia. He has been a consultant on South Asia to a member of the US Senate Foreign Relations Committee, the US Attorney General's Office, defense lawyers, and other agencies in North America and has received five Smithsonian-funded awards for national election studies in India. In September 2003, Professor Wallace served as the expert witness on Sikh violence at the Air India trial in Vancouver, Canada.

His research in India includes a Senior Fulbright Research Award in 1972, and funding from the Ford Foundation, 1988–89, the American Institute of Indian Studies (1980–81), and various government and non-government groups in India. Professor Wallace is the author or editor of eight books and 40+ book chapters and articles. His last co-edited book is *India's 2009 Elections: Coalition Politics, Party Competition and Congress Continuity"* published by SAGE Publications in 2011.

Contributors

Walter K. Andersen is the Administrative Director of the South Asia Studies Program at the School of Advanced International Programs, Johns Hopkins University, and gives lectures in International Relations at Tongji University, Shanghai, China.

Mohita Bhatia is Assistant Professor at the Centre for the Study of Discrimination and Exclusion, Jawaharlal Nehru University, New Delhi.

Nitin Birmal teaches political science at Dr Ambedkar College, Yerawada, Pune. He is a state coordinator for Maharashtra, Lokniti Network. He has been working on politics and political economy of Maharashtra.

Anshu N. Chatterjee is a Faculty Member at the Naval Post-graduate School, Monterey, California. Her work focuses on insurgencies and civil military relations.

Amiya K. Chaudhuri is a Senior Fellow in Maulana Azad Institute of Asian Studies (MAKAIAS) in Kolkata.

Rainuka Dagar is Director (Research), Gender Studies Unit, Institute for Development and Communication (IDC), Chandigarh, and Program Director with Altus Global Justice Alliance, Chandigarh.

Jyotirindra Dasgupta is Professor Emeritus of Political Science at the University of California, Berkeley. His work has focused on language planning and ethnic mobilization in a comparative perspective.

Prakash Desai is Assistant Professor of Political Science, Goa University.

Akhil Ranjan Dutta is Professor of Political Science at Gauhati University, Assam. He is closely associated with Lokniti, Centre for the Study of Developing Societies (CSDS), New Delhi, and a core member of the Foundation for Creative Social Science Research, New Delhi.

Christophe Jaffrelot is Senior Research Fellow at CERI (Centre d'Etudes et de Recherches Internationales) at Sciences Po (Paris), and Research Director at the CNRS (Centre National de la Recherche Scientifique); Professor of Indian Politics and Sociology at the King's India Institute (London); and Global Scholar at Princeton University.

Avinash Kumar is Assistant Professor at the Centre for Informal Sector and Labour Studies, School of Social Sciences, Jawaharlal Nehru University, New Delhi.

Pramod Kumar is Director, Institute for Development and Communication (IDC), Chandigarh. His work focuses on the politics of development and governance, politics of conflict management and resolution, and practice of democracy through empirical methodologies and analysis of public policy and peoples movements.

Sudha Pai is Professor at the Centre for Political Studies and Rector (Pro-Vice Chancellor) Jawaharlal Nehru University, New Delhi. Her research interests include Dalit Politics, State Politics, Agrarian Politics, Globalization, and Legislative Governance.

Suhas Palshikar is Director of Lokniti and Professor in the Department of Politics and Public Administration at the University of Pune.

S.S. Patagundi is Professor of Political Science and Dean, Faculty of Social Sciences, Karnataka University, Dharwad.

Ravi Ranjan is a Political Science Faculty at Zakir Husain Delhi College, Delhi University, and a Fellow at the Developing Countries Research Centre, University of Delhi.

Maneesha Roy is a Faculty Member in the Department of Political Science at Sri Guru Nanak Dev Khalsa College, Delhi University.

Ghanshyam Shah, retired professor from Jawaharlal Nehru University, is at present a National Fellow, Indian Council of Social Science, Research, New Delhi.

Karli Srinivasulu is Professor of Political Science and Dean, Faculty of Social Sciences at Osmania University, Hyderabad, India.

Reeta Chowdhari Tremblay is Professor of Political Science, University of Victoria, Canada. Her research focuses on comparative federalism in South Asia, territorial and cultural identities, and between formal and informal nationalisms.

Gilles Verniers is Assistant Professor of Political Science at Ashoka University, Haryana, and Research Associate at the Centre de Sciences Humaines, New Delhi.

Andrew Wyatt is Senior Lecturer in Politics at the University of Bristol with research interests in party systems, political parties, populism, and nationalism.

Index

coal block allocation, 105
Commonwealth Games, 105, 175, 178
Scheduled Castes (SCs), 16–17, 81–82,
  86–87, 91, 126, 129, 143, 146, 167,
  173, 177, 184, 234, 263, 269, 272–73,
  290, 293, 298, 306, 309–10, 315, 320,
  360, 369, 371, 382, 395–96
Scheduled Tribe (ST), 81, 86, 143, 234,
  263, 273–76, 290, 293, 309–10, 320,
  360, 371, 383, 394, 397–99
School of Advanced International Studies
  (SAIS), 47
Scindia, Vasundhra Raje, 75
seat share, 30
seat-sharing agreements, 37
sectarianism, 81
  religious, 81
secularism, 20, 64, 91, 153, 235, 267
secular realignment, 158
self-identity, 349
Sen, Amartya, 55
Sen, Nirupam, 307, 315
Seva Bharati (Service to India), 16
sexual abuse, 82–83, 85
  appreciation, 85
  exploitation, 83
  harassment, 85
  merchandise, 85
  protection, 90
  violence, 20, 65, 80–81, 83, 87
    protests against, 80
Shah, Amit, 20–21, 23, 44, 49, 52–63,
  119, 129, 131, 133–35, 279, 318
  anti-Muslim remarks, 53
Shakti Pith Pran Prathistha Mahottsav, 266
Shamli, 131
Sharif, Nawaz, 58
Shastri, Lal Bahadur, 12
Shias, 234
Shiromani Akali Dal (SAD), 7, 15–16, 22,
  30, 38, 189–91, 193, 198–99, 204,
  212–14, 216–19, 222, 224–25
Shiromani Gurdwara Parbandhak
  Committee (SGPC), 204
Shiv Sena, 7, 23, 30, 38, 43, 55, 180,
  284–90, 293–95, 297–98
Shiv Sena–BJP alliance, 284, 289
Siddaramaiah, 359–61, 363, 366

Sidhu, Navjot Singh, 51
Sikh Jats, 204
Sikhs, 184, 186, 195, 197–98, 204, 212,
  218, 240
Sikkim, 66
Singh, Amarinder, 16, 204, 212, 217, 224
Singh, Giriraj, 53, 156
  anti-Muslim comments, 53
Singh, Gurnam, 217
Singh, Jaswant, 51–52
Singh, Kalyan, 131
Singh, Maharaja Hari, 238
Singh, Manmohan, 11, 285, 259, 393
Singh, Rajnath, 51–52, 401
Singh, Rajveer, 131
Singh, V.P., 108
Singur, 24, 102, 307–8, 315–17, 320
SMS, 135, 266, 268
social
  activism, 183, 220
  audit, 101, 104
  base, 21, 46, 56, 119, 124, 128, 136,
    150, 341, 347, 354, 360
  coalition, 56, 348–50
  conflicts, 143
  engineering, 145–47, 149, 157, 225,
    359, 389
  equation, 145
  groups, 23, 127–28, 225, 340, 371,
    386
  hierarchy, 82
  justice, 82, 145–46, 153, 155, 187
  media, 135, 267
  order, 83, 86, 88
  organizations, 81
  relationships, 92
  welfare, 46, 54, 150, 177
socialization, 12, 52
Social Media War Room, 135
Social Work and Research Center (SWRC),
  104–5
soft power, 14
Soni, Ambika, 212
Soni, Suresh, 53
Sonowal, Sarbananda, 391, 395
Sri Lanka, 24, 58, 329
Sringeri Shankarcharya Math, 366
Sriramalu, B., 362, 363, 366